TEACHINGS OF PRESIDENTS OF THE CHURCH
# JOSEPH F. SMITH

Published by
The Church of Jesus Christ of Latter-day Saints
Salt Lake City, Utah

Your comments and suggestions about this book would be appreciated. Please submit them to Curriculum Planning, 50 East North Temple Street, Floor 24, Salt Lake City, UT 84150-3200 USA. E-mail: cur-development@ldschurch.org

Please list your name, address, ward, and stake. Be sure to give the title of the book. Then offer your comments and suggestions about the book's strengths and areas of potential improvement.

Page 10: *Joseph Smith*
Courtesy of the RLDS Church, Independence, Missouri

Page 30: *Mary Fielding Smith,* by Sutcliffe Maudsley
Courtesy the Don C. Corbett family

Page 51: *He Is Risen,* by Del Parson
© Del Parson

Page 146: *Christ and the Samaritan Woman,* by Carl Heinrich Bloch
The National Historic Museum at Frederiksborg in Hillerød

Page 233: 20th Ward Choir
Used by permission, Utah State Historical Society. All rights reserved

Page 274: *Prove Me Now Herewith,* by Glen S. Hopkinson
© Glen S. Hopkinson

# Contents

# Introduction

President Joseph F. Smith served for 52 years as a General Authority of the Church—as a member of the Quorum of the Twelve, as a Counselor to four Church Presidents, and for 17 years as the President of the Church. He taught the restored gospel of Jesus Christ with eloquence, tenderness, and conviction, calling for the people to "live in harmony with the designs of our Heavenly Father."[1] His ministry was marked by his powerful witness of Jesus Christ: "I have received the witness of the Spirit in my own heart, and I testify before God, angels and men . . . that I know that my Redeemer lives."[2]

Today his messages and sermons continue to give divine direction on our path of eternal progress. Our work in this world, said President Smith, "is to do good, to put down iniquity under our feet, to exalt righteousness, purity, and holiness in the hearts of the people, and to establish in the minds of our children, above all other things, a love for God and his word."[3] He declared that "to be a Latter-day Saint requires the sacrifice of worldly aims and pleasures; it requires fidelity, strength of character, love of truth, integrity to principle, and zealous desire to see the triumphant, forward march of truth."[4]

The First Presidency and Quorum of the Twelve Apostles have established the series *Teachings of Presidents of the Church* to help Church members deepen their understanding of gospel doctrines and draw closer to Jesus Christ through the teachings of the prophets in this dispensation. This book features the teachings of President Joseph F. Smith, who said: "To be Latter-day Saints, men or women must be thinkers, and workers; they must be men and women who weigh matters in their minds, men and women who consider carefully their course of life and the principles that they have espoused. . . . When people understand the gospel of Jesus Christ, you will see them walking straightforward, according to the word of the Lord, and the law of God, strictly in accordance with that which is consistent, just, righteous, and in every sense acceptable to the Lord."5

Each chapter in this book includes four sections: (1) a statement that briefly summarizes the focus of the chapter; (2) "From the Life of Joseph F. Smith," which illustrates the chapter's teachings by an example from President Smith's life or his wisdom; (3) "Teachings of Joseph F. Smith," which presents important doctrines from his many messages and sermons; and (4) "Suggestions for Study," which encourages personal review and inquiry, further discussion, and application to our lives today through questions.

## How to Use This Book

*For personal study.* This book is intended to enhance each member's understanding of gospel principles taught powerfully by President Joseph F. Smith. By prayerful reading and thoughtful study, each member may receive a personal witness of these truths. This volume will also add to each member's gospel library and will serve as an important resource for family instruction and for study in the home.

*For discussion in Sunday meetings.* This book is the text for Melchizedek Priesthood quorum and Relief Society Sunday meetings. Teachers should focus on the content of the text and related scriptures, drawing from the questions at the end of the chapter to encourage class discussion. Reviewing the questions before studying President Smith's words may give additional insight into his teachings.

The Sunday meetings should concentrate on gospel principles, personal examples that teach these principles, and testimonies of the truth. If teachers humbly seek the Spirit in preparing and directing the lesson, all who participate will be strengthened in their knowledge of the truth. Teachers should remind class members to bring their books to their meetings and should honor the members' preparation by teaching from President Joseph F. Smith's words. Having read the chapter in advance, class members will be prepared to teach and edify each other.

It is not necessary or recommended that members purchase additional commentaries or reference texts to support the material in the text. Members are encouraged to turn to the scriptures that have been suggested for further study of the doctrine.

Since this text is designed for personal study and gospel reference, many chapters are too long to be addressed completely in class. Therefore, study at home becomes essential to receiving the fulness of President Smith's teachings.

In your study, may you come to know this humble, faithful, and fearless prophet of God, President Joseph F. Smith. May you accept his counsel "to choose the right because it is right, and because your heart loves the right, and because it is choice above everything else."[6] May you join President Smith as he testified of the power of the gospel of Jesus Christ: "Our faith in the doctrines that have been restored . . . confirms and strengthens us and establishes beyond a question or doubt, our faith and belief in the divine mission of the Son of God."[7]

## Notes

1. *Deseret News: Semi-Weekly,* 6 Feb. 1893, 2.
2. *Gospel Doctrine,* 5th ed. (1939), 447.
3. *Gospel Doctrine,* 141.
4. "Editor's Table: Principle, Not Popularity," *Improvement Era,* July 1906, 733.
5. In Conference Report, Oct. 1910, 3–4.
6. *Deseret News: Semi-Weekly,* 6 Feb. 1893, 2.
7. *Gospel Doctrine,* 478.

# Historical Summary

This book is not a history, but rather a compilation of gospel principles as taught by President Joseph F. Smith. However, in order to put the teachings in a historical framework, the following list is provided to summarize some of the milestones in his life that have most immediate relationship to his teachings. This summary omits some important events in his personal life, including his marriages (plural marriage was being practiced in the Church at that time) and the births and deaths of his children, to whom he was devoted.

| | |
|---|---|
| 1800, February 9: | Hyrum Smith, Joseph F. Smith's father, born in Tunbridge, Vermont. |
| 1801, July 21: | Mary Fielding, his mother, born in Honeydon, England. |
| 1837, December 24: | Marriage of Hyrum Smith and Mary Fielding, Kirtland, Ohio. |
| 1838, November 13: | Joseph F. Smith born in Far West, Missouri. |
| 1844, June 27: | Joseph and Hyrum Smith martyred, Carthage Jail (5; numbers in parentheses show Joseph F. Smith's age). |
| 1846, September–September 1848: | Mary Fielding Smith family treks from Nauvoo, Illinois, to the Salt Lake Valley (7–9). |
| 1852, May 21: | Joseph F. Smith baptized by President Heber C. Kimball (13). |
| 1852, September 21: | Mary Fielding Smith dies in Salt Lake City (13). |
| 1854–1857: | Serves mission to Sandwich Islands (Hawaii) (15–19). |
| 1860–1863: | Serves mission to Great Britain (21–24). |
| 1864: | Special mission to Hawaii with Elders Ezra T. Benson and Lorenzo Snow (25–26). |
| 1865–66: | Member of territorial legislature; also 1867–70, 1872, 1874, 1880, 1882. |
| 1866, July 1: | Ordained an Apostle and Counselor to the First Presidency (27). |

| | |
|---|---|
| 1867, October 8: | Set apart as a member of the Quorum of the Twelve Apostles (28). |
| 1874–1875, 1877: | Two terms as president of the European Mission (35–36, 38). |
| 1877, August 29: | Death of President Brigham Young, Salt Lake City (38). |
| 1880, October 10: | Sustained as Second Counselor to President John Taylor (41). |
| 1887, July 25: | Death of President John Taylor, Kaysville, Utah (48). |
| 1889, April 7: | Sustained as Second Counselor to President Wilford Woodruff (50). |
| 1890, September 24; October 6: | Manifesto received; Official Declaration 1 accepted by the Church (51). |
| 1893, April 6: | Dedication of the Salt Lake Temple by President Wilford Woodruff (54). |
| 1898, September 2: | President Wilford Woodruff dies, San Francisco, California (59). |
| 1898, September 13: | Sustained Second Counselor to President Lorenzo Snow (59). |
| 1901, October 10: | Death of President Lorenzo Snow, Salt Lake City (62). |
| 1901, October 17: | Ordained and set apart as President of the Church (62). |
| 1901, November 10: | Sustained as President of the Church in a special conference (62). |
| 1906, July–September: | First President of the Church to tour Europe during his administration (67). |
| 1909, November: | First Presidency issues the doctrinal exposition "The Origin of Man" (70). |
| 1911: | YMMIA adopts the Boy Scout program, named MIA Scouts (72). |
| 1912: | Granite Seminary in Salt Lake City is the site of the first released-time classes. |

| | |
|---|---|
| 1913: | YWMIA adopts the Campfire Girls summer program; 1914, replaced with year-round Beehive Girls program (74). |
| 1913, July 27: | Dedicates the site for the Alberta Temple (74). |
| 1915, April 27: | The First Presidency urges members to hold regular home evenings (76). |
| 1915, June 1: | Dedicates the site for the Hawaii Temple (76). |
| 1916, June 30: | First Presidency and the Twelve issue the doctrinal exposition "The Father and the Son" (77). |
| 1918, October 3: | Receives the vision of the redemption of the dead, which became Doctrine and Covenants 138 (79). |
| 1918, November 19: | Dies in the Beehive House, Salt Lake City (80). |
| 1918: | End-of-year statistics: 495,962 members; 75 stakes; 839 wards; 22 missions. |

# The Ministry of Joseph F. Smith

Joseph F. Smith was the sixth President of the Church and the last President to have personally known the Prophet Joseph Smith. "My childhood and youth were spent in wandering with the people of God, in suffering with them and in rejoicing with them. My whole life has been identified with this people," he said.[1] He sought earnestly to know God the Father and His Son, Jesus Christ, and to serve them with whole-souled devotion. Blessed with a profound understanding of the gospel, he was able to lead his people in the principles of eternal truth and to steady the Church through attacks from opponents during the early years of the 20th century. He desired to be "a peacemaker, a preacher of righteousness,"[2] and he vigorously taught obedience, witnessing from his own experience that "all who will yield obedience to the promptings of the Spirit . . . will get a clearer, a more expansive, and a more direct and conclusive knowledge of God's truths than anyone else can obtain."[3]

## A childhood nurtured by faith.

The first child of Mary Fielding and Hyrum Smith, Joseph F. Smith was born on 13 November 1838 in Far West, Caldwell County, Missouri, in the midst of persecution and poverty. Two weeks earlier, his father had been taken prisoner by a mob and unjustly incarcerated. For four long months, Hyrum Smith, his brother the Prophet Joseph Smith, and others suffered privation in Liberty Jail. Mary felt that her husband had been cruelly removed from her "at a time when I needed . . . the kindest care and attention of such a friend, instead of which, the care of a large family was suddenly and unexpectedly left upon myself." A convert to the Church from Canada, she had married Hyrum Smith following the death of his first wife, Jerusha, and she was caring for the five Smith children at the time "my dear little Joseph F. was added to the number."[4]

When the Saints were driven from Missouri during the winter of 1838–39, Joseph F. was a babe in arms. His father was still in prison, and his mother was severely ill and "had to be removed more than two hundred miles, chiefly on [her] bed."[5] Mary's sister, Mercy Fielding Thompson, nursed and cared for Joseph F. along with her own infant daughter. The Saints found refuge in Illinois, and young Joseph F. spent most of his first eight years in Nauvoo, the city the Saints built up on the banks of the Mississippi River. There, within the circle of the Smith family and the community of Saints, he was nurtured in the knowledge of the gospel of Jesus Christ. "I was instructed to believe in the divinity of the mission of Jesus Christ," he later recalled. "I was taught it from my father, from the Prophet Joseph Smith, through my mother . . . and all my boyhood days and all my years in the world I have clung to that belief."[6]

Joseph F.'s father, Hyrum, had helped the Prophet Joseph advance the work of the Restoration since the organization of the Church, and even earlier when Joseph was translating the Book of Mormon. The Prophet relied heavily upon his older brother Hyrum, especially in Nauvoo, where Hyrum was called by revelation both as Church Patriarch and as Assistant President. Hyrum, the Prophet said, possessed "the mildness of a lamb, and the integrity of Job, and in short, the meekness and humility of Christ."[7]

Like his father, Joseph F. developed great love for and loyalty to the Prophet Joseph Smith. In later years, he often shared precious childhood memories of his uncle and constantly testified of his calling as the Prophet of the Restoration: "O, he was full of joy; he was full of gladness; he was full of love. . . . And while he could play with children and amuse himself at simple, innocent games among men, he also communed with the Father and the Son and spoke with angels, and they visited him, and conferred blessings and gifts and keys of power upon him."[8]

Joseph F. was not yet six years old when his uncle Joseph and his father, Hyrum, laid down their lives for the kingdom of God.

Joseph F. Smith, sixth President of The Church of
Jesus Christ of Latter-day Saints. Painting by A. Salzbrenner.

They were assassinated on 27 June 1844 by a violent mob. Nauvoo always evoked for him "sacred memories of the past, made doubly and at the same time Dear and dreadful, by the Sacred resting place of my Fathers Dust, and the Dreadful Scenes that once, (and to my memory Clear as day) brought gloom and Horror upon the honest world and filled 10 thousand Hearts with grief and woe!"[9]

Following the death of Hyrum, Mary and her sister, Mercy, also a widow, worked together to care for a large family and prepare to join the Saints in moving West. Joseph F. Smith recalled that their preparations were cut short in the fall of 1846 when threatening mobs compelled them to ferry "in an open flat boat, across the Mississippi river into Iowa, where we camped under the trees and listened to the bombardment of the city. We had left our comfortable home with all the furniture remaining in the house, together with all our earthly possessions, with no hope or thought of ever seeing them again."[10] His mother repeatedly assured her children, "The Lord will open the way,"[11] and the strength of her conviction nourished their own faith. "We were not far away when we heard the cannonade on the other side of the river," President Smith remembered, "but I felt just as certain in my mind then—as certain as a child could feel—that all was right, that the Lord's hand was in it, as I do today."[12]

As Joseph F. Smith journeyed westward with his family, he observed his mother meet challenge after challenge with faith. When her company captain unkindly insisted that the widow would be a burden to the whole company, she let him know that she would do her part and make her way, and even arrive in the valley before he did. And ultimately, she did! As the family's herd-boy, Joseph F. was keenly aware of the importance of the family's precious cattle, so he never forgot how once through fervent prayer his mother located a lost team. Later, he recalled, she prayed for oxen who had "laid down in the yoke as if poisoned" that they might arise and move forward, and "to the astonishment of all who saw," they "got up and we drove along."[13]

Joseph F. drove one of the family's ox teams into the Salt Lake Valley on 23 September 1848. He was nine years old. The Smiths settled on land south of Salt Lake City at Millcreek, and there young Joseph F. toiled, he recalled, as "teamster, herd-boy, plow-boy, irrigator, harvester, with scythe or cradle, wood-hauler, thresher, winnower . . . [and] general roustabout."[14] The family lived simply in a small cabin, but President Smith later commented, "We were no worse off than thousands of others, and not so bad off as many."[15] He learned to work hard and do his duty, to live without luxuries, to praise God, and to pay tithing on everything the family raised.

Joseph F. Smith forever cherished his mother's labor and sacrifice, her matchless love and faith. He was devastated when, following two months of illness, she died at age 51. "After my mother's death there followed 18 months—from Sept 21st, 1852 to April, 1854 of perilous times for me," he later wrote a childhood friend. "I was almost like a comet or fiery meteor, without attraction or gravitation to keep me balanced or guide me within reasonable bounds." "Fatherless & motherless" at age 13, he recalled, he was "not altogether friendless."[16] His "ever-to-be-loved and remembered Aunt Mercy R. Thompson"[17] continued to nurture him, and he never forgot the solicitude of Brigham Young, Heber C. Kimball, and George A. Smith, his father's cousin. These were men, Joseph F. declared, "whom I learned to love as I loved my father, because of their integrity and love of the Truth."[18]

---

## Called to serve in Hawaii.

When the First Presidency announced at the April 1854 general conference that Joseph F. was called to join a group of missionaries soon to depart, he exercised the faith he had garnered through his childhood and "cheerfully responded" to the call. He later gratefully reflected, "My four years mission to the Sandwich Islands restored my equilibrium, and fixed the laws and metes and bounds which have governed my subsequent life."[19]

Elder Joseph F. Smith arrived at Honolulu in the Sandwich Islands (Hawaii) on 27 September 1854, about six weeks before his 16th birthday. Assigned to the island of Maui, he was soon left alone at Kula to live among the people and learn their language and culture. The young elder "sought earnestly the gift of tongues," he remembered, "and by this gift and by study, in a hundred days after landing upon those islands I could talk to the people in their language as I now talk to you in my native tongue."[20] Extraordinary fluency in the language enabled him to personally minister to the Hawaiian people.

Young though he was, Elder Smith was appointed to preside on the island of Maui, then at Hilo on the island of Hawaii, and later on the island of Molokai. On Molokai, when he contracted a severe fever and was seriously ill for three months, a dear sister, Ma Mahuhii, attended him as lovingly as though he were her own son. She never forgot him, nor he her, and they greeted one another with deep affection whenever they met in later years. "The kindness manifested towards me by many of the good native people of Hawaii"[21] was a blessed remembrance for him.

Elder Joseph F. Smith left Hawaii in October 1857 and accepted the increasing responsibilities President Brigham Young assigned to him. He served a mission to England (1860–63) and a second mission to Hawaii (1864). After his return to Salt Lake City late in 1864, he was employed in the Church Historian's Office, working under the guidance of Elder George A. Smith of the Quorum of the Twelve.

### Service in the Quorum of the Twelve and the First Presidency.

Then in 1866, at the direction of President Young, 28-year-old Joseph F. Smith was ordained an Apostle and called as a Counselor to the First Presidency. He honored President Young as the man "raised up and sustained by the power of Almighty God to continue the mission of [the Prophet] Joseph and to accomplish the work that he laid out during his lifetime."[22] Joseph F. Smith desired with his whole soul to help move forward that "great and glorious work."[23] He taught, "You have embraced the gospel for yourselves, then go and do your whole duty, not by halves, or in part, but your full duty."[24] This is the way to promote "the interests of Zion and the establishment of her cause in the earth."[25]

In addition to other responsibilities as a member of the Quorum of the Twelve, he served two terms as president of the European Mission (1874–75; 1877).

Although Joseph F. Smith's formal schooling was limited, he mastered a large vocabulary and learned to speak with power and persuasion. On 24 June 1866, he spoke in the Salt Lake Tabernacle and, as Elder Wilford Woodruff of the Quorum of the Twelve recorded, "spoke in the Afternoon 1 Hour 15 minutes & the power of God was upon him & he manifested the same spirit that was upon his Uncle Joseph Smith the Prophet & his Father Hyrum Smith."[26] Elder Joseph F. Smith became widely known for the scope and power of his sermons; he desired to teach in accord with the Holy Spirit "to the understanding of those who hear me."[27] It is not "the faultless sentence so much as the spirit accompanying the speaker that awakens life and light in the soul," he taught.[28] "I always tried to make my hearers feel that I and my associates were peacemakers, and lovers of peace and good will, that our mission was to save, and not destroy, to build up and not tear down," he once wrote a missionary son.[29]

From the death of President Brigham Young in 1877 to the time Joseph F. Smith was sustained as President of the Church in 1901, he labored continually to awaken life and light in the souls of the Saints and establish peace and goodwill. During those 24 years, John Taylor, Wilford Woodruff, and Lorenzo Snow each served as President of the Church, and Joseph F. Smith was called as a Counselor in each successive First Presidency. It was a time when Latter-day Saint beliefs and practices were widely misunderstood, and during the 1880s, opponents waged harsh legal battles against the Church and its members. "They do not want us to be, religiously or otherwise, a separate and distinct people from the rest of the world. They want us to become identified and mixed up with the rest of the world, to become like them, thereby thwarting the purposes of God," President Smith explained.[30]

Nevertheless, President Smith beseeched Church members to love and forgive their enemies. "When we forget the object of our calling and step out of the path of duty to return blow for blow, to inflict evil for evil, to persecute because we may be persecuted, we forget the injunctions of the Lord and the covenants we have made with God to keep His commandments," he taught.[31] He reminded discouraged Saints of God's assurance that the destiny of the Church is "onward and upward until the purposes of God concerning this great latter-day work are consummated."[32]

Joseph F. Smith drew very close to those with whom he served. "When I experience the expressions of confidence and love of my brethren and sisters whom I love, it goes directly to my heart," he said.[33] Of all his associations, he prized most his ties to his beloved family. To be a husband and father was for him the greatest of callings. He loved to be at home, to teach his children, to tell them stories, to sing and play and laugh with them. When away on assignments, he longed for his loved ones. In Hawaii, on 1 April 1885, he wrote in his journal: "There is a strong east wind blowing which, in a colder clime, would be wintry and harsh. Is it blowing gently or unkindly upon my loved ones? Are they warm or cold? . . . Are they hungry or fed? In the midst of friends or foes, fretted or peaceful? Peace, be still!"[34] His son Joseph Fielding Smith recalled the precious times he spent by his father's side "discussing principles of the gospel and receiving instruction as only he could give it. In this way the foundation for my own knowledge was laid in truth, so that I too can say I know that my Redeemer lives, and that Joseph Smith is, was, and always will be a prophet of the living God."[35]

He constantly tended to the temporal and spiritual needs of his family and made his presence felt whether he was at home or away. In notes, letters, and poems, he expressed his abiding affection for his loved ones. "My Dear Companion," he wrote to his wife on her 39th birthday, "I think better of you, prize you higher, you are nearer to me and I love you more today than I did . . . twenty years ago. Every hour, week, month and year, strengthens the bond of our union and each child cements it with an eternal seal."[36]

President Smith had great love for the temple and its ordinances that made possible the eternal union of families. "Who are there besides the Latter-day Saints who contemplate the thought that beyond the grave we will continue in the family organization?"[37] On 6 April 1853, at age 14, he had witnessed the laying of the cornerstones for the Salt Lake Temple, and on 6 April 1892, at age 53, he offered the prayer for the laying of the temple's capstone.[38] The following year, on 6 April 1893, President Wilford Woodruff dedicated the magnificent structure, the fourth temple in Utah. Speaking at the dedicatory services, President Smith declared: "This is the sixth temple [including the Kirtland and Nauvoo Temples], but it is not the end."[39] As Church President, he would dedicate sites for the temple at Cardston, Canada (27 July 1913), and the temple at Laie, Hawaii (1 June 1915).

---

## Ministry as President of the Church.

On 17 October 1901, a week after the death of President Lorenzo Snow, the Quorum of the Twelve Apostles ordained and set apart Joseph F. Smith as the sixth President of The Church of Jesus Christ of Latter-day Saints. He would serve as President for 17 years, from 1901 to 1918. In his first address to the Saints as Church President, he declared: "It is our privilege to live nearer to the Lord, if we will, than we have ever done, that we may enjoy a greater outpouring of His Spirit than we have ever enjoyed, and that we may advance faster, grow in the knowledge of the truth more rapidly, and become more thoroughly established in the faith. All this, however, will depend upon the increased faithfulness of the people."[40] His personal visiting among the Saints, his efforts to strengthen the fellowship and teaching in local wards, his own tireless preaching of "the principles of eternal truth" were all means of exalting "righteousness, purity and holiness in the hearts of the people."[41] He knew that only a righteous, pure, and holy people could assist the Savior in bringing forth "the sanctification of the earth and the salvation of the human family."[42]

Church membership nearly doubled during President Smith's administration, from 278,645 in 1901 to 495,962 in 1918. Though the majority of members still lived in the western United States, President Smith felt a strong connection with members in many nations. He visited Europe in 1906, the first President of the Church to do so while in office, returned there in 1910, and made visits to Saints in Canada and the Hawaiian Islands. He and his Counselors in the First Presidency counseled members to be "faithful and true in their allegiance to their governments, and to be good citizens,"[43] and to "remain in their native lands and form congregations of a permanent character."[44] Members of the Church were no longer encouraged to move to Utah to gather with the Saints.

The first generation of Saints had gathered to Zion by geographically separating themselves from the world in order to forge unity and spiritual strength. President Smith emphasized for subsequent generations the importance of living peaceably in the midst of the world while maintaining the legacy of unity and spiritual strength made possible through priesthood order and ordinances.

President Smith spoke and wrote at great length about the incomparable power of the priesthood and strove to help all members understand its significance. At the time Joseph F. Smith was sustained as Church President, the meeting schedules, lessons, and effectiveness of priesthood quorums varied from ward to ward. But President Smith anticipated the day "when every council of the Priesthood in the Church of Jesus Christ of Latter-day Saints will understand its duty; will assume its own responsibility, will magnify its calling, and fill its place in the Church."[45] In the April 1908 general conference, President Smith announced that new efforts were under way "for the benefit and advancement of those who are associated with the various quorums of the Priesthood."[46]

The quorums of the Aaronic Priesthood were of particular concern to him. "We should look after our boys who have been ordained Deacons, Teachers, and Priests in the Church," he advised.[47] Over the next few years bishops provided young priesthood holders with important assignments, many of which are now standard practice. Both Aaronic and Melchizedek Priesthood quorums were strengthened as regular weekly, year-round priesthood meetings were firmly established and a central Church committee issued uniform courses of study for the quorums.

President Smith placed great emphasis on home teaching. "I don't know of any duty that is more sacred, or more necessary, if it is carried out as it should be, than the duties of the teachers who visit the homes of the people, who pray with them, who admonish them to virtue and honor, to unity, to love, and to faith in and fidelity to the cause of Zion," he said.[48] To further strengthen the families of the Church, in 1915 he and his Counselors in the First Presidency introduced a weekly home evening program to the Church, urging parents to use the time to instruct their children in the word of God.

This was also a period of significant advancement in the auxiliary organizations. The general boards of the Sunday School, the organizations for the young men and young women, and the Primary had begun publishing uniform courses of study. Their lessons, President Smith observed, were leading young members "along into greater experiences and better understanding of the principles of the gospel of Jesus Christ."[49] To address the challenge of increasing leisure time for youth, the Boy Scout program was adopted for young men and a new Beehive program was developed for young women. The Relief Society, which since 1902 had encouraged stakes to write lessons for sisters, began publishing uniform lessons in 1914 and special messages for visiting teachers in 1916. These innovations became part of the new *Relief Society Magazine* and better equipped Relief Society women "to look after the spiritual, mental and moral welfare of the mothers and daughters in Zion."[50] For President Smith, it was vital that the auxiliaries work in harmony with priesthood authorities to teach the gospel and strengthen bonds of fellowship among members. "Thus we pull all together a strong pull, a long pull for the establishment of the Church."[51]

One of the greatest challenges Joseph F. Smith faced was dealing with misunderstandings and persecutions directed toward the Church. However, he declared that efforts by detractors "have but been the means, indirectly, of forwarding the work in the world. They have called the attention of the world toward us, and that is just what we want. . . . We want the world to become acquainted with us. We want them to learn our doctrine, to understand our faith, our purposes, and the organization of the Church of Jesus Christ of Latter-day Saints."[52]

Gradually, President Smith's hopes began to be realized and the Church received greater respect in the United States and abroad. In order to provide tourists to Salt Lake City with accurate information about Church beliefs and history, the Church established its first visitors' center on Temple Square in 1902. During the first year of operation, the 25 volunteers at the Bureau of Information and Church Literature were overwhelmed with more than 150,000 visitors. By 1904, the bureau required more workers and a larger building. In 1911 the Tabernacle Choir presented highly praised concerts in 25 cities in the eastern and midwestern United States, including a special concert at the White House for the president of the United States and guests.

"The Lord will all the more exalt and magnify us before the world and make us to assume our real position and standing in the midst of the earth," President Smith promised, in proportion to members' "increased faithfulness" and willingness to become "more thoroughly established in the faith."[53] He therefore continually exhorted Latter-day Saints to become more deeply rooted in their own history and doctrine. President Smith initiated republication of Joseph Smith's *History of the Church* and supported the collection of pioneer diaries and manuscripts for the Church Archives. He also authorized Church officials to purchase historic sites sacred to Latter-day Saints, including Carthage Jail in Illinois, where the Prophet Joseph Smith and his brother Hyrum were martyred in 1844 (1903); part of the temple site at Independence, Missouri (1904); the Vermont farm where Joseph Smith was born in 1805 (1905); and the farm of Joseph Smith Sr. in Manchester, New York, site of the grove where the Prophet first beheld the Father and the Son (1907). He testified, "There is something hallowed about those places, to me and to all, I think, who have accepted the divine mission of Joseph Smith, the Prophet."[54]

President Joseph F. Smith taught Latter-day Saints to honor the Prophet for "lifting the veil of eternity as it were from before their eyes."[55] Likewise, President Smith himself sought to comprehend and teach the expansive truths of the gospel of Jesus Christ. His letters to family and friends, his editorials and responses to questions in Church magazines, and his sermons were all important occasions to expound doctrine. When he and his Counselors in the First Presidency felt that essential doctrines might be misunderstood by Church members or others, they composed and published clarifying explanations. "The Origin of Man" (November 1909)[56] and "The Father and the Son: A Doctrinal Exposition by the First Presidency and the Twelve" (June 1916)[57] became important tools for teaching Latter-day Saints the true nature of our association with Heavenly Father and Jesus Christ.

"I have endeavored from my youth up . . . to be a peacemaker, a preacher of righteousness, and not only to preach righteousness by word, but by example,"[58] President Smith said. From the age of 15 until his death at age 80, he delivered hundreds of gospel talks and discourses to help Saints understand and live the teachings of Jesus Christ. Speaking of his ability to instruct, Charles W. Nibley declared, "As a preacher of righteousness who would compare with him? He was the greatest that I ever heard—strong, powerful, clear, appealing. It was marvelous how the words of living light and fire flowed from him."[59]

Joseph F. Smith rejoiced when Church members heeded his warnings and exhortations as a prophet of God. The willingness of the Saints to move forward in "righteousness, purity and holiness" was of the utmost importance to him.[60] He led the way with his own humility and teachability. "I am only a child, I am only learning," he said in 1916. "I sincerely hope that as I learn little by little, line upon line and precept upon precept, here a little and there a little, day by day, and month by month, and year by year, that there will come a time when I shall have learned indeed the truth and shall know it as God knows it and be saved and exalted in His presence."[61] Always respected for his boldness and certitude, he was revered especially for his compassion. Mrs. Koleka, one of his dear Hawaiian associates, praised him as "the servant of the Most High God, the man of open heart filled with love."[62] He had learned "not only to preach righteousness by word, but by example,"[63] by earnestly seeking to "become conformed to the likeness and image of Jesus Christ."[64]

During the last few months of his life, President Smith felt a particular susceptibility to the Spirit. "I may have physical ailments, but it appears to me that my spiritual status not only remains steadfast as in times past, but is developing, growing,"[65] he said in April 1918. Six months later, on 3 October 1918, as he sat in his room pondering the scriptures and "reflecting upon the great atoning sacrifice that was made by the Son of God, for the redemption of the world,"[66] he received a marvelous manifestation concerning the Savior's visit to the dead while His body was in the tomb. The revelation, later called the vision of the redemption of the dead and canonized as Doctrine and Covenants 138, is a fitting capstone to the life of a prophet who preached unceasingly the importance of bringing to all of God's children the plan of life and salvation.

The glory of God, the divine origin of man and his dependence upon God, the importance of obedience and holy ordinances, loving gratitude, and faithful devotion—these were themes President Smith wove together again and again. Rarely did he address a single gospel principle in isolation from the whole plan of life and salvation. He could preach the gospel in its fulness in a single sermon, sometimes in a single sentence, focusing always on the importance of knowing God the Father and His Son, Jesus Christ. "It is through the love that we have for Them, and through our wish to live in harmony with Their requirements and to become like Them, that we can love one another, and that we can have more pleasure in doing good than we ever could have in doing evil."[67]

## Notes

1. *Deseret News: Semi-Weekly,* 25 Apr. 1882, 1.
2. *Gospel Doctrine,* 5th ed. (1939), 406.
3. In Conference Report, Apr. 1902, 85–86.
4. *Millennial Star,* June 1840, 40.
5. *Millennial Star,* June 1840, 40–41.
6. *Gospel Doctrine,* 494.
7. *History of the Church,* 2:338.
8. In Brian H. Stuy, comp., *Collected Discourses Delivered by President Wilford Woodruff, His Two Counselors, the Twelve Apostles, and Others,* 5 vols. (1987–92), 5:29.
9. Joseph F. Smith's Journal, Leeds, 13 Apr. 1861, holograph, 5; Historical Department Archives, The Church of Jesus Christ of Latter-day Saints.
10. In *Deseret News: Semi-Weekly,* 25 Apr. 1882, 1; spelling modernized.
11. In *Collected Discourses,* 2:348.
12. In *Deseret News: Semi-Weekly,* 10 July 1883, 1.
13. Jos. F. Smith's Journal, 18; spelling modernized; Historical Department Archives, The Church of Jesus Christ of Latter-day Saints.
14. "Editor's Table—In Memoriam, Joseph Fielding Smith (1838–1918)," *Improvement Era,* Jan. 1919, 266.
15. *Life of Joseph F. Smith,* comp. Joseph Fielding Smith (1938), 159.
16. Joseph F. Smith to Samuel L. Adams, 11 May 1888, *Truth and*

*Courage: Joseph F. Smith Letters,* ed. Joseph Fielding McConkie, 2.

17. "Editor's Table—In Memoriam," 266.

18. In James R. Clark, comp., *Messages of the First Presidency of The Church of Jesus Christ of Latter-day Saints,* 6 vols. (1965–75), 5:92.

19. Joseph F. Smith to Samuel L. Adams, 2.

20. In Conference Report, Apr. 1900, 41.

21. In *Messages of the First Presidency,* 4:18.

22. *Gospel Doctrine,* 171.

23. *Gospel Doctrine,* 82.

24. In *Collected Discourses,* 2:280.

25. *Gospel Doctrine,* 90.

26. Journal of Wilford Woodruff, 24 June 1866, Historical Department Archives, The Church of Jesus Christ of Latter-day Saints; spelling modernized.

27. *Gospel Doctrine,* 201.

28. *Gospel Doctrine,* 359.

29. Joseph F. Smith to Hyrum M. Smith, 18 May 1896, *Truth and Courage,* 37.

30. *Deseret News: Semi-Weekly,* 2 Oct. 1883, 1.

31. *Deseret News: Semi-Weekly,* 7 Nov. 1882, 1.

32. *Deseret News: Semi-Weekly,* 25 Apr. 1882, 1.

33. *Life of Joseph F. Smith,* 365.

34. *Life of Joseph F. Smith,* 283.

35. Quoted in Bryant S. Hinckley, "Greatness in Men: Joseph Fielding Smith," *Improvement Era,* June 1932, 459.

36. *Life of Joseph F. Smith,* 453.

37. "General Conference of the Relief Society," *Relief Society Magazine,* June 1917, 316.

38. H. W. Naisbitt, "Temple Building," *Contributor,* Apr. 1892, 257.

39. In *Collected Discourses,* 3:279.

40. In Conference Report, Oct. 1901, 69–70.

41. In Conference Report, Oct. 1901, 70.

42. In *Messages of the First Presidency,* 4:155.

43. In *Messages of the First Presidency,* 4:165.

44. In *Messages of the First Presidency,* 4:222.

45. *Gospel Doctrine,* 159.

46. In Conference Report, Apr. 1908, 5.

47. In Conference Report, Apr. 1908, 6.

48. *Gospel Doctrine,* 189.

49. *Gospel Doctrine,* 393.

50. *Gospel Doctrine,* 386.

51. *Deseret Weekly,* 9 Jan. 1892, 70.

52. In Conference Report, Oct. 1908, 3.

53. In Conference Report, Oct. 1901, 70.

54. In Conference Report, Oct. 1906, 5.

55. *Deseret News: Semi-Weekly,* 27 Feb. 1883, 1.

56. "The Origin of Man, by the First Presidency of the Church," *Improvement Era,* Nov. 1909, 75–81.

57. "The Father and the Son: A Doctrinal Exposition by the First Presidency and the Twelve," *Improvement Era,* Aug. 1916, 934–42.

58. *Gospel Doctrine,* 406.

59. *Gospel Doctrine,* 522.

60. In Conference Report, Oct. 1901, 70.

61. In Conference Report, Apr. 1916, 4.

62. *Life of Joseph F. Smith,* 306.

63. *Gospel Doctrine,* 406.

64. *Gospel Doctrine,* 6.

65. In Conference Report, Apr. 1918, 2.

66. Doctrine and Covenants 138:2.

67. In *Collected Discourses,* 3:218.

The Lord Jesus Christ.
From the painting *Christ and the Rich Young Ruler*, by Heinrich Hofmann.

# I Know That My Redeemer Lives

*Through the witness of the Holy Ghost,*
*each of us can know that Jesus is the Christ,*
*the Son of the living God.*

## From the Life of Joseph F. Smith

For more than half a century, President Joseph F. Smith served as a special witness of the Savior as an Apostle, as a Counselor in the First Presidency, and as President of the Church. His testimony—proclaimed from pulpits at home and in foreign lands, in the councils of the Church, and in the circle of his own family—spoke of a heart and soul committed to Jesus Christ and His glorious gospel. His words were eloquent; his message was clear: "I want to say as a servant of God, independent of the testimonies of all men and of every book that has been written, that I have received the witness of the Spirit in my own heart, and I testify before God, angels and men, without fear of the consequences, that I know that my Redeemer lives, and I shall see him face to face, and stand with him in my resurrected body upon this earth, if I am faithful; for God has revealed this unto me. I have received the witness, and I bear my testimony, and my testimony is true."[1]

At the close of his life, a special graveside funeral service was held in the Salt Lake City Cemetery, where members of the Tabernacle Choir sang in tribute one of his favorite hymns, "I Know That My Redeemer Lives." This phrase was to him the essence of his faith and the focus of his prophetic message: "I know that my Redeemer lives. I feel it in every fiber of my being. I am just as satisfied of it as I am of my own existence. I cannot feel more sure of my own being than I do that my Redeemer lives."[2]

The following testimony is taken from an address that President Smith gave to a conference of the Weber Stake on 18 October 1896.[3]

# Teachings of Joseph F. Smith

### The life and teachings of the Savior
### are proof of His divinity.

We are all familiar with the history of our Savior as it is recorded in the New Testament; how that He was born of a virgin; that He grew in the midst of his brethren to be a man, and what marvelous things He did even in His childhood by the power of His anointing and mission; how He taught the lawyers and the doctors in the synagogue and in the temple, and how He confounded those who sought to make Him an offender for a word. We are all familiar with the power which He displayed in healing the sick, in restoring sight to the blind and hearing to the deaf, and in cleansing the leper, and making the lame to leap with joy.

We are familiar with the doctrines which he taught; and it has always seemed to me that there need be no further proof of the divinity of Jesus Christ than the doctrine which He taught that men should love those who despitefully used them and persecuted them, and that they should return good for evil. Up to His day the doctrine taught in the world was, "an eye for an eye, and a tooth for a tooth." [Matthew 5:38.] This was the philosophy of the age. But Jesus taught directly the opposite of this. He enjoined upon His disciples that they should not return evil for evil, but that they should return good for evil. "Whosoever shall smite thee on thy right cheek, turn to him the other also." [Matthew 5:39.] This doctrine was new to the world. It is a doctrine not in accordance with the fallen nature of man. . . . Therefore, it is not of man. Men could not teach such a doctrine and carry it out in their lives without inspiration and power from on high.

"Blessed are the poor in spirit: for theirs is the kingdom of heaven.

"Blessed are they that mourn: for they shall be comforted.

"Blessed are the meek: for they shall inherit the earth.

looked into the sepulchre and saw two angels in white, "the one at the head, and the other at the feet," [John 20:12] and they said unto her:

"Woman, why weepest thou? She saith unto them, Because they have taken away my Lord, and I know not where they have laid him.

"And when she had thus said, she turned herself back, and saw Jesus standing, and knew not that it was Jesus.

"Jesus saith unto her, Woman, why weepest thou? whom seekest thou? She, supposing him to be the gardener, saith unto him, Sir, if thou have borne him hence, tell me where thou hast laid him, and I will take him away.

"Jesus saith unto her, Mary. She turned herself, and saith unto him, Rabboni; which is to say, Master.

"Jesus saith unto her, Touch me not; for I am not yet ascended to my Father, but go to my brethren, and say unto them, I ascend unto my Father, and your Father; to my God, and your God." [John 20:13–17.]

Mary then went away and told the disciples that she had seen the Lord, and He also appeared unto them.

Now, let us think of this a moment. Here is a historical fact related that Mary went to the tomb, and saw two angels there, and afterwards saw the risen Redeemer Himself. She had the testimony of heavenly messengers, confirmed by the Son of God Himself, that the Redeemer had risen. Her words are handed down to us in testimony. Will you dispute them? Will you doubt her testimony? . . . Afterwards He overtook two disciples who were journeying to Emmaus, and went with them; but "their eyes were holden that they should not know Him." [Luke 24:16.] Jesus asked them what made them so sad, and they replied: "Art thou only a stranger in Jerusalem, and hast not known the things which are come to pass there in these days." [Luke 24:18.] By and by their eyes were opened, and they knew Him.

After this He appeared unto His disciples. One of the disciples heard that Jesus was risen, but said he would not believe it except he saw Him and could thrust his hand into His side and his finger into the prints of the nails in His hands. How very much like mankind today was Thomas. He again appeared unto the disciples, and Thomas was with them.

"Then saith He to Thomas, Reach hither thy finger, and behold my hands; and reach hither thy hand, and thrust it into my side; and be not faithless, but believing.

"And Thomas answered and said unto Him, My Lord and my God.

"Jesus saith unto him, Thomas, because thou hast seen me, thou hast believed; blessed are they that have not seen, and yet have believed." [John 20:27–29.]

---

### By the power of the Holy Ghost we can know that our Redeemer lives.

Jesus administered unto His disciples after He was risen, and confirmed upon their understandings the fact that they were not deceived, but that He was truly the Son of God, now risen from the dead to immortality and eternal life. They saw not with the natural eye. We may see a great many things with our natural sight, but that may be deceived. We may hear with our ears, but they may be deceived. Our natural senses are susceptible to deception. . . . But let me tell you when the Almighty reveals Himself unto man, He does it by the power of the Holy Ghost, and not through the natural eye or the natural ear. He speaks to man as if He were speaking to him independent of his body; He speaks to the spirit. Therefore, if God Almighty speaks to you and bears record of His truth by the power of the Holy Ghost, . . . you will know as God knows. It will not be something that you believe only; something that has been communicated to you through your natural senses, in which you may be mistaken or deceived; but it will be that which God has spoken to the heart, to the living soul, to the eternal being of man, which, like God, is indestructible and eternal.

It was in this way that Jesus opened the spiritual eye and understanding of His disciples after His resurrection, so that they knew that He was both Lord and Christ. They knew that He was risen from the dead. They knew that He was the Son of the living God, because God had revealed it to them. Therefore, they could say as the poet has said,

"O, the sweet joy this sentence gives:
I know that my Redeemer lives."

. . . Who can tell the joy and the satisfaction that comes to the soul of man who has received this witness from Almighty God? No man can utter it. I cannot tell it to you. There are no words of man that can speak it. It can only be felt. It can only be understood by the immortal part of man. Unspeakable is the joy that a man feels who has received this testimony from the Holy Ghost. . . .

The Holy Spirit of God has spoken to me—not through the ear, not through the eye, but to my spirit, to my living and eternal part,—and has revealed unto me that Jesus is the Christ, the Son of the living God. I testify to you that I know that my Redeemer lives. Furthermore, I know that I shall see Him on this earth, and that I shall see Him as He is. . . . For He is coming to visit the earth again; not as He came before, but in power and great glory, taking vengeance upon the wicked and the ungodly who will not hearken to the voice of the Spirit, but who harden their hearts against the truth and close their understanding against the testimonies of the servants of God. They will be judged; not by the hearing of the ear, or by the sight of the eye, but with righteousness shall they be judged, and they will be condemned because the light has come into the world and they love darkness rather than light. . . . The Lord has revealed this to me. He has filled my whole spirit with this testimony, until there is no room for doubt. . . .

We have the testimony of the disciples of Christ on the Asiatic continent and the testimony of the disciples of Jesus on this continent, bearing record to the same truths. Then we have the Book of Doctrine and Covenants, which contains the revelations and testimonies of God to his Servants and Saints in the day in which we live, the third testimony of these things. In addition to all this, . . . we have the testimony of the Holy Spirit in our hearts, which cannot be denied; for he that receiveth this testimony by inspiration of the Holy Ghost cannot be deceived. The Spirit of God does not bear record of that which is not true. Therefore, if you have received the witness of the Holy Spirit in your heart, you know that your Redeemer lives. . . .

. . . I bear you my testimony that the Redeemer lives. May this testimony find a place in your hearts. . . . If we will love each other and do good to each other, we will then carry out the precepts of the Gospel of the Son of God, the doctrine of Christ, which is calculated to redeem and exalt the world and bring back mankind into the presence of God, which may we all have the privilege of receiving and enjoying, is my prayer.

## Suggestions for Study

- What incidents or teachings from the life of the Savior have helped you receive a testimony that He is the Son of God?

- How did Jesus Christ return good for evil when He was persecuted? What blessings result from following His teachings to return good for evil? How can we more effectively follow this doctrine? (See also Matthew 5:38–47.)

- How can we apply the counsel "to plant the word in your hearts, that ye may try the experiment of its goodness" (Alma 34:4) to the passages President Smith referred to from the Sermon on the Mount? (See Matthew 5:3–6.)

- How can meekness be our strength? Why is meekness so difficult for many in the world to develop?

- How did the Savior's final words as He hung on the cross reflect "love, mercy, charity and forgiveness"? How can we follow His example during our own times of trial and testing?

- How is your testimony strengthened by Mary Magdalene's witness of the resurrected Redeemer? (See John 20:11–18.)

- How was Thomas "very much like mankind today"? What blessings do we receive if we "have not seen, and yet have believed"? (John 20:29).

- What have you learned from President Smith about bearing testimony of the Savior?

- How does President Smith's testimony of the Savior make you feel? How can his testimony help you strengthen your own witness of Jesus Christ, the Son of God?

### *Notes*

1. *Gospel Doctrine,* 5th ed. (1939), 447.
2. *Gospel Doctrine,* 69.
3. *Deseret News: Semi-Weekly,* 17 Nov. 1896, 1.

President Joseph F. Smith declared the Prophet Joseph Smith to be
"the instrument chosen of God and endowed with his authority
to restore the holy Priesthood" (*Gospel Doctrine,* 478).

# A Personal Witness of the Prophet Joseph Smith

*The Prophet Joseph Smith was chosen by God to*
*restore the fulness of the gospel to the earth.*

## From the Life of Joseph F. Smith

Early in his life, Joseph F. Smith received a testimony that the Prophet Joseph Smith was chosen to restore the gospel of Jesus Christ in this last dispensation. Years later President Smith recalled: "As a child I knew the Prophet Joseph Smith. As a child I have listened to him preach the gospel that God had committed to his charge and care. As a child I was familiar in his home, in his household, as I was familiar under my own father's roof. I have retained the witness of the Spirit that I was imbued with, as a child, and that I received from my sainted mother, the firm belief that Joseph Smith was a prophet of God; that he was inspired as no other man in his generation, or for centuries before, had been inspired; that he had been chosen of God to lay the foundations of God's Kingdom."[1]

While serving as President, Joseph F. Smith authorized the purchase of landmarks significant to the life of the Prophet Joseph Smith and the growth of the Church, including the Prophet's birthplace in Sharon, Vermont; the jail in Carthage, Illinois; and the Joseph Smith Sr. farm in Manchester, New York.

President Joseph F. Smith said of the Prophet's work: "I bear my testimony to you and to the world, that Joseph Smith was raised up by the power of God to lay the foundations of this great latter-day work, to reveal the fulness of the gospel to the world in this dispensation, to restore the Priesthood of God to the world, by which men may act in the name of the Father, and of the Son, and of the Holy Ghost, and it will be accepted of God; it will be by his authority. I bear my testimony to it; I know that it is true."[2]

# Teachings of Joseph F. Smith

### The Prophet Joseph Smith was God's chosen instrument to restore the gospel of salvation.

Joseph Smith was the instrument chosen of God and endowed with his authority to restore the holy Priesthood, the power of God to bind on earth and in heaven,—the power of the Priesthood by which men may perform ordinances of the gospel of Jesus Christ for the salvation of mankind. Through Joseph Smith the gospel of repentance, baptism in water for the remission of sins, the baptism of the Holy Ghost and by fire have been restored, and the knowledge that Jesus is the Christ, the Only Begotten Son of God, is made manifest through the spirit of truth. We are obligated to this humble servant that the Lord chose to lay the foundation of this work for the ordinances of the gospel of the Son of God, then and still unknown to the world, by which we may become united together as families, as kindreds, under the bonds of the new and everlasting covenant, for time and for all eternity.

We are obligated to the Prophet Joseph Smith, as an instrument in the hand of the Lord, for the knowledge that we possess of the work which is necessary to be done in the house of God, for the salvation of the living and the redemption of the dead, and for the eternal union of souls who are united in this life by the power of God, under the bond of the everlasting covenant. We are indebted, or obligated at least, to the Prophet Joseph Smith, as the instrument in the hands of God, for the knowledge we now possess that a man cannot be exalted into the presence of God and the full enjoyment of his glory, alone. It was not designed for the man to be alone, for the man is not without the woman, neither the woman without the man, in the Lord.[3]

God lives, and Jesus is the Christ, the Savior of the world. Joseph Smith is a prophet of God—living, not dead; for his name will never perish. The angel that visited him and declared God's message unto him, told him that his name should be held for good and for evil throughout the world [see Joseph Smith—History 1:33]. This prediction was made in the days of his youth, before the Church was organized, and before there was any prospect of that which has since been accomplished. The declaration was made, notwithstanding it then seemed an absolute impossibility; but from the day it was spoken until this moment, and from now on until the winding-up scene, the name of Joseph Smith, the prophet of the nineteenth century, has been, is being, and will be heralded abroad to the nations of the earth, and will be held in honor or contempt by the people of the world. . . ; for he did and is doing the work of the Master. He laid the foundations in this dispensation for the restoration of the principles that were taught by the Son of God, who for these principles lived, and taught, and died, and rose from the dead.[4]

Where [Joseph Smith's name] is spoken of for good, it is by those who have had the privilege of hearing the gospel which has come to the earth through him, and who have been sufficiently honest and humble to receive the same. They speak of him with a knowledge which they have received by the inspiration of the Holy Spirit, through obedience to the principles which he taught, as a prophet and as an inspired man. They speak to his praise, to his honor, and they hold his name in honorable remembrance. They revere him, and they love him, as they love no other man, because they know he was the chosen instrument in the hands of the Almighty in restoring the gospel of life and salvation unto them, of opening their understandings of the future, of lifting the veil of eternity, as it were, from before their eyes. Those who have received the principles which he promulgated know they pertain not only to their own salvation, happiness and peace, spiritual and temporal, but to the welfare, happiness, salvation and exaltation of their kindred who have died without a knowledge of the truth.

The work in which Joseph Smith was engaged was not confined to this life alone, but it pertains as well to the life to come, and to the life that has been. In other words, it relates to those who have lived upon the earth, to those who are living and to those who shall come after us. It is not something which relates to man only while he tabernacles in the flesh, but to the whole human family from eternity to eternity. . . . And this is not confined to a village, nor to a state, nor to a nation, but extends to every nation, kindred, tongue and people.[5]

To me it is very strange indeed that there should be so much extreme ill feeling manifested by the world against Joseph Smith. He wronged no man. I am a witness of that, for I know his life. I have seen him in the flesh, and I have read of his sayings. I have read the revelations that the Lord gave to him. I am familiar with his work, and I know that he never wronged a living soul. He did not injure his fellowmen, but he did much to exalt them. And yet, the strange part of it is that people who are absolutely ignorant of him should entertain the most bitter, vindictive and wicked feelings towards him that it is possible for men to feel. I ask myself, Why is this? Men do not feel that way, as a rule, towards impostors, or to the promoters of new, man-made religious organizations. But, strange to say, they nearly always become enraged when the name of the Prophet Joseph Smith is mentioned! While, however, this is strange from a natural standpoint, it is only in accordance with the promise given to him in the beginning by one of the heavenly messengers sent to instruct him. . . .

. . . The foundation of the work laid by the Prophet Joseph Smith was laid in eternal truth. It cannot be overthrown. It is like the house built on the rock. The storms may beat upon it, the rains may descend, the tempests may come, the hearts of men may be stirred up to anger and to persecution against it; but it is as firm as the everlasting hills, because it is built upon the truth [see Matthew 7:24–25]. Honesty, virtue, purity of life, faith in the Lord Jesus Christ and in His resurrection, obedience to the commandments of God, are cardinal principles of our belief. We know that the doctrine is true.[6]

---

**Joseph Smith's First Vision is the greatest event since the Resurrection of the Savior.**

The greatest event that has ever occurred in the world, since the resurrection of the Son of God from the tomb and his ascension on high, was the coming of the Father and of the Son to that boy Joseph Smith, to prepare the way for the laying of the foundation of his kingdom—not the kingdom of man—never more to cease nor to be overturned. Having accepted this truth, I find it easy to accept of every other truth that he enunciated and declared. . . . He never taught a doctrine that was not true. He never practiced a doctrine that he was not commanded to practice. He never advocated error. He was not deceived. He saw; he heard; he did as he was commanded to do; and, therefore, God is responsible for the work accomplished by Joseph Smith—not Joseph Smith. The Lord is responsible for it, and not man.[7]

In the spring of 1820, [Joseph Smith] received the first supernatural or heavenly manifestation. He was then fourteen years of age. Ordinarily we do not expect a very great deal from a boy who is only fourteen years of age, and it is not likely that a boy of that tender age could have become very vicious or wicked, especially when he was born and reared on a farm, apart from the corrupting vices of great cities, and free from contact with the debasing influence of vile associations. It is not likely that he spent many idle moments during the working years of his life, up to fourteen years of age; for his father had to labor for his living and earn it from the soil by the labor of his hands, being a poor man with a large family to support.[8]

Concerning his spiritual manifestations, is it reasonable to suppose that there could have been premeditated deceit on the part of the boy, and such a boy, in his simple statement of what he saw and heard? No; neither could the answer which the heavenly messenger gave to him, have been composed in the child's own mind. Joseph Smith's testimony concerning his heavenly manifestation, in later life, was as simple, straight-forward, plain, and true, as it had been in childhood; the fidelity, courage, and love implanted in and characteristic of his life in boyhood neither faltered nor changed with maturity. His wisdom came in revelations of God to him.[9]

Our critics say it was an apparition that the Prophet Joseph saw, but he did not say so. He said the personages who appeared to him were real men. . . . To us has come the account of the birth, life and work of Christ, and there is nothing in the narrative to cause us to believe it more readily than that story of the

Prophet Joseph Smith. Christ walked and talked and counseled with his friends when he came down from heaven over 1900 years ago. Is there any reason why he could not come again, why he should not visit this earth once more and talk with men to-day? If there is I should be glad to hear it. The thing I want to impress upon you is that God is real, a person of flesh and bones, the same as you are and I am. Christ is the same, but the Holy Ghost is a person of spirit.[10]

---

### The Prophet Joseph Smith translated the Book of Mormon through the gift and power of God.

When [Joseph Smith] was between 17 and 18 years of age, he received another heavenly manifestation, and some great and glorious things were revealed to him, and for four years subsequently he received visits from a heavenly messenger. . . . This personage, he claimed, revealed to him the mind and will of the Lord, and showed him the character of the great work that he, in the hands of God was to be instrumental in establishing in the earth when the time should come. This was the labor that was performed by the angel Moroni, during the four years intervening between 1823 and 1827. In 1827 he received from the hands of the angel Moroni, the gold plates from which this book (Book of Mormon) was translated by him through the inspiration of the Almighty, and the gift and power of God unto him. . . .

Did Joseph Smith during the three years intervening between 1827 and 1830, while he was laboring with his hands for a scanty subsistence, dodging his enemies, and trying to evade the grasp of those who sought to destroy him and prevent the accomplishment of his mission, struggling all the while against untold obstacles and depressing embarrassments to complete the translation of this book, have much chance of becoming wicked or corrupt? I do not think he had. When he had finished translating the Book of Mormon he was still only a boy, yet in producing this book he developed historical facts, prophecies, revelations, predictions, testimonies and doctrines, precepts and principles that are beyond the power and wisdom of the learned world to duplicate or refute. Joseph Smith was an unlearned youth, so far as the learning of the world is concerned. He was taught by the angel Moroni. He received his education from above, from God Almighty, and not from man-made institutions; but to charge him with being ignorant would be both unjust and false; no man or combination of men possessed greater intelligence than he, nor could the combined wisdom and cunning of the age produce an equivalent for what he did. He was not ignorant, for he was taught by him from whom all intelligence flows. He possessed a knowledge of God and of his law, and of eternity.[11]

The Book of Mormon was translated by the gift and power of God, through the instrumentality of a young man; not by a learned man, a man of letters, but by an unlettered, unsophisticated, innocent boy! And that unlettered, unsophisticated, innocent boy was no other than Joseph Smith. He had not the wisdom, the intelligence nor the skill of himself to translate into the English language the inscriptions upon the plates that were hid away by the ancient inhabitants of this continent. He never claimed that he did translate those ancient characters by his own wisdom. On the contrary, he maintained that he did it by the gift and power of God unto him.[12]

---

### The Prophet has done more for the salvation of mankind than anyone who ever lived, save Jesus only.

[Joseph Smith] opened up communication with the heavens in his youth. He brought forth the Book of Mormon, which contains the fulness of the gospel; and the revelations contained in the Book of Doctrine and Covenants; restored the holy Priesthood unto man; established and organized the Church of Jesus Christ of Latter-day Saints, an organization which has no parallel in all the world, and which all the cunning and wisdom of men for ages has failed to discover or produce and never could have done. He founded colonies in the states of New York, Ohio, Missouri and Illinois, and pointed the way for the gathering of the Saints into the Rocky Mountains; sent the gospel into Europe and to the islands of the sea; founded the town of Kirtland, Ohio, and there built a temple that cost scores of thousands of dollars; he founded the city of Nauvoo in the midst of persecution; gathered into Nauvoo and vicinity some 20,000 people, and commenced the building of the temple there, which when completed cost one million dollars; and in doing all this he had to contend against the prejudices of the age, against relentless persecution, mobocracy, and vile calumny and slander, that were heaped upon him from all quarters without stint or measure. In a word, he did more in from fourteen to twenty years for the salvation of man than any other man, save Jesus only, who ever lived [see D&C 135:3], and yet he was accused by his enemies of being an indolent and worthless man!

Where shall we go to find another man who has accomplished a one-thousandth part of the good that Joseph Smith accomplished? . . . No man in the nineteenth century, except Joseph Smith, has discovered to the world a ray of light upon the keys and power of the holy Priesthood, or the ordinances of the gospel, either for the living or the dead. Through Joseph Smith, God has revealed many things which were kept hidden from the foundation of the world in fulfilment of the prophets. . . . And this is strictly in keeping with the objects and character of this great latter-day work, destined to consummate the great purposes and designs of God concerning the dispensation of the fulness of times.[13]

Joseph the Prophet . . . became the means, in God's providence, to restore the old truths of the everlasting gospel of Jesus Christ, the plan of salvation, which is older than the human race. It is true, also, that his teachings were new to the people of his day because they had apostatized from the truth—but the principles of the gospel are the oldest truths in existence. They were new to Joseph's generation, as they are in part to ours, because men had gone astray, been cast adrift, shifted hither and thither by every new wind of doctrine which cunning men—so called progressives—had advanced. This made the Prophet Joseph a restorer, not a destroyer, of old truths. And this does not justify us in discarding the simple, fundamental principles of the gospel and running after modern doctrinal fads and notions.[14]

I declare unto you in all candor, and in all earnestness of soul, that I believe with all my heart in the divine mission of Joseph Smith, the Prophet, that I am convinced in every fiber of my being that God raised him up to restore to the earth the gospel of Christ, which is indeed the power of God unto salvation. I testify to you that Joseph Smith was instrumental in the hand of the Lord in restoring God's truth to the world, and also the holy Priesthood, which is his authority delegated unto man. I know this is true, and I testify of it to you. To me it is all-in-all; it is my life, it is my light; it is my hope, and my joy; it gives me the only assurance that I have for exaltation, for my resurrection from death, with those whom I have loved and cherished in this life, and with whom my lot has been cast in this world—honorable men, pure, humble men, who were obedient unto God and his commands, who were not ashamed of the gospel of Christ, nor of their convictions or knowledge of the truth of the gospel; men who were made of the stuff of which martyrs are made, and who were willing at any moment to lay down their lives for Christ's sake, and for the gospel, if need be, which they had received with the testimony of the Holy Spirit in their hearts. I want to be re-united with these men when I shall have finished my course here. When my mission is done here, I hope to go beyond into the spirit world where they dwell, and be reunited with them. It is this gospel of the Son of God that gives me the hope that I have of this consummation, and the realization of my desire in this direction. I have staked all on this gospel, and I have not done it in vain. I know in whom I trust. I know that my Redeemer lives, and that he shall stand upon the earth in the latter days.[15]

## Suggestions for Study

- In what ways was the Prophet Joseph Smith "an instrument in the hand of the Lord"? In what ways have you been blessed by the things the Lord revealed through the Prophet Joseph Smith?

- Why is it important to have a testimony that Joseph Smith was a prophet of God in this dispensation?

- What significant truths did Joseph Smith learn from the First Vision? What significant truths have you learned from the First

Vision? How is a testimony of the First Vision a foundation for accepting other gospel truths?

• Why is it important to know that the Book of Mormon "was translated by the gift and power of God"?

• What are some of the ways in which the Prophet Joseph Smith did more "for the salvation of man than any other man, save Jesus only"?

• Why is it important to know that the Prophet Joseph Smith was "a restorer, not a destroyer, of old truths"?

• How have you been strengthened by association with men, women, or children who have strong testimonies and are "not ashamed of the gospel of Christ"? How can we strengthen others with our testimonies?

• What most impresses you about President Joseph F. Smith's testimonies of the Prophet? What is your own witness of the divine mission of the Prophet Joseph Smith?

## Notes

1. *Gospel Doctrine*, 5th ed. (1939), 493.
2. *Gospel Doctrine*, 168–69.
3. *Gospel Doctrine*, 478–79; paragraphing added.
4. *Gospel Doctrine*, 479.
5. *Gospel Doctrine*, 480–81.
6. *Proceedings at the Dedication of the Joseph Smith Memorial Monument: At Sharon, Windsor County, Vermont, December 23rd, 1905*, 41–42.
7. *Gospel Doctrine*, 495–96.
8. *Gospel Doctrine*, 482.
9. *Gospel Doctrine*, 488–89.
10. *Gospel Doctrine*, 478.
11. *Gospel Doctrine*, 483–84.
12. *Proceedings at the Dedication of the Joseph Smith Memorial Monument*, 38–39.
13. *Gospel Doctrine*, 484–85.
14. *Gospel Doctrine*, 489.
15. *Gospel Doctrine*, 501.

# True, Faithful, Earnest Prayer

*True prayer arises from the heart to God*
*in the name of Jesus Christ.*

## From the Life of Joseph F. Smith

In the fall of 1847, nine-year-old Joseph F. Smith; his widowed mother, Mary Fielding Smith; and his uncle Joseph Fielding were camped along the Missouri River on the way to Winter Quarters. The next morning they discovered that their best team of oxen was missing.

Joseph F. and his uncle searched long and hard for the oxen, becoming "soaked to the skin, fatigued, disheartened and almost exhausted." Joseph F. said: "In this pitiable plight I was the first to return to our wagons, and as I approached I saw my mother kneeling down in prayer. I halted for a moment and then drew gently near enough to hear her pleading with the Lord not to suffer us to be left in this helpless condition, but to lead us to recover our lost team, that we might continue our travels in safety. When she arose from her knees I was standing nearby. The first expression I caught upon her precious face was a lovely smile, which discouraged as I was, gave me renewed hope and an assurance I had not felt before."

She cheerfully encouraged Joseph and his uncle to sit and enjoy the breakfast she had prepared and said, "I will just take a walk out and see if I can find the cattle." Despite her brother's protests that further searching would be fruitless, Mary set out, leaving him and Joseph F. to eat breakfast. She encountered a nearby herdsman who indicated that he had seen the lost oxen in the direction opposite to her course. Joseph F. said, "We heard plainly what he said, but mother went right on, and did not even turn her head to look at him." She soon beckoned to Joseph F.

and his uncle, who ran to the spot where she stood. There they saw the oxen fastened to a clump of willows.

President Joseph F. Smith later said, "It was one of the first practical and positive demonstrations of the efficacy of prayer I had ever witnessed. It made an indelible impression upon my mind, and has been a source of comfort, assurance and guidance to me throughout all of my life."[1]

# Teachings of Joseph F. Smith

### Know how to approach God in prayer.

I pray that you will know how to approach God in prayer. It is not such a difficult thing to learn how to pray. It is not the words we use particularly that constitute prayer. Prayer does not consist of words, altogether. True, faithful, earnest prayer consists more in the feeling that rises from the heart and from the inward desire of our spirits to supplicate the Lord in humility and in faith, that we may receive his blessings. It matters not how simple the words may be, if our desires are genuine and we come before the Lord with a broken heart and contrite spirit to ask him for that which we need.[2]

He is not afar off. It is not difficult to approach Him, if we will only do it with a broken heart and a contrite spirit, as did Nephi of old. This was the way in which Joseph Smith, in his boyhood, approached Him. He went into the woods, knelt down, and in humility he sought earnestly to know which church was acceptable to God. He received an answer to his prayer, which he offered from the depths of his heart, and he received it in a way that he did not expect.

My brethren and sisters, do not learn to pray with your lips only. Do not learn a prayer by heart, and say it every morning and evening. That is something I dislike very much. It is true that a great many people fall into the rut of saying over a ceremonious prayer. They begin at a certain point, and they touch at all the points along the road until they get to the winding up scene; and when they have done, I do not know whether the prayer has ascended beyond the ceiling of the room or not.[3]

My brethren and sisters, let us remember and call upon God and implore his blessings and his favor upon us. Let us do it, nevertheless, in wisdom and in righteousness, and when we pray we should call upon him in a consistent and reasonable way. We should not ask the Lord for that which is unnecessary or which would not be beneficial to us. We should ask for that which we need, and we should ask in faith, "nothing wavering, for he that wavereth," as the apostle said, "is like the wave of the sea, driven by the wind and tossed. For let not that man think that he shall receive anything of the Lord" [James 1:6–7]. But when we ask of God for blessings let us ask in the faith of the gospel, in that faith that he has promised to give to those who believe in him and obey his commandments.[4]

I was greatly impressed and moved by [President Heber C. Kimball's] manner of praying in his family. I have never heard any other man pray as he did. He did not speak to the Lord as one afar off, but as if conversing with him face to face. Time and again I have been so impressed with the idea of the actual presence of God, while he was conversing with him in prayer, that I could not refrain from looking up to see if he were actually present and visible.[5]

---

## Go before the Lord often in humility and faith.

We . . . accept without any question the doctrines we have been taught by the Prophet Joseph Smith and by the Son of God himself, that we pray to God, the Eternal Father, in the name of his only begotten Son, to whom also our father Adam and his posterity have prayed from the beginning.[6]

I think that it is desirable for us to look well to our words when we call upon the Lord. He hears us in secret, and can reward us openly. We do not have to cry unto him with many words. We do not have to weary him with long prayers. What we do need, and what we should do as Latter-day Saints, for our own good, is to go before him often, to witness unto him that we remember him and that we are willing to take upon us his name, keep his commandments, work righteousness; and that we desire his Spirit to help us. Then, if we are in trouble, let us go to the Lord and ask him directly and specifically to help us out of the trouble that we are in; and let the prayer come from the heart, let it not be in words that are worn into ruts in the beaten tracks of common use, without thought or feeling in the use of those words.

Let us speak the simple words, expressing our need, that will appeal most truly to the Giver of every good and perfect gift. He can hear in secret; and he knows the desires of our hearts before we ask, but he has made it obligatory, and a duty that we shall call upon his name—that we shall ask that we may receive; and knock that it may be opened to us; and seek that we may find [see Matthew 7:7]. Hence, the Lord has made it a loving duty that we should remember him, that we should witness unto him morning, noon, and night, that we do not forget the Giver of every good gift unto us.[7]

Observe that great commandment given of the Master, always to remember the Lord, to pray in the morning, and in the evening, and always remember to thank him for the blessings that you receive day by day.[8]

No limit should be or can be set to the offering of prayer and the rendering of praise to the Giver of Good, for we are specially told to pray without ceasing, and no special authority of the Priesthood or standing in the Church is essential to the offering of prayer.[9]

A man may fast and pray till he kills himself, and there isn't any necessity for it; nor wisdom in it. I say to my brethren, when they are fasting, and praying for the sick, and for those who need faith and prayer, do not go beyond what is wise and prudent in fasting and prayer. The Lord can hear a simple prayer offered in faith, in half a dozen words, and he will recognize fasting that may not continue more than twenty-four hours, just as readily and as effectually as he will answer a prayer of a thousand words and fasting for a month.[10]

What shall we do if we have neglected our prayers? Let us begin to pray. If we have neglected any other duty, let us seek unto the Lord for his Spirit, that we may know wherein we have erred and lost our opportunities, or let them pass by us unimproved.

Let us seek unto the Lord in humility, determined to forsake every-thing that would be an obstruction to our receiving the intelligence and the light that we need, and an answer to our prayers, that we may approach him confident that his ears will be open to our petitions, that his heart will be turned unto us in mercy, that our sins may be forgiven, our minds enlightened by the influence and power of God, that we may comprehend our duty and have a disposition to perform it, not to postpone it, not to set it aside.[11]

We should carry with us the spirit of prayer throughout every duty that we have to perform in life. Why should we? One of the simple reasons that appeals to my mind with great force is that man is so utterly dependent upon God! How helpless we are without him; how little can we do without his merciful providence in our behalf![12]

If you do not forget to pray God will not forget you, and He will not withdraw Himself from you if you do not withdraw yourselves from Him. Why do men apostatize? Why do they lose the faith? Why do their minds become darkened? Because they wander from the right path; they neglect their duties and forget to pray, and to acknowledge the Lord and He withdraws His Spirit from them and they are left in the dark. . . . [This will not happen] to the man who will pray morning, noon and night and humble himself before the Lord, and pray to the Lord in his prosperity just as he would pray to Him in his adversity. That man will never apostatize.[13]

---

**Home is the temple of the family for
prayer and praise to God.**

The typical "Mormon" home is the temple of the family, in which the members of the household gather morning and evening, for prayer and praise to God, offered in the name of Jesus Christ, and often accompanied by the reading of scripture and the singing of spiritual songs.[14]

It is a simple thing to pray, yet how generally this duty is neglected. Parents forget to call together their households and invoke upon them the blessings of God; they are too often in a hurry, or are perplexed so much with the affairs of life as to forget the obligations they are under to the Almighty. Prayer in the family circle may be looked upon by some Latter-day Saints as a very simple thing, but its neglect will produce very serious results. . . . Some Latter-day Saints remember Him only when adversity overtakes them; in prosperity they forget him. Now the Lord may conclude to forget us when we most need his help, and if he should do so we would find ourselves in an unfortunate condition. Never forget God; seek him in prayer morning and night. . . . Be prayerful in storm and sunshine, then when darkness overtakes you, relief will assuredly come.[15]

Fathers, pray with your families; bow down with them morning and at night; pray to the Lord, thank him for his goodness, mercy and Fatherly kindness, just as our earthly fathers and mothers have been extremely kind to us poor, disobedient and wayward children.

Do you pray? What do you pray for? You pray that God may recognize you, that he may hear your prayers, and that he may bless you with his Spirit, and that he may lead you into all truth and show you the right way; that he will warn you against wrong and guide you into the right path; that you may not fall astray, that you may not veer into the wrong way unto death, but that you may keep in the narrow way.[16]

When a little child bows down in its perfect simplicity and asks the Father for a blessing, the Father hears the voice, and will answer in blessings upon his head, because the child is innocent and asks in full trust and confidence. These are simple principles that I have sought to impress upon your minds. They are simple, but necessary, and essential.[17]

We are directed to call upon God in the name of Jesus Christ. We are told that we should remember him in our homes, keep his holy name fresh in our minds, and revere him in our hearts; we should call upon him from time to time, from day to day; and, in fact, every moment of our lives we should live so that the desires of our hearts will be a prayer unto God for righteousness, for truth, and for the salvation of the human family.[18]

## Let your soul go out in prayer for the good of others.

When we come together each should have a prayerful spirit and let his soul go out, not alone for himself, but toward the whole church. If this were done, none would go away from the house of worship without experiencing the spirit of God. . . . [When prayer is offered,] everyone . . . should endorse it by a verbal amen.[19]

When a man seeks the spirit of wisdom and of inspiration from the Almighty, . . . the Lord will build him up, because he has the fear of God before his eyes, because he loves his neighbor as he loves himself, and he is not praying: "O Lord, bless me and my wife, my son John and his wife; us four, and no more. Amen." Such a man does not pray in this way, but he prays for the welfare of Zion, and the longevity of these men who have been raised up of the Lord to be our leaders, our counselors and our advisers in the principles of the Gospel. He prays for his neighbor.[20]

The man who is prayerful before the Lord will set an example before all others who see and know his conduct.[21]

I never pray to the Lord without remembering His servants who are in the nations of the earth preaching the Gospel. The burden of my prayer is, "O God, keep them pure and unspotted from the world; help them to maintain their integrity, that they may not fall into the hands of their enemies and be overcome; lead them to the honest in heart." This has been my prayer ever since I was in the mission field, and I will continue to pray thus as long as I live.[22]

[To his missionary son Joseph Fielding, Joseph F. Smith wrote on 18 July 1899:] Our hearts are full of blessing for you and . . . together with all your companions we hold you up in remembrance before the Lord whenever we pray. O! God, my Father, bless, comfort, sustain and make efficient my sons, and all thy servants in the mission field. When doors are shut in their faces, give them grace, forbearance and forgiving hearts. When coldly spurned by scornful men, warm them by thy precious love, when cruelly treated and persecuted be thou present to shield them by thy power. Make thy servants to know Thou art God, and to feel thy presence. Feed them with spiritual life and with perfect love which casteth out all fear and may all their bodily needs be supplied. Help them to store their minds with useful knowledge, and their memories to retain thy truth as a well filled treasure. May they be humble before Thee and meek and lowly as thy glorious Son! Put their trust in Thee, in thy word, and in thy gracious promises. And may wisdom and judgment, prudence and presence of mind, discretion and charity, truth and purity, and honor and dignity characterise their ministry and clothe them as with holy garments. O, God, bless abundantly thy young servants with every needed gift and grace and holy thought, and power to become thy Sons in very deed![23]

## Suggestions for Study

- What does it mean to "supplicate the Lord in humility and in faith"? What does it mean to have a broken heart and a contrite spirit? How do a broken heart and a contrite spirit help us to approach Heavenly Father in prayer?

- Why is faith necessary as we pray? (See also Helaman 10:5.) Why should we avoid repetitious prayers? What can we do to make our prayers more meaningful?

- Why must we be willing to "forsake everything that would be an obstruction" to receiving an answer to prayer? What are some of these obstructions?

- How can we "carry with us the spirit of prayer throughout every duty that we have to perform in life"?

- What "serious results" might we face if we neglect family prayer?

- What makes a child's prayer so effective? How can we be more childlike in our prayers?

- Why is it important to "endorse" the prayers of others "by a verbal amen"?

- Why is it important to pray for others? How does praying for the general and local leaders of the Church bless them? How does it bless us and our families?

## Notes

1. *Life of Joseph F. Smith,* comp. Joseph Fielding Smith (1938), 131–34.

2. *Gospel Doctrine,* 5th ed. (1939), 219.

3. In Conference Report, Oct. 1899, 71–72.

4. *Gospel Doctrine,* 218.

5. *Gospel Doctrine,* 198.

6. In Conference Report, Oct. 1916, 6.

7. *Gospel Doctrine,* 221; paragraphing added.

8. *Gospel Doctrine,* 218.

9. *Gospel Doctrine,* 205.

10. *Gospel Doctrine,* 368.

11. *Deseret News* (weekly), 8 Dec. 1875, 4.

12. *Gospel Doctrine,* 218.

13. "Discourse by President Joseph F. Smith," *Millennial Star,* 25 Oct. 1906, 674.

14. In Conference Report, Apr. 1907, 7.

15. In Brian H. Stuy, comp., *Collected Discourses Delivered by President Wilford Woodruff, His Two Counselors, the Twelve Apostles, and Others,* 5 vols. (1987–92), 2:280.

16. *Gospel Doctrine,* 215.

17. *Gospel Doctrine,* 216; paragraphing altered.

18. *Gospel Doctrine,* 503–4.

19. In *Collected Discourses,* 2:365.

20. "Discourse by President Joseph F. Smith," *Millennial Star,* 11 Nov. 1897, 709.

21. *Gospel Doctrine,* 116.

22. "Discourse by President Joseph F. Smith," *Millennial Star,* 1 Nov. 1906, 691–92.

23. Joseph F. Smith to Joseph Fielding Smith, 18 July 1899, in Joseph Fielding Smith Papers 1854–1918, Historical Department Archives, The Church of Jesus Christ of Latter-day Saints.

President Joseph F. Smith said of his mother, Mary Fielding Smith,
"My mother was a Saint, . . . a woman of God, pure and faithful"
*(Deseret News: Semi-Weekly,* 5 Jan. 1892, 3).

# The Influence of Mothers

*Mothers who have the gospel in their hearts will lead their children in the paths of righteousness and truth.*

## From the Life of Joseph F. Smith

President Joseph F. Smith had the highest esteem for mothers. His own mother was an example to him of faith and resolve. Describing her noble influence, he said: "I can remember my mother in the days of Nauvoo [1839–46]. I remember seeing her and her helpless children hustled into a flat boat with such things as she could carry out of the house at the commencement of the bombardment of the city of Nauvoo by the mob. I remember the hardships of the Church there and on the way to Winter Quarters, on the Missouri river, and how she prayed for her children and family on her wearisome journey. . . . I can remember all the trials incident to our endeavors to move out with the Camp of Israel, coming to these valleys of the mountains without teams sufficient to draw our wagons; and being without the means to get those teams necessary, she yoked up her cows and calves, and tied two wagons together, and we started to come to Utah in this crude and helpless condition, and my mother said—'The Lord will open the way;' but how He would open the way no one knew. . . .

"Do you not think that these things make an impression upon the mind? Do you think I can forget the example of my mother? No; her faith and example will ever be bright in my memory. What do I think! Every breath I breathe, every feeling of my soul rises to God in thankfulness to Him that my mother was a Saint, that she was a woman of God, pure and faithful, and that she would suffer death rather than betray the trust committed to her; that she would suffer poverty and distress in the wilderness and try to hold her family together rather than remain in

Babylon. That is the spirit which imbued her and her children. Would not her children be unworthy of such a mother did they not hearken to and follow her example? Therefore I say God bless the mothers in Israel."[1]

# Teachings of Joseph F. Smith

### A mother's influence extends from generation to generation.

How I love and cherish true motherhood! Nothing beneath the celestial kingdom can surpass my deathless love for the sweet, true, noble, soul who gave me birth—my own, own, mother! O she was good! She was true! She was pure! She was indeed a Saint! A royal daughter of God! To her I owe my very existence as also my success in life, coupled with the favor and mercy of God![2]

As a rule the mothers in Zion, the mothers of Israel, are the very best women that live in the world, the best that can be found anywhere. . . . The good influence that a good mother exercises over her children is like leaven cast into the measure of meal, that will leaven the whole lump; and as far as her influence extends, not only to her own children, but to the associates of her children, it is felt, and good is the result accomplished by it.

And, sisters, you do not know how far your influence extends. A mother that is successful in raising a good boy, or girl, to imitate her example and to follow her precepts through life, sows the seeds of virtue, honor and integrity and of righteousness in their hearts that will be felt through all their career in life; and wherever that boy or girl goes, as man or woman, in whatever society they mingle, the good effects of the example of that mother upon them will be felt; and it will never die, because it will extend from them to their children from generation to generation. And especially do we hope for this in the Gospel of Jesus Christ.[3]

In my childhood . . . I was instructed to believe in the divinity of the mission of Jesus Christ. I was taught by my mother, a Saint indeed—that Jesus Christ is the Son of God; that he was indeed no other than the Only Begotten of God in the flesh, and that,

transgression and from temptation that will lead them astray. May the power of God be over all the household of faith.[16]

I look upon these mothers in Israel, who have been endowed with the gift of the Holy Ghost, who have been born again, . . . the daughters of Israel have been born of the water and of the Spirit, and they have been endowed with the gift of the Holy Ghost, by the laying on of hands of those who had authority to convey that power and that gift to the daughters of Zion, as well as to the sons of Zion. I believe that every mother has the right to . . . know what to do in her family and in her sphere, over her children, in their guidance and direction; and that mother and every mother possessing that spirit has the gift of revelation, the gift of inspiration and the gift of knowledge, which is the spirit of prophecy, the spirit of discernment, a gift of God to them, to govern their households and lead their children in the path of righteousness and truth.[17]

I feel in my heart to bless you, mothers and sisters, with all my heart and with all the power and right that I possess in the priesthood which is after the order of the Son of God. . . . I have the right and the authority in the priesthood to bless Israel, and to bless those who are faithful, especially; and I feel in my heart to say I bless you.[18]

## Suggestions for Study

- What impresses you about President Smith's description of his mother? What qualities of righteousness do you see exemplified by mothers you know?

- Why does motherhood lie "at the foundation of happiness in the home, and of prosperity in the nation"? What are the "sacred obligations" of men and women "with respect to motherhood"?

- How does our understanding of eternal families influence our actions and attitudes toward mothers and motherhood?

- How can a mother influence the minds and hearts of her children for righteousness? How have you been blessed by the influence of a mother in Zion?

• What challenges do parents face today in bringing up children "in the love of truth, in obedience to [God's] commands"? How can parents deal with these challenges?

• What spiritual blessings does President Smith say are the right of mothers who have received the gift of the Holy Ghost? How can mothers use these gifts to help their children walk in the paths of righteousness?

• How can the love and teachings of a mother become "a defense, a barrier between [us] and temptation"?

## Notes

1. *Deseret News: Semi-Weekly,* 5 Jan. 1892, 3; paragraphing added.

2. *Life of Joseph F. Smith,* comp. Joseph Fielding Smith (1938), 452.

3. *Deseret News: Semi-Weekly,* 5 Jan. 1892, 3.

4. *Gospel Doctrine,* 5th ed. (1939), 494.

5. *Gospel Doctrine,* 288.

6. "General Conference of the Relief Society," *Relief Society Magazine,* June 1917, 316.

7. *Deseret News: Semi-Weekly,* 5 Jan. 1892, 3.

8. In Conference Report, Apr. 1912, 7.

9. *Gospel Doctrine,* 300–301.

10. *Gospel Doctrine,* 290.

11. "General Conference of the Relief Society," 316–17.

12. *Gospel Doctrine,* 314–15.

13. *Gospel Doctrine,* 264.

14. *Gospel Doctrine,* 463.

15. *Gospel Doctrine,* 429.

16. In Conference Report, Apr. 1907, 118.

17. Address at the home of A. W. McCune, 14 Nov. 1913, Historical Department Archives, The Church of Jesus Christ of Latter-day Saints.

18. "General Conference of the Relief Society," 320.

# The Inspiration and Divinity of the Scriptures

*Members of the Church should faithfully study the scriptures and diligently live by the principles taught in the standard works.*

## From the Life of Joseph F. Smith

Throughout the trek to the Salt Lake Valley in 1848, Mary Fielding Smith sat with her son Joseph and other family members and studied the scriptures by lamp and firelight. These were the days of Joseph's earliest spiritual education, obtained from his mother in the tent, in the camp, and on the prairie.[1] Later in life, President Joseph F. Smith recalled: "As a child I was impressed, deeply, with the thought, and firmly with the belief, in my soul that the revelations that had been given to and through Joseph the Prophet . . . were the word of God, as were the words of the ancient disciples when they bore record of the Father and of the Son. That impression made upon me in my childhood has followed through all the vicissitudes of more than sixty years of actual and practical experience in the mission field, throughout the nations of the world, and at home in the midst of the authorized servants of God."[2]

At the general conference held on 10 October 1880, the First Presidency of the Church—President John Taylor and his Counselors George Q. Cannon and Joseph F. Smith—presented to the Church the Pearl of Great Price and some additional sections of the Doctrine and Covenants "as revelations from God to the Church of Jesus Christ of Latter-day Saints, and to all the world."[3] By unanimous vote, the Church members accepted these revelations, thus expanding the canon of scriptures of the Church. For President Smith, the scriptures remained a constant source of "spiritual wealth."[4] He wove the scriptures into his teaching throughout his life, and it was while pondering the scriptures that he received the great revelation now known as Doctrine and Covenants section 138.

# Teachings of Joseph F. Smith

### The scriptures convey words of love and spiritual wealth.

To [those who are] at a loss to know what to do, among all the various teachings that are extant in the world, I would say: Search the Scriptures, seek God in prayer, and then read the doctrines that have been proclaimed by Christ in his sermon on the mount, as found in Matthew, and as reiterated to the ancient saints upon this [the American] continent (III Nephi). Having studied these splendid standards, and searched deeply the significance of these matchless sentiments, you may defy the philosophies of the world, or any of its ethics to produce their equal. The wisdom of men is not to be compared with them. They lead to the rest of the peaceable followers of Christ, and enable mankind to become perfect as he is perfect. No other philosopher has ever said as Jesus said, "Come unto me." From the beginning of the world until the present time, no other philosopher has ever cried unto the people such words of love, nor guaranteed and declared power within himself to save. "Come unto me, all ye that labor and are heavy laden, and I will give you rest," is his call to all the sons and daughters of men [Matthew 11:28].

The Latter-day Saints have answered the call, and thousands thereby have found rest and peace surpassing all understanding; and this notwithstanding the outward, fiery ordeals, the turmoil and the strife, through which they have passed. They rest in the knowledge that no man could declare or teach such doctrine; it is the truth of God.[5]

That which characterizes above all else the inspiration and divinity of the Scriptures is the spirit in which they are written and the spiritual wealth they convey to those who faithfully and conscientiously read them. Our attitude, therefore, toward the Scriptures should be in harmony with the purposes for which they were written. They are intended to enlarge man's spiritual endowments

President Joseph F. Smith's copy of the first Hawaiian edition of the
Book of Mormon, 1905. Also the Hawaiian translation of the Doctrine and
Covenants and Pearl of Great Price, presented to him at the dedication
of the Hawaii Temple site in 1915.

and to reveal and intensify the bond of relationship between him and his God. The Bible, as all other books of Holy Writ, to be appreciated must be studied by those spiritually inclined and who are in quest of spiritual truths.[6]

The greatest achievement mankind can make in this world is to familiarize themselves with divine truth, so thoroughly, so perfectly, that the example or conduct of no creature living in the world can ever turn them away from the knowledge that they have obtained. "In the footsteps of the Master," the greatest of all the teachers that this world has ever received, is the safest and surest course to pursue that I know of in the world. We can absorb the precepts, the doctrines and the divine word of the Master, without any fear that the exemplar will fail of carrying out and executing his own precepts and fulfilling his own doctrines and requirements.[7]

---

## Modern scriptures teach us the word of God and testify that Jesus is the Christ.

By the testimony of the Holy Spirit of God to me, I know that this book, the Book of Doctrine and Covenants, which I hold in my hand, is the word of God through Joseph Smith to the world, and especially to the members of the Church of Jesus Christ of Latter-day Saints throughout the world, and that by the gift and power of God he translated this book (the Book of Mormon) from its original language, and from the engravings upon the golden plates into the language which we now read within the lids of this book; and it contains the fullness of the everlasting Gospel. It will lead men to the obtaining of the knowledge of truth whereby they may be saved and brought back again into the presence of God and partake of His glory and of endless lives.[8]

Christ himself burst the barriers of the tomb, conquered death and the grave and came forth "the first fruits of them that slept." [1 Corinthians 15:20.] . . . [His] disciples witness and testify to the resurrection, and their testimony can not be impeached. It therefore stands good, and is true and faithful.

But is this the only evidence we have to depend on? Have we nothing but the testimony of the ancient disciples to rest our hopes upon? Thank God we have more. And the additional evidence which we possess enables us to become witnesses to the truth of the testimony of the ancient disciples. We go to the Book of Mormon; it testifies of the death and resurrection of Jesus Christ in plain and unmistakable terms; we may go to the book of Doctrine and Covenants containing the revelations of this dispensation, and we shall find clear and well defined evidence there. We have the testimony of the Prophet Joseph Smith, the testimony of Oliver Cowdery, and the testimony of Sidney Rigdon, that they saw the Lord Jesus—the same that was crucified in Jerusalem—and that he revealed himself unto them [see D&C 76:22–24].[9]

The Book of Mormon [is] a book of scripture that was translated by the gift and power of God, for the voice of God declared to the three witnesses that it had been translated by the gift and power of God and that it was true. The three witnesses declared and testified to its truth, and eight other witnesses, besides the Prophet Joseph, declared that they beheld the plates and handled them, and saw the engravings on them, and that they do know that Joseph Smith did have the plates from which the Book of Mormon was translated.[10]

The Book of Mormon, which Joseph Smith was the instrument in the hands of God in bringing forth to this generation, has been translated into the German, French, Danish, Swedish, Welsh, Hawaiian, Hindustani, Spanish, and Dutch languages, and this book will be translated into other languages, for according to the predictions it contains, and according to the promises of the Lord through Joseph Smith it is to be sent unto every nation, and kindred, and people under the whole heavens, until all the sons and daughters of Adam shall have the privilege of hearing the gospel as it has been restored to the earth in the dispensation of the fulness of times.[11]

That God will manifest his purposes to the Lamanites in his own time and way there can be no doubt in the minds of those who believe in the divine origin of the Book of Mormon—for in that book this fact is made unmistakably clear, but just how he will do so in every particular, and just what agencies he will use to bring about his purposes in this regard, may be matters of conjecture beyond what has actually been revealed. One of the agencies, we know, will be the Book of Mormon itself.[12]

I say to my brethren that the book of Doctrine and Covenants contains some of the most glorious principles ever revealed to the world, some that have been revealed in greater fulness than they were ever revealed before to the world; and this, in fulfilment of the promise of the ancient prophets that in the latter times the Lord would reveal things to the world that had been kept hidden from the foundation thereof; and the Lord has revealed them through the Prophet Joseph Smith.[13]

I believe in the divinity of Jesus Christ, because more than ever I come nearer the possession of the actual knowledge that Jesus is the Christ, the Son of the living God, through the testimony of Joseph Smith contained in this book, the Doctrine and Covenants, that he saw Him, that he heard Him, that he received instructions from Him, that he obeyed those instructions, and that he today stands before the world as the last great, actual, living witness of the divinity of Christ's mission and His power to redeem man from the temporal death and also from the second death which will follow man's own sins, through disobedience to the ordinances of the gospel of Jesus Christ.[14]

---

### Study the standard works to obtain a knowledge of the word of God.

I have found very often in my experience in reading over passages of Scripture that the Spirit has brought to my mind new light, and has shown up to my understanding thoughts and views which seemed to be new to me, notwithstanding I had been familiar with those Scriptures and had read them over and over again. In fact, there is a peculiarity which I have found accompanies the reading of the word of God, that whenever read it is calculated to refresh the soul, to revive the spirit of man, and to draw him nearer, if possible, to the fountain of light, truth, wisdom, love and knowledge. Therefore, it is a good thing for the Latter-day Saints to read very often the word of God as it is recorded in the Bible, the Book of Mormon and Doctrine and

Covenants, and as it has been discussed also by the leading Elders of the Church with a view to making plain the laws of God to the understanding of the children of men.

And in reading the word of the Lord we should take into consideration its application to us under the circumstances and in the conditions in which we find ourselves, and we should reflect as to whether we are complying with the requirements of the Gospel or not, and whether we have the Spirit in our hearts which accompanies the work and word of the Lord. We should not read merely to say that we have read; but we should read with the spirit and with the understanding, in order that we may be profited, and that the truth may be revealed, as far as possible, unto our understanding, and may be so impressed upon our minds that it will never depart from us, but will be in us like a fountain which springeth up unto everlasting life, and which shall be an unfailing source of truth, of light, of joy and of peace in our hearts continually.[15]

All members of the Church of Jesus Christ of Latter-day Saints should be as familiar as possible with the words that are recorded in the New Testament, especially with reference to those things spoken as recorded by the apostles, and the Savior Himself. The Book of Mormon should be read carefully, and the book of Doctrine and Covenants should be read very carefully by the Latter-day Saints. These are standard works of the Church and they contain truth, not error, not the mere words and opinions of men, not novels or novelettes, not suppositions, but the truth, God's word, for God's word is truth, and these are things which our daughters, and our sons, our fathers and mothers should thoroughly understand. Let us know the truth for the truth makes us and will make us free from error, from superstition, from false tradition, from false science or so-called science, and from the vagaries of men and the vain philosophies of the world. If we can learn the truth then we will be free from those errors and from the power of error that is so potent in the world.

. . . We want our sons and our daughters to know God's truth and not the vagaries of the world and we want you to study those books from whence you will obtain a knowledge of the word of the Lord to us.

Some of our good people read many of the books that are published today, popular fiction so-called but they haven't time to read the Word of the Lord. Many of these books are beautiful, but often many ideas are expressed which are only pretty words, well-connected sentences or sentiments that are like flowers blooming on the stem without root. Real truth you can gain from books that have been adopted as standard works of the Church. I see too many of our people who are very much better read in the things that are written by some of the popular authors of books than they are in the things of God. They don't know one thing about the real essence of the Gospel of Jesus Christ, they don't know or comprehend one thing about the rites of the Priesthood and the principles of government that God has revealed to the children of men to maintain the kingdom of God in the earth. They know more about novels than they do about the Bible, the Book of Mormon, and the Doctrine and Covenants—yes, far more.[16]

It is surprising to hear the multitude of questions that are continuously sent to the Presidency of the Church, and to others of my brethren who are in leading positions, for information upon some of the most simple things that pertain to the Gospel. Hundreds of questions, communications, and letters are sent to us from time to time asking information and instruction on matters that are so plainly written in the revelations of God—contained in the Book of Mormon, the Doctrine and Covenants, the Pearl of Great Price, and the Bible—it seems that any one who can read should understand.[17]

We have in the gospel the truth. If that is the case, and I bear my testimony that so it is, then it is worth our every effort to understand the truth, each for himself, and to impart it in spirit and practice to our children. . . . This should be done every day, and in the home, by precept, teaching and example. . . . Spend ten minutes in reading a chapter from the words of the Lord in the Bible, the Book of Mormon, the Doctrine and Covenants, before you retire, or before you go to your daily toil. Feed your spiritual selves at home, as well as in public places.[18]

# Suggestions for Study

- How do the scriptures "lead to the rest of the peaceable followers of Christ" and enable us to become perfect? How have they helped you to become a peaceable follower of Christ?

- What are the "purposes for which [the scriptures] were written"? How do they "intensify the bond of relationship" between us and God?

- How do you feel when you study the scriptures? With what attitude should we study the scriptures?

- What passages in the Book of Mormon, Doctrine and Covenants, or Pearl of Great Price have most strengthened your testimony that Jesus is the Christ? What passages have strengthened your testimony of the divine calling of the Prophet Joseph Smith?

- How are God's purposes being made manifest today among the descendants of Book of Mormon peoples?

- What are some of the "most glorious principles ever revealed to the world" that are found in the Book of Mormon, Doctrine and Covenants, and Pearl of Great Price? What difference have these principles made in your life?

- What does it mean to read the scriptures very carefully? Why should we do so? How have you been most successful in reading and studying them?

- How can we ensure that we and our families do not allow popular books, television, and other entertainment to take priority over study of the scriptures?

- What is the value of daily personal and family scripture study? How have you or others successfully incorporated scripture study into busy personal and family lives?

## Notes

1. See Edward H. Anderson, "A Biographical Sketch," in *Gospel Doctrine*, 5th ed. (1939), 529.

2. *Gospel Doctrine*, 493.

3. "Fiftieth Semi-Annual Conference," *Millennial Star*, 15 Nov. 1880, 724.

4. *Gospel Doctrine*, 45.

5. *Gospel Doctrine*, 128.

6. *Gospel Doctrine*, 45–46.

7. *Gospel Doctrine*, 3–4.

8. In Brian H. Stuy, comp., *Collected Discourses Delivered by President Wilford Woodruff, His Two Counselors, the Twelve Apostles, and Others,* 5 vols. (1987–92), 5:29.

9. *Gospel Doctrine*, 444–45; paragraphing altered.

10. *Gospel Doctrine*, 466.

11. *Gospel Doctrine*, 481.

12. *Gospel Doctrine*, 378.

13. *Gospel Doctrine*, 45.

14. *Gospel Doctrine*, 495.

15. *Deseret News: Semi-Weekly,* 6 Feb. 1893, 2; paragraphing added.

16. "Reading," *Young Woman's Journal,* Aug. 1917, 412–13.

17. In Conference Report, Apr. 1915, 138.

18. *Gospel Doctrine*, 301–2.

# Faith: The Foundation of All Righteousness

*Faith in God the Father and in His Son, Jesus Christ,
is the first principle of our religion and the
foundation of all righteousness.*

## From the Life of Joseph F. Smith

Joseph F. Smith centered his faith in his Father in Heaven, in the Lord Jesus Christ, and in the simple and constant truths of the gospel. When Joseph F. Smith was young, his faith was greatly strengthened by his mother's devotion to duty and to righteousness.

He said: "I recollect most vividly a circumstance that occurred in the days of my childhood. My mother was a widow, with a large family to provide for. One spring [between 1849 and 1852] when we opened our potato pits, she had her boys get a load of the best potatoes and she took them to the tithing office; potatoes were scarce that season. I was a little boy at the time, and drove the team. When we drove up to the steps of the tithing office, ready to unload the potatoes, one of the clerks came out and said to my mother, 'Widow Smith, it's a shame that you should have to pay tithing.' . . . He chided my mother for paying her tithing, called her anything but wise or prudent; and said there were others who were strong and able to work that were supported from the tithing office. My mother turned upon him and said: ' . . . Would you deny me a blessing? If I did not pay my tithing, I should expect the Lord to withhold his blessings from me. I pay my tithing, not only because it is a law of God, but because I expect a blessing by doing it.' "

President Smith explained: "She prospered because she obeyed the laws of God. . . . Then that widow had her name recorded in the book of the law of the Lord. That widow was entitled to the privileges of the house of God. No ordinance of the gospel could be denied her, for she was obedient to the laws of God, and she would not fail in her duty."[1]

# Teachings of Joseph F. Smith

### It is necessary to have faith in God and in His Son, Jesus Christ.

We believe in God, the Father of our Lord and Savior Jesus Christ, the Maker of heaven and earth, the Father of our spirits. We believe in him without reserve, we accept him in our heart, in our religious faith, in our very being. We know that he loves us, and we accept him as the Father of our spirits and the Father of our Lord and Savior Jesus Christ.[2]

First . . . it is necessary to have faith in God, faith being the first principle in revealed religion, and the foundation of all righteousness.

Faith in God is to believe that he is, and "that he is the only supreme Governor and independent Being, in whom all fulness and perfection and every good gift and principle dwell independently," and in whom the faith of all other rational beings must centre for life and salvation; and further, that he is the great Creator of all things, that he is omnipotent, omniscient, and by his works and the power of his Spirit omnipresent [see Joseph Smith, comp., *Lectures on Faith* (1985), 10].

Not only is it necessary to have faith in God, but also in Jesus Christ, his Son, the Savior of mankind and the Mediator of the New Covenant; and in the Holy Ghost, who bears record of the Father and the Son, "the same in all ages and forever."[3]

Our faith in Jesus Christ lies at the foundation of our religion, the foundation of our hope for remission of sins, and for exaltation after death, and for the resurrection from death to everlasting life. Our faith in the doctrines that have been restored through the instrumentality of the Prophet Joseph Smith confirms and strengthens us and establishes beyond a question or doubt, our faith and belief in the divine mission of the Son of God.[4]

*He Is Risen,* by Del Parson. President Joseph F. Smith taught that it is
"necessary to have faith in God, . . . in Jesus Christ, his Son, the Savior of mankind
and the Mediator of the New Covenant; and in the Holy Ghost"
(*Gospel Doctrine,* 100).

Faith, Paul tells us, is the substance of things hoped for and the evidence of things not seen [see Hebrews 11:1]. Faith in God [is] to believe that He is, and is the rewarder of them that seek after Him and that love Him. Faith in God would lead men to all knowledge and to all fulness and to all fidelity before them. . . .

We are all babes in this principle of the gospel. We are only beginning, the best of us, to know something of this principle of life and salvation, this principle of power. By faith, we are told, the worlds were made. Who of us have faith to do much of anything? Our faith is so limited that we can scarcely live the little principles of the gospel that God has revealed to us that are necessary for social peace and enjoyment. We have scarcely faith to carry out these little principles that are revealed to us for the government of our every day lives. The Lord has to bear with us and to be patient with us and to teach us here a little and there a little, line upon line and precept upon precept that we may eventually gain that faith that was once delivered to the Saints by which the mouths of lions were stopped, and the heat of the fiery furnace was assuaged. . . . Our great teacher, Jesus Christ, . . . is trying to teach us the principles of life and salvation which are principles of power, teaching men to rise from the depths of sorrow, from the depths of humanity to the heights of glory and knowledge of God.[5]

The truth is, every son and daughter of God must first have faith in God—faith that He is, that He is righteous, that He is almighty, that He governs all things, and that in Him all perfection dwells. You may not have a knowledge of this, but you must have faith that this is true. This is the first principle of revealed religion. It is written that without faith it is impossible to please God. It is also written that the just shall live by faith. Therefore I say it is necessary for all men to have faith in God, the Maker and Creator of all things, the Ruler of heaven and earth. Without faith worlds could not have been made; without it they could not be held in their positions; but by faith all things are possible with God and with man.[6]

God, in his revelation to man, has made his word so simple that the humblest of men, without special training, may enjoy great faith, comprehend the teachings of the gospel, and enjoy undisturbed their religious convictions.[7]

No man's faith, no man's religion, no religious organization in all the world, can ever rise above the truth. The truth must be at the foundation of religion, or it is in vain and it will fail of its purpose. I say that the truth is at the foundation, at the bottom and top of, and it entirely permeates this great work of the Lord that was established through the instrumentality of Joseph Smith, the prophet.[8]

---

### Faith, a gift of God, is obtained by obedience.

Faith is always a gift of God to man, which is obtained by obedience, as all other blessings are. The man or woman in this Church who desires to enrich his or her faith to the highest possible degree will desire to observe every rite and ordinance in the Church in conformity to the law of obedience to the will of God. In these things, and through them, man gains a more perfect knowledge of God's purposes in the world. An enriched faith means an enlarged power, and though man may not have in this life an occasion to exercise all the powers that come to him through the enrichment of his faith, those powers may be exercised in their fulness in eternity, if not in time.[9]

It is said that faith is a gift of God, and so it is; but faith does not come without works; faith does not come without obedience to the commandments of God.[10]

A leading mission of the Church is to teach the gospel of Christ in the world. It has an important message to deliver, which not only includes the spiritual salvation of men, but also their temporal welfare. It not only teaches that faith is necessary, but also that works are required. Belief in Jesus is well and good, but it must be of a living kind which induces the believer to work out his own salvation, and to aid others to do the same.[11]

We believe it is necessary to live our religion every day in the week, every hour in the day, and every moment. Believing and acting thus, we become strengthened in our faith, the Spirit of God increases within us, we advance in knowledge, and we are better able to defend the cause we are engaged in.[12]

I pray you, my brethren and sisters, who have children in Zion, and upon whom rests the greater responsibility, teach them the principles of the gospel, teach them to have faith in the Lord Jesus Christ, and in baptism for the remission of sins when they shall reach the age of eight years.[13]

---

### Faith in God will sustain us in times of adversity.

In order to successfully overcome anxieties in reference to questions that require time for their solution, an absolute faith and confidence in God and in the triumph of his work are essential.[14]

The need of one's having a keen knowledge of the truth is paramount. So also is it that every Latter-day Saint should have a deep-rooted conviction of the justice of God, and an implicit confidence and faith in his being and mercy. To rightfully understand the gospel and to be able to keep his commandments such knowledge is absolutely necessary. Let each person ask himself if in his soul there is a sharp and immovable conviction of these facts. Could anything that might occur to you . . . change your faith in the purposes, and in the absolute justice and mercy, of the Lord, or in the saving power of his gospel, the message of his salvation? If so, your faith is not deep-rooted, and there is strong need of your becoming convinced.

The scriptures abound in examples of men who were unflinchingly grounded in an abiding faith in God. There is need of every young man leaning upon such a pillar of strength.

In the loss of all his earthly goods, and even in the severer bereavement which befell him in the loss of his children, Job yet implicitly trusted in the Almighty. . . .

In Abraham we have another example of devotion to the word of God, and faith in ultimately sharing his goodness. . . . In Abraham's willingness to trust in God in the greatest trial that could come to a father—the sacrifice of his son—we observe deep-rooted faith and abiding confidence in the Almighty being able and willing to fulfill his promises, no matter how improbable it might appear under the most trying circumstances. . . . So will he do with all who trust him, for the promise is to all.

Such knowledge, faith, and confidence, supply an important part in revealed religion. . . . Abraham learned the great truth, which we also must impress upon our hearts, that God is just, and will fulfill his promises to the uttermost. And so he was blessed, as we shall be also, in trying circumstances, because he trusted the Lord and obeyed his voice. It was further told to him, Thus saith the Lord: "That in blessing I will bless thee, and in multiplying I will multiply thy seed as the stars of the heaven, and as the sand which is upon the sea-shore; and thy seed shall possess the gate of his enemies; and in thy seed shall all the nations of the earth be blessed." [Genesis 22:17–18.]

The situation is the same today; unless the Saints have an actual knowledge that the course which they are pursuing is in harmony with the will of God, they will grow weary in trial, and will faint under persecution. . . . But, on the contrary, with this trust in God burned into their souls, no matter what comes, they are happy in doing his will, knowing full well that at last the promise shall be theirs. Thus is the world overcome, and the crown of glory obtained which God has laid away for those who love, honor and obey him. . . .

No person can realize the fullness of the blessings of God, unless he can approach, in some degree, at least, the standard of faith in God's justice, exemplified in the examples quoted. He must have founded in his own soul belief and confidence in the justice and mercy of God. It must be individual, no man can act for another. Lessons of this class need be taught and held up before the youth of Zion, to bring forcibly to their minds the truth which alone will make them free and able to stand firm in the faith. Let them, as they are called together in their assemblies, present themselves before God, and be reminded of his gracious benefits, in bringing forth the Book of Mormon, in the scenes of Kirtland, in Zion [Jackson County, Missouri], in Nauvoo, in the trying days of the exodus, and in the wilderness. This that they might count the mercies of God in his promises, and behold how past affliction and sore trial have been turned to the well-being of his people; and so renew their covenants, filled with a deep-rooted, immovable conviction of the goodness and mercy of the Lord. Each individual must learn this lesson, it must be impressed upon his soul, so deep, and be so well-founded that nothing can separate him from a knowledge of the love of God, though death and hell stand in the way. . . .

God is good; his promises never fail; to implicitly trust his goodness and mercy, is a correct principle. Let us, therefore, put our trust in Him.[15]

There are people fond of saying that women are the weaker vessels. I don't believe it. Physically, they may be; but spiritually, morally, religiously and in faith, what man can match a woman who is really convinced? Daniel had faith to sustain him in the lion's den, but women have seen their sons torn limb from limb, and endured every torture satanic cruelty could invent because they believed. They are always more willing to make sacrifices, and are the peers of men in stability, Godliness, morality, and faith.[16]

To stand firm in the face of overwhelming opposition, when you have done all you can, is the courage of faith. The courage of faith is the courage of progress. Men who possess that divine quality go on; they are not permitted to stand still if they would. They are not simply the creatures of their own power and wisdom; they are instrumentalities of a higher law and a divine purpose.[17]

---

**By faith we can enter into God's rest.**

The ancient prophets speak of "entering into God's rest" [see Alma 12:34; D&C 84:23–24]; what does it mean? To my mind, it means entering into the knowledge and love of God, having faith in his purpose and in his plan, to such an extent that we know we are right, and that we are not hunting for something else, we are not disturbed by every wind of doctrine, or by the cunning and craftiness of men who lie in wait to deceive. We know of the doctrine that it is of God, and we do not ask any questions of anybody about it; they are welcome to their opinions, to their ideas and to their vagaries. The man who has reached that degree of faith in God that all doubt and fear have been cast from him, he has entered into "God's rest."[18]

Without the aid of the Holy Ghost no man can know the will of God, or that Jesus is the Christ—the Redeemer of the world, or that the course he pursues, the work he performs, or his faith, are acceptable to God, and such as will secure to him the gift of eternal life, the greatest of all gifts.[19]

No man can obtain the gift of eternal life unless he is willing to sacrifice all earthly things in order to obtain it. We cannot do this so long as our affections are fixed upon the world.

. . . But if we will lay up our treasures in heaven; if we will wean our affections from the things of this world, and say to the Lord our God, "Father, not my will, but thine be done," [see Luke 22:42] then may the will of God be done on earth as it is done in heaven, and the kingdom of God in its power and glory will be established upon the earth. Sin and Satan will be bound and banished from the earth, and not until we attain to this condition of mind and faith will this be done.[20]

## Suggestions for Study

- What is faith? Why is faith in God and in Jesus Christ "the foundation of our religion"?

- What do we know about God and Jesus Christ that help us to have faith in them? Why must our faith be based upon truth? (See Alma 32:21.)

- How is faith obtained? How can we enrich and strengthen our faith? What is the relationship between faith and works?

- How can we effectively help our children develop faith in Jesus Christ?

- To endure adversity, why must every Latter-day Saint have complete faith in the "absolute justice and mercy" of the Lord and in "the saving power of his gospel"?

- What can we learn about faith from the examples of Abraham, Job, and the early leaders and members of this dispensation? In the midst of your most challenging experiences, how has trusting in the Lord strengthened and blessed you?

- Why is it important for us to know that the course we are pursuing is "in harmony with the will of God"? How can we know this?

- What is the "courage of faith," and how can it be effective in our daily lives?

- Why must we be willing to sacrifice all earthly things in order to obtain the gift of eternal life?

- What does it mean to enter into God's rest? How can we enter into this rest now?

## Notes

1. *Gospel Doctrine,* 5th ed. (1939), 228–29.
2. *Gospel Doctrine,* 138.
3. *Gospel Doctrine,* 100.
4. *Gospel Doctrine,* 478.
5. In Brian H. Stuy, comp., *Collected Discourses Delivered by President Wilford Woodruff, His Two Counselors, the Twelve Apostles, and Others,* 5 vols. (1987–92), 2:299–300; paragraphing added.
6. "Discourse by President Joseph F. Smith," *Millennial Star,* 26 Sept. 1895, 609.
7. *Gospel Doctrine,* 9.
8. *Gospel Doctrine,* 1.
9. *Gospel Doctrine,* 212–13; paragraphing altered.
10. In Conference Report, Oct. 1903, 4.
11. *Gospel Doctrine,* 236.
12. *Gospel Doctrine,* 82.
13. *Gospel Doctrine,* 293–94.
14. *Gospel Doctrine,* 155.
15. "Editor's Table," *Improvement Era,* Nov. 1903, 53–56.
16. *Gospel Doctrine,* 352.
17. *Gospel Doctrine,* 119.
18. *Gospel Doctrine,* 58.
19. *Gospel Doctrine,* 101.
20. *Gospel Doctrine,* 261.

# The Glorious Work of Repentance and Baptism

*Repentance and baptism are essential to becoming heirs of the celestial kingdom.*

## From the Life of Joseph F. Smith

Joseph F. Smith was baptized on 21 May 1852 in City Creek near the northeast corner of Temple Square in Salt Lake City. The ordinance was performed by President Heber C. Kimball, a member of the First Presidency and a close friend of Joseph's martyred father. In describing that day, Joseph F. Smith said: "I felt in my soul that if I had sinned—and surely I was not without sin—that it had been forgiven me; that I was indeed cleansed from sin; my heart was touched, and I felt that I would not injure the smallest insect beneath my feet. I felt as if I wanted to do good everywhere to everybody and to everything. I felt a newness of life, a newness of desire to do that which was right. There was not one particle of desire for evil left in my soul. I was but a little boy, it is true, when I was baptized; but this was the influence that came upon me, and I know that it was from God, and was and ever has been a living witness to me of my acceptance of the Lord."[1]

Throughout his life, President Smith sought to honor the covenants he made at his baptism. He taught that repentance from sin was essential to keeping these covenants: "I believe in the principle of repentance, because I have tested it and I know it to be good. If in an evil moment I have said or done anything that has given offense to my brother, I never could be satisfied or feel free from a certain degree of bondage until I went to that brother whom I had wronged, repented of my sin and made it right with him. Then the load would be lifted and I would at once feel the good effect of repentance of sin."[2]

59

# Teachings of Joseph F. Smith

## Repentance and baptism are true principles of the gospel.

I want to say to you that the principles of the gospel are always true—the principles of faith in God, of repentance from sin, of baptism for the remission of sins by authority of God, and the laying on of hands for the gift of the Holy Ghost; these principles are always true and are always absolutely necessary for the salvation of the children of men, no matter who they are or where they are. . . . No man can enter into the kingdom of heaven except he be born again of the water and of the Spirit. These principles are indispensable, for God has declared them. Not only has Christ declared them by his own voice, and his disciples from generation to generation, in the olden time, but in these latter days, they have taken up the same testimony and declared these things to the world. They are true today as they were true then, and we must obey these things.[3]

We must obey the will of the Father. I frequently hear people say, "All that is required of a man in this world is to be honest and square," and that such a man will attain to exaltation and glory. But those who say this do not remember the saying of the Lord, that "Except a man be born again he cannot see the kingdom of heaven." [See John 3:3.] . . . No matter how good, how honorable, how honest he is, he must pass through that door in order to enter into the kingdom of God. The Lord requires it. Therefore, if he refuses or declines to enter through the door of the sheepfold, he can never become an heir of God and a joint heir with Jesus Christ.[4]

Repentance of a sin is an eternal principle, and is as essential in its place, and is as much an integral part of the gospel of Jesus Christ as: "thou shalt not kill," or, "thou shalt have no other gods before me."

Baptism for the remission of sin, by one having authority, is an eternal principle, for God devised it, and commanded it, and Christ himself was not above obeying it; he had to obey it in order to fulfil the law of righteousness.[5]

The Lord taught through Joseph Smith; repentance of sin, then baptism by immersion with Christ, being buried with Him in the water, in the liquid grave, and coming forth again out of the liquid grave in likeness of His resurrection from death to life, baptism by immersion, and the baptism of the Holy Ghost, by the laying on of hands; these are necessary for the salvation of the children of men.[6]

---

### Only true repentance is acceptable to God.

Men can only be saved and exalted in the kingdom of God in righteousness, therefore we must repent of our sins, and walk in the light as Christ is in the light, that his blood may cleanse us from all sins, and that we may have fellowship with God and receive of his glory and exaltation.[7]

Does repentance consist of sorrow for wrong doing? Yes, but is this all? By no means. True repentance only is acceptable to God, nothing short of it will answer the purpose. Then what is true repentance? True repentance is not only sorrow for sins, and humble penitence and contrition before God, but it involves the necessity of turning away from them, a discontinuance of all evil practices and deeds, a thorough reformation of life, a vital change from evil to good, from vice to virtue, from darkness to light. Not only so, but to make restitution, so far as it is possible, for all the wrongs we have done, to pay our debts, and restore to God and man their rights—that which is due to them from us. This is true repentance, and the exercise of the will and all the powers of body and mind is demanded, to complete this glorious work of repentance; then God will accept it.[8]

No mouth profession of repentance is acceptable to God unless it is carried out in practice. We must have works as well as faith; we must *do* as well as *pretend* to do.[9]

Who can say in his heart, in the presence of God and man, "I have truly repented of all my sins." . . . I have many weaknesses and imperfections. I have as many weaknesses as many of you, and I do not know but what I have more than a great many of you. . . . I have not been able yet to live up to and honor this second principle of the gospel of Jesus Christ; and I would like to see the man who has. I would like to see the human preacher who has done it. But I am trying, I want you to understand, my brethren and sisters, I am still trying.[10]

You cannot take a murderer, . . . an adulterer, a liar, or one who was or is thoroughly abominable in his life here, and simply by the performance of an ordinance of the gospel, cleanse him from sin and usher him into the presence of God. God has not instituted a plan of that kind, and it cannot be done. He has said you shall repent of your sins. The wicked will have to repent of their wickedness. Those who die without the knowledge of the gospel will have to come to the knowledge of it, and those who sin against light will have to pay the uttermost farthing for their transgression and their departure from the gospel, before they can ever get back to it. Do not forget that. Do not forget it, you elders in Israel, nor you, mothers in Israel, either; and, when you seek to save either the living or the dead, bear it in mind that you can only do it on the principle of their repentance and acceptation of the plan of life.[11]

A time for reconciliation has come . . . that we shall . . . plead with the Lord for the spirit of repentance, and, having obtained it, follow its promptings; so that in humbling ourselves before Him and seeking forgiveness from each other, we shall yield that charity and generosity to those who crave our forgiveness that we ask for and expect from Heaven.[12]

While there is life there is hope, and while there is repentance there is a chance for forgiveness; and if there is forgiveness, there is a chance for growth and development until we acquire the full knowledge of these principles that will exalt and save us and prepare us to enter into the presence of God the Father.[13]

---

## By baptism we enter into the Church and kingdom of God.

Having thus repented, the next thing requisite is baptism, which is an essential principle of the gospel—no man can enter into the gospel covenant without it. It is the door of the Church of Christ, we cannot get in there in any other way, for Christ hath said it, "sprinkling," or "pouring," is not baptism. Baptism means immersion in water, and is to be administered by one having authority, in the name of the Father, and of the Son, and of the Holy Ghost. Baptism without divine authority is not valid. It is a symbol of the burial and resurrection of Jesus Christ, and must be done in the likeness thereof, by one commissioned of God, in the manner prescribed, otherwise it is illegal and will not be accepted by him, nor will it effect a remission of sins, the object for which it is designed, but whosoever hath faith, truly repents and is "buried with Christ in baptism," by one having divine authority, shall receive a remission of sins, and is entitled to the gift of the Holy Ghost by the laying on of hands.[14]

We are baptized in the name of the Father and of the Son and of the Holy Ghost. We are initiated into the Church and Kingdom of God in the name of the Father and of the Son and of the Holy Ghost, and we worship the Father. We seek to obey the Son and follow in his footsteps.[15]

It is the duty of Latter-day Saints to teach their children the truth, to bring them up in the way they should go, to teach them the first principles of the gospel, the necessity of baptism for the remission of sins, and for membership in the Church of Christ.[16]

Baptism by immersion for the remission of sins, by one having authority, is a true principle, because Christ taught it; Christ obeyed it, and would not fail, for anything, to fulfil it—not that He was sinful and needed to be baptized for the remission of sins, but He only needed to do it to fulfill all righteousness, that is, to fulfil the law.[17]

Jesus himself attended to the ordinance of baptism; he instituted the sacrament of the Lord's supper, and ordained its observance; and performed other rites which he thought essential to man's salvation. In the case of Nicodemus, he so emphasized baptism that he made the birth of water and the Spirit essential to man's salvation [see John 3:1–5].[18]

There appears to be, among some of our people, an inadequate conception of the sanctity attending certain of the ordinances of the Holy Priesthood. True, the ministrations of those in authority among us are not attended with . . . pomp and worldly ceremony . . . , but the fact that the Church of Jesus Christ of Latter-day Saints is in possession of the Priesthood is sufficient to make any and every ordinance administered by due authority within the Church an event of supreme importance. In performing any such ordinance the one who officiates speaks and acts, not of himself and of his personal authority, but by virtue of his ordination and appointment as a representative of the powers of heaven. We do not . . . make the ordinance of baptism a spectacular display; but the simplicity of the order established in the Church of Christ ought rather to add to than take from the sacred character of the several ordinances.[19]

---

## God will exalt those who repent, are baptized, and continue faithful.

There are blessings which pertain to the gospel of Jesus Christ and to the world to come, which cannot be secured by personal influence, nor be bought with money, and which no man by his own intelligence or wisdom can obtain except through compliance with certain ordinances, laws and commandments which have been given. And it is well, in my judgment, for the Latter-day Saints to continue to bear in mind that the inestimable blessings of the gospel have been bestowed upon them through their faith, that a remission of sins has been obtained by baptism and repentance, and that it is only through continuing faithful that they can retain the gifts and blessings which pertain to eternal life.[20]

Then, we say to you who have repented of your sins, who have been buried with Christ in baptism, who have been raised from the liquid grave to newness of life, born of the water and of the Spirit, and who have been made the children of the Father, heirs of God and joint heirs with Jesus Christ—we say to you, if you will observe the laws of God, and cease to do evil, . . . and have faith in God, believe in the truth and receive it, and be honest before God and man, that you will be set up on high, and God will put you at the head, just as sure as you observe these commandments. Whoso will keep the commandments of God, no matter whether it be you or any other people, they will rise and not fall,

by every wind of doctrine; but shall "know of the doctrine" whether it be of God or of man [see Ephesians 4:14; John 7:17].[5]

The Holy Ghost, who bears record of the Father and the Son, who takes of the things of the Father and shows them unto men, who testifies of Jesus Christ, and of the everliving God, the Father of Jesus Christ, and who bears witness of the truth—this Spirit, this Intelligence, is not given unto all men until they repent of their sins and come into a state of worthiness before the Lord [see 3 Nephi 28:11]. Then they receive the gift of the Holy Ghost by the laying on of the hands of those who are authorized of God to bestow his blessings upon the heads of the children of men.[6]

The presentation or "gift" of the Holy Ghost simply confers upon a man the right to receive at any time, when he is worthy of it and desires it, the power and light of truth of the Holy Ghost, although he may often be left to his own spirit and judgment.[7]

---

**The Holy Ghost is a lamp to light our onward march.**

The office of the Holy Ghost is to bear record of Christ, or to testify of him, and confirm the believer in the truth, by bringing to his recollection things that have passed, and showing or revealing to the mind things present and to come. "But the Comforter, which is the Holy Ghost, whom the Father will send in my name, he shall teach you all things, and bring all things to your remembrance, whatsoever I have said unto you." [John 14:26.] "He will guide you into all truth." [John 16:13.][8]

It is the duty of Latter-day Saints to teach their children . . . the necessity of receiving the gift of the Holy Ghost by the laying on of hands, which will lead them into all truth, and which will reveal to them things that have passed and things which are to come, and show to them more clearly those things which are present with them, that they may comprehend the truth, and that they may walk in the light as Christ is in the light; that they may have fellowship with him and that his blood may cleanse them from all sin.[9]

There is a course marked out for us to walk in—it is that strait and narrow path which leads back to the presence of God; the lamp to light our onward march is the Holy Ghost, which we received on or after our new birth. If we falter and turn aside, our lamp will burn dim and finally go out, when lo, the Comforter, the source of revelation, will leave us, and darkness will take its place; then how great will be that darkness! In proportion to the light we possessed will darkness overpower us, and unless a speedy repentance is made the darkness will increase within us until we lose sight of our calling and forget Him who redeemed us and claimed us for his own.[10]

The office of the Holy Spirit is to enlighten the minds of the people with regard to the things of God, to convince them at the time of their conversion of their having done the will of the Father, and to be in them an abiding testimony as a companion through life, acting as the sure and safe guide into all truth and filling them day by day with joy and gladness, with a disposition to do good to all men, to suffer wrong rather than to do wrong, to be kind and merciful, long suffering and charitable. All who possess this inestimable gift, this pearl of great price, have a continual thirst after righteousness. Without the aid of the Holy Spirit no mortal can walk in the straight and narrow way, being unable to discern right from wrong, the genuine from the counterfeit, so nearly alike can they be made to appear. Therefore it behooves the Latter-day Saints to live pure and upright, in order that this Spirit may abide in them; for it is only possessed on the principle of righteousness. I cannot receive it for you, nor you for me; every one must stand for him or her self, whether of high or humble birth, learned or unlearned, and it is the privilege of all alike to be made partakers of it.[11]

The Holy Ghost descends only upon the righteous and upon those who are forgiven of their sins. . . . So long as the Latter-day Saints are content to obey the commandments of God, to appreciate the privileges and blessings which they enjoy in the Church, and will use their time, their substance, in honor to the name of God, to build up Zion, and to establish truth and righteousness in the earth, so long our heavenly Father is bound by his oath and covenant to protect them from every opposing foe, and to help them to overcome every obstacle that can possibly be arrayed against them, or thrown in their pathway; but the moment a community begin to be wrapt up in themselves, become selfish, become engrossed in the temporalities of life, and put their faith in riches, that moment the power of God begins to withdraw from them, and if they repent not the Holy Spirit will depart from them entirely, and they will be left to themselves.[12]

You who have obeyed the requirements of the everlasting Gospel, and have been chosen out of the world, having received the gift of the Holy Ghost through the laying on of hands, it is your privilege to receive the witness of the Spirit for yourselves; it is your privilege to discern the mind and will of the Father respecting your own welfare, and respecting the final triumph of the work of God.[13]

---

### Through the power of the Holy Ghost, we are born again.

The Savior said to Nicodemus, "Except a man be born again, he cannot see the kingdom of God," [see John 3:3] and that is true today. A man must be born from ignorance into truth, today. . . . If he is not so born, he is more blind than the one whom Christ healed, for having eyes he sees not, and having ears, hears not.[14]

That change comes today to every son and daughter of God who repents of his or her sins, who humble themselves before the Lord, and who seek forgiveness and remission of sin by baptism by immersion, by one having authority to administer this sacred ordinance of the gospel of Jesus Christ. For it is this new birth that was spoken of by Christ to Nicodemus as absolutely essential that men might see the kingdom of God, and without which no man could enter into the kingdom. Each of us can remember, perhaps, the change that came into our hearts when we were baptized for the remission of our sins. . . . I speak of the influence and power of the Holy Spirit that I experienced when I had been baptized for the remission of my sins. The feeling that came upon me was that of pure peace, of love and of light. . . .

Oh! that I could have kept that same spirit and that same earnest desire in my heart every moment of my life from that day to this. Yet many of us who have received that witness, that new birth, that change of heart, while we may have erred in judgment or have made many mistakes, and often perhaps come short of the true standard in our lives, we have repented of the evil, and we have sought from time to time forgiveness at the hand of the Lord; so that until this day the same desire and purpose which pervaded our souls when we were baptized and received a remission of our sins, still holds possession of our hearts, and is still the ruling sentiment and passion of our souls. Though at times we may be stirred to anger, and our wrath move us to say and do things which are not pleasing in the sight of God, yet instantly on regaining our sober senses and recovering from our lapse into the power of darkness, we feel humble, repentant, and to ask forgiveness for the wrong that we have done to ourselves, and perchance to others. The great, earnest, overwhelming desire, which is born of the truth and of the witness of the Holy Spirit in the hearts of the people who obey the truth, assumes sway and again takes possession of our souls, to lead us on in the path of duty. This is my testimony and I know it is true.[15]

---

### The unpardonable sin is to willfully deny and defy the Holy Ghost after having received His witness.

No man can sin against light until he has it; nor against the Holy Ghost, until after he has received it by the gift of God through the appointed channel or way. To sin against the Holy Ghost, the Spirit of Truth, the Comforter, the Witness of the Father and the Son, wilfully denying him and defying him, after having received him, constitutes [the unpardonable sin].[16]

No man can possibly commit the unpardonable sin in ignorance. A man must be brought to a knowledge of Christ; he must receive a testimony of Christ in his heart, and possess light and power, knowledge and understanding, before he is capable of committing that sin. But when a man turns away from the truth, violates the knowledge that he has received, tramples it under his feet, puts Christ again to open shame, denies His atonement, denies the power of the resurrection, denies the miracles that He has wrought for the salvation of the human family, and says in his heart, "It is not true", and abides in that denial of the truth, after having received the testimony of the Spirit, he commits the unpardonable sin.[17]

[Following the Savior's Crucifixion,] why were [the Apostles] forgetful and seemingly ignorant of all they had been taught by the Savior respecting the objects of his mission to the earth? Because they lacked one important qualification, they had not yet been "endowed with power from on high." [See Luke 24:49.] They had not yet obtained the gift of the Holy Ghost. . . .

If the disciples had been endowed with the "gift of the Holy Ghost," or "with power from on high," at this time, their course would have been altogether different . . . , as the sequel abundantly proved. If Peter, who was the chief apostle, had received the gift of the Holy Ghost, and the power and testimony thereof prior to the terrible night on which he cursed and swore and denied his Lord [see Matthew 26:69–75], the result would have been very different with him, for then he would have sinned against "light and knowledge," and "against the Holy Ghost," for which there is no forgiveness. The fact, therefore, that he was forgiven, after bitter tears of repentance, is an evidence that he was without the witness of the Holy Ghost, never having received it. The other disciples or apostles of Christ were precisely in the same condition, and it was not until the evening of the day on which Jesus came out of the grave that he bestowed upon them this inestimable gift [see John 20:22].[18]

Just before the risen Redeemer left the earth he commanded his disciples to tarry in the city of Jerusalem until they should be endowed with power from on high. They did so, and agreeable to promise, the Comforter came whilst they were met together, filling their hearts with unspeakable joy, insomuch that they spake in tongues and prophesied; and the inspiring influence of this holy being accompanied them in all their ministerial duties, enabling them to perform the great mission to which they had been called by the Savior.[19]

Saul, of Tarsus, possessing extraordinary intelligence and learning, brought up at the feet of Gamaliel, taught according to the perfect manner of the law, persecuted the Saints unto death, binding and delivering unto prisons both men and women; and when the blood of the Martyr Stephen was shed, Saul stood by keeping the raiment of those who slew him, and consented unto his death. And "he made havoc of the Church, entering into every house, and haling men and women committed them to prison." [Acts 8:3.] And when they were put to death, he gave his voice against them, and he "punished them oft in every synagogue, and compelled them to blaspheme; and being exceedingly mad against them, persecuted them even unto strange cities," [Acts 26:11] and yet this man committed no unpardonable sin, because he knew not the Holy Ghost.[20]

If any people on earth are capable of committing the unpardonable sin, you will find them among those who have, or will, come to a knowledge of the truth. . . . You and I have received the light. We have received the Holy Priesthood. We have received the testimony of the Holy Spirit, and have been brought from death unto life. Therefore, we are now on very safe or on dangerous ground,—dangerous if we are trifling with these sacred things that have been committed to our care. Hence I warn you, my brethren and sisters, especially my brethren, against trifling with your [priesthood]. . . . If you do, as God lives He will withdraw His Spirit from you, and the time will come when you will be found kicking against the light and knowledge which you have received, and you may become sons of perdition. Therefore, you had better beware lest the second death shall be passed upon you.[21]

## Suggestions for Study

- What is the difference between the temporary influence or manifestation of the Holy Ghost and the gift of the Holy Ghost? (See also Moroni 10:4.) How can we receive the gift of the Holy Ghost? What blessings come to us when we honor this gift?

- How can the Holy Ghost guide us into all truth? (See John 16:13.) What truths has the Holy Ghost testified of to you?

- Why is a lamp a good symbol to represent the Holy Ghost? What can we do to ensure that this lamp burns brightly in our lives?

- What can we do to increase the influence of the Holy Ghost in our lives? How can we help others understand how the Holy Ghost blesses their lives?

- What must we do to receive the new birth spoken of by the Savior? (See John 3:5.) What feelings accompany this new birth? How can we retain these feelings? (See Alma 5:14–16, 26.)

- What is the unpardonable sin? What does it mean to trifle with the "sacred things that have been committed to our care"?

## Notes

1. Joseph F. Smith Journal, 1856, Historical Department Archives, The Church of Jesus Christ of Latter-day Saints; spelling modernized.
2. *Deseret News: Semi-Weekly,* 29 Jan. 1878, 1.
3. *Gospel Doctrine,* 5th ed. (1939), 61.
4. In James R. Clark, *Messages of the First Presidency of The Church of Jesus Christ of Latter-day Saints,* 6 vols. (1965–75), 5:4.
5. *Gospel Doctrine,* 59–60.
6. *Gospel Doctrine,* 67.
7. *Gospel Doctrine,* 60–61.
8. *Gospel Doctrine,* 101.
9. *Gospel Doctrine,* 291.
10. *Deseret News: Semi-Weekly,* 28 Nov. 1876, 1.
11. *Deseret News: Semi-Weekly,* 28 Nov. 1876, 1.
12. *Gospel Doctrine,* 50–51.
13. *Deseret News: Semi-Weekly,* 22 Apr. 1884, 1.
14. *Gospel Doctrine,* 97.
15. *Gospel Doctrine,* 96–97.
16. *Gospel Doctrine,* 434.
17. *Deseret Evening News,* 9 Feb. 1895, 9.
18. *Gospel Doctrine,* 20–21.
19. *Gospel Doctrine,* 92.
20. *Gospel Doctrine,* 433–34.
21. *Deseret Evening News,* 9 Feb. 1895, 9.

# Our Missionary Duty

*Missionaries go into the world to testify of Jesus Christ
and to sow the precious seed of eternal life.*

## From the Life of Joseph F. Smith

Shortly after his arrival in Hawaii on 20 October 1854, Joseph
F. Smith wrote a letter to his father's cousin George A. Smith, the
member of the Quorum of the Twelve who had ordained him an
elder. The young missionary pledged himself to the work of the
Lord, saying, "I am happy to say that I am ready to go through
thick and thin for this cause in which I am engaged; and truly
hope and pray that I may prove faithful to the end."[1] His faith
would be tried many times.

At one time a fire destroyed most of his belongings, including
"clothing, copies of the first edition (European) of the Book of
Mormon, the Doctrine and Covenants, which had been given as
a present to the Patriarch Hyrum Smith. In one of these books
Elder Joseph F. Smith had placed his Elder's certificate. When
the house was destroyed with its contents, Elder Smith's trunk,
and every article in it was reduced to ashes except his missionary certificate. In some remarkable manner it was preserved intact, except that it was scorched around the edges, but not one
word was obliterated even though the book in which it was contained was entirely consumed. Not only were the books destroyed but also Elder Smith's journals which he had faithfully
kept."

Out of this experience came an amusing incident, which was
serious at the time. The missionaries' clothing was destroyed, so
Joseph F. Smith and his companion for a short time had to share
one suit between them. One elder stayed at home while the
other wore the suit and went to meetings. Then the situation
was reversed and the other elder stayed at home while his com-

panion went to meetings. "Of course this did not continue but for a short time, but it was one amusing story that was frequently told in later years, when time had removed the suffering Elders far from the scene of their embarrassment and difficulties."[2]

# Teachings of Joseph F. Smith

### Missionaries should live so that they have constant communion with the Spirit of God.

One of the indispensable qualifications of the elders who go out into the world to preach is humility, meekness and love unfeigned, for the well-being and the salvation of the human family, and the desire to establish peace and righteousness in the earth among men. We can not preach the gospel of Christ without this spirit of humility, meekness, faith in God and reliance upon his promises and word to us. You may learn all the wisdom of men, but that will not qualify you to do these things like the humble, guiding influence of the Spirit of God will. "Pride goeth before destruction, and an haughty spirit before a fall." [Proverbs 16:18.]

It is necessary for the elders who go out into the world to preach to study the spirit of the gospel, which is the spirit of humility, the spirit of meekness and of true devotion to whatever purpose you set your hand or your mind to do. If it is to preach the gospel, we should devote ourselves to the duties of that ministry, and we ought to strive with the utmost of our ability to qualify ourselves to perform that specific labor, and the way to do it is to live so that the spirit of God will have communion and be present with us to direct us in every moment and hour of our ministry, night and day.[3]

My brethren, you are engaged in the work of God; you are in the harness; you receive to a great extent the Spirit of the Gospel because you are engaged in it exclusively. You are ministers of the everlasting covenant. You pray; you don't forget your prayers, surely. An Elder cannot forget his prayers; he cannot forget the Lord; he will certainly remember Him if he is in the line of his duty. If he places himself in a position where he can accomplish the most good, he cannot forget the Lord morning, noon and night. He prays to the Lord, and humbles himself before Him and acknowledges Him. If you are in this line you are enjoying His Spirit.[4]

A missionary should have in himself the testimony of the Spirit of God—the witness of the Holy Ghost. . . . Men are not converted by eloquence or oratory; they are convinced when they are satisfied that you have the truth and the Spirit of God.[5]

### Missionaries should be honest, virtuous, and faithful to their covenants.

It is deemed inconsistent to send men out into the world to promise to others through obedience to the gospel that which they have not themselves received. Neither is it considered proper to send men out to reform them. Let them first reform at home if they have not been strictly keeping the commandments of God. This applies to the Word of Wisdom as well as to all other laws of heaven. No objection is offered to men being called who in earlier years may have been rough or wayward, if in later years they have lived a godly life and brought forth the precious fruits of repentance.[6]

We want young men . . . who have kept themselves unspotted from the world, and can go into the nations of the earth and say to men, "Follow me, as I follow Christ." Then we would like to have them know how to sing, and to pray. We expect them to be honest, virtuous, and faithful unto death to their covenants, to their brethren, to their wives, to their fathers and mothers, to their brothers and sisters, to themselves and to God. Where you get men like this to preach the gospel to the world, whether they know much to begin with or not, the Lord will put his Spirit into their hearts, and he will crown them with intelligence and power to save the souls of men. For the germ of life is in them. It has not been vitiated or corrupted; it has not been driven away from them.[7]

It is not necessary that our young people should know of the wickedness carried on in any place. Such knowledge is not elevating, and it is quite likely that more than one young man can trace the first step of his downfall to a curiosity which led him

Joseph F. Smith at about age 19 just after his return from the
Hawaiian Mission in 1858.

into questionable places. Let the young men of Zion, whether they be on missions or whether they be at home, shun all dens of infamy. It is not necessary that they should know what is going on in such places. No man is better or stronger for such knowledge. Let them remember that "the knowledge of sin tempteth to its commission," and then avoid those temptations that in time to come may threaten their virtue and their standing in the Church of Christ.[8]

The characteristics of a good missionary are: A man who has sociability—whose friendship is permanent and sparkling—who can ingratiate himself into the confidence and favor of men who are in darkness. This cannot be done offhand. You must get acquainted with a man, learn him and gain his confidence and make him feel and know that your only desire is to do him good and bless him; then you can tell him your message, and give him the good things you have for him, kindly and lovingly. Therefore, in selecting missionaries, choose such as have sociability, who have friendship and not enmity towards men; and if you have not any such in your ward, train and qualify some young men for this work.[9]

---

### Missionaries are to teach the gospel of life by the Spirit with simplicity.

Our elders are instructed here, and they are taught from their childhood up, that they are not to go out and make war upon the religious organizations of the world when they are called to go out to preach the gospel of Jesus Christ, but to go and bear with them the message which has been given to us through the instrumentality of the Prophet Joseph, in this latter dispensation, whereby men may learn the truth, if they will.

They are sent out to offer the olive branch of peace to the world, to offer the knowledge that God has spoken from the heavens once more to his children upon the earth; that God has in his mercy restored again to the world the fulness of the gospel of his Only Begotten Son, in the flesh, that God has revealed and restored to mankind the divine power and authority from himself, whereby they are enabled and authorized to perform the ordinances of the gospel of Jesus Christ necessary for their salvation; and their performance of these ordinances must of necessity be acceptable unto God who has given to them the authority to perform them in his name.

Our elders are sent out to preach repentance of sin, to preach righteousness, to preach to the world the gospel of life, of fellowship, and of friendship among mankind, to teach men and women to do that which is right in the sight of God and in the presence of all men, to teach them the fact that God has organized his Church, a Church of which he, himself, is the author and the founder.[10]

The question often arises in the minds of young men who find themselves in the mission field, "What shall I say?" And another follows closely upon it, "How shall I say it?" . . . While no specific rule may be given, experience has taught that the simplest way is the best. Having learned the principles of the gospel, through a prayerful spirit and by careful study, these should be presented to men in humility, in the simplest forms of speech, without presumption or arrogance and in the spirit of the mission of Christ. This cannot be done if a young missionary waste his effort in a vain-glorious attempt to become a noisy orator. This is the point I wish to impress upon the elders, and to advise that all oratorical effort be confined to appropriate times and places. The mission field is not the place for such effort. The gospel is not successfully taught by ostentatious display of words and argument, but rather is expressed by modest and rational statements of its simple truth, uttered in a way that will touch the heart and appeal, as well, to reason and sound sense.

. . . The spirit must first be with the missionary, if he shall succeed in awakening its response in his hearers; and this is true whether the words be spoken in conversation, face to face, or in public gatherings. The spirit will not manifest itself in the person who devotes his time to deliver what he has to say in pompous words or with display of oratory. He hopes to please artificially, and not effectively through the heart.[11]

No man is able to preach the Gospel of Jesus Christ of himself; for the things of God knoweth no man but by the Spirit of

God which is in him [see 1 Corinthians 2:11]. For any man to attempt to preach the word of the Lord by his own wisdom and knowledge, independent of inspiration, is simply mockery. No man can preach God and godliness and the truth as it is in Christ Jesus except he be inspired by the Holy Spirit. The disciples in ancient time walked and conversed with the Savior during His mission among the children of men, and yet . . . they were commanded to tarry in Jerusalem and to go not out to preach until they were endowed with power from on high; in other words, until the Holy Spirit should be poured out upon them by which their minds would be quickened, their understandings enlarged, the testimony of Jesus Christ planted in their hearts, that they might bear that testimony to those unto whom they should come.[12]

The individual elder is left largely to the guidance of the spirit of his calling, with which he should be imbued. If he fail to cultivate that spirit, which is the spirit of energy and application, he will soon become torpid, indolent and unhappy. Every missionary should strive to devote part of each day to study and prayerful thought on the principles of the gospel and the theology of the Church. He should read and reflect and pray. True, we are opposed to the preparing of set sermons to be delivered with the thought of oratorical effect and rhetorical display; yet when an elder arises to address a congregation at home or abroad, he should be thoroughly prepared for his sermon. His mind should be well stored with thoughts worth uttering, worth hearing, worth remembering; then the spirit of inspiration will bring forth the truths of which his auditors are in need, and give to his words the ring of authority.[13]

It is to be earnestly recommended that elders abroad on missions, as indeed Latter-day Saints in general, avoid contentious argument and debate regarding doctrinal subjects. The truth of the gospel does not depend for its demonstration on heated discussion; the message of truth is most effectively delivered when expressed in words of simplicity and sympathy.

. . . A testimony of the truth is more than a mere assent of the mind, it is a conviction of the heart, a knowledge that fills the whole soul of its recipient.

Missionaries are sent forth to preach and teach the first principles of the gospel, Christ and him crucified, and practically nothing more in the way of theological doctrine. They are not commissioned to expound their own views on intricate questions of theology, nor to mystify their hearers with a show of profound learning. Teachers they are and must be, if they meet in any degree the responsibilities of their high calling; but they should teach as nearly as they can after the manner of the Master—seeking to lead by love for their fellows, by simple explanation and persuasion; not trying to convince by force.

Brethren, leave these themes of profitless discussion alone; keep closely to the teachings of the revealed word, as made plain in the standard works of the Church and through the utterances of the living prophets; and let not a difference of views on abstruse matters of doctrine absorb your attention, lest thereby you become estranged from one another and separated from the Spirit of the Lord.[14]

---

### Missionary service is as necessary at home as it is abroad.

It is a pity that after so many of our boys who go abroad and fill good missions return home, they should be apparently dropped or ignored by the presiding authorities of the Church and be permitted to drift away again into carelessness and indifference, and eventually, perhaps, to wander entirely away from their Church duties. They should be kept in the harness, they should be made active in the work of the ministry, in some way, that they may better keep the spirit of the gospel in their minds and in their hearts and be useful at home as well as abroad.

There is no question as to the fact that missionary service is required and is as necessary in Zion, or here at home, as it is abroad. We see too many boys that are falling into very careless, if not into pernicious, ways and habits. Every missionary boy who returns from his mission full of faith and good desire should take it upon himself to become a savior as far as possible of his young and less experienced associates at home. When a returned missionary sees a boy falling into bad ways and is becoming accustomed to bad habits, he should feel that it is his duty to take hold of him, in connection with the presiding authorities of the stake or of the ward in which he lives, and exercise all the power and influence he can for the salvation of that erring young man who has not the experience that our elders abroad have had, and thus become a means of saving many and of establishing them more firmly in the truth.[15]

One's labor in the missionary field broadens his field of vision, vitalizes his energies, enlarges his capacity for good work in any direction and makes of him in every way a stronger and more useful citizen, as well as a more devoted member of the Church. While a missionary is actually engaged in the field he should be wholly a missionary, devoting the best of his energies to the special duties assigned him. When he returns to his home community he is still a missionary in the general sense; but he must remember that he has again taken his place in the ranks of the toilers, to earn his bread by the sweat of his brow. . . . Returned missionaries ought to be in demand where brave hearts, strong minds and willing hands are wanted. The genius of the gospel is not that of negative goodness—mere absence of what is bad; it stands for aggressive energy well directed, for positive goodness—in short, for work.[16]

As bearers and sowers of the precious seed of eternal life, let our lives correspond with our professions, our words be consonant with the truth we bear, and our acts agreeable to the revealed will of God; for [unless] these fruits do follow in some degree our professions of faith, we, as Elders or Saints, are only obstacles to the progress of the work, stumbling-blocks in the way of the practically-minded observer, and are not only not enhancing the prospects of the salvation of others, but are jeopardizing our own.[17]

## Suggestions for Study

- Why are "humility, meekness and love unfeigned" indispensable qualifications of missionaries? What other characteristics help elders and sisters become effective missionaries? (See also D&C 4.) How can similar characteristics help us be effective member missionaries?

- Why is it vital that missionaries keep themselves "unspotted from the world"? How does the Lord bless those missionaries who do so?

- How can we gain the confidence of our nonmember friends and neighbors and help them know that our "only desire is to do [them] good and bless [them]"? How can we more effectively share the gospel with our nonmember friends?

- What truths should missionaries be prepared to teach?

- What are the dangers of missionaries' using argument, debate, and profitless discussion when teaching the gospel? Why is there greater power in teaching simply with the Spirit? (See D&C 100:5–8.)

- How can a missionary cultivate "the spirit of his calling"? How can we as members obtain and cultivate the "spirit of energy and application" in sharing the gospel?

- How can returned missionaries remain "in the harness"? What can Church leaders and other Church members do to help returned missionaries remain "active in the work of the ministry"? In what ways can a returned missionary "become a means of saving many and of establishing them more firmly in the truth"?

## Notes

1. George Albert Smith Papers, 1834–75, Historical Department Archives, The Church of Jesus Christ of Latter-day Saints, 3; spelling and punctuation modernized.
2. *Life of Joseph F. Smith*, comp. Joseph Fielding Smith (1938), 183–84.
3. *Gospel Doctrine*, 5th ed. (1939), 356.
4. "Discourse by President Joseph F. Smith," *Millennial Star*, 25 Oct. 1906, 674.
5. *Gospel Doctrine*, 357.
6. *Gospel Doctrine*, 355.
7. *Gospel Doctrine*, 356.
8. *Gospel Doctrine*, 373–74.
9. *Gospel Doctrine*, 356–57.
10. *Gospel Doctrine*, 357; paragraphing added.
11. *Gospel Doctrine*, 358–59.
12. "Discourse by President Joseph F. Smith," *Millennial Star*, 19 Sept. 1895, 593.
13. *Gospel Doctrine*, 363.
14. *Gospel Doctrine*, 364.
15. *Gospel Doctrine*, 369.
16. "Counsel to Returning Missionaries," *Millennial Star*, 2 Oct. 1913, 646–47.
17. *Life of Joseph F. Smith*, 231–32.

# Jesus Christ Redeems All Mankind from Temporal Death

*The Atonement of Jesus Christ unconditionally overcomes temporal death and gives to all people the gift of resurrection and immortality.*

## From the Life of Joseph F. Smith

As a missionary and throughout his life, Joseph F. Smith shared the message of the restored gospel of salvation with those who would listen. He taught that the Atonement of Jesus Christ is the central and most significant act of all human history.

The Atonement of our Savior unconditionally overcomes temporal death and provides all people with the gift of resurrection and immortality. In addition, the Atonement of Jesus Christ overcomes spiritual death by redeeming us from our sins and making possible our exaltation if we repent and keep the commandments. The unconditional aspects of the Atonement are addressed in this chapter; the conditional aspects are addressed in the following chapter.

At the death of his 19-year-old daughter Alice, his "Darling Alibo," on 29 April 1901, Joseph F. Smith conveyed his faith in the Atonement in a letter to his son: "Our hearts are still bowed down in the earth where the remains of our Sweet girl and those of her little Brothers and Sisters repose in dust. . . . But we will do the best we can, by the help of the Lord, and from our hearts we feel that our Sleeping treasures are all in His holy keeping and will soon awake from the dust to immortality and eternal life. But for the precious assurance and glorious hope in the Gospel of Christ, life would not only *not* be worth the living, but it would be an infamous and damning *farce!* But, 'O, what joy this sentence gives, I *know* that *my Redeemer lives!*' Thank God."[1]

# Teachings of Joseph F. Smith

### Jesus Christ wrought the glorious redemption
### for the salvation of mankind.

We believe in the Lord Jesus and in his divine, saving mission into the world, and in the redemption, the marvelous, glorious redemption, that he wrought for the salvation of men.[2]

Jesus had not finished his work when his body was slain, neither did he finish it after his resurrection from the dead; although he had accomplished the purpose for which he then came to the earth, he had not fulfilled all his work. And when will he? Not until he has redeemed and saved every son and daughter of our father Adam that have been or ever will be born upon this earth to the end of time, except the sons of perdition. That is his mission.[3]

Jesus Christ, the Son of the living God, is the true standard for all men to follow, the example for all men. He was not a sinner; He was not wicked. In Him there was not any wickedness, nor unbelief, nor folly whatever. He was thoroughly endowed with the wisdom of God from the cradle to the tomb, and after His resurrection He became possessed of the glory of the Father, and became like God himself, possessed of power as God possesses power, for He declared that all power had been given unto Him, and He sits upon the right hand of the Almighty, and is our Mediator, our Elder Brother, and we must follow Him and nobody else.[4]

No other name under heaven is given but that of Jesus Christ, by which you can be saved or exalted in the kingdom of God.[5]

There are some great truths in the plan of redemption that are fundamental. They cannot be ignored; none others can be placed before them. The fatherhood of God, the efficacy of the atonement of our Lord and Savior, the restoration of the gospel in these latter days, must be accepted with our whole hearts.[6]

### Adam's Fall brought death into the world.

Death is not an unmixed horror. With it are associated some of the profoundest and most important truths of human life. Although painful in the extreme to those who must suffer the departure of dear ones, death is one of the grandest blessings in divine economy.

We are born that we may put on mortality, that is, that we may clothe our spirits with a body. Such a blessing is the first step toward an immortal body, and the second step is death. Death lies along the road of eternal progress; and though hard to bear, no one who believes in the gospel of Jesus Christ, and especially in the resurrection, would have it otherwise. . . . Death is really a necessity as well as a blessing, and . . . we would not and could not be satisfied and supremely happy without it.[7]

When man [Adam] transgressed that heavenly law, which forbade that he should partake of the elements of this earth, whereby he should become of the earth, earthy, then he brought upon himself temporal death, just as God declared he would do, if he should partake of the "forbidden fruit."[8]

For death was the penalty of the law transgressed, which man was powerless to avert, that fiat of God being, "In the day that thou eatest thereof thou shalt surely die," [Moses 3:17] and this penalty was to follow upon all flesh, all being as helpless and dependent as he was in this matter.[9]

We are called mortal beings because in us are seeds of death, but in reality we are immortal beings, because there is also within us the germ of eternal life. Man is a dual being, composed of the spirit which gives life, force, intelligence and capacity to man, and the body which is the tenement of the spirit and is suited to its form, adapted to its necessities, and acts in harmony with it, and to its utmost capacity yields obedience to the will of the spirit. The two combined constitute the soul. The body is dependent upon the spirit, and the spirit during its natural occupancy of the body is subject to the laws which apply to and govern it in the mortal state. In this natural body are the seeds of weakness and decay, which, when fully ripened or untimely plucked up, in the language of scripture, is called "the temporal death."[10]

Every man born into the world will die. It matters not who he is, nor where he is, whether his birth be among the rich and the noble, or among the lowly and poor in the world, his days are numbered with the Lord, and in due time he will reach the end. We should think of this. Not that we should go about with heavy hearts or with downcast countenances; not at all. I rejoice that I am born to live, to die, and to live again. I thank God for this intelligence. It gives me joy and peace that the world cannot give, neither can the world take it away. God has revealed this to me, in the gospel of Jesus Christ. I know it to be true. Therefore, I have nothing to be sad over, nothing to make me sorrowful.

All that I have to do with in the world is calculated to buoy me up, to give me joy and peace, hope and consolation in this present life, and a glorious hope of salvation and exaltation in the presence of my God in the world to come. I have no reason to mourn, not even at death. It is true, I am weak enough to weep at the death of my friends and kindred. I may shed tears when I see the grief of others.

I have sympathy in my soul for the children of men. I can weep with them when they weep; I can rejoice with them when they rejoice; but I have no cause to mourn, nor to be sad because death comes into the world. I am speaking now of the temporal death, the death of the body. . . . [Latter-day Saints] know that as death came upon them by the transgression of Adam, so by the righteousness of Jesus Christ shall life come unto them, and though they die, they shall live again.[11]

---

### The Atonement of Jesus Christ overcomes temporal death through the resurrection of all people.

Death came upon us without the exercise of our agency; we had no hand in bringing it originally upon ourselves; it came because of the transgression of our first parents. Therefore, man, who had no hand in bringing death upon himself, shall have no hand in bringing again life unto himself; for as he dies in consequence of the sin of Adam, so shall he live again, whether he will or not, by the righteousness of Jesus Christ, and the power of his resurrection. Every man that dies shall live again.[12]

Jesus Christ . . . is the first fruits of the resurrection from the dead, as he was raised up, so will he raise up all the children of his Father upon whom the curse of Adam came. For as by one man came temporal death upon all men, so by the righteousness of Christ all shall come to life, through the resurrection from the dead upon all men; whether they be good or whether they be evil, whether they be black or white, bond or free, learned or unlearned, or whether they be young or old, it matters not [see 1 Corinthians 15:21–22; Alma 11:44]. The death that came by the fall of our first parents is eradicated by the resurrection of the Son of God, and you and I cannot help it.[13]

We all know that [the Son of God] was lifted upon the cross; that he was pierced in the side, and that his life blood flowed from the body; and that he groaned upon the cross and gave up the spirit; that his body was taken from the cross . . . and wrapped in clean linen and laid in a new sepulchre wherein the body of no man had ever been laid.[14]

Christ himself burst the barriers of the tomb, conquered death and the grave and came forth "the first fruits of them that slept." [1 Corinthians 15:20.][15]

He came into the world . . . clothed with double power—power to die, which He derived from His mother; and power to resist death, if He had so willed it, which He had inherited from His Father. Thus He had power both to live forever and also power to pass through the ordeal of death, that He might suffer it for all men, and come forth out of the grave to a newness of life—a resurrected being, to be clothed with immortality and eternal life, that all men might come forth out of the grave unto life eternal, if they will obey Him. They will come forth anyhow, either as vessels of honor or as vessels of dishonor. They will come forth from the grave whether they will or not. They can't help themselves. We could not help the curse of mortal death coming upon us, neither shall we be able to avoid or to prevent the resurrection of this body from that grave; for as God raised from the dead, so will all mankind.[16]

We distinctly believe that Jesus Christ himself is the true, and only true type of the resurrection of men from death unto life. We believe there is no other form of resurrection from death to life; that as he rose, and as he preserved his identity, even to the scars of the wounds in his hands and feet and side, that he could prove himself to those that were skeptical of the possibility of rising from the dead, that he was indeed himself, the Lord crucified, buried in the tomb, and raised again from death to life, so it will be with you and with every son and daughter of Adam, born into the world.[17]

We [will] come forth out of the grave, when the trump shall sound, and these our bodies shall rise and our spirits shall enter into them again, and they shall become living souls, no more to be dissolved or separated, but to become inseparable, immortal, eternal.[18]

The elements which compose this temporal body will not perish, will not cease to exist, but in the day of the resurrection these elements will come together again, bone to bone, and flesh to flesh. The body will come forth as it is laid to rest, for there is no growth or development in the grave. As it is laid down, so will it arise, and changes to perfection will come by the law of restitution. But the spirit will continue to expand and develop, and the body, after the resurrection will develop to the full stature of man.[19]

The spirit and the body will be reunited. We shall see each other in the flesh, in the same tabernacles that we have here while in mortality. Our tabernacles will be brought forth as they are laid down, although there will be a restoration effected; every organ, every limb that has been maimed, every deformity caused by accident or in any other way, will be restored and put right. Every limb and joint shall be restored to its proper frame. We will know each other and enjoy each other's society throughout the endless ages of eternity, if we keep the law of God.[20]

What a glorious thought it is, to me at least, and it must be to all who have conceived of the truth or received it in their hearts, that those from whom we have to part here, we will meet again and see as they are. We will meet the same identical being that we associated with here in the flesh—not some other soul, some other being, or the same being in some other form, but the same identity and the same form and likeness, the same person we knew and were associated with in our mortal existence, even to the wounds in the flesh. Not that a person will always be marred by scars, wounds, deformities, defects or infirmities, for these will be removed in their course, in their proper time, according to the merciful providence of God. Deformity will be removed; defects will be eliminated, and men and women shall attain to the perfection of their spirits, to the perfection that God designed in the beginning. It is his purpose that men and women, his children, born to become heirs of God, and joint heirs with Jesus Christ, shall be made perfect, physically as well as spiritually, through obedience to the law by which he has provided the means that perfection shall come to all his children.[21]

So far as the stages of eternal progression and attainment have been made known through divine revelation, we are to understand that only resurrected and glorified beings can become parents of spirit offspring. Only such exalted souls have reached maturity in the appointed course of eternal life; and the spirits born to them in the eternal worlds will pass in due sequence through the several stages or estates by which the glorified parents have attained exaltation.[22]

I cannot conceive of any more desirable thing than is vouchsafed to us in the gospel of Jesus Christ—that though we die, yet we shall live again, and though we die and dissolve into the native elements of which our tabernacles are composed, yet these elements will again be restored to each other and be reorganized, and we will become again living souls just as the Savior did before us; and his having done so has made it possible for all the rest of us.[23]

## Suggestions for Study

- What is the "divine, saving mission" of Jesus Christ in the plan of redemption?

- Why must the reality and power of the Atonement "be accepted with our whole hearts"? What blessings come to those who do this?

- How is man a "dual being"? (See also D&C 88:15–16.) What blessings come to us because we know this?

- What is temporal death? How does it help you to know that "death lies along the road of eternal progress"?

- What doctrines help us to remove the fear of temporal death from our lives? Why can we rejoice that we are "born to live, to die, and to live again"?

- In what way was Jesus Christ "clothed with double power"?

- What does it mean to be resurrected? In what form will our bodies appear when we are resurrected?

- How do you feel when you realize that Jesus Christ has made it possible for you to be resurrected and live forever? How does this realization help you keep the covenants you have made with God?

- Why is it important to remember that one day we really will die and be resurrected?

## Notes

1. Joseph F. Smith to Jos. R. Smith, 14 May 1901, Historical Department Archives, The Church of Jesus Christ of Latter-day Saints.
2. *Gospel Doctrine,* 5th ed. (1939), 138.
3. *Gospel Doctrine,* 442.
4. In Brian H. Stuy, comp., *Collected Discourses Delivered by President Wilford Woodruff, His Two Counselors, the Twelve Apostles, and Others,* 5 vols. (1987–92), 5:54.
5. *Gospel Doctrine,* 39.
6. *Gospel Doctrine,* 117.
7. *Gospel Doctrine,* 296–97.
8. "Latter-day Saints Follow Teachings of the Savior," *Scrap Book of Mormon Literature,* 2 vols. (n.d.), 2:555.
9. *Gospel Doctrine,* 202.
10. *Gospel Doctrine,* 14.
11. *Gospel Doctrine,* 428; paragraphing added.
12. *Gospel Doctrine,* 69.
13. *Gospel Doctrine,* 469.
14. *Gospel Doctrine,* 463.
15. *Gospel Doctrine,* 444.
16. "Latter-day Saints Follow Teachings of the Savior," 2:558.
17. *Gospel Doctrine,* 435.
18. *Gospel Doctrine,* 450–51.
19. "Editor's Table: On the Resurrection," *Improvement Era,* June 1904, 623–24.
20. *Gospel Doctrine,* 447.
21. *Gospel Doctrine,* 23.
22. *Gospel Doctrine,* 69–70.
23. *Gospel Doctrine,* 458.

*Christ in Gethsemane,* by Harry Anderson.
Through His Atonement, Jesus Christ redeemed all mankind from
physical death. He also redeems the repentant from sin.

## Jesus Christ Redeems the Repentant from Spiritual Death

*The Atonement of Jesus Christ redeems those who are repentant and faithful from spiritual death.*

## From the Life of Joseph F. Smith

"I am young and inexperienced at present," Joseph F. Smith wrote while on his mission in Hawaii. "Therefore I wish to be humble, prayerful before the Lord, that I may be worthy of the blessings and love of God."[1] Early in his service in Hawaii, the young missionary had a spiritual experience that illustrates the cleansing and comforting power of the Atonement of Jesus Christ: He said that he was "very much oppressed" on his mission and in a "condition of poverty, lack of intelligence and knowledge."

"While in that condition I dreamed that I was on a journey, and I was impressed that I ought to hurry—hurry with all my might, for fear I might be too late. I rushed on my way as fast as I possibly could, and I was only conscious of having just a little bundle, a handkerchief with a small bundle wrapped in it. I did not realize just what it was, when I was hurrying as fast as I could; but finally I came to a wonderful mansion, if it could be called a mansion. It seemed too large, too great to have been made by hand, but I thought I knew that was my destination. As I passed towards it, as fast as I could, I saw a notice, 'Bath.' I turned aside quickly and went into the bath and washed myself clean. I opened up this little bundle that I had, and there was a pair of white, clean garments, a thing I had not seen for a long time. . . . I put them on. Then I rushed to what appeared to be a great opening, or door. I knocked and the door opened, and the man who stood there was the Prophet Joseph Smith. He looked at me a little reprovingly, and the first words he said: 'Joseph, you are late.' Yet I took confidence and said:

" 'Yes, but I am clean—I am clean!'

" . . . That vision, that manifestation and witness that I enjoyed at that time has made me what I am, if I am anything that is good, or clean, or upright before the Lord, if there is anything good in me. That has helped me out in every trial and through every difficulty."[2]

# Teachings of Joseph F. Smith

## Through the Fall of Adam, spiritual death came into the world.

I want to speak a word or two in relation to another death, which is a more terrible death than that of the body. When Adam, our first parent, partook of the forbidden fruit, transgressed the law of God, and became subject unto Satan, he was banished from the presence of God. . . . This was the first death. Yet living, he was dead—dead to God, dead to light and truth, dead spiritually; cast out from the presence of God; communication between the Father and the Son cut off. He was as absolutely thrust out from the presence of God as was Satan and the hosts that followed him. That was spiritual death.[3]

I want to impress upon your minds—"wherein [Adam] became spiritually dead." Now what was his condition when he was placed in the Garden of Eden? He had access to the Father. He was in His presence. He walked and talked with Him face to face, as one man walks and talks with another. This was the condition of Adam and Eve when they were in the garden. But when they partook of the forbidden fruit they were cast out and banished from the presence of God, . . . "Wherein they became spiritually dead, which is the first death." [See D&C 29:41.] And it was impossible for Adam in that condition to extricate himself from the position in which he had placed himself. He was within the grasp of Satan. . . . He was "spiritually dead"—banished from the presence of God. And if there had not been a way of escape provided for him, his death would have been a perpetual, endless, eternal death, without any hope of redemption therefrom.[4]

**No one can be saved in the kingdom of God in sin.**

No man can be ushered into the presence of God in his sins, and no man can receive a remission of his sins except he repent and [be buried] with Christ [see Romans 6:4]. For God has made us free agents, to choose good or evil, to walk in the light or in the darkness, as we choose, and he has ordained it thus that we might become like Him, that if we prove ourselves worthy of everlasting life and glory in His presence, it will be because we have repented of our sins and have obeyed and kept His commandments.[5]

No man can be saved in the kingdom of God in sin. No man will ever be forgiven of his sins by the just Judge, except he repent of his sins. No man will ever be freed from the power of [spiritual] death unless he is born again as the Lord Almighty has decreed.[6]

God has given to all men an agency and has granted to us the privilege to serve him or serve him not, to do that which is right or that which is wrong, and this privilege is given to all men irrespective of creed, color or condition. The wealthy have this agency, the poor have this agency, and no man is deprived by any power of God from exercising it in the fullest and in the freest manner. This agency has been given to all. This is a blessing that God has bestowed upon the world of mankind, upon all his children alike. But he will hold us strictly to an account for the use that we make of this agency, and as it was said of Cain, so it will be said of us; "If thou doest well, shalt thou not be accepted? and if thou doest not well, sin lieth at the door" (Gen. 4:7). . . . While God has bestowed upon all men, irrespective of condition, this agency to choose good or evil, he has not and will not bestow upon the children of men a remission of sins but by their obedience to law. Therefore, the whole world lies in sin and is under condemnation, inasmuch as light has come unto the world and men will not place themselves in a proper position before the Lord.[7]

## The Atonement of Christ redeems us from
## spiritual death through repentance and obedience.

The Lord designed in the beginning to place before man the knowledge of good and evil, and gave him a commandment to cleave to good and abstain from evil. But if he should fail, he would give to him the law of sacrifice and provide a Savior for him, that he might be brought back again into the presence and favor of God and partake of eternal life with him. This was the plan of redemption chosen and instituted by the Almighty before man was placed on the earth. And when man did fall by transgressing the law which was given him, the Lord gave to him the law of sacrifice, and made it clear to his understanding, that it was for the purpose of reminding him of that great event that should transpire in the meridian of time, whereby he and all his posterity might be brought forth by the power of redemption and resurrection from the dead, and partake of eternal life with God in his kingdom.[8]

There was a plan laid for [Adam's] redemption. It was decreed by the Almighty that he should not suffer the temporal death until he should be taught the way of escape from the spiritual death that had come upon him by reason of sin. Therefore the angel came and taught him the Gospel of salvation, held up before him Christ, the Redeemer of the world, who was to come in the meridian of time possessed of power to conquer death and to redeem Adam and his posterity from the fall, and from the grasp of Satan. . . . Somebody else had to reach down and help him up. Some other and higher power than his had to bring him forth out of the condition in which he had placed himself: for he was subject unto Satan and powerless and helpless in and of himself.

The Gospel was, therefore, preached to him, and a way of escape from that spiritual death given unto him. That way of escape was through faith in God, repentance of sin, baptism for the remission of sins, the gift of the Holy Ghost by the laying on of hands. Thereby he received a knowledge of the truth and a testimony of Jesus Christ, and was redeemed from the spiritual death that came upon him, which was the first death, and a complete and perfect death, so far as spirit was concerned, although he lived and moved and had his being, as he did before he partook of the forbidden fruit and became spiritually dead; he had his entity and his organization; but he was spiritually dead, and he had to be redeemed from that condition.[9]

Adam . . . had to be redeemed from [spiritual death] by the blood of Christ, and by faith and obedience to the commands of God. By this means Adam was redeemed from the first death, and brought back again into the presence of God, back again into the favor of the Almighty, back again into the channel of eternal increase and progress.[10]

If the Lord has revealed to the world the plan of salvation and redemption from sin, by which men may be exalted again into his presence and partake of eternal life with him, I submit, as a proposition that cannot be controverted, that no man can be exalted in the presence of God and attain to a fulness of glory and happiness in his kingdom and presence, save and except he will obey the plan that God has devised and revealed.[11]

If we live in harmony with the designs of our Heavenly Father, if our hearts are drawn out toward Him, and toward our Elder Brother, the Son of God, our glorious Redeemer, through Him we are raised not only from the dead, but are also redeemed, or may be redeemed, from spiritual death, and be brought back into the presence of God.[12]

Christ was divinely appointed and sent into the world to relieve mankind of sin through repentance; to relieve mankind from the death which came upon them by the sin [transgression] of the first man. I believe it with all my soul.[13]

When we commit sin, it is necessary that we repent of it and make restitution as far as lies in our power. When we cannot make restitution for the wrong we have done, then we must apply for the grace and mercy of God to cleanse us from that iniquity.

Men cannot forgive their own sins; they cannot cleanse themselves from the consequences of their sins. Men can stop sinning and can do right in the future, and so far their acts are acceptable before the Lord and worthy of consideration. But who shall repair the wrongs they have done to themselves and to others, which it seems impossible for them to repair themselves? By the atonement of Jesus Christ the sins of the repentant shall be washed away; though they be crimson they shall be made white as wool [see Isaiah 1:18]. This is the promise given to you.[14]

---

### Through the Atonement and our faithfulness, we can become joint heirs with Jesus Christ.

We shall stand before the bar of God to be judged. So says the Bible, so says the Book of Mormon, and so say the revelations which have come direct to us through the Prophet Joseph Smith. And then those who have not been subject and obedient to the celestial law will not be quickened by the celestial glory. And those who have not been subject and obedient to the terrestrial law will not be quickened by the terrestrial glory. And those who have not been subject and obedient to the telestial law, will not be quickened by a telestial glory; but they will have a kingdom without glory.[15]

All the bodies that lie in the graves are called forth; not all at the first resurrection, nor in the morning of the first resurrection, but some perhaps in the last resurrection; and every soul will be required to go before the bar of God and be judged according to the deeds done in the body. If his works have been good, then he receives the reward of well doing; if [they have] been evil, then he will be banished from the presence of the Lord.[16]

We live, then; we do not die; we do not anticipate death but we anticipate life, immortality, glory, exaltation, and to be quickened by the glory of the celestial kingdom, and receive of the same even a fulness. This is our destiny; this is the exalted position to which we may attain and there is no power that can deprive or rob us of it, if we prove faithful and true to the covenant of the gospel.[17]

The object of our earthly existence is that we may have a fulness of joy, and that we may become the sons and daughters of God, in the fullest sense of the word, being heirs of God and joint heirs with Jesus Christ, to be kings and priests unto God, to inherit glory, dominion, exaltation, thrones and every power and attribute developed and possessed by our Heavenly Father. This is the object of our being on this earth. In order to attain unto this exalted position, it is necessary that we go through this mortal experience, or probation, by which we may prove ourselves worthy, through the aid of our elder brother Jesus.[18]

Men can only be saved and exalted in the kingdom of God in righteousness, therefore we must repent of our sins, and walk in the light as Christ is in the light, that his blood may cleanse us from all sins, and that we may have fellowship with God and receive of his glory and exaltation.[19]

## By partaking of the sacrament, we remember Jesus Christ and His Atonement.

Adam, after he was cast out of the garden, was commanded to offer sacrifices to God; by this act, he and all who participated in the offerings of sacrifices, were reminded of the Savior who should come to redeem them from death which, were it not for the atonement wrought out by him, would forever exclude them from dwelling in the presence of God again. But in his coming and death, this commandment was fulfilled; and he instituted the Supper and commanded his followers to partake of this in all time to come, in order that they may remember him, bearing in mind that he had redeemed them, also that they had covenanted to keep his commandments and to walk with him in the regeneration. Hence it is necessary to partake of the Sacrament, as a witness to him that we do remember him, are willing to keep the commandments he has given us, that we may have his Spirit to be with us always—even to the end, and also that we may continue in the forgiveness of sins.[20]

When Jesus came and suffered, "the just for the unjust," he that was without sin for him that had sinned, and was subjected to the penalty of the law which the sinner had transgressed, the law of sacrifice was fulfilled, and instead thereof he gave another law, which we call the "Sacrament of the Lord's Supper," by which his life and mission, his death and resurrection, the great sacrifice he had offered for the redemption of man, should be kept in everlasting remembrance, for, said he, "this do ye . . . in remembrance of me, for as often as ye eat this bread and drink this cup, ye do shew the Lord's death till he come." Therefore this law is

101

to us what the law of sacrifice was to those who lived prior to the first coming of the Son of Man, until he shall come again. Therefore, we must honor and keep it sacredly, for there is a penalty attached to its violation [see 1 Corinthians 11:25–29].[21]

The Sacrament of the Lord's Supper . . . is a principle of the Gospel, one as necessary to be observed by all believers, as any other ordinance of the Gospel. What is the object of it? It is that we may keep in mind continually the Son of God who has redeemed us, from eternal death, and brought us to life again through the power of the Gospel. Before the coming of Christ to the earth, this was borne in mind by the inhabitants of the earth to whom the Gospel was preached, by another ordinance, which involved the sacrifice of animal life, an ordinance which was a type of the great sacrifice that should take place in the meridian of time.[22]

## Suggestions for Study

- What is the Atonement? When have you felt strongly the power of the Atonement in your life?

- What is spiritual death? Why is it "a more terrible death than that of the body"?

- If "there had not been a way of escape provided" for Adam and his posterity, what would have been the consequence for us? (See also 2 Nephi 9:6–9.)

- What has the Savior done to make possible our escape from spiritual death? What must we do to overcome spiritual death? How can we "apply for the grace and mercy of God to cleanse us from . . . iniquity"?

- What blessings have come into your life because you know that Jesus Christ can cleanse the wrongs we do to ourselves and others? How have you seen these same blessings in the lives of others?

- What does it mean to be quickened? How can we be spiritually quickened now? (See Moses 6:64–68.) What blessings come to those who are "quickened by the glory of the celestial kingdom"? (See also D&C 88:28–29.)

- What is the "object of our earthly existence"?

- How does partaking of the sacrament help us overcome spiritual death? How can we always remember the Savior? What can we do to honor the sacrament and keep it sacred?

- How might we gratefully receive the gift of the Atonement in our lives?

## Notes

1. *Life of Joseph F. Smith*, comp. Joseph Fielding Smith (1938), 180–81.
2. *Gospel Doctrine*, 5th ed. (1939), 542–43.
3. *Gospel Doctrine*, 432.
4. *Deseret Evening News*, 9 Feb. 1895, 9.
5. "Latter-day Saints Follow Teachings of the Savior," *Scrap Book of Mormon Literature*, 2 vols. (n.d.), 2:563.
6. *Gospel Doctrine*, 250.
7. *Gospel Doctrine*, 49.
8. *Gospel Doctrine*, 202.
9. *Deseret Evening News*, 9 Feb. 1895, 9; paragraphing added.
10. *Deseret Evening News*, 9 Feb. 1895, 9.
11. *Gospel Doctrine*, 6.
12. *Deseret News: Semi-Weekly*, 6 Feb. 1893, 2.
13. *Gospel Doctrine*, 420.
14. *Gospel Doctrine*, 98–99.
15. *Gospel Doctrine*, 451.
16. *Deseret Evening News*, 9 Feb. 1895, 9.
17. *Gospel Doctrine*, 443.
18. *Gospel Doctrine*, 439.
19. *Gospel Doctrine*, 250–51.
20. *Gospel Doctrine*, 103–4.
21. *Gospel Doctrine*, 204.
22. *Deseret News: Semi-Weekly*, 19 Feb. 1878, 1.

# Valiant in the Cause of Christ

*We must be valiant in the cause of Christ and true to*
*our covenants, to our God, and to the work of Zion.*

## From the Life of Joseph F. Smith

In the fall of 1857 Joseph F. Smith, just 19 years of age, left his
mission in Hawaii to return home. He came home by way of San
Francisco, Los Angeles, and San Bernardino. "In southern California, just after the little train of wagons had traveled only a
short distance and made their camp, several anti-'Mormon'
toughs rode into the camp on horseback, cursing and swearing
and threatening what they would do to the 'Mormons.' Joseph F.
was a little distance from the camp gathering wood for the fire,
but he saw that the few members of his own party had cautiously
gone into the brush down the creek, out of sight. When he saw
that, . . . the thought came into his mind, 'Shall I run from these
fellows? Why should I fear them?' With that he marched up with
his arm full of wood to the campfire where one of the ruffians,
still with his pistol in his hand, shouting and cursing about the
'Mormons,' in a loud voice said to Joseph F.

" 'Are you a "Mormon"?'

"And the answer came straight, 'Yes, siree; dyed in the wool;
true blue, through and through.'

"At that the ruffian grasped him by the hand and said:

" 'Well, you are the ——— ——— pleasantest man I ever met!
Shake, young fellow, I am glad to see a man that stands up for
his convictions.' "[1]

President Smith lived a life true to the Lord, no matter what
the obstacles or difficulties. Close friend and Presiding Bishop of

adulation, from that which will in any degree tarnish that which they call honor or a good name.[8]

Let the spirit of this gospel be so imbedded in my soul that though I go through poverty, through tribulation, through persecution, or to death, let me and my house serve God and keep his laws. However, the promise is that you shall be blessed through obedience. God will honor those who honor him, and will remember those who remember him. He will uphold and sustain all those who sustain truth and are faithful to it. God help us, therefore, to be faithful to the truth, now and forever.[9]

---

**We can be valiant warriors in the cause of Christ.**

While listening to the brethren this afternoon I was led to reflect upon some of our friends who have passed away. When we look back and think of President Young, Heber C. Kimball, Willard Richards, George A. Smith, Orson Pratt, Parley Pratt, President John Taylor, Erastus Snow, and the thousands of faithful, valiant Saints of God who passed through the persecutions in Ohio, in Missouri, and in Illinois, and were driven from their homes time and time and time again, and finally out into the wilderness, with no knowledge, except the promises of the Holy Spirit in their hearts, that they would ever find a resting place for their weary feet—driven from their homes, their kindred, and their friends, with the dimmest prospect in the world, so far as human knowledge or prescience was concerned, of ever reaching a haven of rest, but trudging across the plains with weary step, yet with unshaken confidence in God and unwavering faith in His word—when we look back and think of those scenes we cannot forget the faithful men and women who passed through them. They did not faint by the way; they did not backslide; they did not turn from the truth. The harder the trial, the more difficult the journey, the greater the obstacles, the more firm and determined they were.[10]

I have served from my youth up along with such men as Brigham Young, Heber C. Kimball, Willard Richards, George A. Smith, Jedediah M. Grant, Daniel H. Wells, John Taylor, George Q. Cannon, and Wilford Woodruff and his associates, and Lorenzo Snow and his associates, the members of the twelve apostles, the seventies, and the high priests in the Church of Jesus Christ of Latter-day Saints for more than sixty years; and, that my word may be heard by every stranger within the sound of my voice, I want to testify to you that better men than these have never lived within the range of my acquaintance. I can so testify because I was familiar with these men, grew up from babyhood with them, associated with them in council, in prayer and supplication, and in travel from settlement to settlement through our country here, and in crossing the plains. I have heard them in private and in public, and I bear my testimony to you that they were men of God, true men, pure men, God's noblemen.[11]

Here are our sisters engaged in the Relief Society work. . . . Here are sisters who are connected with the Mutual Improvement associations, and those also connected with the Primary work and our Sunday school interests. . . . They all have our blessings, because we have confidence in them. We believe that they know the truth themselves and do not have to borrow light from somebody else. We know that their integrity is unimpeachable; we know they love God and the truth and that they love the work more than their own personal interest. We know many of them and we know these are their feelings. We love them; they have our respect, our full confidence; the blessings of the Lord will attend them.[12]

The sisters of the Relief Society, always active and helpful, have been found at hand everywhere in time of need, aiding the poor, comforting the afflicted, visiting the widow and the fatherless, and traveling to distant points imparting valuable instruction.[13]

President Heber C. Kimball was one of God's noblemen. True as steel to every trust. Pure as refined gold. Fearless of foes or of death. Keen of perception, full of the spirit of the prophets. Inspired of God. Valiant in the testimony of Christ; a lifelong, undeviating friend and witness of the divine calling and mission of Joseph Smith. He was called by the grace of God, ordained by living authority, and lived and died an apostle of the Lord Jesus Christ.[14]

I believe that the brethren of the Twelve who have been at their posts, performing their duty, stand solid for the advancement of the kingdom of God, and are united in their views and labors for the upbuilding of Zion. . . . They are worthy of the confidence of the Latter-day Saints, are valiant in their testimony for the truth, are earnest and vigilant in their watchcare over the interests of Zion.[15]

Now, God bless you. May peace abide in your souls, and the love of truth abound in you. May virtue garnish all your ways. May you live uprightly and honestly before the Lord, keep the faith, and be valiant in the testimony of Jesus Christ; for he that is valiant will receive his reward. God bless you, is my prayer in the name of Jesus. Amen.[16]

## Suggestions for Study

- What does it mean to be valiant in the testimony of Christ? How can we show in our daily lives a willingness to be true to our religion and to our God?

- Why is the religion of Christ "not a Sunday religion" only? How can we teach our religion to our children "from our hearts to their hearts and from our affections to their affections"?

- How might we as members of the Church sometimes attempt to "popularize" the gospel "at the risk of principle"?

- How can we show proper tolerance for other people's opinions and lifestyles without sacrificing integrity to principle?

- How can we teach principles such as courage, integrity to principle, and valiant living of the gospel to others, including our children?

- What are some of the ways in which the early Church leaders were valiant in their testimonies? What can we learn about being courageous and valiant from the lives of these leaders?

- What is the "courage of faith"? When have you shown this courage in times of opposition?

- How can we be valiant in fulfilling our Church callings?

- What blessings come to us and our families as a result of our valiant living of the gospel? (See also D&C 14:7.) What are the eternal consequences for those who are not valiant in the testimony of Jesus? (See also D&C 76:79.)

## Notes

1. Charles W. Nibley, "Reminiscences," in *Gospel Doctrine,* 5th ed. (1939), 518.
2. Charles W. Nibley, "Reminiscences," 525.
3. *Gospel Doctrine,* 257.
4. *Gospel Doctrine,* 394–95; paragraphing added.
5. *Gospel Doctrine,* 155.
6. "Editor's Table: Principle, Not Popularity," *Improvement Era,* July 1906, 731, 733.
7. *Gospel Doctrine,* 119–20.
8. *Gospel Doctrine,* 211.
9. *Gospel Doctrine,* 251.
10. *Deseret News: Semi-Weekly,* 9 Aug. 1898, 1.
11. *Gospel Doctrine,* 169.
12. In Conference Report, Oct. 1906, 9.
13. In James R. Clark, comp., *Messages of the First Presidency of The Church of Jesus Christ of Latter-day Saints,* 6 vols. (1965–75), 4:296.
14. *Gospel Doctrine,* 198–99.
15. In Conference Report, Apr. 1906, 2.
16. In Conference Report, Apr. 1906, 8.

# Stand by the Truth Lest You Be Deceived

*We must abide by the pure, truthful principles*
*of the gospel of Jesus Christ and avoid the falsehoods*
*and errors of deceivers.*

## From the Life of Joseph F. Smith

Joseph F. Smith had been home from a mission to Great Britain just five months when President Brigham Young called him to serve his third mission—his second to the Hawaiian Islands. Because of his fluency with the Hawaiian language, President Young asked him to serve as an interpreter for Elders Ezra T. Benson and Lorenzo Snow, members of the Quorum of the Twelve. When they left for Hawaii in the spring of 1864, Joseph F. Smith was 24 years of age.

Joseph F. Smith said of this mission: "The special object of our errand [was] to put a stop to the fraudulent operations of [an] imposter . . . who was deceiving the . . . native members of the Church, not only in matters of doctrine, but with grotesquely false representations of his own power and authority. He had reorganized the Church according to his own fancies, ordained Twelve Apostles and other officers, selling them their ordinations, and imposing himself upon the people as a priestly and kingly ruler, to whom they must pay abject homage. We confronted him, charged him with his misdeeds, and labored faithfully to reclaim him, but he proved obdurate and impenitent and was therefore cut off from the Church. We then directed our energies towards reclaiming those whom he had misled, and in this work, under the blessing of God, we were very successful."[1] After Elders Benson and Snow left the islands, Joseph F. Smith remained until the following winter to continue to put the affairs of the Church in order. During this time he counseled with members of the Church who had been led into error by this apostate and wanted to repent. For the rest of his life President Smith taught the Saints the importance of recognizing and resisting false teachings.

# Teachings of Joseph F. Smith

## Latter-day Saints must stand by the truth, no matter what may come.

We should have gained sufficient experience by this time to realize that no man, no individual, no clique, and no secret organization can combine with force and power sufficient to overturn the purposes of the Almighty, or to change the course of His work. Many and many an individual has arisen in times past, and these individuals have been falsely impressed with the idea that they were going to work a wonderful reformation in the Church; they anticipated that in a very short time the whole people would desert their standard, the standard of truth to which they had gathered and around which they had rallied from the beginning of the Church until then. These persons thought the people would follow the "new shepherds," but the people of God know the voice of the true shepherd, and the stranger's voice they will not heed, nor the counsels of him who assumes authority that does not belong to him. None such will they ever follow. The Latter-day Saints know the spirit of the Gospel; they understand the spirit of truth. They have learned their duty, and they will stand by the truth, no matter what may come.

From the beginning until now, we have had to face the entire world; and the whole world, comparatively, is or has been arrayed against the work of the Lord, not all on account of hatred, not solely with the intent or desire in their hearts to do evil or to fight the truth, but because they were ignorant of the truth, and because they knew not what they were doing. Many are deceived by the voice of false shepherds, and are misled by false influences. They are deceived; they know not the truth; they understand not what they do and, therefore, they are arrayed, as it were, against the truth, against the work of the Lord; so it has been from the beginning. From the day that the Prophet Joseph

Smith first declared his vision until now, the enemy of all righteousness, the enemy of truth, of virtue, of honor, uprightness, and purity of life; the enemy to the only true God, the enemy to direct revelation from God and to the inspirations that come from the heavens to man, has been arrayed against this work.

You have never found the friend to righteousness, the friend to revelation, the friend to God, the friend to truth, the friend to righteous living and purity of life, or he who is devoted to righteousness and is broad enough to comprehend truth from error and light from darkness—I say you have never found such as these arrayed against the cause of Zion. To be arrayed against the cause of Zion is to be arrayed against God, against revelation from God, against that spirit that leads men into all truth that cometh from the source of light and intelligence, against that principle that brings men together and causes them to forsake their sins, to seek righteousness, to love God with all their hearts, mind and strength, and to love their neighbors as themselves.[2]

---

### Beware of false teachings.

Some men there will be who would limit the power of God to the power of men, and we have some of these among us and they have been among our school teachers. They would have you disbelieve the inspired accounts of the Scriptures, that the winds and the waves are subject to the power of God; and believe the claim of the Savior to cast out devils, raise the dead, or perform miraculous things, such as cleansing the leper, is only a myth. They would make you believe that God and his Son Jesus Christ did not appear in person to Joseph Smith, that this was simply a myth, but we know better; the testimony of the Spirit has testified that this is the truth. And I say, beware of men who come to you with heresies that things come by laws of nature of themselves, and that God is without power.[3]

Among the Latter-day Saints, the preaching of false doctrines disguised as truths of the gospel, may be expected from people of two classes, and practically from these only; they are:

First—The hopelessly ignorant, whose lack of intelligence is due to their indolence and sloth, who make but feeble effort, if indeed any at all, to better themselves by reading and study; those who are afflicted with a dread disease that may develop into an incurable malady—laziness.

Second—The proud and self-vaunting ones, who read by the lamp of their own conceit; who interpret by rules of their own contriving; who have become a law unto themselves, and so pose as the sole judges of their own doings. More dangerously ignorant than the first.

Beware of the lazy and the proud.[4]

The Latter-day Saints by this time should be so well settled in the conviction that God has established his Church in the earth for the last time, to remain, and no more to be thrown down or destroyed; and that God's house is a house of order, of law, of regularity, that erratic disturbers of that order of men of restless temperament, who, through ignorance and egotism, become vain babblers, yet make great pretensions to prophetic powers and other spiritual graces and gifts, ought not to have any influence with them, nor ought the Saints to be disturbed in their spirit by such characters and their theories. The Church of Christ is with the Saints. It has committed to it the law of God for its own government and perpetuation. It possesses every means for the correction of every wrong or abuse or error which may from time to time arise, and that without anarchy, or even revolution; it can do it by process of evolution—by development, by an increase of knowledge, wisdom, patience and charity.

The presiding quorums of the Church will always be composed of such men, they will be chosen in such manner, that the Saints can be assured that solid wisdom, righteousness, and conscientious adherence to duty, will characterize the policy of those who are entrusted with the administration of the affairs of the Church.[5]

From the days of Hiram Page (Doc. and Cov., Sec. 28), at different periods there have been manifestations from delusive spirits to members of the Church. Sometimes these have come to men and women who because of transgression became easy prey to the Arch-Deceiver. At other times people who pride themselves on their strict observance of the rules and ordinances and ceremonies of the Church are led astray by false spirits, who exercise an influence so imitative of that which proceeds from a Divine source that even these persons, who think they are "the very elect," find it difficult to discern the essential difference [Matthew 24:24]. Satan himself has transformed himself to be apparently "an angel of light" [2 Corinthians 11:14; 2 Nephi 9:9].

When visions, dreams, tongues, prophecy, impressions or any extraordinary gift or inspiration conveys something out of harmony with the accepted revelations of the Church or contrary to the decisions of its constituted authorities, Latter-day Saints may know that it is not of God, no matter how plausible it may appear. Also they should understand that directions for the guidance of the Church will come, by revelation, through the head. All faithful members are entitled to the inspiration of the Holy Spirit for themselves, their families, and for those over whom they are appointed and ordained to preside. But anything at discord with that which comes from God through the head of the Church is not to be received as authoritative or reliable.[6]

The gifts of the Spirit and the powers of the holy Priesthood are of God, they are given for the blessing of the people, for their encouragement, and for the strengthening of their faith. This Satan knows full well, therefore he seeks by imitation-miracles to blind and deceive the children of God. Remember what the magicians of Egypt accomplished in their efforts to deceive Pharaoh as to the divinity of the mission of Moses and Aaron. . . .

That the power to work wonders may come from an evil source is declared by Christ in his prophecy regarding the great judgment: "Many will say to me in that day, Lord, Lord, have we not prophesied in thy name? and in thy name have cast out devils? and in thy name done many wonderful works? And then will I profess unto them, I never knew you; depart from me, ye that work iniquity." (Matt. 7:22–23.)

The danger and power for evil in witchcraft is not so much in the witchcraft itself as in the foolish credulence that superstitious people give to the claims made in its behalf. It is outrageous to believe that the devil can hurt or injure an innocent man or woman, especially if they are members of the Church of Christ—

[unless] that man or woman has faith that he or she can be harmed by such an influence and by such means. If they entertain such an idea, then they are liable to succumb to their own superstitions. There is no power in witchcraft itself, only as it is believed in and accepted.[7]

---

### Avoid religious hobbies.

Brethren and sisters, don't have [religious] hobbies. Hobbies are dangerous in the Church of Christ. They are dangerous because they give undue prominence to certain principles or ideas to the detriment and dwarfing of others just as important, just as binding, just as saving as the favored doctrines or commandments.

[Religious] hobbies give to those who encourage them a false aspect of the gospel of the Redeemer; they distort and place out of harmony its principles and teachings. The point of view is unnatural. Every principle and practice revealed from God is essential to man's salvation, and to place any one of them unduly in front, hiding and dimming all others is unwise and dangerous; it jeopardizes our salvation, for it darkens our minds and beclouds our understandings. Such a view, no matter to what point directed, narrows the vision, weakens the spiritual perception, and darkens the mind, the result of which is that the person thus afflicted with this perversity and contraction of mental vision places himself in a position to be tempted of the evil one, or, through dimness of sight or distortion of vision, to misjudge his brethren and give way to the spirit of apostasy. He is not square before the Lord.

We have noticed this difficulty: that Saints with hobbies are prone to judge and condemn their brethren and sisters who are not so zealous in the one particular direction of their pet theory as they are. The man with the Word of Wisdom only in his brain, is apt to find unmeasured fault with every other member of the Church who entertains liberal ideas as to the importance of other doctrines of the gospel.

There is another phase of this difficulty—the man with a hobby is apt to assume an "I am holier than thou" position, to feel puffed

place, let your virtue, your integrity, your honesty, your ability, your religious teachings, implanted in your hearts at the knees of your devoted "Mormon" mothers, "so shine before men, that they may see your good works, and glorify your Father which is in heaven." [Matthew 5:16.][11]

May the Lord bless our government and lead those that hold the power in their hands to do that which is righteous, pleasing and acceptable unto God.[12]

---

### We hold to the doctrine of separation of Church and state.

Church members are commanded by Divine revelation . . . : "Let no man break the laws of the land, for he that obeys the laws of God hath no need to break the laws of the land." [D&C 58:21.][13]

With reference to the laws of the Church, it is expressly said: . . .

"Behold, the laws which ye have received from my hand are the laws of the Church, and in this light ye shall hold them forth." [D&C 58:23.]

That is to say, no law or rule enacted, or revelation received by the Church, has been promulgated for the State. Such laws and revelations as have been given are solely for the government of the Church.

The Church of Jesus Christ of Latter-day Saints holds to the doctrine of the separation of church and state; the non-interference of church authority in political matters; and the absolute freedom and independence of the individual in the performance of his political duties. If at any time there has been conduct at variance with this doctrine, it has been in violation of the well-settled principles and policy of the Church.

We declare that from principle and policy, we favor: The absolute separation of church and state; No domination of the state by the church; No church interference with the functions of the state; No state interference with the functions of the church, or with the free exercise of religion; The absolute freedom of the individual from the domination of ecclesiastical authority in political affairs; The equality of all churches before the law.[14]

The Church does not engage in politics; its members belong to the political parties at their own pleasure. . . . They are not asked, much less required, to vote this way or that. . . . But they cannot justly be denied their rights as citizens, and there is no reason why they should be, for, on the average, they are as loyal, as sober, as well educated, as honest, as industrious, as virtuous, as moral, as thrifty, and as worthy in every other respect as any people in the nation, or on the earth.[15]

---

### We are subject to the powers that be until the advent of the kingdom of God.

The Bible, which is one of the written standards of the "Mormon" Church, teems with predictions and promises of the establishment of Divine rule on the earth; of the advent of a reign of righteousness extending over all the face of the globe. Christ is to be King and all nations and peoples are to serve and obey Him. That is to be the Kingdom of God in very deed. The Church of Jesus Christ of Latter-day Saints is set up preparatory to that Kingdom. Its gospel is "the gospel of the kingdom." Its principles, ordinances, authority and gifts are of heavenly origin. It is therefore the spiritual "kingdom of heaven," bearing within it the influence and power that are to open the way for the fulfilment of the prophecies concerning the universal dominion of the Son of God.[16]

It is sometimes pointed out, that the members of the Church are looking for the actual coming of a Kingdom of God on earth, that shall gather all the kingdoms of the world into one visible, divine empire, over which the risen Messiah shall reign.

All this, it is held, renders it impossible for a "Mormon" to give true allegiance to his country, or to any earthly government.

. . . We deny that our belief in divine revelation, or our anticipation of the coming kingdom of God weakens in any degree the genuineness of our allegiance to our country. When the divine empire will be established, we may not know any more than other Christians who pray, "Thy kingdom come, Thy will be done, in earth as it is in heaven;" [Matthew 6:10] but we do know that our allegiance and loyalty to our country are strengthened by the fact that while awaiting the advent of the Messiah's kingdom, we are under a commandment from God to be subject to the powers that be, until He comes "whose right it is to reign." [D&C 58:22.][17]

# Suggestions for Study

- Why should Latter-day Saints be loyal to the country in which they live? (See also D&C 134:5.) How can we demonstrate loyalty and honor to our country even though we may disagree with some of its policies?

- How can we teach our children to be good citizens? What are our responsibilities as citizens? Why should a faithful Latter-day Saint be "one of the best citizens of any country"?

- How does personal righteousness exalt a nation? Why is personal righteousness an important element of good citizenship? What part should personal righteousness play in the lives of those seeking or holding public office?

- How does the separation of church and state help people exercise their religious beliefs? (See also D&C 134:7, 9.) Why is it important to have individual freedom from ecclesiastical authority in political matters?

- What is the kingdom of God yet to come, and who will be subject to this kingdom?

## Notes

1. See James R. Clark, comp., *Messages of the First Presidency of The Church of Jesus Christ of Latter-day Saints,* 6 vols. (1965–75), 4:165.
2. *Gospel Doctrine,* 5th ed. (1939), 404.
3. *Gospel Doctrine,* 409–10.
4. In *Messages of the First Presidency,* 5:55.
5. "Discourse by President Joseph F. Smith," *Millennial Star,* 27 Sept. 1906, 610.
6. In Conference Report, Apr. 1905, 46.
7. In *Messages of the First Presidency,* 4:150.
8. In Conference Report, Apr. 1910, 8.
9. In *Messages of the First Presidency,* 4:147.
10. In *Messages of the First Presidency,* 4:154.
11. "Editor's Table: Congress and the 'Mormons,' " *Improvement Era,* Apr. 1903, 473.
12. In Conference Report, Oct. 1908, 127.
13. In *Messages of the First Presidency,* 4:81.
14. In *Messages of the First Presidency,* 4:153; paragraphing altered.
15. "Editor's Table: The Probable Cause," *Improvement Era,* June 1903, 626.
16. In *Messages of the First Presidency,* 4:81.
17. In *Messages of the First Presidency,* 4:154.

# The Salvation of Little Children

*Little children who die*
*before they reach the years of accountability*
*are redeemed by the blood of Christ.*

## From the Life of Joseph F. Smith

Although President Joseph F. Smith knew firsthand the anguish, loneliness, and love that attend the death of a child, his teachings on the salvation of little children were inspiring and reassuring. Between 1869 and 1898, he buried nine little children of his own.

Following the death of his firstborn child, Mercy Josephine, on 6 June 1870, he expressed his great sorrow: "O God only knows how much I loved my girl, and she the light and the joy of my heart. The morning before she died, after being up with her all night, for I watched her every night, I said to her, 'My little pet did not sleep all night.' She shook her head and replied, 'I'll sleep today, papa.' Oh! how those little words shot through my heart. I knew though I would not believe, it was another voice, that it meant the sleep of death and she did sleep. And, Oh! the light of my heart went out. The image of heaven graven in my soul was almost departed. . . . Thou wert a heavenly gift directly to my heart of hearts."[1]

On 6 July 1879, Joseph F. Smith wrote in his journal of his grief at the death of his daughter Rhonda: "I took her on a pillow and walked the floor with her, she again revived but only lingered about an hour and died in my arms at 1:40 a.m. Now God only knows how deeply we mourn. This is the 5th death in my family. All my little ones most beloved! O! God help us to bear this trial!"[2]

But he found comfort in the knowledge that, through the Atonement of the Savior, all was well with his beloved children. At the death of his daughter Ruth, on 17 March 1898, he received a glorious revelation: "O my soul! I see my own sweet mother's arms extended welcoming to her embrace the ransomed glorious spirit of my own sweet babe! O my God! For this glorious vision, I thank Thee! And there too are gathered to my Father's mansion all my darling lovely ones; not in infantile helplessness, but in all the power and glory and majesty of sanctified spirits! Full of intelligence, of joy and grace, and truth."[3]

## Teachings of Joseph F. Smith

### Little children who pass away before they are accountable are redeemed.

With little children who are taken away in infancy and innocence before they have reached the years of accountability, and are not capable of committing sin, the gospel reveals to us the fact that they are redeemed, and Satan has no power over them. Neither has death any power over them. They are redeemed by the blood of Christ, and they are saved just as surely as death has come into the world through the fall of our first parents. . . .

. . . Our beloved friends who are now deprived of their little one, have great cause for joy and rejoicing, even in the midst of the deep sorrow that they feel at the loss of their little one for a time. They know he is all right; they have the assurance that their little one has passed away without sin. Such children are in the bosom of the Father. They will inherit their glory and their exaltation, and they will not be deprived of the blessings that belong to them; for, in the economy of heaven, and in the wisdom of the Father, who doeth all things well, those who are cut down as little children are without any responsibility for their taking off, they, themselves, not having the intelligence and wisdom to take care of themselves and to understand the laws of life; and, in the wisdom and mercy and economy of God our Heavenly Father, all that could have been obtained and enjoyed by them if they had been permitted to live in the flesh will be provided for them hereafter. They will lose nothing by being taken away from us in this way. . . .

With these thoughts in my mind, I take consolation in the fact that I shall meet my children who have passed behind the veil; I have lost a number, and I have felt all that a parent can feel, I think, in the loss of my children. I have felt it keenly, for I love children, and I am particularly fond of the little ones, but I feel thankful to God for the knowledge of these principles, because now I have every confidence in his word and in his promise that I will possess in the future all that belongs to me, and my joy will be full. I will not be deprived of any privilege or any blessing that I am worthy of and that may be properly entrusted to me. But every gift, and every blessing that it is possible for me to become worthy of I shall possess, either in time or in eternity, and it will not matter, so that I acknowledge the hand of God in all these things, and say in my heart, "The Lord giveth and the Lord taketh away, blessed be the name of the Lord" [see Job 1:21]. This is the way we should feel with regard to our children, or our relatives, or friends, or whatever vicissitudes we may be called to pass through.[4]

---

### After the resurrection, a child's body will grow to match the stature of the spirit.

Would we be satisfied to see the children we bury in their infancy remain as children only, throughout the countless ages of eternity? No! Neither would the spirits that did possess the tabernacles of our children be satisfied to remain in that condition. But we know our children will not be compelled to remain as a child in stature always, for it was revealed from God, the fountain of truth, through Joseph Smith the prophet, in this dispensation, that in the resurrection of the dead the child that was buried in its infancy will come up in the form of the child that it was when it was laid down; then it will begin to develop. From the day of the resurrection, the body will develop until it reaches the full measure of the stature of its spirit, whether it be male or female. If the spirit possessed the intelligence of God and the aspirations of mortal souls, it could not be satisfied with anything less than this. You will remember we are told that the spirit of Jesus Christ visited one of the ancient prophets and revealed himself to him, and he declared his identity, that he was the same Son of God that was to come in the meridian of time. He said he would appear in the flesh just as he appeared to that prophet [see Ether 3:9, 16–17]. He was not an infant; he was a grown, developed spirit; possessing the form of man and the form of God, the same form as when he came and took upon him a tabernacle and developed it to the full stature of his spirit.[5]

Every spirit that comes to this earth to take upon it a tabernacle is a son or a daughter of God, and possesses all the intelligence and all the attributes that any son or daughter can enjoy, either in the spirit world, or in this world, except that in the spirit, and separated from the body, they lacked just the tabernacle of being like God the Father. It is said that God is a spirit, and they who worship him must worship him in spirit and in truth [see John 4:24]. But he is a spirit possessing the tabernacle of flesh and bones, as tangible as a man's and therefore to be like God and Jesus all men must have a body. It matters not whether these tabernacles mature in this world, or have to wait and mature in the world to come, according to the word of the Prophet Joseph Smith, the body will develop, either in time or in eternity, to the full stature of the spirit, and when the mother is deprived of the pleasure and joy of rearing her babe to manhood or to womanhood in this life, through the hand of death, that privilege will be renewed to her hereafter, and she will enjoy it to a fuller fruition than it would be possible for her to do here. When she does it there, it will be with the certain knowledge that the results will be without failure; whereas here, the results are unknown until after we have passed the test.[6]

The spirits of our children are immortal before they come to us, and their spirits, after bodily death, are like they were before they came. They are as they would have appeared if they had lived in the flesh, to grow to maturity, or to develop their physical bodies to the full stature of their spirits. If you see one of your children that has passed away it may appear to you in the form in which you would recognize it, the form of childhood; but if it came to you as a messenger bearing some important truth, it would perhaps come as the spirit of Bishop Edward Hunter's son (who died when a little child) came to him, in the stature of full-grown manhood, and revealed himself to his father, and said: "I am your son."

Bishop Hunter did not understand it. He went to my father and said: "Hyrum, what does that mean? I buried my son when he was only a little boy, but he has come to me as a full-grown man—a noble, glorious, young man, and declared himself my son. What does it mean?"

Father (Hyrum Smith, the Patriarch) told him that the Spirit of Jesus Christ was full-grown before he was born into the world; and so our children were full-grown and possessed their full stature in the spirit, before they entered mortality, the same stature that they will possess after they have passed away from mortality, and as they will also appear after the resurrection, when they shall have completed their mission.

Joseph Smith taught the doctrine that the infant child that was laid away in death would come up in the resurrection as a child; and, pointing to the mother of a lifeless child, he said to her: "You will have the joy, the pleasure, and satisfaction of nurturing this child, after its resurrection, until it reaches the full stature of its spirit." There is restitution, there is growth, there is development, after the resurrection from death. I love this truth. It speaks volumes of happiness, of joy and gratitude to my soul. Thank the Lord he has revealed these principles to us.[7]

---

### All is well with little children who pass away.

If we have received the testimony of the spirit of truth in our souls we know that all is well with our little children who pass away, that we could not, if we would, better their condition; and least of all would it better their condition if we could call them back here, for the reason that so long as man is in the world, clothed with mortality, surrounded by the evils that are in the world, he runs chances and is subject to risks, and there are responsibilities resting upon him which may prove fatal to his future prosperity, happiness and exaltation.[8]

It is a very difficult matter to say anything at a time of sorrow and bereavement like the present that will give immediate relief to the sorrowing hearts of those who mourn. Such griefs can only be fully relieved by the lapse of time and the influence of the good spirit upon the hearts of those that mourn, by which they can obtain comfort and satisfaction in their hopes of the future. . . . I have learned that there are a great many things which are far worse than death. With my present feelings and views and the understanding that I have of life and death I would far rather follow every child I have to the grave in their innocence and purity, than to see them grow up to man and womanhood and degrade themselves by the pernicious practices of the world, forget the Gospel, forget God and the plan of life and salvation, and turn away from the only hope of eternal reward and exaltation in the world to come.[9]

---

### If we are faithful, we will be reunited with our children beyond the veil.

The prophet Elijah was to plant in the hearts of the children the promises made to their fathers, foreshadowing the great work to be done in the temples of the Lord in the Dispensation of the Fulness of Times, for the redemption of the dead and the sealing of the children to their parents, lest the whole earth be smitten with a curse and utterly wasted at his coming.[10]

If we live and turn away from the truth we will be separated throughout the countless ages of eternity from the society of those we love. We will have no claim upon them, and they will have no claim upon us. There will be an impassable gulf between us over which we can not pass, one to the other. If we die in the faith, having lived righteous lives, we are Christ's, we have the assurance of eternal reward, being in possession of the principles of eternal truth and shall be clothed with glory, immortality and eternal lives. While we sojourn in the flesh we pass a great portion of our life in sorrow; death separates us for a short time, some of us pass behind the vail, but the time will come when we will meet with those who have gone, and enjoy each other's society forever. The separation is but for a moment as it were. No power can separate us then. God having joined us together we have a claim upon each other—an undeniable claim—inasmuch as we have been united by the power of the priesthood in the Gospel of Christ. Therefore it is better to be separated in this life for a little season, although we have to pass through deprivation, sorrow, trouble, toil, widowhood, orphanage and many other vicissitudes, than to be separated for all eternity.[11]

We are begotten in the similitude of Christ himself. We dwelt with the Father and with the Son in the beginning, as the sons and daughters of God; and at the time appointed, we came to this earth to take upon ourselves tabernacles, that we might become conformed to the likeness and image of Jesus Christ and become like him; that we might have a tabernacle, that we might pass through death as he has passed through death, that we might rise again from the dead as he has risen from the dead. . . . The thought of meeting my children who have preceded me beyond the veil, and of meeting my kindred and my friends, what happiness it affords! For I know that I shall meet them there. God has shown me that this is true. He has made it clear to me, in answer to my prayer and devotion, as he has made it clear to the understanding of all men who have sought diligently to know him.[12]

[To Elder Joseph H. Dean in Oahu, Hawaii, President Joseph F. Smith wrote:] I heard with deep sympathy of the death of your baby at home. I knew how to sympathize, for I passed thro the same kind of bitter experience myself while there. I would have written you, but I judged you by myself and refrained from doing so. Under such circumstances I feel more like going into some distant quiet, lonely retreat, where no eye but that of God beheld me, and there, alone, feel and sense my grief, God only knowing it. . . . Time, and time only—that great healer of wounds—can touch my soul, and I think you would no doubt feel the same. But when the first poignant throes of grief are passed and the soul is calmed by time and fate, then a word fitly spoken may touch the tender chord of fellowship flowing from heart to heart in kindred sorrows. The Lord truly knows best and we know that the innocents who have been recalled from earth, so soon after their coming untainted by the sordid elements of this fallen world return to Him from whom they came, pure and holy, redeemed from the foundation, by the sacrifice of one who said "of such is the kingdom of heaven." My most earnest, heartfelt prayer is, O! God help me to live and be worthy to join my innocent children in their home with thee![13]

# Suggestions for Study

- What blessings are promised to little children who die before the age of accountability? (See also D&C 29:46.) How can this bring us comfort and hope when we mourn the death of a little child?

- If a little child dies, what is the state of his or her spirit? When will the child's body develop and mature?

- Who will be responsible for raising a child who dies young? What blessings are promised in the next life to righteous parents whose children died young?

- How can understanding the principles of the plan of salvation comfort and assist those who are grieving for the death of a little child?

- How can the sealing ordinances of the temple bring comfort and hope to parents when a child dies? What must we do to be reunited with our little children who have died?

- How can "a word fitly spoken" bring comfort to a sorrowing soul at the death of a loved one? How can we prepare to speak such words?

## Notes

1. *Life of Joseph F. Smith,* comp. Joseph Fielding Smith (1938), 456–57; paragraphing added.
2. *Truth and Courage: The Joseph F. Smith Letters,* ed. Joseph Fielding McConkie (n.d.), 56.
3. *Life of Joseph F. Smith,* 463.
4. *Gospel Doctrine,* 5th ed. (1939), 452–54.
5. *Gospel Doctrine,* 24.
6. *Gospel Doctrine,* 453–54.
7. *Gospel Doctrine,* 455–56.
8. *Gospel Doctrine,* 452.
9. *Deseret News: Semi-Weekly,* 24 Apr. 1883, 1.
10. *Gospel Doctrine,* 475.
11. *Deseret News: Semi-Weekly,* 24 Apr. 1883, 1.
12. *Gospel Doctrine,* 428–29.
13. *Truth and Courage: The Joseph F. Smith Letters,* 57.

President Joseph F. Smith in the 1860s, a member of the Quorum of the Twelve Apostles and Counselor to President Brigham Young.

# Priesthood, the Divine Government

*The holy priesthood is the authority and power of God delegated to man to govern and bless His people.*

## From the Life of Joseph F. Smith

By age 28, Joseph F. Smith was serving as secretary to the Council of the First Presidency and Quorum of the Twelve. On 1 July 1866, as the regular prayer meeting of the Council was adjourning, President Brigham Young announced to his brethren: "I always feel well to do as the Spirit constrains me. It is my mind to ordain Brother Joseph F. Smith to the Apostleship, and to be one of my counselors." He called on each of the Brethren to express their feelings about the calling, and they all supported President Young with "hearty approval."

They then laid their hands on the head of Joseph F., and President Young said: "Brother Joseph F. Smith, we lay our hands upon your head in the name of Jesus Christ, and by virtue of the Holy Priesthood we ordain you to be an Apostle in the Church of Jesus Christ of Latter-day Saints, and to be a special witness to the nations of the earth. We seal upon your head all the authority, power and keys of this holy Apostleship; and we ordain you to be a counselor to the First Presidency of the Church and Kingdom of God upon the earth. These blessings we seal upon you in the name of Jesus Christ and by the authority of the Holy Priesthood. Amen."[1]

On 8 October 1867, Joseph F. Smith was sustained and set apart as a member of the Quorum of the Twelve Apostles during a general conference, a milestone in his lifelong labor as a member of the governing priesthood councils of the Church. During his service of more than 50 years, his great experience and wisdom in priesthood and Church government benefited the Church throughout the world.

# Teachings of Joseph F. Smith

### The priesthood is the authority by which God governs and blesses His people.

The Holy Priesthood is that authority which God has delegated to man, by which he may speak the will of God as if the angels were here to speak it themselves; by which men are empowered to bind on earth and it shall be bound in heaven, and to loose on earth and it shall be loosed in heaven; by which the words of man, spoken in the exercise of that power, become the word of the Lord, and the law of God unto the people, scripture, and divine commands. . . . It is the authority by which the Lord Almighty governs his people, and by which, in time to come, he will govern the nations of the world.[2]

A great deal may be said in relation to the authority and rights of the priesthood. It is the grand principle of government and of organization, by which the energies and forces of the people of God in all ages have been and will be directed. It is that principle by which God Almighty governs throughout all His universe. It is the principle by which the Church of Jesus Christ of Latter-day Saints is governed. . . . It is the authority which God has revealed and restored to the children of men for their government and guidance in the building up of Zion and in the proclamation of the Gospel to the nations of the earth, until every son and daughter of Adam shall have the privilege of hearing the sound of the Gospel, and of being brought to the knowledge of the truth, not only upon this earth, but in the spirit world.[3]

[The] Melchizedek or Holy Priesthood . . . is the authority by which individuals or the . . . quorums . . . composing the priesthood of the Church, may legitimately act in the name of the Lord; or the moving, directing, controlling, governing or presiding agency, right and authority, which is vested in the Godhead and delegated unto man for the purpose of his instruction, initiation into the Church, spiritual and temporal guidance, government and exaltation.[4]

The Lord has established on earth the Priesthood in its fulness . . . by direct revelation and commandment from heaven; . . . he has instituted an order or government that is beyond the capacity, and that is superior to the wisdom and learning and understanding of man, so far, indeed, that it seems impossible for the human mind, unaided by the Spirit of God, to comprehend the beauties, powers, and character of the Holy Priesthood. It seems difficult for men to comprehend the workings of the Priesthood, its legitimate authority, its scope and power; and yet by the light of the spirit it is easily comprehended.[5]

However imperfect they may be, men have been clothed with this authority, by which they can speak and act in the name of the Father and the Son, and God is bound, if they speak by His spirit in the discharge of their duties as His servants, to respect and fulfil that which they say, because they speak by the authority that He has given. . . . Of course, all things must be done in righteousness. No man can do anything in unrighteousness that God is bound to respect. But when a man who holds the Priesthood does that which is righteous, God is bound to acknowledge it as though He had done it Himself.[6]

The pith of the matter is: the Lord has established his Church, organized his priesthood, and conferred authority upon certain individuals, councils and quorums, and it is the duty of the people of God to live so that they shall know that these are acceptable unto him.[7]

---

**Although the priesthood is bestowed only upon men, both men and women partake of its blessings.**

The Priesthood was originally exercised in the patriarchal order; those who held it exercised their powers firstly by right of their fatherhood. It is so with the great Elohim. This first and strongest claim on our love, reverence and obedience is based on the fact that he is the Father, the Creator, of all mankind. . . . Man possessing the holy Priesthood is typical of him. But as men on earth cannot act in God's stead as his representatives without the authority, appointment and ordination naturally follow. No man has the right to take this honor to himself, except he be called of God through the channels that he recognizes and has empowered.[8]

The patriarchal order is of divine origin and will continue throughout time and eternity. . . . Men, women and children should understand this order and this authority in the households of the people of God, and seek to make it what God intended it to be, a qualification and preparation for the highest exaltation of his children.[9]

Whatever honors, privileges, or glory are attained by the man through the Priesthood, are those shared with and enjoyed by the wife. She being one with him in Christ, all his honors are her honors, his blessings are her blessings, his glory is her glory, for they are one—inseparably. . . . As Paul said, "The man is not without the woman nor the woman without the man in the Lord." [See 1 Corinthians 11:11.] In other words, the man cannot attain to glory, honor or exaltation without the woman, nor the woman without the man. They are but two complements of one whole. . . . The Priesthood of the Son of God is bestowed upon the man, that attaining to the same eminence and perfection, he may act as Christ and God act. . . . While man . . . is the direct object on whom the power and honor of the Priesthood are bestowed, and he is the active medium of its operations, she partakes of its benefits, its blessings, its powers, its rights and privileges, with him as the complement of himself. . . . The power is not given to the woman to act independent of the man, nor is it given to the man to act independent of Christ.[10]

Women are responsible for their acts just as much as men are responsible for theirs, although the man, holding the authority of the priesthood, is regarded as the head, as the leader. . . . Furthermore, when we speak of the men, we speak of the women, too, for the women are included with the men and are an inseparable part of mankind.[11]

## The keys of the priesthood are required for the government of the Church.

The Priesthood in general is the authority given to man to act for God. Every man ordained to any degree of the Priesthood has this authority delegated to him.

But it is necessary that every act performed under this authority shall be done at the proper time and place, in the proper way, and after the proper order. The power of directing these labors constitutes the *keys* of the Priesthood. In their fulness, the keys are held by only one person at a time, the prophet and president of the Church. He may delegate any portion of this power to another, in which case that person holds the keys of that particular labor. Thus, the president of a temple, the president of a stake, the bishop of a ward, the president of a mission, the president of a quorum, each holds the keys of the labors performed in that particular body or locality. His Priesthood is not increased by this special appointment; . . . the president of an elders' quorum, for example, has no more Priesthood than any member of that quorum. But he holds the power of directing the official labors performed in the . . . quorum, or in other words, the *keys* of that division of that work.[12]

[The] President is the mouthpiece of God, the revelator, the translator, the seer, and the Prophet of God to the whole Church. It is he who holds the keys of this Holy Priesthood—the keys which unlock the doors of the Temples of God and of the ordinances of His house for the salvation of the living and the redemption of the dead. It is he who holds the sealing power, by which man may bind on earth and it shall be bound in heaven, and by which men duly authorized and appointed of him who holds the keys may loose on earth and it will be loosed in heaven. This is the order of the Holy Priesthood.[13]

## The priesthood governs by the law of love.

The Lord revealed the great principle of organization, by which His Church is to be governed, which the Lord Himself established in the Church, the authority of the Holy Priesthood, that of the High Priesthood, the Apostleship, the Seventies, and the Elders, and then the organizations of the Lesser Priesthood—the Bishops, the Priests, the Teachers and the Deacons—God established these organizations in the Church for the government of the people. What for? To oppress them? No. To injure them? No, a thousand times, no. What for? That they and their children might have the benefits of these organizations for instruction, for admonition, for guidance, for revelation, and for inspiration to do that which the Lord requires at their hands, that they may become perfect in their lives.[14]

We are governed by law, because we love one another, and are actuated by long-suffering and charity, and good will; and our whole organization is based upon the idea of self-control; the principle of give and take, and of rather being willing to suffer wrong than to do wrong. Our message is peace on earth and good will towards men; love, charity and forgiveness, which should actuate all associated with the Church of Jesus Christ of Latter-day Saints. Ours is a Church where law is dominant, but the law is the law of love.[15]

No man should be oppressed. No authority of the Priesthood can be administered or exerted in any degree of unrighteousness, without offending God. Therefore, when we deal with men we should not deal with them with prejudice in our minds against them.[16]

There is not a man holding any position of authority in the Church who can perform his duty as he should in any other spirit than in the spirit of fatherhood and brotherhood toward those over whom he presides. Those who have authority should not be rulers, nor dictators; they should not be arbitrary; they should gain the hearts, the confidence and love of those over whom they preside, by kindness and love unfeigned, by gentleness of spirit, by persuasion, by an example that is above reproach and above the reach of unjust criticism. In this way, in the kindness of their hearts, in their love for their people, they lead them in the path of righteousness, and teach them the way of salvation, by saying to them, both by precept and example: Follow me, as I follow our head.[17]

---

## Honor the power and authority of the holy priesthood.

It is a proper thing for us to accept and honor the Holy Priesthood that has been restored to the earth in this dispensation, through Joseph the Prophet. I know that is good, because it is calculated to uphold the truth, and sustain the Church, and develop men in knowledge, in good works, in fidelity to the purposes of the Lord, and it is essential to the proper government of the people of God in the earth, and for our own individual government, the government of our families, the government of our temporal and spiritual affairs, individually as well as collectively.[18]

Honor that power and authority which we call the Holy Priesthood, which is after the order of the Son of God, and which has been conferred upon man by God himself. Honor that Priesthood. What is that Priesthood? It is nothing more and nothing less than divine authority committed unto man from God. That is the principle that we should honor. . . . The Priesthood of the Son of God cannot be exercised in any degree of unrighteousness; neither will its power, its virtue and authority abide with him who is corrupt, who is treacherous in his soul toward God and toward his fellowmen. It will not abide in force and power with him who does not honor it in his life by complying with the requirements of heaven.[19]

Do you honor this Priesthood? . . . Would you, holding that Priesthood, and possessing the right and authority from God to administer in the name of the Father, and of the Son, and of the Holy Ghost, violate the confidence and the love of God, the hope and desire of the Father of all of us? For, in bestowing that key and blessing upon you, he desires and expects you to magnify your calling.[20]

If you will honor the holy Priesthood in yourself first, you will honor it in those who preside over you, and those who administer in the various callings, throughout the Church.[21]

It is . . . not good that the Latter-day Saints and the children of the Latter-day Saints should treat lightly this sacred principle of authority which has been revealed from the heavens in the dispensation in which we live. . . . It is sacred, and it must be held sacred by the people. It should be honored and respected by them, in whomsoever it is held, and in whomsoever responsibility is placed in the Church. The young men and young women and the people generally should honor this principle and recognize it as something that is sacred, and that cannot be trifled with nor spoken lightly of with impunity. Disregard of this authority leads to darkness and to apostasy, and severance from all the rights and privileges of the house of God; for it is by virtue of this authority that the ordinances of the gospel are performed throughout the world and in every sacred place, and without it they cannot be performed. Those also who hold this authority should honor it in themselves. They should live so as to be worthy of the authority vested in them and worthy of the gifts that have been bestowed upon them.[22]

## Suggestions for Study

- What is the priesthood? For what purposes did the Lord delegate to man the authority of the priesthood?

- How can we come to "comprehend the workings of the Priesthood"?

- In what ways do the men and women of God partake of the blessings, powers, and privileges of the priesthood?

- How has the priesthood blessed your life? How has it blessed those in your home?

- What are the keys of the priesthood? Why are they given? Who holds all of the priesthood keys? Who holds keys at the ward and stake level?

- In what spirit should priesthood holders perform their duties? (See D&C 121:41–46.) What influence does a priesthood holder have in the home and the Church when he shows "love unfeigned" and "gentleness of spirit"?

- How can we honor the priesthood and hold it sacred? In what ways might we "treat lightly" this sacred authority?

- How does the example of the Savior help us understand how to exercise and honor priesthood authority?

## Notes

1. *Life of Joseph F. Smith*, comp. Joseph Fielding Smith (1938), 227.
2. *Gospel Doctrine*, 5th ed. (1939), 140–41.
3. *Deseret News: Semi-Weekly*, 23 Aug. 1892, 6.
4. *Gospel Doctrine*, 190.
5. *Gospel Doctrine*, 40–41.
6. *Deseret News: Semi-Weekly*, 23 Aug. 1892, 6.
7. *Gospel Doctrine*, 45.
8. *Gospel Doctrine*, 147.
9. *Gospel Doctrine*, 287.
10. Letter to Susa Young Gates, 7 July 1888, in *Truth and Courage: The Joseph F. Smith Letters*, ed. Joseph Fielding McConkie (n.d.), 11–12.
11. In James R. Clark, comp., *Messages of the First Presidency of The Church of Jesus Christ of Latter-day Saints*, 6 vols. (1965–75), 5:80.
12. *Gospel Doctrine*, 136.
13. *Deseret News: Semi-Weekly*, 27 Apr. 1897, 1.
14. In Conference Report, Oct. 1911, 7.
15. *Gospel Doctrine*, 143–44.
16. *Gospel Doctrine*, 149.
17. *Gospel Doctrine*, 150–51.
18. In Conference Report, Apr. 1912, 9.
19. *Gospel Doctrine*, 160.
20. *Gospel Doctrine*, 165.
21. *Gospel Doctrine*, 165.
22. *Gospel Doctrine*, 140–41.

*Christ and the Samaritan Woman,* by Carl Bloch. The Savior taught the Samaritan woman near Jacob's Well that He was the Savior of the world (see John 4:5–30).

# The Great Plan of Life and Salvation

*Our Father in Heaven has provided a plan for
His sons and daughters to become like Jesus Christ
and to enjoy exaltation.*

## From the Life of Joseph F. Smith

In 1874 shortly after his arrival in England to preside over the European Mission and on the occasion of his 36th birthday, Joseph F. Smith recorded in his diary:

"The day was cold, bleak and dreary, a fit and proper anniversary of the dark and trying day of my birth; When my father [Hyrum] and his brother [Joseph] were confined in a dungeon for the gospel's sake and the saints were being driven from their homes in Missouri by a merciless mob. The bright sunshine of my soul has never thoroughly dispelled the darkening shadows cast upon it by the lowering gloom of that eventful period.

"Yet the merciful hand of God and his kindliest providences have ever been extended visibly toward me, even from my childhood, and my days grow better and better thru humility and the pursuit of wisdom and happiness in the kingdom of God; The objects of my life becoming more apparent as time advances and experience grows. Those objects being the proclamation of the gospel, or the establishment of the kingdom of God on the earth; The salvation of souls, and most important of which to me—that of myself and family."[1]

With knowledge and conviction, President Joseph F. Smith taught and testified of our Heavenly Father's eternal plan of salvation. "There is nothing under the heavens," he declared, "of so much importance to me or to the children of men as the great plan of life and salvation."[2]

# Teachings of Joseph F. Smith

## Our Heavenly Father designed the plan of salvation so that we can be exalted.

The Lord Almighty lives; he made the heavens and the earth, and the fountains of water; and we are his children, his offspring, and we are not here by chance. The Lord designed our coming, and the object of our being. He designs that we shall accomplish our mission, to become conformed to the likeness and image of Jesus Christ, that, like him, we may be without sin unto salvation, like him we may be filled with pure intelligence, and like him we may be exalted to the right hand of the Father, to sit upon thrones and have dominion and power in the sphere in which we shall be called to act. I testify to this doctrine, for the Lord has made me to know and feel the truth of it from the crown of my head to the soles of my feet.[3]

Man will be held responsible in the life to come for the deeds that he has done in this life, and will have to answer for the stewardships entrusted to his care here, before the Judge of the quick and the dead, the Father of our spirits, and of our Lord and Master. This is the design of God, a part of his great purpose. We are not here to live a few months or years, to eat, drink and sleep, then to die, pass away and perish. The Lord Almighty never designed man to be so ephemeral, useless and imperfect as this.[4]

Had we not known before we came [to earth] the necessity of our coming, the importance of obtaining tabernacles, the glory to be achieved in posterity, the grand object to be attained by being tried and tested—weighed in the balance, in the exercise of the divine attributes, god-like powers and free agency with which we are endowed; whereby, after descending below all things, Christ-like, we might ascend above all things [see D&C 88:6], and become like our Father, Mother and Elder Brother, Almighty and Eternal!—we never would have come.[5]

There is nothing under the heavens of so much importance to me or to the children of men as the great plan of life and salvation which was devised in the heavens in the beginning, and which has been handed down from period to period through the inspiration of holy men called of God until the day of the coming of the Son of Man, for this gospel and this plan of salvation was revealed to our first parents. The angel of God carried to them the plan of redemption, and of salvation from death and sin that has been revealed from time to time by divine authority to the children of men, and it has undergone no change. There was nothing in it, in the beginning, that was superfluous or unnecessary; nothing in it that could be dispensed with; it was a complete plan devised in the beginning by the wisdom of the Father and the holy ones for the redemption of the human race and for their salvation and exaltation in the presence of God. . . . Through all the generations of time, the same gospel, the same plan of life and salvation, the same ordinances, burial with Christ, remembrance of the great sacrifice to be offered for the sins of the world and for man's redemption, have been handed down from time to time, from the time of the creation.[6]

It is the plan of life that the Almighty has restored to man in the latter days for the salvation of the souls of men, not only in the world to come, but in our present life, for the Lord has instituted his work that his people may enjoy the blessings of this life to the utmost; that they should be saved in this present life, as well as in the life to come, that they should lay the foundation here for immunity from sin and all its effects and consequences, that they may obtain an inheritance in the kingdom of God beyond this vale of tears. The gospel of Jesus Christ is the power of God unto salvation.[7]

God did speak to His servant Joseph Smith, and did reveal Himself unto him; not only the Father, but the Son also. They did reveal themselves unto him, and they gave him commandments and their law, their Gospel and their plan of life eternal. . . . This plan contemplated not only salvation from sin and from the effects of sin here and hereafter, but exaltation, glory, power and dominion, that will come to the children of God through their obedience to the laws and principles of the gospel.[8]

## We came to earth to prepare ourselves for eternal life.

The object of our earthly existence is that we may have a fulness of joy, and that we may become the sons and daughters of God, in the fullest sense of the word, being heirs of God and joint heirs with Jesus Christ [see Romans 8:14–17], to be kings and priests unto God, to inherit glory, dominion, exaltation, thrones and every power and attribute developed and possessed by our Heavenly Father. This is the object of our being on this earth. In order to attain unto this exalted position, it is necessary that we go through this mortal experience, or probation, by which we may prove ourselves worthy, through the aid of our elder brother Jesus.[9]

The object of our being here is to do the will of the Father as it is done in heaven, to work righteousness in the earth, to subdue wickedness and put it under our feet, to conquer sin and the adversary of our souls, to rise above the imperfections and weaknesses of poor, fallen humanity, by the inspiration of Almighty God and his power made manifest, and thus become indeed the saints and servants of the Lord in the earth.[10]

We shall all die. But is that the end of our being? If we had an existence before we came here we certainly shall continue that existence when we leave here. The spirit will continue to exist as it did before, with the additional advantages derived from having passed through this probation. It is absolutely necessary that we should come to the earth and take upon us tabernacles; because if we did not have tabernacles we could not be like God, or like Jesus Christ. . . . We are destined to come forth out of the grave as Jesus did, and to obtain immortal bodies as he did—that is, that our tabernacles are to become immortal as his became immortal, that the spirit and the body may be joined together and become one living being, indivisible, inseparable, eternal.[11]

I am looking forward to the time when I shall have passed away from this stage of existence, there I shall be permitted to enjoy more fully every gift and blessing that have contributed to my happiness in this world; everything. I do not believe that there is one thing that was designed or intended to give me joy or make me happy, that I shall be denied here after, provided I continue faithful; otherwise my joy cannot be full. . . . I refer to the happiness experienced in seeking to do the will of God on earth as it is done in heaven. We expect to have our wives and husbands in eternity. We expect our children will acknowledge us as their fathers and mothers in eternity. I expect this; I look for nothing else. Without it, I could not be happy.[12]

The principles of the gospel which the Lord has revealed in these days will lead us to eternal life. This is what we are after, what we were created for, what the earth was created for. The reason that we are here is that we may overcome every folly and prepare ourselves for eternal life in the future. . . .

Then let us be faithful and humble; let us live the religion of Christ, put away our follies and sins and the weaknesses of the flesh, and cleave to God and his truth with undivided hearts, and with full determination to fight the good fight of faith and continue steadfast to the end.[13]

---

## One of the main purposes of our existence is to conform to the image and likeness of Jesus Christ.

I believe that our Savior is the ever-living example to all flesh. . . . The works he did, we are commanded to do. We are enjoined to follow him, as he followed his Head; that where he is, we may be also; and being with him, may be like him.[14]

The important consideration is not how long we can live but how well we can learn the lesson of life, and discharge our duties and obligations to God and to one another. One of the main purposes of our existence is that we might conform to the image and likeness of him who sojourned in the flesh without blemish—immaculate, pure, and spotless! Christ came not only to atone for the sins of the world, but to set an example before all men and to establish the standard of God's perfection, of God's law, and of obedience to the Father.[15]

No doctrine was ever as perfect as that of Jesus. . . . He has revealed to us the way of salvation, from the beginning, and through all the meanderings of this life to never-ending exaltation and glory in his kingdom, and to a newness of life therein. . . .

Happy is the man, indeed, who can receive this soul-satisfying testimony, and be at rest, and seek for no other road to peace than by the doctrines of Jesus Christ. His gospel teaches us to love our fellowmen, to do to others as we would have others do to us, to be just, to be merciful, to be forgiving, and to perform every good act calculated to enlarge the soul of man. . . .

. . . "Come unto me, all ye that labor and are heavy laden, and I will give you rest," [Matthew 11:28] is his call to all the sons and daughters of men.[16]

Christ is the great example for all mankind, and I believe that mankind were as much foreordained to become like him, as that he was foreordained to be the Redeemer of man. . . . We are . . . in the form of God, physically, and may become like him spiritually, and like him in the possession of knowledge, intelligence, wisdom and power.

The grand object of our coming to this earth is that we may become like Christ, for if we are not like him, we cannot become the sons of God, and be joint heirs with Christ.[17]

Let us follow the Son of God. Make him our exemplar, and our guide. Imitate him. Do his work. Become like unto him, as far as it lies within our powers to become like him that was perfect and without sin.[18]

---

### We have hope of eternal life only through Christ and by our obedience to His gospel.

No other name, under heaven, is given, but that of Jesus Christ, by which you can be saved or exalted in the Kingdom of God.[19]

The man who passes through this probation, and is faithful, being redeemed from sin by the blood of Christ, through the ordinances of the gospel, and attains to exaltation in the kingdom of God, is not less but greater than the angels.[20]

We have entered into the bond of that new and everlasting covenant agreeing that we would obey the commandments of God in all things whatsoever he shall command us. This is an everlasting covenant even unto the end of our days. . . . We shall never see the day in time nor in eternity, when it will not be obligatory, and when it will not be a pleasure as well as a duty for us, as his children, to obey all the commandments of the Lord throughout the endless ages of eternity. It is upon this principle that we keep in touch with God, and remain in harmony with his purposes. It is only in this way that we can consummate our mission, and obtain our crown and the gift of eternal lives, which is the greatest gift of God. Can you imagine any other way?[21]

There is no salvation but in the way God has pointed out. There is no hope of everlasting life but through obedience to the law that has been affixed by the Father of life, "with whom there is no variableness, neither shadow of turning" [James 1:17]; and there is no other way by which we may obtain that light and exaltation. Those matters are beyond peradventure, beyond all doubt in my mind; I know them to be true.[22]

Every blessing, privilege, glory, or exaltation is obtained only through obedience to the law upon which the same is promised. If we will abide the law, we shall receive the reward; but we can receive it on no other ground.[23]

Even Christ himself was not perfect at first; he received not a fulness at first, but he received grace for grace, and he continued to receive more and more until he received a fulness [see D&C 93:11–13]. Is not this to be so with the children of men? Is any man perfect? Has any man received a fulness at once? Have we reached a point wherein we may receive the fulness of God, of his glory, and his intelligence? No; and yet, if Jesus, the Son of God, and the Father of the heavens and the earth in which we dwell, received not a fulness at the first, but increased in faith, knowledge, understanding and grace until he received a fulness, is it not possible for all men who are born of women to receive little by little, line upon line, precept upon precept, until they shall receive a fulness, as he has received a fulness, and be exalted with him in the presence of the Father?[24]

I am living for my own salvation now and hereafter; next to my own comes that of my children and their beloved and precious mothers. Nothing that I can do in the world that will secure this glorious end can be called a sacrifice. It is a labor of love, an aim for life eternal and the fulness of joy. "He that hath eternal life is rich." [D&C 6:7.][25]

# Suggestions for Study

- Who is the author of the plan of salvation? How can this knowledge help us during our mortal lives?

- What are the purposes of our life here on earth? How does your life reflect that knowledge?

- Why is the same plan of salvation revealed by the Lord in every dispensation? How does the gospel plan work for our salvation "in this present life, as well as in the life to come"?

- Why was it necessary for each of us to receive a body? (See also D&C 93:33–34.) How can we use our bodies to accomplish God's will?

- In what ways is the Savior our "great example"? What are we to do to become conformed to the "image and likeness" of Christ and eventually become like Him?

- Why is keeping the commandments of God obligatory in time and eternity? How can obedience to the Lord be a "pleasure as well as a duty"?

- What does it mean to you to receive "grace for grace"? (See also D&C 93:12.) In what ways have you grown more like the Savior "little by little, line upon line, precept upon precept"?

- Why is nothing a sacrifice if it is done for our own salvation or the salvation of others?

## Notes

1. Joseph F. Smith's diary, 13 Nov. 1874, quoted in Francis M. Gibbons, *Joseph F. Smith: Patriarch and Preacher, Prophet of God* (1984), 98.
2. *Gospel Doctrine*, 5th ed. (1939), 11.
3. *Gospel Doctrine*, 6.
4. *Gospel Doctrine*, 21–22.
5. *Gospel Doctrine*, 13.
6. *Gospel Doctrine*, 11.
7. *Gospel Doctrine*, 72–73.
8. In Conference Report, Oct. 1909, 3.
9. *Gospel Doctrine*, 439.
10. *Gospel Doctrine*, 249.
11. *Gospel Doctrine*, 32–33.
12. *Gospel Doctrine*, 65.
13. *Gospel Doctrine*, 85.
14. *Gospel Doctrine*, 13.
15. *Gospel Doctrine*, 270.
16. *Gospel Doctrine*, 127–28.
17. *Gospel Doctrine*, 18.
18. *Gospel Doctrine*, 180.
19. *Gospel Doctrine*, 3.
20. *Gospel Doctrine*, 18.
21. *Gospel Doctrine*, 210.
22. *Gospel Doctrine*, 503.
23. *Gospel Doctrine*, 441.
24. *Gospel Doctrine*, 68.
25. Joseph F. Smith to one of his sons, 1907, quoted in *Life of Joseph F. Smith*, comp. Joseph Fielding Smith (1938), 454.

# Chastity and Purity

*The Lord commands us to be pure and to honor*
*the sanctity of the marriage covenant.*

## From the Life of Joseph F. Smith

President Joseph F. Smith was saddened when in 1875, as president of the European Mission, he had to release a missionary who had broken the law of chastity. As he contemplated the regret and heartache that faced the young man, he wrote, "Thus a man may almost fill a mission or live a lifetime honorably and faithfully, and at the last moment, as it were by a single act or crime, or folly, or error, overturn and destroy it all in a moment, turning all the sweetness in the cup of life into gall and bitterness."

President Smith then went on to reflect on his gratitude for the protecting hand of the Lord in helping him to remain true to his covenants. "O, how I thank my God for His protecting, watchful care, . . . preserving me from the deadly sins of the world, and many thousand times from my own weaknesses and proneness to err." He was determined to be the kind of person who could "look his fellows in the face, and with a clean conscience before God stand erect in honest pride of truth, morally and sexually pure." He rejoiced that he lived "in the pure unsullied love" of his family and said, "I would not abuse their love and confidence for all I have or am."[1]

## Teachings of Joseph F. Smith

### Chastity brings strength and power to the peoples of the earth.

We believe that God lives, and that he is a judge of the quick and the dead. We believe that his eye is upon the world, and that he beholds his groveling, erring and weak children upon this earth. We believe that we are here by his design . . . ; that we are here to fulfil a destiny, and not to fulfil a whim, or for the gratification of mortal lusts.[2]

Personal purity and proper thoughts . . . are the bases of all proper action. I wish that all young [people] could appreciate the value there is in this practice, and in giving their youthful days to the service of the Lord. Growth, development, progress, self-respect, the esteem and admiration of men naturally follow such a course in youth. The Savior set a striking example in this matter, and was early about his Father's business. . . . Samuel, the prophet, had so prepared himself by a pure, self-respecting childhood that he was perfectly attuned to the whisperings of God.[3]

There appears to be a something beyond and above the reasons apparent to the human mind why chastity brings strength and power to the peoples of the earth, but it is so.[4]

We believe in one standard of morality for men and women. If purity of life is neglected, all other dangers set in upon us like the rivers of waters when the flood gates are opened.[5]

We desire with holy zeal to emphasize the enormity of sexual sins. Though often regarded as insignificant by those not knowing the will of God, they are, in his eyes an abomination, and if we are to remain his favored people they must be shunned as the gates of hell. The evil results of these sins are so patent in vice, crime, misery and disease that it would appear that all, young and old, must perceive and sense them. They are destroying the world. If we are to be preserved we must abhor them, shun them, not practice the least of them, for they weaken and enervate, they kill man spiritually, they make him unfit for the company of the righteous and the presence of God.[6]

We hold that sexual sin is second only to the shedding of innocent blood in the category of personal crimes. . . . We proclaim as the word of the Lord: "Thou shalt not commit adultery." [Exodus 20:14.] "He that looketh on a woman to lust after her, or if any shall commit adultery in their hearts, they shall not have the Spirit, but shall deny the faith." [D&C 63:16.][7]

Like many bodily diseases, sexual crime drags with itself a train of other ills. As the physical effects of drunkenness entail the deterioration of tissue, and disturbance of vital functions, and so render the body receptive to any distemper to which it may be exposed, and at the same time lower the powers of resistance even to fatal deficiency, so does unchastity expose the soul to divers spiritual maladies, and rob it of both resistance and recuperative ability. The adulterous generation of Christ's day were deaf to the voice of truth, and through their diseased state of mind and heart, sought after signs and preferred empty fable to the message of salvation [see Matthew 16:4].[8]

Unchastity, furthermore, not only fixes its penalty on the one who transgresses, but reaches out unerring punishment to the third and fourth generation, making not only the transgressor a wreck, but mayhap involving scores of people in his direct line of relationship, disrupting family ties, breaking the hearts of parents, and causing a black stream of sorrow to overwhelm their lives.[9]

## The law of chastity is vitally important to men, women, and children.

The law of chastity is one of the most vital importance, both to children, and to men and to women. It is a vitally important principle to the children of God in all their lives, from the cradle to the grave. God has fixed dreadful penalties against the transgression of his law of chastity, of virtue, of purity. When the law of God shall be in force among men, they will be cut off who are not absolutely pure and unsoiled and spotless—both men and women. We expect the women to be pure, we expect them to be spotless and without blemish, and it is as necessary and important for man to be pure and virtuous as for woman.[10]

Waiting to serve the Lord until the wild oats of youth are sown, is reprehensible. . . . It is better far that a man should late turn from evil, than to continue in sin all his days, but . . . there are regrets and heartburnings in repenting late in life from the follies and sins of youth.[11]

It is a deplorable fact that society persists in holding women to stricter account than men in the matter of sexual offense. What shadow of excuse, not to speak of justification, can be found for this outrageous and cowardly discrimination? . . .

So far as woman sins it is inevitable that she shall suffer, for retribution is sure, whether it be immediate or deferred. But in so far as man's injustice inflicts upon her the consequence of his offenses, he stands convicted of multiple guilt. And man is largely responsible for the sins against decency and virtue, the burden of which is too often fastened upon the weaker participant in the crime. . . .

We accept without reservation or qualification the affirmation of Deity, through an ancient Nephite prophet: "For I, the Lord God, delight in the chastity of women. And whoredoms are an abomination before me; thus saith the Lord of Hosts." (Jacob 2:28.)[12]

We raise our voices against prostitution, and against all forms of immorality. We are not here to practice immorality of any kind. Above all things, sexual immorality is most heinous in the sight of God. . . . Therefore, we raise our voices against sexual immorality, and against all manner of obscenity.[13]

---

### Our marriage vows are most sacred.

The lawful association of the sexes is ordained of God, not only as the sole means of race perpetuation, but for the development of the higher faculties and nobler traits of human nature, which the love-inspired companionship of man and woman alone can insure. The word of Scripture is explicit as to the Divine intent and command with respect to the sexes. It is not good for man to be alone; and therefore hath it been ordained that "a man leave his father and his mother and shall cleave unto his wife; and they shall be one flesh." [See Genesis 2:18, 24.]

The precept that marriage is honorable is as true today as when uttered by the Apostle of old [see Hebrews 13:4]. . . .

Sexual union is lawful in wedlock, and, if participated in with right intent is honorable and sanctifying. *But without the bonds of marriage, sexual indulgence is a debasing sin, abominable in the sight of Deity.*[14]

Today a flood of iniquity is overwhelming the civilized world. One great reason therefor is the neglect of marriage; it has lost its sanctity in the eyes of the great majority. It is at best a civil contract, but more often an accident or a whim, or a means of gratifying the passions. And when the sacredness of the covenant is ignored or lost sight of, then a disregard of the marriage vows, under the present moral training of the masses, is a mere triviality, a trifling indiscretion.[15]

Infidelity to marriage vows is a fruitful source of divorce, with its long train of attendant evils, not the least of which are the shame and dishonor inflicted on unfortunate though innocent children. The dreadful effects of adultery cannot be confined to the erring participants. Whether openly known or partly concealed under the cloak of guilty secrecy, the results are potent in evil influence. The immortal spirits that come to earth to tabernacle in bodies of flesh have the right to be well born, through parents who are free from the contamination of sexual vice.[16]

## The sin against chastity is intensified by the breaking of sacred covenants.

The law as given, we believe to be general, applying to all the Saints. But undoubtedly when, in addition to the actual offense against the laws of chastity, covenants are broken, then the punishment for the double offense will, either in this life or that which is to come, be correspondingly greater and more severe.[17]

There are said to be more shades of green than of any other color, so also we are of the opinion there are more grades or degrees of sin associated with the improper relationship of the sexes than of any other wrongdoing of which we have knowledge. They all involve a grave offense—the sin against chastity, but in numerous instances this sin is intensified by the breaking of sacred covenants, to which is sometimes added deceit, intimidation or actual violence.

Much as all these sins are to be denounced and deplored, we can ourselves see a difference both in intent and consequence between the offense of a young couple who, being betrothed, in an unguarded moment, without premeditation fall into sin, and that of the man, who having entered into holy places and made sacred covenants, plots to rob the wife of his neighbor of her virtue either by cunning or force and accomplish his vile intent.

Not only is there a difference in these wrongs, judging from the standpoint of intent, but also from that of the consequences. . . . In the [case of the man who has made covenants], others are most disastrously involved, families are broken up, misery is forced upon innocent parties, society is affected . . . ; altogether, wrongs are committed both to the living and the dead, as well as to the yet unborn, which it is out of the power of the offenders to repair or make right.[18]

---

### The gospel offers hope to those determined to be pure.

It is only the vicious and the truly wicked who do not desire purity; they do not love purity and truth. I do not know whether it is possible for any soul to become so debased as to lose all regard for that which is pure and chaste, good and true and godlike. I believe that there still lingers in the heart of the most vicious and wicked, at times at least, a spark of that divinity that has been planted in the souls of all the sons of God. Men may become so corrupt that they do not have more than mere glimpses of that divine inspiration that strives to lead them toward and to love good; but I do not believe there is a soul in the world that has absolutely lost all conception and admiration of that which is good and pure, when he sees it. It is hard to believe that a human being may become so depraved that he has lost all desire that he might also be good and pure, if it were possible; but many people have abandoned themselves to evil and have come to the conclusion that there is no chance for them. While there is life there is hope, and while there is repentance there is a chance for forgiveness.[19]

The gospel of Jesus Christ is the Divinely ordained panacea for the ills that afflict humanity, and preeminently so for the dread affliction of sexual sin.[20]

Then, we say to you who have repented of your sins, who have been buried with Christ in baptism, who have been raised from the liquid grave to newness of life, born of the water and of the Spirit, and who have been made the children of the Father, heirs of God and joint heirs with Jesus Christ—we say to you, if you will observe the laws of God, and cease to do evil, cease to be obscene, cease to be immoral, sexually or otherwise, cease to be profane, cease to be infidel, and have faith in God, believe in the truth and receive it, and be honest before God and man, that you will be set up on high, and God will put you at the head, just as sure as you observe these commandments. Whoso will keep the commandments of God, no matter whether it be you or any other people, they will rise and not fall, they will lead and not follow, they will go upward and not downward. God will exalt them and magnify them before the nations of the earth, and he will set the seal of his approval upon them, will name them as his own. This is my testimony to you.[21]

## Suggestions for Study

- What is the Lord's law of chastity? In what ways does chastity bring "strength and power" to people?

- How can we nurture "personal purity and proper thoughts" in ourselves? How can personal purity be a blessing to ourselves, our families, and the world?

- Why do you think that violation of the law of chastity is "second only to the shedding of innocent blood"? (See also Alma 39:5.)

- What things are included in the "train of other ills" that accompanies violations of the law of chastity? How do violations of the law of chastity affect many more people than just the transgressors?

- What can we do to "raise our voices against sexual immorality, and against all manner of obscenity"?

- For what purposes is the "lawful association of the sexes . . . ordained of God"?

- Why is the neglect of the sanctity of marriage a "great reason" for the "flood of iniquity . . . overwhelming the civilized world"?

- How does breaking the law of chastity constitute a "double offense" for those who have made sacred covenants with God? What are the consequences of this double offense?

• What hope is in the gospel of Jesus Christ for those who are determined to purify themselves and observe the law of chastity?

## Notes

1. *Life of Joseph F. Smith,* comp. Joseph Fielding Smith (1938), 450–51.
2. *Gospel Doctrine,* 5th ed. (1939), 312.
3. *Gospel Doctrine,* 334.
4. *Gospel Doctrine,* 274.
5. *Gospel Doctrine,* 313.
6. *Gospel Doctrine,* 275–76.
7. *Gospel Doctrine,* 310; paragraphing altered.
8. *Gospel Doctrine,* 309–10.
9. *Gospel Doctrine,* 335.
10. *Gospel Doctrine,* 273–74.
11. *Gospel Doctrine,* 335.
12. *Gospel Doctrine,* 309–10.
13. *Gospel Doctrine,* 312.
14. "Unchastity the Dominant Evil of the Age," *Improvement Era,* June 1917, 739.
15. *Gospel Doctrine,* 274.
16. *Gospel Doctrine,* 309.
17. *Gospel Doctrine,* 311.
18. *Gospel Doctrine,* 310–11.
19. *Gospel Doctrine,* 27–28.
20. "Unchastity the Dominant Evil of the Age," 743.
21. *Gospel Doctrine,* 312.

# Thrift, the Foundation of Prosperity

*We should pay our debts and save our means so that we are better able to serve in the kingdom of God.*

## From the Life of Joseph F. Smith

In 1918 Joseph F. Smith wrote a letter to his son in which he recalled Christmas experiences from his own youth when he was "always penniless." He said about his early married life: "I owed no man through all those days, and I *had* to work—I could not be idle." He said that he and his family labored "tugging away with all our mights to keep soul and body together." It was under these conditions that he went out just before Christmas with the intent of doing something special for his children. He said, "I wanted something to please them, and to mark the Christmas day from all other days—but not a cent to do it with! I walked up and down Main Street, looking into the shop windows . . . and then slunk out of sight of humanity and sat down and wept like a child, until my poured-out grief relieved my aching heart; and after awhile returned home, as empty as when I left, and played with my children, grateful and happy only for them. . . .

"After these trials, my pathway became more smooth. I began to pick up; by hard work, rigid economy, self-denial, and the love of God, I prospered."[1]

Bishop Charles W. Nibley, who worked closely with President Smith, said: "He was always careful with his expenditures. . . . He abhorred debt, and no man have I ever known who was so prompt to pay an obligation to the last penny. . . . He resolutely set his face against debt; and would not, under any conditions or circumstances, involve the Church in that way. Neither would he himself become involved in debt in his own individual affairs, but he stuck persistently to the old motto, 'Pay as you go.' "[2]

President Smith emphasized the practicality of the gospel when he taught, "It has always been a cardinal teaching with the Latter-day Saints, that a religion which has not the power to save people temporally and make them prosperous and happy here, cannot be depended upon to save them spiritually, to exalt them in the life to come."[3]

# Teachings of Joseph F. Smith

### Avoid debt and you will be financially as well as spiritually free.

Now, I believe sincerely that one of the principal causes of the distress that exists among us—and I believe the same thing will apply almost universally throughout the land—is that people have gone beyond their means. They have borrowed largely, mortgaged their homes, their farms, and nearly everything they possess, to keep pace with their neighbors, competing one with another in putting on appearances and in carrying on their business on the credit basis that is so much in vogue in the world. . . .

. . . Many of us that have borrowed means . . . that we might put on an appearance at least equal to that of our neighbor, if we had not done so, but had lived within our means, and in addition had laid a little aside for a rainy day, today we would be the most independent people upon this continent. . . . So far as I am concerned, I would like to see . . . that whenever we buy a dollar's worth of goods we either pay a dollar for it or something that represents a dollar, and that we do it without crippling ourselves at home or placing a mortgage upon us and upon our children. Every man that lives by credit is placing shackles upon himself and upon his family. . . .

Did you ever see anybody who went in debt and mortgaged and bonded that which he possessed, as free, as independent, as happy as the man who paid for what he had as he went along? We should live according to our means, and lay a foundation upon which we can build, and upon which our children can build after us, without paying interest on bonded debts incurred by us. I am aware that I am not preaching the financial gospel of the world. I suppose I am laying myself open to the charge of

To encourage economic self-reliance, the pioneer Saints built up enterprises
such as Zion's Cooperative Mercantile Institution.

being called a mossback, non-progressive, and so on. All these epithets are hurled at the men that dare to tell the people to live within their means. . . . Sometimes we are put in a position where it is necessary to go into debt. When it is necessary, so may it be. . . . But I have never yet been convinced that it was essential for the welfare of the present or future generation that my children should be brought in bondage by my acts.[4]

What a blessed condition would result in Zion if the evil of going into debt . . . could be made very clear to every Latter-day Saint, young and old! Well, indeed, would it be if some of the burdens of the mortgage and its accompanying sorrows, could be felt and understood by every man who has in contemplation the pawning of his home and land for money—that he might comprehend its slavery and terror—as thoroughly prior to the deed as he is sure to feel it after.[5]

In the time of prosperity, . . . it is highly proper for the Latter-day Saints to get out of debt. . . . I would say, in connection with this subject, that one of the best ways that I know of to pay my obligations to my brother, my neighbor, or business associate, is for me first to pay my obligations to the Lord. I can pay more of my debts to my neighbors, if I have contracted them, after I have met my honest obligations with the Lord, than I can by neglecting the latter; and you can do the same. If you desire to prosper, and to be free men and women and a free people, first meet your just obligations to God, and then meet your obligations to your fellowmen.[6]

Now is the time for all the people to study true economy, and to begin to retrench and free themselves from debt, and become a free and independent people. . . . If we will only do our duty as Latter-day Saints and be wise in the use of our means, circumstances will be overruled for us, our labors will be blessed unto us, the land will be made fruitful, and we will reap bountiful harvests and rejoice in them; for God will bestow His favors upon His faithful children. . . . Now is the time to curtail expenses. Now is the time to cut down extravagance and to deny ourselves a little worldly pleasure. But let us be charitable. Do not condemn one another. . . . Do not go and take your fellow-

bondage of debt, and it may be difficult for us to get out of it; but if we possibly can get out of it in honor, let us bend all our efforts to that end and do it; that when we are called to go on missions we can say, "Yes I am ready and willing to go," and what is more, "I do not owe anybody, and I have the means to go with, and to provide for my family."[20]

I believe that it is our business to prepare against the day of famine, of pestilence, of tempests and earthquakes, and the time when the sea shall heave itself beyond its bounds. How shall we do it? . . . By studying and carrying out the principles of true economy in our lives, and by a system of fraternity and love by which each one will help his brother, and all stand united, so that none shall suffer from want when it is within the power of others to alleviate it. One of the great promises that the Lord has made concerning His people, as contained in the Book of Doctrine and Covenants, is that they shall become the richest of all people [see D&C 38:39]. Now, how can this be fulfilled if every day we spend all that we earn, and borrow a little besides of our neighbor? . . .

. . . Let us be industrious and economical, and save our means. Not that we build our hopes upon our riches, not that we make that our god; but for what? That we may be able, when perilous times shall come, to meet the necessities of the times and the obligations that may rest upon the people of God to consummate the purposes of the Almighty in the land.[21]

## Suggestions for Study

- If we desire to prosper spiritually and temporally, what must we do? How can covetousness destroy prosperity?

- What blessings result from avoiding debt? What problems can come to those who unwisely accumulate debt? What rationalizations do people sometimes use for accumulating unwise debt?

- What can we do in "the time of prosperity" to free ourselves from debt? What are our financial obligations to the Lord? Why should we meet them first?

- Although homes must frequently be purchased through "periodical payments," what cautions should we observe regarding mortgages? How can the "spirit of extravagance" lead people to jeopardize their homes and financial security? How can we avoid these things?

- How do selfishness and pleasure-seeking separate us from God? What are the dangers of loving money more than God?

- How can we prepare temporally and spiritually "against the day of famine"?

- How can we use our means to "consummate the purposes of the Almighty"? How does financial preparedness enable us to be of service?

- How can we teach our children the principles of wise money management?

## Notes

1. "Editor's Table: In Memoriam—Joseph Fielding Smith," *Improvement Era*, Jan. 1919, 266–67.
2. Charles W. Nibley, "Reminiscences," in *Gospel Doctrine*, 5th ed. (1939), 519.
3. "The Truth about Mormonism," *Out West: A Magazine of the Old Pacific and the New*, Sept. 1905, 242.
4. *Deseret Weekly*, 19 Aug. 1893, 282.
5. *Gospel Doctrine*, 307.
6. *Gospel Doctrine*, 259–60.
7. *Deseret Weekly*, 19 Aug. 1893, 283.
8. *Gospel Doctrine*, 299–300.
9. *Gospel Doctrine*, 306–7; paragraphing altered.
10. *Deseret News: Semi-Weekly*, 1 May 1883, 1.
11. In Conference Report, Oct. 1911, 128–29.
12. *Deseret News: Semi-Weekly*, 8 Aug. 1884, 1.
13. In Conference Report, Oct. 1903, 5.
14. *Deseret News: Semi-Weekly*, 21 Jan. 1896, 1.
15. *Gospel Doctrine*, 323–24.
16. *Deseret Weekly*, 19 Aug. 1893, 283.
17. *Deseret News: Semi-Weekly*, 1 May 1883, 1.
18. *Deseret News: Semi-Weekly*, 11 Mar. 1884, 1; paragraphing added.
19. *Deseret News: Semi-Weekly*, 8 Aug. 1884, 1.
20. *Deseret News: Semi-Weekly*, 20 Nov. 1894, 1.
21. *Deseret Weekly*, 19 Aug. 1893, 283.

# The Eternal Union of Husband and Wife

*The man and woman who are sealed for eternity under the authority of the holy priesthood can, through their faithfulness, attain exaltation in the celestial kingdom of God.*

## From the Life of Joseph F. Smith

While serving as a Counselor to President John Taylor, Joseph F. Smith traveled to Hawaii with his wife Julina, who he said was "as true as steel; as constant as the pole star, as faithful as time and better than gold."[1] In Hawaii President Smith suffered from a serious illness, and Julina nursed him back to health. Several months later, in March of 1887, it became necessary for Julina and their children to return to the mainland while Joseph F. remained on the islands.

On March 15 he recorded in his journal: "The steamer cut loose at 12 p.m. and at exactly 12:15 she commenced her course out of the harbor; and I took the last look at the receding forms of my loved and loving ones until God in his mercy shall permit us to meet again. When the ship passed the line of sight, I hastened [to a better vantage point] . . . to look again at the speeding steamer *Australia* with her precious sacred treasures until lost behind Diamond Head. When once alone, my soul burst forth in tears and I wept their fountains dry and felt all the pangs and grief of parting with my heart's best treasures on earth."[2]

Despite the pain of such separations, President Smith knew the power and promise of the eternal principle revealed to the world by the Prophet Joseph Smith: "What is it? The union of husband and wife for time and for all eternity. . . . Who understood the responsibility that dwells with the union of husband and wife, till Joseph Smith revealed it in the simplicity and plainness with which he has revealed it to the world? . . . It has opened my eyes. If anything in the world could have made me a better man, or a better husband, . . . it is that principle that the Lord has revealed, which shows me the obligations that I am under."[3]

# Teachings of Joseph F. Smith

### God instituted marriage for our eternal glory and exaltation.

God instituted marriage in the beginning. He made man in his own image and likeness, male and female, and in their creation it was designed that they should be united together in sacred bonds of marriage, and one is not perfect without the other.[4]

The lawful union of man and woman [is] the means through which they may realize their highest and holiest aspirations. To the Latter-day Saints, marriage is not designed by our heavenly Father to be merely an earthly union, but one that shall survive the vicissitudes of time, and endure for eternity, bestowing honor and joy in this world, glory and eternal lives in the worlds to come.[5]

[The gospel] takes men and women and it joins them together in an eternal covenant of matrimony, holy and pure, given of God, which supplies the necessities and meets the purest and strongest desires of the soul. It makes men and women complete—husbands and wives for time and for all eternity. What a glorious thought this is![6]

God not only commends but he commands marriage. While man was yet immortal, before sin had entered the world, our heavenly Father himself performed the first marriage. He united our first parents in the bonds of holy matrimony, and commanded them to be fruitful and multiply and replenish the earth. This command he has never changed, abrogated or annulled; but it has continued in force throughout all the generations of mankind.[7]

[People] . . . are more and more being imbued with the selfish and ungodly idea that marriage is wrong and children a disgrace. The Church of Jesus Christ of Latter-day Saints takes an entirely opposite view, and believes in, and teaches as gospel truth, the first great scriptural commandment of God to man: "Be fruitful, and multiply and repenish the earth, and subdue it." [Genesis 1:28.]

*Rebekah at the Well,* by Michael Deas. Abraham's servant sought a wife for Isaac, son of Abraham, among God's covenant people. Rebekah drew water from a well for the camels of the servant, thus fulfilling his prayer that he would be led to find a righteous young woman.

. . . God has commanded, authorized and instituted the marriage relation. This was made very plain in the revelation of God to the Prophet Joseph Smith, as witness this language in the Doctrine and Covenants, section 49:15: "And, again, I say unto you, that whoso forbiddeth to marry is not ordained of God, for marriage is ordained of God unto man."[8]

Marriage is . . . a principle or ordinance of the gospel, most vital to the happiness of mankind, however unimportant it may seem, or lightly regarded by many. There is no superfluous or unnecessary principle in the plan of life, but there is no principle of greater importance or more essential to the happiness of man—not only here, but especially hereafter, than that of marriage.[9]

---

### It is a glorious privilege to be united as man and wife for time and all eternity.

It is a glorious privilege to be permitted to go into a Temple of God to be united as man and wife in the bonds of holy wedlock for time and all eternity by the authority of the Holy Priesthood, which is the power of God, for they who are thus joined together "no man can put asunder," for God hath joined them.[10]

The man and the woman who engage in this ordinance of matrimony are engaging in something that is of such far-reaching character, and is of such vast importance, that thereby hangs life and death, and eternal increase. Thereupon depends eternal happiness, or eternal misery.[11]

Why did [God] teach us the principle of eternal union of man and wife? . . . So that the man receiving his wife by the power of God, for time and for all eternity, would have the right to claim her and she to claim her husband, in the world to come.[12]

Men and women may be saved singly, but men and women will not be exalted separately. They must be bound together in that union which has been revealed in this great latter dispensation. The man is not without the woman in the Lord, and neither is the woman without the man in the Lord. Whatever men and women may say or think in relation to this, they cannot obtain an exaltation in the kingdom of God single and alone. . . .

We have come here to be conformed to the likeness of God. He made us in the beginning in His own image and in His own likeness, and He made us male and female. We never could be in the image of God if we were not both male and female. . . . When we become like Him you will find that we will be presented before Him in the form in which we were created, male and female. The woman will not go there alone, and the man will not go there alone, and claim exaltation. They may attain a degree of salvation alone, but when they are exalted they will be exalted according to the law of the celestial kingdom. They cannot be exalted in any other way.[13]

There is no union for time and eternity that can be perfected outside of the law of God, and the order of his house. Men may desire it, they may go through the form of it, in this life, but it will be of no effect except it be done and sanctioned by divine authority, in the name of the Father and of the Son and of the Holy Ghost.[14]

The Latter-day Saints marry for time and eternity, not merely until death parts husband and wife. Marriages performed under the civic law and by ministers of other denominations are regarded as honorable and effectual so far as relates to this life, but in order to be effectual in the life to come such covenants must be made for eternity, such unions must be formed according to God's law and under his authority, or they will have no force or effect hereafter. The family is the foundation of eternal glory, the nucleus of a kingdom without end. The husband will have his wife, the wife her husband, parents their children, forever, provided they secure them in the manner prescribed by him whose right it is to regulate all things pertaining to his kingdom.[15]

---

**Marry in the faith, at the appropriate time,
and in the house of the Lord.**

We say to our young people, get married, and marry aright. Marry in the faith, and let the ceremony be performed in the place God has appointed. Live so that you may be worthy of this blessing.[16]

I want the young men of Zion to realize that this institution of marriage is not a man-made institution. It is of God. It is honorable. . . . It is not simply devised for the convenience alone of man, to suit his own notions, and his own ideas; to marry and then divorce, to adopt and then to discard, just as he pleases. There are great consequences connected with it, consequences which reach beyond this present time, into all eternity, for thereby souls are begotten into the world, and men and women obtain their being in the world. Marriage is the preserver of the human race. Without it, the purposes of God would be frustrated; virtue would be destroyed to give place to vice and corruption, and the earth would be void and empty.[17]

Bachelorhood and small families carry to the superficial mind the idea that they are desirable because they bring with them the minimum of responsibility. The spirit that shirks responsibility shirks labor. Idleness and pleasure take the place of industry and strenuous effort. The love of pleasure and of an easy life in turn make demands upon young men who refuse to look upon marriage and its consequent family enlargement as a sacred duty. . . .

. . . This loss to the home is a loss the nation must feel, as years go on. Time will vindicate the laws of God and the truth that individual human happiness is found in duty and not in pleasure and freedom from care.

The spirit of the world is contagious. We cannot live in the midst of such social conditions without suffering from the effects of their allurements. Our young people will be tempted to follow the example of the world about them. There is already a strong tendency to make sport of the obligations to marry. Pretexts of ambition are set up as an excuse to postpone marriage till some special object is attained. Some of our leading young men desire to complete first a course of study at home or abroad. Being natural leaders in society their example is dangerous and the excuse is one of questionable propriety. It were better far that many such young men never went to college than that the excuse of college life be made the reason for postponing marriage beyond the proper age.[18]

Young men want to get homes that are palatial, that are fine in all their appointments, and as modern as anybody else's before they will get married. I think it is a mistake. I think that young men and young women, too, should be willing, even at this day, and in the present condition of things, to enter the sacred bonds of marriage together and fight their way together to success, meet their obstacles and their difficulties, and cleave together to success, and cooperate in their temporal affairs, so that they shall succeed. Then they will learn to love one another better, and will be more united throughout their lives, and the Lord will bless them more abundantly.[19]

The Church authorities and the teachers of our associations should inculcate the sacredness, and teach the duty of marriage, as it has been revealed in the latter days to us. There should be a . . . sentiment created in favor of honorable marriage, and that would prevent any young man, or any young woman, who is a member of the Church, from marrying except by that authority which is sanctioned of God.[20]

## Marriage should be built upon principles of love and sacred devotion.

There should be no difficulty in holding in the highest reverence and exalted thought, the home, if it can be built upon the principles of purity, of true affection, of righteousness and justice. The man and his wife who have perfect confidence in each other, and who determine to follow the laws of God in their lives and fulfil the measure of their mission in the earth, would not be, and could never be, contented without the home. Their hearts, their feelings, their minds, their desires would naturally trend toward the building of a home and family and of a kingdom of their own; to the laying of the foundation of eternal increase and power, glory, exaltation and dominion, worlds without end.[21]

A home is not a home in the eye of the gospel, unless there dwell perfect confidence and love between the husband and the wife. Home is a place of order, love, union, rest, confidence, and absolute trust; where the breath of suspicion of infidelity can not enter; where the woman and the man each have implicit confidence in each other's honor and virtue.[22]

Zion is no place for a war of the sexes. God intended them to be one, and so declared. It is not doing His work to keep them separate, or to cause them to feel that they have diverse and opposed interests, and that separation, not union, is the object of their creation.[23]

What then is an ideal home—model home, such as it should be the ambition of the Latter-day Saints to build . . . ? It is one in which all worldly considerations are secondary. One in which the father is devoted to the family with which God has blessed him, counting them of first importance, and in which they in turn permit him to live in their hearts. One in which there is confidence, union, love, sacred devotion between father and mother and children and parents. One in which the mother takes every pleasure in her children, supported by the father—all being moral, pure, God-fearing.[24]

Parents . . . should love and respect each other, and treat each other with respectful decorum and kindly regard, all the time. The husband should treat his wife with the utmost courtesy and respect. The husband should never insult her; he should never speak slightly of her, but should always hold her in the highest esteem in the home, in the presence of their children. . . . The wife, also should treat the husband with the greatest respect and courtesy. . . . The wife should be a joy to her husband, and she should live and conduct herself at home so the home will be the most joyous, the most blessed place on earth to her husband. This should be the condition of the husband, wife, the father and the mother, within the sacred precinct of that holy place, the home.[25]

Brethren and sisters, nothing should be permitted to come in between you—father and mother, husband and wife; there never should be a shade of difference of feeling; there never should be a thing permitted to come between you and estrange you one from another; you should not allow it. This is essential to your welfare and happiness and to the union that should exist in your home. We all have our weaknesses and failings. Sometimes the husband sees a failing in his wife, and he upbraids her with it. Sometimes the wife feels that her husband has not done just the right thing, and she upbraids him. What good does it do? Is not forgiveness better? Is not charity better? Is not love better? Isn't it better not to speak of faults, not to magnify weaknesses by iterating and reiterating them? Isn't that better? and will not the union that has been cemented between you and the birth of children and by the bond of the new and everlasting covenant, be more secure when you forget to mention weaknesses and faults one of another? Is it not better to drop them and say nothing about them—bury them and speak only of the good that you know and feel, one for another, and thus bury each other's faults and not magnify them; isn't that better?[26]

What can there be more joyous to think of than the fact that [a man] who loved his wife and whom she loved, to whom he was true and who was true to him all her days of association with him as wife and mother, will have the privilege of coming up on the morning of the first resurrection clothed with immortality and eternal life, and resume the relationship that existed between them in this life, the relationship of husband and wife, father and mother, parents to their children, having laid the foundation for eternal glory and eternal exaltation in the kingdom of God![27]

It is marriage, sanctified and God-sanctioned, upon which glorified home is founded—that blesses, happifies, exalts, and leads at length to companionship with our Heavenly parents, and to eternal, united life, and increase.[28]

## Suggestions for Study

- For what purposes was marriage instituted by God? How does eternal marriage enable us to realize our "highest and holiest aspirations"?

- Why is marriage "most vital to the happiness of mankind"? Why is it regarded as unimportant by many?

- How do eternal increase and eternal happiness depend on the eternal union of man and wife? How does it make you feel to know that you will have claim on your husband or wife for all eternity?

- Why should we seek to marry in the temple?

- What might be the consequences to ourselves and to others of breaking the bond of the new and everlasting covenant of marriage?

- What allurements or distractions might lead some people to postpone or avoid marriage? How can we know when it is appropriate for us to marry?

- President Joseph F. Smith prophesied that the shirking of the responsibilities of marriage is a "loss the nation must feel, as years go on." How are nations now feeling this loss?

- How can the covenant of eternal marriage strengthen couples when they face "their obstacles and their difficulties"?

- Why is "absolute trust" between husband and wife important? What other attributes should be cultivated between husbands and wives? How do negative behaviors—such as criticism, sarcasm, failure to forgive, and pride—weaken marital relationships?

- What does it mean for a husband and wife to be one? What sacrifices might couples need to make to become one? What other things can couples do to strengthen their eternal union?

## Notes

1. *Life of Joseph F. Smith,* comp. Joseph Fielding Smith (1938), 453.
2. Quoted in Francis M. Gibbons, *Joseph F. Smith: Patriarch and Preacher, Prophet of God* (1984), 153.
3. In Conference Report, Oct. 1911, 8.
4. *Gospel Doctrine,* 5th ed. (1939), 272.
5. In James R. Clark, comp., *Messages of the First Presidency of The Church of Jesus Christ of Latter-day Saints,* 6 vols. (1965–75), 4:147.
6. "Discourse by President Joseph F. Smith," *Millennial Star,* 15 Feb. 1900, 98.
7. *Gospel Doctrine,* 274.
8. "Editor's Table: Marriage God-Ordained and Sanctioned," *Improvement Era,* July 1902, 713; paragraphing altered.
9. *Gospel Doctrine,* 105.
10. *Deseret News: Semi-Weekly,* 10 Sept. 1878, 1.
11. *Gospel Doctrine,* 273.
12. *Gospel Doctrine,* 277.
13. *Deseret News: Semi-Weekly,* 28 June 1898, 1.
14. *Gospel Doctrine,* 272.
15. In *Messages of the First Presidency,* 4:250.
16. *Gospel Doctrine,* 275.
17. *Gospel Doctrine,* 272.
18. *Gospel Doctrine,* 281.
19. *Gospel Doctrine,* 278.
20. *Gospel Doctrine,* 273.
21. *Gospel Doctrine,* 304.
22. *Gospel Doctrine,* 302.
23. "Editorial Thoughts: The Righteousness of Marriage, and Its Opposite," *Juvenile Instructor,* 1 July 1902, 402.
24. *Gospel Doctrine,* 302–3.
25. In Conference Report, Apr. 1905, 84–85.
26. "Sermon on Home Government," *Millennial Star,* 25 Jan. 1912, 49–50.
27. *Gospel Doctrine,* 458.
28. "Editor's Table: Marriage God-Ordained and Sanctioned," 717–18.

help the sisters fulfill their responsibilities? How does this knowledge help priesthood holders support the Relief Society?

- How can Relief Society sisters "lead . . . the women of the world" in everything that is praiseworthy, uplifting, and purifying? (See also Articles of Faith 1:13.)

- How can Relief Society sisters fulfill their "callings as angels of mercy to the suffering and the down-trodden"? How can we be led to those who "suffer in silence"?

- How can the Relief Society as an organization administer comfort? How can it teach the principles of right living? How can it increase women's understanding of their family responsibilities?

- Why are the greater things the spiritual things? How can "well-directed charity" and "simple deeds of mercy" help us lead souls to "higher planes of faith and spiritual excellence"?

- What impresses you about the Relief Society sisters described in this chapter?

- How is the Relief Society blessed by the direction of the priesthood?

- How has the "noble cause" of Relief Society blessed your life?

## Notes

1. Minutes of the General Board of the Relief Society, 17 Mar. 1914, Historical Department Archives, The Church of Jesus Christ of Latter-day Saints, 54.
2. Minutes, 17 Mar. 1892, 233–34.
3. Minutes, 17 Mar. 1914, 51.
4. Minutes, 17 Mar. 1914, 54–55.
5. Minutes, 17 Mar. 1914, 55–56.
6. In Conference Report, Apr. 1914, 3–4.
7. *Gospel Doctrine,* 5th ed. (1939), 385.
8. Minutes, 17 Mar. 1914, 49–51; paragraphing added.
9. "Epistle to the Relief Society Concerning These War Times," *Relief Society Magazine,* July 1917, 364.
10. *Woman's Exponent,* May 1903, 93; paragraphing added.
11. *Woman's Exponent,* May 1903, 93; paragraphing added.
12. *Woman's Exponent,* May 1903, 93.
13. Minutes, 17 Mar. 1914, 57.
14. Minutes, 17 Mar. 1914, 58–60; paragraphing added.
15. *Gospel Doctrine,* 290.
16. Minutes, 17 Mar. 1914, 63.
17. In Conference Report, Oct. 1906, 9.
18. *Gospel Doctrine,* 383.
19. " 'Peace on Earth, Good Will to Men,' " *Relief Society Magazine,* Jan. 1915, 16.

# Charity in Our Souls

*We are to care for those in need and be filled
with kindness and love toward all people.*

## From the Life of Joseph F. Smith

President Joseph F. Smith beseeched Latter-day Saints to love
their neighbors and to look upon one another's needs—temporal and spiritual—with mercy and pure charity. "The moment that
a Latter-day Saint learns his duty, he will learn that it is his business . . . to be filled with the spirit of kindness, love, charity, and
forgiveness," he taught.[1]

He was the recipient of great service himself, as evidenced
when he visited Hawaii as President of the Church with Bishop
Charles W. Nibley. Bishop Nibley later described the experience:

"As we landed at the wharf in Honolulu, the native Saints were
out in great numbers with their wreaths of *leis,* beautiful flowers
of every variety and hue. We were loaded with them, he, of
course, more than anyone else. The noted Hawaiian band was
there playing welcome. . . . It was a beautiful sight to see the
deep-seated love, the even tearful affection, that these people had
for him. In the midst of it all I noticed a poor, old, blind woman,
tottering under the weight of about ninety years, being led in.
She had a few choice bananas in her hand. It was her all—her offering. She was calling, 'Iosepa, Iosepa.' Instantly, when he saw
her, he ran to her and clasped her in his arms, hugged her, and
kissed her over and over again, patting her on the head saying,
'Mama, Mama, my dear old Mama.'

"And with tears streaming down his cheeks he turned to me
and said, 'Charlie, she nursed me when I was a boy, sick and without anyone to care for me. She took me in and was a mother to
me.'

## God has made provision in His Church for the care of those in need.

God has made provision in His Church, in the complete organization of it, so that every faithful soul in it may be looked after and nurtured and cared for in the hour of need.[13]

God has commanded this people to remember the poor, and to give means for their support. . . . We do not believe in charity as a business; but rather we depend on mutual helpfulness. While the gospel message requires faith and repentance, it requires also that temporal necessities must be met. So the Lord has revealed plans for the temporal salvation of the people.

For the benefit of the poor we have the fast instituted, a leading object of which among other things is to provide the poor with food and other necessities until they may help themselves. For it is clear that plans which contemplate only relieving present distress are deficient. The Church has always sought to place its members in a way to help themselves, rather than adopting the method of so many charitable institutions of providing for only present needs. When the help is withdrawn or used up, more must be provided from the same source, thus making paupers of the poor and teaching them the incorrect principle of relying upon others' help, instead of depending upon their own exertions. . . . Our idea of charity, therefore, is to relieve present wants and then to put the poor in a way to help themselves so that in turn they may help others. The funds are committed for distribution to wise men, generally to bishops of the Church, whose duty it is to look after the poor.

We submit the equitable fast-day plan of the Lord to the churches of the world as a wise and systematic way of providing for the poor. . . . It would be a simple matter for people to comply with this requirement to abstain from food and drink one day each month, and to dedicate what would be consumed during that day to the poor, and as much more as they pleased. The Lord has instituted this law; it is simple and perfect, based on reason and intelligence, and would not only prove a solution to the question of providing for the poor, but it would result in good to those who observe the law. It would . . . place the body in subjection to the spirit, and so promote communion with the Holy Ghost, and insure a spiritual strength and power which the people of the nation so greatly need. As fasting should always be accompanied by prayer, this law would bring the people nearer to God, and divert their minds once a month at least, from the mad rush of worldly affairs and cause them to be brought into immediate contact with practical, pure and undefiled religion—to visit the fatherless and the widow, and keep themselves unspotted from the sins of the world [see James 1:27].[14]

It is evident that the acceptable fast is that which carries with it the true spirit of love for God and man; and that the aim in fasting is to secure perfect purity of heart and simplicity of intention—a fasting unto God in the fullest and deepest sense—for such a fast would be a cure for every practical and intellectual error; vanity would disappear, love for our fellows would take its place, and we would gladly assist the poor and the needy.[15]

---

**The gospel makes us unselfish and willing to sacrifice our own desires for the welfare of others.**

We admonish, we beseech our brothers and sisters in the gospel of Jesus Christ, not only to honor themselves by a proper course of living, but also to honor and love and be charitable to your neighbors, every one of you.[16]

I think we ought to live our religion. We should keep the commandments of God. We should possess and enjoy the spirit of the gospel in our hearts and bear the fruits of the spirit in our lives; faith, hope and charity, love, humility and forgiveness in our souls one for another, and avoid, as far as possible, the spirit of accusation, of contention, that leads to strife, to confusion and division among men, and the spirit of hatred. Oh, banish hatred from you. Hatred harbored in our hearts, or envy or jealousy, will injure those who permit them to abide in their souls and rancor in their thoughts a thousand-fold more than it will injure others. So let us banish those things from our hearts, and from our thoughts. Let us live righteous lives, let the husband love his wife and be true and kind to her, and the wife be true and kind to her husband, and they be true and loving and solicitous for the welfare of their children; let them be united as a family unit in the Church and as that condition extends abroad to the borders of Zion, we will have the millennial reign among us, and there will be peace on earth and good will to men everywhere.[17]

The Gospel is calculated to remove from us everything that is not consistent with God and the plan of salvation which he has revealed to men. It is designed to qualify us to live so that we may enjoy a fulness of the light of truth, and understand the purposes of God, and be able to live so near to Him that we may be in harmony with His wishes constantly. The principles of the Gospel are calculated to make us unselfish, to broaden our minds, to give breadth to our desires for good, to remove hatred, animosity, envy and anger from our hearts, and make us peaceful, tractable, teachable, and willing to sacrifice our own desires, and perchance our own interests, for the welfare of our fellow-creatures, and for the advancement of the Kingdom of God. A man who cannot sacrifice his own wishes, who cannot say in his heart, "Father, Thy will be done, not mine," is not a truly and thoroughly converted child of God; he is still, to some extent, in the grasp of error and in the shades of darkness that hover around the world, hiding God from the presence of mankind.[18]

## Suggestions for Study

- What are the two greatest commandments? (See also Matthew 22:37–40.) Why are these commandments so fundamental?

- What is charity? (See also Moroni 7:45–48.) What can we do so that charity pervades all our actions and dwells in our hearts? Why do you think that "charity never faileth"? (See Moroni 7:46.)

- What is our responsibility toward those who are unfortunate or needy or "lack the sympathies of mankind"?

- How can we increase our ability to truthfully say, "I love my neighbor as I love myself"? How should we deal with the failings we perceive in others? (See also Luke 6:41–42.) How can we magnify the virtues in others?

- What blessings result from observing the monthly fast day and contributing fast offerings? Prayerfully consider how you might contribute to the Church's care of the needy through such efforts as seeking out new or lonely members, volunteering in the community, increasing fast offerings, or participating in welfare and humanitarian aid projects.

- What are the "fruits of the spirit in our lives"? (See also Galatians 5:22–23.) What blessings come to us and to others when we are willing to sacrifice our own desires for the good of others?

- How does the gospel of Jesus Christ "remove hatred, animosity, envy and anger from our hearts" and help us be charitable toward others?

## Notes

1. In Conference Report, Apr. 1915, 4.
2. Charles W. Nibley, "Reminiscences," in *Gospel Doctrine,* 5th ed. (1939), 519–20.
3. *Deseret Weekly,* 19 Aug. 1893, 284.
4. *Gospel Doctrine,* 282–83.
5. In Conference Report, Apr. 1898, 47–48; paragraphing added.
6. In Conference Report, Apr. 1917, 4.
7. *Deseret News: Semi-Weekly,* 31 Mar. 1896, 1; paragraphing added.
8. *Gospel Doctrine,* 270.
9. In James R. Clark, comp., *Messages of the First Presidency of The Church of Jesus Christ of Latter-day Saints,* 6 vols. (1965–75), 5:91.
10. In *Messages of the First Presidency,* 5:93.
11. "The Gospel in Precept and Example," *Millennial Star,* 15 Mar. 1906, 162.
12. "Discourse by President Joseph F. Smith," *Millennial Star,* 11 Nov. 1897, 706–7.
13. In Conference Report, Apr. 1915, 7.
14. *Gospel Doctrine,* 236–38; paragraphing altered.
15. "Editor's Table," *Improvement Era,* Dec. 1902, 147.
16. In *Messages of the First Presidency,* 5:53.
17. In Conference Report, Oct. 1916, 8.
18. "Blind Obedience and Tithing," *Millennial Star,* 20 Jan. 1893, 79.

# Receiving a Testimony of Jesus Christ

*It is necessary for us to have the testimony of Jesus Christ in our hearts and to do the things that He has commanded.*

## From the Life of Joseph F. Smith

Throughout his ministry President Joseph F. Smith testified that Jesus is the Christ, the Son of the living God. He taught that all the sons and daughters of God could receive this personal revelation, this gift of the Spirit.

"When I as a boy first started out in the ministry," he explained, "I would frequently go out and ask the Lord to show me some marvelous thing, in order that I might receive a testimony. But the Lord withheld marvels from me, and showed me the truth, line upon line, precept upon precept, here a little and there a little, until he made me to know the truth from the crown of my head to the soles of my feet, and until doubt and fear had been absolutely purged from me. He did not have to send an angel from the heavens to do this, nor did he have to speak with the trump of an archangel. By the whisperings of the still small voice of the Spirit of the living God, he gave to me the testimony I possess. And by this principle and power he will give to all the children of men a knowledge of the truth that will stay with them, and it will make them to know the truth, as God knows it, and to do the will of the Father as Christ does it."[1]

President Smith testified: "I have received the witness of the Spirit of God in my own heart, which exceeds all other evidences, for it bears record to me, to my very soul, of the existence of my Redeemer, Jesus Christ. I know that he lives, and that in the last day he shall stand upon the earth, that he shall come to the people who shall be prepared for him."[2]

# Teachings of Joseph F. Smith

### A testimony of Jesus Christ comes as a glorious gift of God.

I consider that every principle of the Gospel which we have received is in itself a glorious gift of God unto the children of men. The gift of wisdom, the gift of understanding, the gift of prophecy, the gift of tongues, the gift of healing, the gift of testimony, the gift of knowledge, all these are designed by the Almighty to come to us through our obedience to the principles of life and salvation.[3]

Men do not receive the gift of . . . a testimony of the Spirit of the Living God in their hearts, [unless] they seek for it. The principle is: Thou shalt knock and it shall be opened unto thee; thou shalt ask and receive; thou shalt seek if thou wilt find [see Matthew 7:7–8]; and if you want wisdom, ask for it, as Solomon did; if you want knowledge and the testimony of the spirit in your hearts, seek for it earnestly. Put yourself in a position whereby you will be worthy to receive it, then it will come to you as a gift of God, and His name should be praised for the same.[4]

[A testimony] comes to us . . . because we put ourselves in harmony with the principle of communication from God to man. We believe, we repent of and confess our sins, we do that which the Lord requires in order to gain a remission of our sins, and thus we receive the gift of the Holy Spirit. Our minds become attuned to the Spirit of God, and to the method which God has instituted for revealing His mind to the children of men.

Now, it is a great thing for one to receive the witness in his heart of the divine mission of the Son of God and of the divine mission of the Prophet Joseph Smith. . . . We feel in our souls the truth of the principles which were restored through the Prophet Joseph Smith, and we feel it because we have, in some degree at least, put ourselves in a position to be in communication with the Spirit and hear the voice thereof when it speaks to us. The

Spirit of God speaks to our spirits. The Lord does not communicate to us very often through our natural senses, but when He speaks He speaks to the immortal part; the spirit of man receives the communications the Lord sends to His children, and we must therefore be in harmony to receive them.[5]

We must obtain this light [of testimony] by revelation, we cannot do it by our own wisdom. God will give us knowledge and understanding, he will lead us in the path of truth if we put our whole trust in him and not in man.[6]

A gift from God, if neglected, or unworthily used, is in time withdrawn; the testimony of the truth will not remain with one who, having received, uses not the sacred gift in the cause of individual and general advancement.[7]

This unmistakable assurance, which is derived through yielding obedience to and practising the principles of eternal life, is continually being confirmed, as it were, by "line upon line and precept upon precept," through the revelations of the Holy Spirit, which is a continuous and unfailing source of intelligence, of joy and happiness, drawing him who possesses it nearer unto God, and will eventually cause him to appear like unto his Maker.[8]

---

**The Holy Ghost bears witness in our hearts
that Jesus is the Christ.**

Jesus . . . is our fore-runner, he is our exemplar. The path which he marked out we have got to walk in, if we ever expect to dwell, and be crowned with him in his kingdom. We must obey and put our trust in him, knowing that he is the Savior of the world.

It is not a difficult thing for me to believe this; I read the Bible in which I find narrations of many of his doings, sayings, precepts, and examples. And I do not believe that any upright, honest man or woman, possessing common intelligence, can read the gospels of the New Testament and the testimonies therein given of the Savior, without intuitively feeling that he was what he professed to be. For every upright, honest person is possessed, more or less, of the Holy Spirit, and this holy messenger in the hearts of men bears record of the word of God; and when all such read these inspired writings, with honesty of heart and meekness of spirit, divested of prejudices and the false conceptions arising from traditions and erroneous training, the Spirit of the Lord bears witness in unmistakable language that burns with conviction, therefore, I believe that Jesus was the Christ, the Savior, the only begotten of the Father; and this too through reading the Bible.

But do we depend upon the Bible for this conviction and knowledge? No, thank the Lord we do not. What else have we to impart this knowledge and confirm this testimony? We have the Book of Mormon, the "stick of Ephraim," which has come to us by the gift and power of God, which also testifies of him, and which reveals an account of his mission to and dealings with the inhabitants of this continent, after his resurrection from the dead, when he came to this land to visit his "other sheep," to unite them in the one fold, that they might also be his sheep and he their great shepherd. Besides the conviction that the Book itself carries with it, we have the collateral testimony of him who translated it, who sealed his testimony with his blood; also that of other witnesses, who testify to the whole world that they saw the plates and the engravings thereon, from which the Book was translated. . . .

Here, then, are two witnesses—the Bible and the Book of Mormon, both bearing record of the same truth, that Jesus was the Christ, that he died and lives again, having burst the bands of death and triumphed over the grave. This latter additional evidence the Latter-day Saints have of this fact, over and above that possessed by the Christian world who do not believe in the Book of Mormon.

But is this all? No. We have here another book, the Doctrine and Covenants, which contains revelations from God through the prophet Joseph Smith, who lived contemporary with ourselves. They are Christ's words, declaring that he was the same that came to the Jews, that was lifted up on the cross, was laid in the tomb, burst the bands of death and came forth out of the grave. . . . Here, then, is another testimony of this divine truth; hence we have three witnesses. In the mouth of two or three witnesses, we are told, all things shall be established; and by the testimony of two or three witnesses shall we stand, or be condemned.

But would this satisfy me? It might, if I could obtain no further light or knowledge. But when greater light comes, and I have the privilege to make myself possessor of it, I could not remain satisfied with the lesser. We could never be satisfied nor happy hereafter, unless we receive a fulness of the light and blessings prepared for the righteous. . . .

It is given to us to know these things for ourselves. God has said he will show these things unto us; and for this purpose the Holy Ghost has been imparted to all who are entitled to it through submission, which bears record of the Father and the Son, and also takes of the things of God and shows them unto man. Convictions that we may previously have had respecting the truth the Holy Ghost confirms, giving us a positive assurance of their correctness, and through it we obtain a personal knowledge, not as one that has been told, but as one that has seen, felt, heard, and that knows for himself.

Then, in standing before you, my brethren and sisters, as a humble instrument in the hands of God, I testify, not by virtue of the knowledge I may have derived from books, but by the revelations of God to me, that Jesus is the Christ. I know that my Redeemer lives; I know that although the worms may destroy this body, that I shall in my flesh see God, and I shall behold him for myself and not for another. This light has come to me, and is in my heart and mind, and of it I testify, and through and by it I testify, and I know whereof I speak. . . .

Am I alone? No; there are tens of thousands to-day that can bear this testimony. They, too, know it for themselves; God has shown it to them, they have received the Holy Ghost, which has borne witness of these things in their hearts, and they likewise are not dependent upon books, nor upon the words of another, for they have received a knowledge from God themselves, and know as he knows and see as he sees in relation to these plain and precious things.[9]

## A testimony of Jesus Christ inspires us to do the things He has commanded.

We speak of the Savior, of Jesus the Son of God, and we feel safe and solid in him, and that our feet have rested on the very foundation of eternal truth when the spirit of Christ is in our hearts.

I want to say to my brethren and sisters, that if there is a man in all the world who has received more deeply and more keenly in his soul the love of Christ than I have, I would love to see him, I would love to be associated with such a man. Christ is indeed the Savior of my soul, the Savior of mankind. He has sacrificed his life for us that we might be saved, he has broken the bands of death, and has bid defiance to the grave, and bids us follow him. He has come forth from death unto life again, he has declared himself to be the way of salvation, the light and the life of the world, and I believe it with all my heart. I not only believe it, but as I know that the sun shines, so I know that belief in him inspires to good and not to evil; and as I know that his spirit prompts to purity of life, to honor, to uprightness, to honesty and to righteousness, and not to evil, so I know by all the proofs that it is possible for me to grasp that Jesus is the Christ, the Son of the living God, the Savior of mankind.

Yet with all this, with this assurance in my heart, with this knowledge that I have received, if I stop here, what good will it do me? Of what good will this knowledge be to me? What will this knowledge alone avail? It will avail this, that having received that testimony in my heart, having received in my soul the witness of the spirit of the living God, that Jesus is the Christ, and I stop there and go not any further, that very witness in my soul will add to my eternal damnation. Why? Because it is not only our duty to know that Jesus is the Christ but to keep the influence of his spirit in our souls. It is not only necessary to have his testimony in our hearts, but it is necessary that we should do the things that he has commanded, and the works of righteousness that he did, in order that we may attain to the exaltation that is in store for his children who do as well as believe; and those who stop short of this will most assuredly fail. "Not every one that saith unto me, Lord,

Lord, shall enter into the kingdom of heaven; but he that *doeth* the will of my Father which is in heaven." [Matthew 7:21.]

The Savior said: "Many will say to me in that day, Lord, Lord, have we not prophesied in thy name? and in thy name have cast out devils? and in thy name done many wonderful works? And then will I profess unto them, I never knew you; depart from me, ye that work iniquity." [Matthew 7:22–23.] And why? Because you profess to love me, with your lips, you professed to receive me, with your mouths, or with your words, but you did not the things that I commanded you to do; you did not repent of your sins, you did not love God with all your heart, mind and strength, you failed to love your neighbor as yourself, you failed to be baptized by one having authority to baptize for the remission of sins; you failed to receive the gift of the Holy Ghost by the laying on of hands; you failed to identify yourselves with my people; you did not come into my fold; you are not numbered with my chosen ones, and I do not know you, "depart from me, ye that work iniquity." To know to do good and not do it is sin. (James 4:17). This will be the case with those who simply believe. Believing, why don't you do the things that he requires? . . .

. . . It will not do for you to assume that you are Latter-day Saints while in your practices, in your course of life, in your deeds or acts, you are imitating . . . the unbeliever in God and in the divine mission of Jesus Christ. It will not do. The devil will take advantage of you, he will mislead you, and destroy you if you do not repent of deeds or acts that are not in harmony, or are inconsistent, with the gospel that you have received.[10]

---

## Our whole heart and soul should go out in love for the Savior.

A pure testimony is a tower of strength through all time.[11]

My brethren and sisters, I desire to bear my testimony to you; for I have received an assurance which has taken possession of my whole being. It has sunk deep into my heart; it fills every fiber of my soul; so that I feel to say before this people, and would be pleased to have the privilege of saying it before the whole world, that God has revealed unto me that Jesus is the Christ, the Son of the living God, the Redeemer of the world.[12]

I have absolute confidence in [Jesus Christ]. My whole heart and soul goes out with love for him. My hopes are built upon His glorious character and His word. He was without sin; He was spotless, and possessed power unto life eternal; He opened the way from the grave to everlasting life for me and all the children of men. My confidence in Him is boundless. My love for Him surpasses all else on earth, when I possess the Spirit of the Gospel as I should, and He to me is first and foremost. He is the greatest of all that has ever sojourned in this world of ours, and He came to be our beacon light, our guide and exemplar, and it is our business to follow Him.[13]

## Suggestions for Study

- What is a testimony? How do we receive a testimony of Jesus Christ? What part does "obedience to the principles of life and salvation" play in the development of a testimony?

- How has your testimony grown "line upon line and precept upon precept"? What blessings come to those who receive the continual revelations of the Holy Spirit?

- Under what conditions might the gift of testimony be withdrawn? How can we nurture our testimonies? What consequences follow the failure to nurture our testimonies?

- How can we show gratitude for the gift of testimony?

- How does studying the scriptures help us gain a testimony of Jesus Christ? In what spirit should we approach the scriptures in order for our testimonies to grow?

- How can we gain a personal knowledge that Jesus is the Christ, "not as one that has been told, but as one that . . . knows for himself"?

- How does a testimony received through the Holy Ghost exceed all other evidences? When you have been blessed with a witness from the Holy Ghost, how have you felt?

- Why is it necessary to do the things that the Savior has commanded as well as believe in Him? How has your testimony been strengthened by works of righteousness? How can we "keep the influence of [the Savior's] spirit in our souls"?

- How has President Smith's powerful witness of the Savior touched your heart? How have the testimonies of the First Presidency and the Quorum of the Twelve Apostles blessed you? As we bear our own testimonies, why should we center our thoughts on Jesus Christ?

## *Notes*

1. *Gospel Doctrine,* 5th ed. (1939), 7.
2. *Gospel Doctrine,* 506–7.
3. *Deseret News: Semi-Weekly,* 14 May 1895, 1.
4. In Conference Report, Oct. 1903, 4.
5. "Discourse by President Joseph F. Smith," *Millennial Star,* 6 Sept. 1906, 561–62.
6. *Deseret News: Semi-Weekly,* 29 Jan. 1878, 1.
7. *Gospel Doctrine,* 206.
8. *Deseret News: Semi-Weekly,* 28 Nov. 1876, 1.
9. *Deseret News: Semi-Weekly,* 30 Apr. 1878, 1; paragraphing added.
10. "Testimony," *Improvement Era,* Aug. 1906, 806–8; paragraphing added.
11. In Brian H. Stuy, comp., *Collected Discourses Delivered by President Wilford Woodruff, His Two Counselors, the Twelve Apostles, and Others,* 5 vols. (1987–92), 2:356.
12. *Gospel Doctrine,* 501.
13. In *Collected Discourses,* 5:55–56.

# Sustaining Those Who Are Called to Preside

*We should honor and sustain in truth and in deed our priesthood leaders who are called to preside.*

## From the Life of Joseph F. Smith

President Joseph F. Smith sustained his priesthood leaders in his heart and in his actions. Repeatedly his labors echoed the faithful words of Nephi: "I will go and do the things which the Lord hath commanded" (1 Nephi 3:7).

In October 1873, President Brigham Young again called him to serve a mission. Joseph F. Smith said of this time: "I was called on a mission after I had served four years on a homestead and it was only necessary for me to remain one year more to prove up and get my title to the land; but President Young said he wanted me to go to Europe on a mission, to take charge of the mission there. I did not say to him, 'Brother Brigham, I cannot go; I have got a homestead on my hands, and if I go I will forfeit it.' I said to Brother Brigham, 'All right, President Young; whenever you want me to go I will go; I am on hand to obey the call of my file leader.' And I went. I lost the homestead, and yet I never complained about it; I never charged Brother Brigham with having robbed me because of this. I felt that I was engaged in a bigger work than securing 160 acres of land. I was sent to declare the message of salvation to the nations of the earth. I was called by the authority of God on the earth, and I did not stop to consider myself and my little personal rights and privileges; I went as I was called, and God sustained and blessed me in it."[1]

# Teachings of Joseph F. Smith

## We raise our hands in token of a covenant to uphold and sustain our leaders.

In my judgment, one of the most important acts performed at the conferences of the Church is that in which we hold up our hands before the Lord to sustain the authorities of the Church and the organization thereof as it exists. But it is one of the important things that we do which rests with little weight upon some people. In other words, some people go away after holding up their hands to sustain the authorities of the Church and think no more about it, and act in many respects as though they had merely gone through a form to which they did not attach any importance whatever. I conceive this to be a wrong principle. . . . Those who covenant to keep the commandments of the Lord, and then violate that covenant by failing to observe those commandments, do no more than they do who raise their hands in token of a covenant to uphold and sustain the authorities of the Church and then fail to do it. The principle is the same in both cases: it is a violation of the covenant we make.[2]

It is a serious wrong in the presence of the Almighty for one to vote to sustain the authorities of the Church and then to go away and oppose them and trample under foot the counsels that they give; and we will be judged of the Lord for it.[3]

It is an important duty resting upon the Saints who vote to sustain the authorities of the Church, to do so not only by the lifting of the hand, the mere form, but in deed and in truth. There never should be a day pass but all the people composing the Church should lift up their voices in prayer to the Lord to sustain His servants who are placed to preside over them. . . . These men should have the faith of the people to sustain them in the discharge of their duties, in order that they may be strong in the Lord. . . .

. . . It is the command of the Lord that we shall meet together to . . . sustain the authorities of the Church, thus renewing our covenant to uphold God's authority which He has instituted in the earth for the government of His Church. And I cannot emphasize too strongly the importance of Latter-day Saints honoring and sustaining in truth and in deed the authority of the Holy Priesthood which is called to preside. The moment a spirit enters into the heart of a member to refrain from sustaining the constituted authorities of the Church, that moment he becomes possessed of a spirit which inclines to rebellion or dissension; and if he permit that spirit to take a firm root in his mind, it will eventually lead him into darkness and apostasy.[4]

It is well understood that we meet together in general conference twice a year for the purpose of presenting the names of those who have been chosen as presiding officers in the Church, and it is understood that those who occupy these positions are dependent upon the voice of the people for the continuance of the authority, the rights and privileges they exercise. The female members of this Church have the same privilege of voting to sustain their presiding officers as the male members of the Church, and the vote of a sister in good standing counts in every way equal with the vote of a brother.[5]

### As Latter-day Saints, we sustain and honor the General Authorities who are called to preside.

Now, while the commandments of God are to all the world, there are some special commandments that are applicable to the Latter-day Saints only. What are they? One of these commandments is, that we shall honor those who preside over us; in other words, we shall honor the Priesthood. I ask no man to honor me, unless I do that which is strictly in accord with the spirit of my calling and the priesthood which I hold. No member of the Church is bound to honor me if I step beyond that priesthood and authority which has been conferred upon me by the choice of God and the voice of the Church. But when I do speak by the Spirit of the Lord in accordance with the duties of my office, it is proper for every member of the Church to hearken to that which I say. For if it is said by the Spirit of God and in accordance with my duty, it is the word and will of the Almighty.

"And whatsoever they shall speak when moved upon by the Holy Ghost, shall be Scripture, shall be the will of the Lord, shall

President Joseph F. Smith with his son Joseph Fielding Smith, who was a member of the Quorum of the Twelve Apostles at the time of this picture in 1914 and later became the tenth President of the Church.

be the mind of the Lord, shall be the voice of the Lord, and the power of God unto salvation.

"Behold this is the promise of the Lord unto you; O ye my servants" [D&C 68:4–5].

It is the privilege of all to know whether I speak the truth by the Spirit of God or not. To the Church of Jesus Christ of Latter-day Saints it is given as a commandment that we shall hearken to the voice of the Spirit made manifest through those channels that God has appointed for the guidance of His people. . . . If I counsel in unrighteousness, I will be brought to judgment. No man can teach wickedness to this people and continue in it long; for God will detect him and will reveal the secrets of his heart; his purpose and intent will be made manifest to the Saints, and he will stand judged of the Spirit of God before the Saints. If you acknowledge . . . the President of the Church and he and his counselors as the presiding authority, then the member who does not give heed to their counsel deserves pity, for he is in transgression. These men will not counsel you wrong. . . .

. . . I never want to see the day come when these men, to whom you have entrusted the right and power to preside, shall have their mouths closed so that they dare not reprove sin or rebuke iniquity. . . . It is our duty to do it. We are here for that purpose. We are watchmen upon the towers of Zion [see Ezekiel 3:17–19]. It is our business and duty to point out errors and follies among men; and if men will not receive it, they must go their own way and abide the consequences. Those who will not obey righteous counsels will be the sufferers, and not those who rebuke iniquity.[6]

We propose to do our duty according to the light we possess, by the help of the loving Father. I propose to do nothing that I have not the most positive assurance is right, through the unanimity of my counselors, our seeing eye to eye, and our understanding alike together. . . . I do not propose to do anything, or suffer anything to be done or sanctioned which will affect the kingdom of God in the earth, except by common consent, or unless we can see eye to eye upon it, then I know we shall have strength behind us, that the power of God will be with us, and the Saints will uphold and sustain our hands.[7]

Men may become dissatisfied one with another, they may become dissatisfied towards the Presidency, the Quorum of the Twelve, or others, and may say in their hearts, "I do not like such an one; I do not believe he is as good as he should be, he has too many faults and weaknesses and, therefore, I cannot and will not acknowledge his authority, as I have not faith in the man." Doubtless there are those, too many perhaps, who feel that way, but the trouble is, . . . just because they have become dissatisfied with the individual and harbored feelings of bitterness in their hearts against their brethren, they lose sight of the designs of the Almighty; they turn against the authority of the Holy Priesthood; and through their blindness allow themselves to be led astray, and at last turn away from the Church.

Now how should it be? I will tell you. In the first place every person should know that the Gospel is true, as this is every one's privilege who is baptized and receives the Holy Ghost. A man may be grieved in his feelings because of some personality between him and [the President of the Church and his Counselors]; he may have feelings in his heart which lead him to think that he could not sustain us in his faith and prayers; but if this should be the case, what is the course for him to pursue? He should say in his heart, "God has established His Kingdom, and His Priesthood is upon the earth; and notwithstanding my dislike for certain men, I know that the Gospel is true and that God is with His people; and that if I will do my duty and keep His commandments, the clouds will roll by and the mists will disappear, the spirit of the Lord will come more fully to my relief and by and by I will be able to see,—if I am in error, wherein I erred, and then I will repent of it, for I know that every wrong thing will yet be made right." I think all men should feel that way.[8]

---

### Let us sustain our local authorities and listen to their counsel.

As the Presidency of the Church preside over the whole Church—over all the stakes, all the wards, and all the missionary fields in the world—so these men [the stake presidency] preside over this Stake of Zion, and all the wards and branches therein;

and when they call upon the people to sustain them in that which is right, if the people fail to sustain them the consequences shall be upon the heads of the people and not upon the heads of these men. It is their duty to rebuke iniquity and to reprove unrighteousness. It is their duty to counsel and exhort the people to be faithful and diligent throughout all their Stake. . . . I want you to distinctly understand this. . . . [The stake president has the] right to preside, to counsel, to direct, and to watch over the interests of the people here. . . .

. . . We have the written word for example, for instruction, for admonition, for reproof, for counsel and for exhortation. Every man should read and understand them, and then all will know that the oracles of God are in their midst. But when they do not read the word of God nor understand it, when the oracles speak they may not listen to them. The Stake Presidency are your oracles here. They are chosen of the Lord. . . . You ought to sustain and uphold them, and listen to their counsels. They will not guide you wrong; they will not direct you in wickedness; they will make no mistake in their counsel to you; for they stand as a beacon light to the people—not the only beacon light, but they stand in their place as the presidents of the Church in this Stake of Zion, and God will make Himself manifest through them to the people. Furthermore, it is the right of every man and woman to have revelation and wisdom from the Almighty, to know these men are good men, and are doing their duty.[9]

A bishop is the presiding officer of his ward, and where the bishop is in the ward, his counselors and those who are members of his ward are subject to his presidency. He cannot yield it up. He cannot give it to another; or, if he does, he violates one of the sacred principles of the government of the priesthood.[10]

Here is a man who says: "I do not have any faith in the bishop. I do not like the bishop. I do not believe in him, he is incompetent; he is partial; he is unjust; and I will not sustain him in his position in the Church." . . . Don't you forget it; [the bishop and his counselors] are there, not because we of our own will put them there. They are there because the Lord has designated that as the order of presidency in a ward, by divine authority, and the bishop holds authority there from God, not from man. . . .

. . . When a man says: "I am a Latter-day Saint; I am a member of the Church, in good standing, because I know what the principles of the gospel are, and I know what the principles of government are in the Church," for that man to say, "I oppose the bishop because I don't like him" or "because I haven't faith in him," is proof by that very act that he does not understand the principle of government and submission to divine authority. He therefore becomes obstreperous, unyielding, ungovernable, undesirable, and worthy to be dealt with according to his merits or demerits.[11]

A man may not have confidence in his Bishop or in one or both of his Counselors; . . . but because he may feel so, would it be right or consistent in him as an Elder in Israel, to set himself up as the judge of the Bishop or his Counselors and the whole Church? If one were to get in a position of this kind he would be like some [men who had apostatized from the Church]. . . . Do you think you could convince those of this class that they had apostatized from the Church? No; these men are firmly convinced in their own minds that they never apostatized. They stoutly and indignantly deny that they ever apostatized or turned away from the Church. . . . If I were to raise my hand against my Bishop, against the Twelve or the First Presidency, because I did not like them, that moment I should place myself in the position that these men now occupy, and that scores of others who have passed away have occupied, and say: "The Church has apostatized, Joseph Smith and Brigham Young, and John Taylor, have apostatized, but I am firm in the faith; all the people have gone astray because they will not acknowledge me." There is where the man is who rebels against the authority of the Priesthood, and at the same time endeavors to hold on to the faith. Never is there but one appointed at a time to hold the keys of the kingdom of God pertaining to the earth.[12]

Therefore, I say to you, honor the Presidency of the Stake and your Bishops, and all who are placed to preside in your midst. Sustain them in their positions by your faith and your prayers, and show them that you will help them in every good word and work, and God will bless you for it.[13]

**Sustaining our leaders is an evidence of goodwill, faith, and fellowship on our part.**

I believe it to be the duty of the Church to recognize and acknowledge every man who holds an official position in it, in his sphere and in his calling. I hold to the doctrine that the duty of a teacher is as sacred as the duty of an apostle, in the sphere in which he is called to act, and that every member of the Church is as much in duty bound to honor the teacher who visits him in his home, as he is to honor the office and counsel of the presiding quorum of the Church. They all have the Priesthood; they are all acting in their callings, and they are all essential in their places, because the Lord has appointed them and set them in his Church. We cannot ignore them; or, if we do, the sin will be upon our heads.[14]

We should not permit ourselves to go about from day to day with a spirit of murmuring and fault-finding in our hearts against those who are presented before us to be sustained in responsible positions. If we have anything in our hearts against any of these brethren, it is our duty, as conscientious members of the Church, first, as the Scriptures direct, to go to them alone and make known to them our feeling toward them and show them the cause of such feeling; not with a desire in our hearts to widen or increase the difficulty, but we should go to them in the spirit of reconciliation and brotherly love, in a true Christian spirit, so that if any feeling of bitterness exists within us it may be absolutely removed; and if we have cause against our brother, that he may be in a position to remedy the evil. We should seek to love one another and to sustain each other as children of God and as brothers and sisters in the cause of Zion.[15]

My brethren and sisters, I want to thank you . . . for the unanimity that has been manifested here by the uplifted hands of this vast congregation. I understand this as an evidence of good will, of faith and of fellowship on the part of this vast congregation to all the authorities, both general and local, or auxiliary, that have been presented before you, and that you will all abide the pledge you have given to the Lord and to one another by the

him to this work, that He should pass him by and go to some-body else to accomplish the same purpose. No sensible person would accept for one moment such a proposition. To seriously contemplate any such idea would be charging the Almighty with inconsistency, and with being the author of confusion, discord and schism. The Kingdom of God never could be established on earth in any such way.[21]

If [the President of the Church] should become unfaithful, God would remove him out of his place. I testify in the name of Israel's God that He will not suffer the head of the Church, him whom He has chosen to stand at the head, to transgress His Laws and apostatize; the moment he should take a course that would in time lead to it, God would take him away. Why? Because to suf-fer a wicked man to occupy that position, would be to allow, as it were, the fountain to become corrupted, which is something He will never permit.[22]

## God will honor and magnify His servants.

[This] is not the work of man but of God Almighty; and it is His business to see that the men who occupy this position are men after His own heart, men that will receive instructions from Him, and that will carry out the same according to the counsels of His will.[23]

[God's] priesthood will ever be found to be composed of the right men for the place, of men whose backs will be fitted for the burden, men through whom he can work and regulate the affairs of his Church according to the counsels of his own will. And the moment that individuals look to any other source, that moment they throw themselves open to the seductive influences of Satan, and render themselves liable to become servants of the devil; they lose sight of the true order through which the blessings of the Priesthood are to be enjoyed; they step outside of the pale of the kingdom of God, and are on dangerous ground.[24]

God will honor and magnify his servants in the sight of the people. He will sustain them in righteousness. He will lift them on high, exalt them into his presence, and they will partake of his glory forever and ever.[25]

227

I bear my testimony to the divine authority of those who have succeeded the Prophet Joseph Smith in the presidency of this Church. They were men of God. . . . I can bear testimony to the integrity, to the honor, to the purity of life, to the intelligence, and to the divinity of the mission and calling of Brigham [Young], of John [Taylor], of Wilford [Woodruff], and of Lorenzo [Snow]. They were inspired of God to fill the mission to which they were called, and I know it. I thank God for that testimony and for the Spirit that prompts me and impels me towards these men, toward their mission, toward this people, toward my God and my Redeemer.[26]

My brethren and sisters, my business, my duty, is to preach the Gospel of Jesus Christ and Him crucified and risen from the dead and sitting enthroned in power, glory and majesty on the right hand of his Father, our God. . . . I must do the best I can, the best I know how, for those whom God has entrusted to my care. I must also do my duty toward the people of God to whom He has willed that I should be a humble minister and teacher of the Gospel.[27]

It is the Lord's work, and I plead with you not to forget it. I implore you not to disbelieve it; for it is true. All that the Lord said concerning this latter-day work will come to pass. The world cannot prevent it. . . . God is at the helm, and he will lead his people to victory.[28]

Whenever, if ever, I say a word that is acceptable to God, whenever I speak His truth, it is by the presence and influence of His Spirit, and it is to His honor and to His glory that I do it. I never have taken any honor unto myself. I want no honor; I claim none except that of being a member of the Church of Christ, the honor of having a standing unsullied, undefiled, unshaken, and immovable, in the kingdom of my God and His Christ.[29]

It is the kingdom of God or nothing, so far as I am concerned. I cut no figure personally in this work, and I am nothing except in the humble effort to do my duty as the Lord gives me the ability to do it. But it is the kingdom of God. What I mean by the kingdom of God is the organization of the Church of Jesus Christ of Latter-day Saints, of which Jesus Christ is the king and the head.[30]

# Suggestions for Study

- Who leads the Church? Why is it important for us to understand that "no *man* will lead God's people nor his work"?

- What blessings are promised to the members of the Church when they faithfully follow the President of the Church? (See also D&C 21:4–6.) In what ways have you been blessed by following the counsel of the living prophets?

- How can you sustain the First Presidency and the Quorum of the Twelve Apostles in their work?

- What do the "exalted titles" of prophet, seer, and revelator mean? To whom do these titles apply?

- What are the keys of the priesthood? What does it mean to sustain the President of the Church as the only person on earth who possesses and is authorized to exercise all priesthood keys?

- Why is it vital to know that only the President of the Church is appointed to receive revelation for the entire Church? How can we guard against believing false prophets and false revelations?

- Why can we be assured that the President of the Church will always lead us according to God's will?

## Notes

1. See Conference Report, Oct. 1901, 71.
2. *Gospel Doctrine,* 5th ed. (1939), 169.
3. *Gospel Doctrine,* 154.
4. *Gospel Doctrine,* 76.
5. *Gospel Doctrine,* 210.
6. *Gospel Doctrine,* 138–39.
7. In Conference Report, Oct. 1902, 87.
8. In Conference Report, Apr. 1898, 69.
9. *Gospel Doctrine,* 176.
10. In James R. Clark, comp., *Messages of the First Presidency of The Church of Jesus Christ of Latter-day Saints,* 6 vols. (1965–75), 4:248.
11. In *Messages of the First Presidency,* 4:307.
12. *Gospel Doctrine,* 177–78.
13. *Gospel Doctrine,* 136.
14. *Gospel Doctrine,* 176.
15. *Gospel Doctrine,* 43–44.
16. *Gospel Doctrine,* 175–76.
17. *Gospel Doctrine,* 174.
18. In *Messages of the First Presidency,* 4:270.
19. In *Messages of the First Presidency,* 4:154.
20. *Gospel Doctrine,* 41–42.
21. *Deseret News: Semi-Weekly,* 26 June 1883, 1.
22. *Deseret News: Semi-Weekly,* 26 June 1883, 1.
23. *Deseret News: Semi-Weekly,* 26 June 1883, 1.
24. *Gospel Doctrine,* 42.
25. *Gospel Doctrine,* 502.
26. *Gospel Doctrine,* 169.
27. In Conference Report, Oct. 1915, 6–7.
28. *Gospel Doctrine,* 502.
29. In Conference Report, Apr. 1912, 137–38.
30. *Gospel Doctrine,* 154.

# Observing the Sabbath:
# That Your Joy May Be Full

*The Sabbath is a day set apart by God for us to worship,*
*to pray, and to pay our devotions to the Most High.*

## From the Life of Joseph F. Smith

President Joseph F. Smith recognized and taught the great responsibility Latter-day Saints have to honor the Sabbath day. He taught the Saints to worship the Lord on the Sabbath and to use the time to teach and bless their families. He said: "On the Sabbath days, as far as I am concerned, between the hours of service, I would love to have the privilege of sitting down in my home with my family and conversing with them, and visiting with them, and becoming better acquainted with them. I would like to have the privilege of occupying as much time as I could conveniently on the Sabbath day for this purpose; to get acquainted with my children, keep in touch with them, and to keep them in touch with the scriptures, and to think of something besides fun and jokes and laughter and merriment, and such things as these."[1]

He also taught the consequences of desecrating the day hallowed by the Lord. On Sunday, 12 June 1898, in the Salt Lake City Tabernacle he said: "As I came to this meeting I overtook one of the brethren, and he remarked to me that as he passed by the station he saw a vast crowd of people there ready to go out to some pleasure resort. . . . If any of those profess to be Latter-day Saints, then the course they are pursuing today is contrary to the law of God, contrary to the covenants they have made in the waters of baptism, and contrary to the covenants entered into in the most sacred places to which Latter-day Saints are admitted. They are violating the Sabbath day, they are dishonoring a commandment of the Lord; they are proving themselves disobedient to the law, and they are doing that which is not pleasing in the sight of God, and which will result eventually in their injury, if not in their apostasy."[2]

# Teachings of Joseph F. Smith

### The Lord has set apart and hallowed one day in seven.

God made or designated the Sabbath day for a day of rest, a day of worship, a day for goodly deeds, and for humility and penitence, and the worship of the Almighty in spirit and in truth.[3]

There is a growing tendency throughout the land to disregard the observance of the Sabbath day. The command: "Remember the Sabbath day to keep it holy," is as much the law to-day as when it was given to Israel on Mount Sinai [Exodus 20:8].[4]

The Sabbath is a day of rest and of worship, designated and set apart by special commandment of the Lord to the Church of Jesus Christ of Latter-day Saints, and we should honor and keep it holy. We should also teach our children this principle.[5]

One day in seven has been set apart and hallowed for a day of worship, a day of solemn thought, a day of prayer and thanksgiving, and to partake of the Lord's Supper in memory of Him and His matchless atonement. Let us teach our children that they should observe the Sabbath to keep it holy, and that, too, because they love to do it as also because God has commanded it. Then they will get recreation and rest, change and pleasure, in a legitimate way on other days. . . . Let us not desecrate the Sabbath.[6]

### What shall we do on the Sabbath day?

Honor the Sabbath day, and keep it holy. Worship the Lord on the Sabbath day. Do not work. Go not out to seek vain pleasures on the Sabbath. Rest, and refresh the mind in prayer, study, and thought upon the principles of life and salvation. These are legitimate labors for the Sabbath day. . . .

Let the people go from here to their homes and take this with them, and extend it to the absent members of their families. Say to them that the presidency of the Church of Jesus Christ of Latter-day Saints are against the violation of the Sabbath day.[7]

To observe the Sabbath day properly is the plain duty of every Latter-day Saint—and that includes the young men and young women and the boys and girls. It may seem strange that it should be necessary to repeat this often-asserted fact. But there appear to be some people, and sometimes whole communities, who neglect this duty, and therefore stand in need of this admonition.

What are we required to do on the Sabbath day? The revelations of the Lord to the Prophet Joseph are very plain on this subject, and these should govern us, for they are in strict harmony with the teachings of the Savior. Here are some of the simple requirements:

The Sabbath is appointed unto you to rest from your labors.

The Sabbath is a special day for you to worship, to pray, and to show zeal and ardor in your religious faith and duty—to pay devotions to the Most High.

The Sabbath is a day when you are required to offer your time and attention in worship of the Lord, whether in meeting, in the home, or wherever you may be—that is the thought that should occupy your mind.

The Sabbath day is a day when, with your brethren and sisters, you should attend the meetings of the Saints, prepared to partake of the sacrament of the Lord's supper; having first confessed your sins before the Lord and your brethren and sisters, and forgiven your fellows as you expect the Lord to forgive you.

On the Sabbath day you are to do no other thing than to prepare your food with singleness of heart, that your fasting may be perfect, and your joy may be full. This is what the Lord calls fasting and prayer [see D&C 59:13–14].

The reason for this required course upon the Sabbath day is also plainly stated in the revelations. It is that one may more fully keep himself unspotted from the world; and to this end, also, the Saints are required to go to the house of prayer and offer up their sacraments on the Sabbath day [see D&C 59:9]. . . .

The Lord is not pleased with people who know these things and do them not.

The Salt Lake 20th Ward choir in the early 1900s. President Joseph F. Smith regarded the music sung by the "choirs of the Saints" as "gracious praise of God," which is important to our worship on the Sabbath day (*Gospel Doctrine*, 259).

Men are not resting from their labors when they plow, and plant and haul and dig. They are not resting when they linger around the home all day on Sunday, doing odd jobs that they have been too busy to do on other days.

Men are not showing zeal and ardor in their religious faith and duty when they hustle off early Sunday morning . . . to the canyons, the resorts, and to visit friends or places of amusement with their wives and children. They are not paying their devotions in this way to the Most High.

Not in seeking pleasure and recreation do they offer their time and attention in the worship of the Lord; nor can they thus rejoice in the spirit of forgiveness and worship that comes with partaking of the holy sacrament.

Boys and young men are not fasting with singleness of heart that their joy may be full when they spend the Sabbath day loafing around the village ice-cream stand or restaurant, playing games, or in buggy riding, fishing, shooting, or engaged in physical sports, excursions and outings. Such is not the course that will keep them unspotted from the world, but rather one that will deprive them of the rich promises of the Lord, giving them sorrow instead of joy, and unrest and anxiety instead of the peace that comes with works of righteousness.[8]

We derive, or would derive all the benefit if we would only devote every hour on the Sabbath to some work, or some pursuit, or some study, that would improve our minds and make us more fully acquainted with our duties in the Church, with the law of the Church, with the commandments of God, and with the precepts of the gospel of Jesus Christ. . . .

My belief is that it is the duty of Latter-day Saints to honor the Sabbath day and keep it holy, just as the Lord has commanded us to do. Go to the house of prayer. Listen to instructions. Bear your testimony to the truth. Drink at the fountain of knowledge and of instruction, as it may be opened for us from those who are inspired to give us instruction. When we go home, get the family together. Let us sing a few songs. Let us read a chapter or two in the Bible, or in the Book of Mormon, or in the book of Doctrine and Covenants. Let us discuss the principles of the gospel which pertain to advancement in the school of divine knowledge, and in this way occupy one day in seven. . . .

I think it is a good thing for us to take our children under our wings, so to speak, at least one day in the week, and teach them honor and honesty, and reverence for that which is right and divine, and teach them to respect age and infirmity, and to be kind to the stranger who is within our gates. . . . We should teach them politeness. We should teach our boys to be gentlemen, and our girls to be ladies. And when I speak of a lady or a gentleman, I mean a boy or a girl, or a man or a woman, who observes genuine modesty, meekness, mildness, patience, love and kindness toward the children of men. . . .

There are a great many things that we can do on the Sabbath day that would entertain, interest, and instruct our children at home, between the hours of service. . . . Let them have amusements at the proper time, but let them be taught better things on the Sabbath day.[9]

## Saturday evening may be wisely set apart as an introduction to the Lord's day.

It is incumbent on members of the Church to so plan their work that there shall be no excuse for robbing the Lord's day of its sanctity. To this end let the boys and girls have [time] during the week, which may be profitably used for recreations, leaving the Sabbath for spiritual culture and worship. It is equally obligatory that we so plan our amusements that these shall not interfere with our worship.[10]

Saturday evening may be wisely set apart as a time for thoughtful conversation or helpful reading as an introduction to the Sabbath day.[11]

A good modern . . . commandment might read something like this: Do not so overwork and fret on Saturday as to deprive the Sabbath of the devotions and worship that belong to it as a day of rest.

In the home, Saturday is the day set apart for house cleaning, for extra cooking, for mending and all sorts of repairs that the Sabbath is thought to require. In business, Saturday is a day for picking up all loose ends, for closing up all the unfinished details of a week's work.

The consequences of our modern treatment of the last day of the week are too often manifested in an indolence and supine indifference that make our feelings and a total lack of energy almost incompatible with the spirit of worship. No worn-out man or woman, by the excessive toil of an early Saturday morning and a late Saturday night, can properly worship God in spirit and in truth.[12]

## Persons who habitually desecrate the Lord's day will lose the Spirit of the Lord.

Thou shalt honor the Sabbath day and keep it holy. Do we do it? Is it necessary to do it? It is absolutely necessary to do so in order that we may be in harmony with God's law and commandments; and whenever we transgress that law or that commandment we are guilty of transgressing the law of God. And what will be the result, if we continue? Our children will follow in our footsteps; they will dishonor the command of God to keep one day holy in seven; and will lose the spirit of obedience to the laws of God and his requirements, just as the father will lose it if he continues to violate the commandments.[13]

Persons who habitually desecrate the Lord's day cannot be held in fellowship, and members of the Church who neglect public worship and the partaking of the Sacrament and do not remember the Sabbath day to keep it holy, will become weak in the faith and spiritually sickly, and will lose the Spirit and favor of God, and ultimately forfeit their standing in the Church and their exaltation with the obedient and faithful.[14]

The Lord has said, "Remember the Sabbath day, to keep it holy." It is a law of God, not only unto this people, but unto all mankind. The member of the Church who does not honor the Sabbath day and keep it holy is in transgression; he continues not in the word of truth; he is not in very deed a disciple of Christ; he will not know the truth, and the truth cannot make him free unless he does know it and live by it.[15]

Theaters and various public amusements are now held on the Sabbath day contrary to the revelations of the Lord, and they prove a potent factor in destroying the faith of those who participate in this practice. The parents of the youth of Zion should guard their children against this and all other evils, for they will be held responsible should their children go astray through their neglect.[16]

It is as much the duty of the Latter-day Saints to honor the Sabbath day, and to attend to those duties which are required at their hands upon the Sabbath, as it is for them to be honest with their neighbors and otherwise to live righteous lives. . . . It is also the duty of the parents to set an example before their children in honoring the Sabbath day, in prayerfulness in the family circle, and in attending to every duty as Latter-day Saints. The father and mother who neglect to teach their children and to encourage them to perform their duties, will live to regret their own folly.[17]

## Those who honor the Sabbath enjoy great temporal and spiritual blessings.

Sunday is a day of rest, a change from the ordinary occupations of the week, but it is more than that. It is a day of worship, a day in which the spiritual life of man may be enriched. A day of indolence, a day of physical recuperation is too often a very different thing from the God-ordained day of rest. Physical exhaustion and indolence are incompatible with a spirit of worship. A proper observance of the duties and devotions of the Sabbath day will, by its change and its spiritual life, give the best rest that men can enjoy on the Sabbath day.[18]

I sincerely desire . . . that we may be strengthened in our faith; and that we may become better Latter-day Saints than we have been in the past. This is one of the principal objects we have in meeting together on the Sabbath day. . . . I am persuaded that we have fallen into a habit of coming to meeting without any special contrition of heart. This may be considered a hard saying, and it may not apply to all of us, but I am convinced that many come to meeting listlessly, without a special purpose. I think that we should come to acknowledge before the Lord that we remember the Sabbath day and that we propose to learn of His ways. . . .

I think all should be imbued with the thought that there is a portion of this work [that] depends on every person. It is for each to realize that he or she will reap what is sown. Therefore, each should labor with a determination and when we come together each should have a prayerful spirit and let his soul go out, not alone for himself, but toward the whole church. If this were done, none would go away from the house of worship without experiencing the spirit of God.[19]

Now, what is the promise to the Saints who observe the Sabbath? The Lord declares that inasmuch as they do this with cheerful hearts and countenances, the fulness of the earth is theirs: "the beasts of the field and the fowls of the air, and that which climbeth upon the trees and walketh upon the earth. Yea, and the herb, and the good things which cometh of the earth, whether for food or for raiment, or for houses, or for barns, or for orchards, or for gardens, or for vineyards." [D&C 59:16–17.]

These are all made for the benefit and use of man to please the eye and to gladden the heart, to strengthen the body and to enliven the soul. All are promised to those who keep the commandments, and among the commandments is this important one, to observe properly the Sabbath day. . . .

Let us play and take recreation to our hearts' content during other days, but on the Sabbath let us rest, worship, go to the house of prayer, partake of the sacrament, eat our food with singleness of heart, and pay our devotions to God, that the fulness of the earth may be ours, and that we may have peace in this world and eternal life in the world to come.[20]

## Suggestions for Study

- For what purposes has the Lord "set apart and hallowed" the Sabbath day? What are the blessings of having a day of rest and worship?

- What does it mean to rest from our labors on the Sabbath? What are "legitimate labors for the Sabbath day"? How can we teach our family members to honor the Sabbath?

- What does it mean to be "unspotted from the world"? How does Sabbath observance help us do this?

- How are joy and rejoicing a part of Sabbath observance? (See also D&C 59:13–14.) How can dishonoring the Sabbath lead to unhappiness, loss of the Spirit, and apostasy?

- What are our family responsibilities on the Sabbath? On the Sabbath, how can we teach our children "reverence for that which is right and divine"?

- How can our activities on Saturday add to or detract from our Sabbath worship?

- What is our responsibility when we go to Sunday meetings? What blessings do we receive when we have the true spirit of worship at our meetings?

- What spiritual blessings do we enjoy when we honor the Sabbath? What temporal blessings are we promised? (See also D&C 59:9–23.)

We have a glorious destiny before us; we are engaged in a glorious work. It is worth all our attention, it is worth our lives and everything the Lord has put into our possession, and then ten thousand times more. Indeed, there is no comparison, it is all in all, it is incomparable. It is all that is and all that ever will be. The gospel is salvation, and without it there is nothing worth having.[7]

---

### We are each responsible to do all we can to gain our salvation.

Let us work out our salvation in fear and trembling before our Father, and be faithful to the end. Remember that you have enlisted in this work for time and for all eternity. There is no backing out of it, no falling away from it, except in sin, and then comes the penalty of transgression. But if you expect exaltation; if you expect fathers and mothers, brothers and sisters, kindred and friends; if you expect glory, intelligence and endless lives, you must get them in God's work; for nowhere outside can you get them. Therefore, let every sympathy and interest be centered in this cause. Let all your love go out toward this cause, and this alone. Let the world go.[8]

The gospel of Jesus Christ is the power of God unto salvation, and it is absolutely necessary for every man and woman in the Church of Christ to work righteousness, to observe the laws of God, and keep the commandments that he has given, in order that they may avail themselves of the power of God unto salvation in this life.[9]

We believe it is necessary that men in this age should live and act and be in touch with God the Father and with the Son, and that they should know them, whom to know is eternal life. We believe in order to know them and be in touch with them it is necessary in this age that we should live as the Saints did in ancient times, so that we may enjoy the same blessings which they did, and be taught of Him day by day, line upon line, precept upon precept, here a little and there a little, until we come to a knowledge of the Father and know Him for ourselves. It is impossible for me to know for you, or for any man to know for me. The Spirit of God does not reveal to you the Gospel, or bear witness to you of the Father, for me. I cannot save you; you cannot save me. No man can be a savior in this sense to any other man. Yet the man who has the testimony of the Spirit in his heart and who has a knowledge of the first principles of the Gospel may declare them to another, and by so declaring another soul may be convinced of the truth and be led to embrace it for himself. But it is *his* obedience to the Gospel and *his* own works of righteousness which save him, and not those of the man that bears testimony to him. It is only in this way that the man can be saved.[10]

You must not only believe, but you must obey and do the things that [God] commands. You must not only do that, but you must give your heart, your affection and your whole soul with a willing mind to God. You must give up your will to the will of the Father, and you must do all things that He requires at your hands, if you will be saved and exalted in His presence.[11]

---

### We are to labor to save our own.

Oh! God, let me not lose my own. I can not afford to lose mine, whom God has given to me and whom I am responsible for before the Lord, and who are dependent upon me for guidance, for instruction, for proper influence. Father, do not permit me to lose interest in my own, in trying to save others. Charity begins at home. Life everlasting should begin at home. I should feel very badly to be made to realize, by and by, that through my neglect of home, while trying to save others, I have lost my own. I do not want that. The Lord help me to save my own, so far as one can help another. I realize I cannot save anybody, but I can teach them how to be saved. I can set an example before my children how they can be saved, and it is my duty to do that first. I owe it more to them than to anybody else in the world. Then, when I have accomplished the work I should do in my own home circle, let me extend my power for good abroad just as far as I can.[12]

Our mission in this world is to do good, to put down iniquity under our feet, to exalt righteousness, purity, and holiness in the hearts of the people, and to establish in the minds of our children, above all other things, a love for God and his word, that shall be in them as a fountain of light, strength, faith and power, leading them on from childhood to old age, and making them firm believers in the word of the Lord, in the restored gospel and Priesthood, and in the establishment of Zion, no more to be thrown down or given to another people. If there is anything that I desire above another in this world, it is that my children shall become established in this knowledge and faith, so that they can never be turned aside from it.[13]

A soul saved out in the world is as precious in the sight of God as a soul saved at home. But we have work to do right at home, at our own doors; and it will not do for us to neglect the work necessary to be done at our own thresholds, and then go out into the world to do work that is no more necessary. Let us do our duty everywhere.[14]

---

### We are to labor for the salvation of the living and the dead.

Let us sustain Christ, his people, and his cause of righteousness and redemption; let us sustain one another in the right, and kindly admonish one another in regard to wrongdoing, that we may be friends and saviors on Mount Zion, one for another, and that we may help the weak and strengthen them, encourage the doubtful and bring light to their right understanding as far as it is possible, that we may be instrumental in the hands of God of being saviors among men. Not that we have power to save men. We have not; but we have power to show them how they can obtain salvation through obedience to the laws of God. We can show them how to walk in order to be saved, for we have the right to do that, we have knowledge and understanding as to how to do it, and it is our privilege to teach it . . . by example as well as by precept among our associates wherever we are in the world.[15]

Our mission has been to save men. We have been laboring . . . to bring men to a knowledge of the gospel of Jesus Christ, to bring them to repentance, to obedience to the requirements of God's law. We have been striving to save men from error, to persuade them to turn away from evil and to learn to do good.[16]

Our mission is to save, to preserve from evil, to exalt mankind, to bring light and truth into the world, to prevail upon the people of the earth to walk righteously before God, and to honor him in their lives.[17]

The test . . . of our soul's greatness is . . . to be sought in our ability to comfort and console, our ability to help others, rather than in our ability to help ourselves and crowd others down in the struggle of life.[18]

We should always aim to help [others] to victory—not to defeat them! Our aim is life eternal—our object to lift up mankind—not to debase them.[19]

Our business is to save the world, to save mankind; to bring them into harmony with the laws of God and with principles of righteousness and of justice and truth, that they may be saved in the kingdom of our God, and become, eventually, through obedience to the ordinances of the gospel, heirs of God and joint heirs with Jesus Christ. That is our mission.[20]

We will not finish our work until we have saved ourselves, and then not until we shall have saved all depending upon us; for we are to become saviors upon Mount Zion, as well as Christ. We are called to this mission. The dead are not perfect without us, neither are we without them. We have a mission to perform for and in their behalf; we have a certain work to do in order to liberate those who, because of their ignorance and the unfavorable circumstances in which they were placed while here, are unprepared for eternal life; we have to open the door for them, by performing ordinances which they cannot perform for themselves, and which are essential to their release from the "prison-house," to come forth and live according to God in the spirit, and be judged according to men in the flesh.[21]

The work for our dead, which the Prophet Joseph laid upon us with more than ordinary injunction, instructing us that we should look after those of our kinfolk and our ancestors who have died without the knowledge of the gospel, should not be neglected. We should avail ourselves of those sacred and potent ordinances of the gospel which have been revealed as essential to the happiness, salvation and redemption of those who have lived in this world when they could not learn the gospel and have died without the knowledge of it, and are now waiting for us, their children, who are living in an age when these ordinances can be performed, to do the work necessary for their release from the prison-house. Through our efforts in their behalf their chains of bondage will fall from them, and the darkness surrounding them will clear away, that light may shine upon them and they shall hear in the spirit world of the work that has been done for them by their children here, and will rejoice with you in your performance of these duties.[22]

There is never a time, there never will come a time to those who hold the Priesthood in the Church of Jesus Christ of Latter-day Saints, when men can say of themselves that they have done enough. So long as life lasts, and so long as we possess ability to do good, to labor for the upbuilding of Zion, and for the benefit of the human family, we ought, with willingness, to yield with alacrity to the requirements made of us to do our duty, little or great.[23]

## Suggestions for Study

- Why is it important to know that every person has been sent into the world "to accomplish a mission"? Why is it impossible for us to accomplish our missions by "laboring exclusively" for ourselves?

- How can we make God's work our work? Why is the work of the Lord worth "all our attention"? How should our choices reflect our commitment to the Lord's work?

- What must we do beyond believing and obeying to be "saved and exalted in [God's] presence"? What does it mean to you to give "your heart, your affection and your whole soul with a willing mind to God"? After all our effort, how do we receive salvation? (See also 2 Nephi 25:23.)

- What things should we seek to establish in the minds of our family members "above all other things"?

- How can we strive to save our own and still fulfill our other service responsibilities? How can our service to others in the Church and elsewhere be a blessing to our family?

- How can we seek "to exalt mankind"? What can we do to assist others to be faithful to the laws of God?

- What can we do to remove the "chains of bondage" from those who have died without a knowledge of the gospel? How does it make you feel to know that the people you help "rejoice with you in your performance of these duties"?

- Why is "the test . . . of our soul's greatness" found in "our ability to help others"? Why do you think this is so? How and when have you made sacrifices for the good of others? How did you feel when you did this?

## Notes

1. In Conference Report, Oct. 1918, 2.
2. In Conference Report, Oct. 1901, 69.
3. *Gospel Doctrine*, 5th ed. (1939), 460.
4. *Gospel Doctrine*, 249.
5. *Gospel Doctrine*, 115–16.
6. *Gospel Doctrine*, 397.
7. *Gospel Doctrine*, 84.
8. *Deseret Weekly*, 5 May 1894, 608.
9. *Gospel Doctrine*, 73.
10. "Discourse by President Joseph F. Smith," *Millennial Star*, 19 Sept. 1895, 596–97.
11. *Deseret News: Semi-Weekly*, 9 Aug. 1898, 1.
12. *Gospel Doctrine*, 462.
13. *Gospel Doctrine*, 141–42.
14. *Gospel Doctrine*, 390.
15. *Gospel Doctrine*, 255.
16. *Gospel Doctrine*, 72.
17. *Gospel Doctrine*, 73.
18. *Gospel Doctrine*, 265.
19. Joseph F. Smith to his son Hyrum M. Smith, 31 July 1896, in *Truth and Courage: Letters of Joseph F. Smith*, ed. Joseph Fielding McConkie (n.d.), 52.
20. *Gospel Doctrine*, 150.
21. *Gospel Doctrine*, 442.
22. *Gospel Doctrine*, 469–70.
23. *Gospel Doctrine*, 188.

# The Wrongful Road of Abuse

*We should never abuse others*
*but should show compassion and tenderness to all,*
*especially to family members.*

## From the Life of Joseph F. Smith

President Joseph F. Smith was a tender and gentle man who expressed sorrow at any kind of abuse. He understood that violence would beget violence, and his own life was an honest expression of compassion and patience, warmth and understanding.

On one occasion President Smith said: "I witnessed a little circumstance in our meeting this afternoon in the aisle; a little child was sitting by its mother on a seat. Somebody came along and took the little child off its seat, and occupied the seat himself, leaving the child to stand. I want to say to you, my brethren and sisters, that that act sent a pang to my heart. I would not, for anything . . . grieve the heart of a little child in the house of God, lest an impression should be left upon its mind that would make the house of worship a distasteful place, and it would prefer not to come within its walls, than to come and be offended."[1]

President Smith often counseled his brothers and sisters to treat each other with the greatest kindness. Violence or behavior that demeaned another person was unthinkable to him. Husbands and wives were to hold one another in the highest esteem and teach their children by example to respect family members and all other people.

# Teachings of Joseph F. Smith

## We should treat each other with the greatest respect and courtesy.

Let us conquer ourselves, and then go to and conquer all the evil that we see around us, as far as we possibly can. And we will do it without using violence; we will do it without interfering with the agency of men or of women. We will do it by persuasion, by long-suffering, by patience, and by forgiveness and love unfeigned, by which we will win the hearts, the affections and the souls of the children of men to the truth as God has revealed it to us.[2]

[God] has made us in his own form and likeness, and here we are male and female, parents and children. And we must become more and more like him—more like him in love, in charity, in forgiveness, in patience, long-suffering and forbearance, in purity of thought and action, intelligence, and in all respects, that we may be worthy of exaltation in his presence.[3]

Parents . . . should love and respect each other, and treat each other with respectful decorum and kindly regard, all the time. The husband should treat his wife with the utmost courtesy and respect. The husband should never insult her; he should never speak slightly of her, but should always hold her in the highest esteem in the home, in the presence of their children. . . . The wife, also should treat the husband with the greatest respect and courtesy. Her words to him should not be keen and cutting and sarcastic. She should not pass slurs or insinuations at him. She should not nag him. She should not try to arouse his anger or make things unpleasant about the home. The wife should be a joy to her husband, and she should live and conduct herself at home so the home will be the most joyous, the most blessed place on earth to her husband. This should be the condition of the husband, wife, the father and the mother, within the sacred precinct of that holy place, the home.

Then it will be easy for the parents to instill into the hearts of their children not only love for their fathers and their mothers, not only respect and courtesy towards their parents, but love

*Christ with the Children*, by Harry Anderson. Jesus Christ loved little children and taught that "whosoever shall offend one of these little ones that believe in me, it is better for him that a millstone were hanged about his neck, and he were cast into the sea" (Mark 9:42).

251

and courtesy and deference between the children at home. The little brothers will respect their little sisters. The little boys will respect one another. The little girls will respect one another and the girls and boys will respect one another, and treat one another with that love, that deference and respect that should be observed in the home on the part of the little children. Then . . . the foundation of a correct education has been laid in the heart and mind of the child at home.[4]

## Husbands should treat their wives with tenderness.

Think what it means to hold keys of authority which—if exercised in wisdom and in righteousness—are bound to be respected by the Father, the Son, and the Holy Ghost! Do you honor this Priesthood? . . . Would you, as an elder in the Church of Jesus Christ, dishonor your wife or your children? Would you desert the mother of your children, the wife of your bosom, the gift of God to you, which is more precious than life itself? For without the woman the man is not perfect in the Lord, no more than the woman is perfect without the man.[5]

I can not understand how a man can be unkind to any woman, much less to the wife of his bosom, and the mother of his children, and I am told that there are those who are absolutely brutal, but they are unworthy the name of men.[6]

When I think of our mothers, the mothers of our children, and realize that under the inspiration of the Gospel they live virtuous, pure, honorable lives, true to their husbands, true to their children, true to their convictions of the Gospel, oh, how my soul goes out in pure love for them; how noble and how God-given, how choice, how desirable and how indispensable they are to the accomplishment of God's purposes and the fulfilment of his decrees! My brethren, can you mistreat your wives, the mothers of your children? Can you help treating them with love and kindness? Can you help trying to make their lives as comfortable and happy as possible, lightening their burdens to the utmost of your ability, making life pleasant for them and for their children in their homes? How can you help it? How can any one help feeling an intense interest in the mother of his children, and also in his children? If we possess the Spirit of God, we can not do otherwise. It is only when men depart from the right spirit, when they digress from their duty, that they will neglect or dishonor any soul that is committed to their care. They are bound to honor their wives and children.[7]

Intelligent men, men of business, men of affairs, men who are involved constantly in the labors of life, and have to devote their energies and thought to their labors and duties, may not enjoy as many comforts with their families as they would like, but if they have the Spirit of the Lord with them in the performance of their temporal duties, they will never neglect the mothers of their children, nor their children.[8]

---

**Fathers and mothers, do not drive your children away.**

Oh! my brethren, be true to your families, be true to your wives and children. Teach them the way of life. Do not allow them to get so far from you that they will become oblivious to you or to any principle of honor, purity or truth. . . . If you will keep your boys close to your heart, within the clasp of your arms; if you will make them to feel that you love them, that you are their parents, that they are your children, and keep them near to you, they will not go very far from you, and they will not commit any very great sin. But it is when you turn them out of the home, turn them out of your affection—out into the darkness of the night into the society of the depraved or degraded; it is when they become tiresome to you, or you are tired of their innocent noise and prattle at home, and you say, "Go off somewhere else," it is this sort of treatment of your children that drives them from you.[9]

Our children are like we are; we couldn't be driven; we can't be driven now. We are like some other animals that we know of in the world. You can coax them; you can lead them, by holding out inducements to them, and by speaking kindly to them, but you can't drive them; they won't be driven. We won't be driven. Men are not in the habit of being driven; they are not made that way. . . .

You can't force your boys, nor your girls into heaven. You may force them to hell, by using harsh means in the efforts to make them good, when you yourselves are not as good as you should be. The man that will be angry at his boy, and try to correct him while he is in anger, is in the greatest fault; he is more to be pitied and more to be condemned than the child who has done wrong. You can only correct your children by love, in kindness, by love unfeigned, by persuasion, and reason.[10]

Fathers, if you wish your children to be taught in the principles of the gospel, if you wish them to love the truth and understand it, if you wish them to be obedient to and united with you, love them! and prove to them that you do love them by your every word or act to them. For your own sake, for the love that should exist between you and your boys—however wayward they might be, or one or the other might be, when you speak or talk to them, do it not in anger, do it not harshly, in a condemning spirit. Speak to them kindly; get them down and weep with them if necessary and get them to shed tears with you if possible. Soften their hearts; get them to feel tenderly toward you. Use no lash and no violence, but . . . approach them with reason, with persuasion and love unfeigned.[11]

May the fathers in Israel live as they should live; treat their wives as they should treat them; make their homes as comfortable as they possibly can; lighten the burden upon their companions as much as possible; set a proper example before their children; teach them to meet with them in prayer, morning and night, and whenever they sit down to partake of food, to acknowledge the mercy of God in giving them the food that they eat and the raiment that they wear, and acknowledge the hand of God in all things.[12]

## Suggestions for Study

- What does it mean to "conquer ourselves"? How can we "win the hearts" of our children and others to the truth?

- How can husbands and wives treat each other with "utmost courtesy" and "the greatest respect"? What are the benefits of doing so? When parents treat each other with respect and courtesy, how does their behavior affect the behavior of their children?

• What are the best ways in which we can influence others to live righteously? (See D&C 121:41–44.) What are some kinds of abusive behavior that contradict this counsel from the Lord?

• How do we sometimes drive our children away from us? What might happen to us and our children if we drive them away?

• Why is the parent who corrects a child in anger at greater fault than the child? What might a parent do when he or she feels anger at children?

• How did the Savior treat little children? (See Matthew 19:13–15; 3 Nephi 17:11–24.) What was His warning to those who abuse little children? (See Matthew 18:1–6.)

• How can we keep our children close to us and to the principles of the gospel? What are the blessings that come to those who keep their children "close to [their] heart"?

*Notes*

1. *Gospel Doctrine*, 5th ed. (1939), 283.

2. *Gospel Doctrine*, 253–54.

3. *Gospel Doctrine*, 276.

4. *Gospel Doctrine*, 283–84; paragraphing added.

5. *Gospel Doctrine*, 165.

6. *Gospel Doctrine*, 352.

7. In Conference Report, Apr. 1915, 6–7.

8. *Gospel Doctrine*, 285.

9. *Gospel Doctrine*, 281–82.

10. *Gospel Doctrine*, 316–17.

11. *Gospel Doctrine*, 316.

12. *Gospel Doctrine*, 288.

Even as He suffered on the cross, Jesus Christ bore no malice
toward His persecutors, but prayed, "Father, forgive them; for they
know not what they do" (Luke 23:34).

We love all men. We have nothing against mankind, and will never oppose them so long as they will leave us alone. We do not make war upon the tenets of others; we do not make war upon their churches, nor upon their religious beliefs. It is not our purpose to do it, and it is not any part of our mission to do so, let them worship how or what or where they please. . . . Our duty is simply to go straight ahead, do our duty, preach the gospel by good example as well as by precept, and let our light so shine upon their understanding that they may see the light as God sees it, and accept it, and walk in it, if they will.[11]

---

### The work of the Lord has its enemies, but God will not let our efforts fail.

There are enemies to the work of the Lord, as there were enemies to the Son of God. There are those who speak only evil of the Latter-day Saints. There are those . . . who will shut their eyes to every virtue and to every good thing connected with this latter-day work, and will pour out floods of falsehood and misrepresentation against the people of God.[12]

"If ye were of the world, the world would love its own; but because ye are not of the world, but I have chosen you out of the world, therefore the world hateth you." (John 15:19) The followers of Jesus were his chosen people, and because they were chosen by him, the world hated them. . . . Contempt is the heritage of a chosen people. Ought we therefore to court the contempt of the world? By no means. On the other hand, we should not be discouraged because it comes to us unsought.[13]

I do not believe there ever was a people who were guided by revelation, or acknowledged of the Lord as his people, who were not hated and persecuted by the wicked and the corrupt.[14]

From the day that the Prophet Joseph Smith first declared his vision until now, the enemy of all righteousness, the enemy of truth, of virtue, of honor, uprightness, and purity of life, the enemy of the only true God, the enemy to direct revelation from God and to the inspirations that come from the heavens to man has been arrayed against this work.[15]

Personally I have no enemies. My enemies are not *mine,* they are his whom I am trying to serve! The devil does not care much about *me.* I am insignificant, but he hates the *Priesthood,* which is after the order of the Son of God![16]

In truth the gospel is carrying us against the stream of passing humanity. We get in the way of purely human affairs and disturb the current of life in many ways and in many places. People who are comfortably located and well provided for, do not like to be disturbed. It angers them. . . . The Saints are never safe in following the protests and counsels of those who would have us ever and always in harmony with the world. We have our particular mission to perform; and that we may perform it in consonance with divine purposes, we are running counter to the ways of man. We are made unpopular. The contempt of the world is on us.[17]

Have no fear; slacken not your labors for the truth; live as becometh Saints. You are in the right way, and the Lord will not let your efforts fail. This Church stands in no danger from opposition and persecution from without. There is more to fear in carelessness, sin and indifference, from within; more danger that the individual will fail in doing right and in conforming his life to the revealed doctrines of our Lord and Savior Jesus Christ. If we do the right, all will be well, the God of our fathers will sustain us, and every opposition will tend only to the further spread of the knowledge of truth.[18]

---

### Let us leave our enemies in God's hands.

It is written, and I believe it is true, that although it must needs be that offenses come, woe unto them by whom they come [see Matthew 18:7]; but they are in the hands of the Lord as we are. We bring no railing accusation against them. We are willing to leave them in the hands of the Almighty to deal with them as seemeth him good. Our business is to work righteousness in the earth, to seek for the development of a knowledge of God's will and of God's ways, and of his great and glorious truths which he has revealed through the instrumentality of Joseph, the prophet, not only for the salvation of the living but for the redemption and salvation of the dead.[19]

God will deal with [our enemies] in his own time and in his own way, and we only need to do our duty, keep the faith ourselves, to work righteousness in the world ourselves, and leave the results in the hands of him who overruleth all things for the good of those who love him and keep his commandments.[20]

We have no ill feelings in our hearts toward any living creature. We forgive those who trespass against us. Those who have spoken evil of us, and who have misrepresented us before the world, we have no malice in our hearts toward them. We say, let God judge between them and us; let him recompense them for their work [see D&C 64:11]. We will not raise a hand against them; but we will extend the hand of fellowship and friendship to them, if they will repent of their sins and come unto the Lord and live. No matter how malicious they may have been, or how foolish they may have acted, if they will repent of it we will receive them with open arms and we will do all we can to help them to save themselves.[21]

## Suggestions for Study

- How have you felt when you have forgiven those who have offended you? Why do you think that Latter-day Saints who fail to forgive are more guilty than those who have sinned against them? (See also D&C 64:9–11.)

- If we are aware that someone has hard feelings against us, what should we do?

- How does "magnify[ing] the good" in other people help us better fulfill "our mission . . . to save mankind"?

- Why are we to have mercy and compassion even for our enemies? What might we include in our prayers for our enemies?

- Why may the Saints often experience "the contempt of the world"? How should we react to this contempt? Why does the Church stand "in no danger from opposition and persecution from without"?

- When we are hurt by others, why should we be willing to leave their punishment "in the hands of the Almighty"?

- How did the Savior treat His enemies? (See Luke 23:34.) How can we follow His example in extending the "hand of fellowship and friendship" to our enemies?

## Notes

1. *Gospel Doctrine,* 5th ed. (1939), 271.
2. Quoted in Norman S. Bosworth, "Remembering Joseph F. Smith," *Ensign,* June 1983, 22.
3. *Deseret News: Semi-Weekly,* 31 Mar. 1896, 9.
4. *Gospel Doctrine,* 256.
5. *Gospel Doctrine,* 255–56.
6. *Deseret News: Semi-Weekly,* 31 Mar. 1896, 9.
7. *Gospel Doctrine,* 254.
8. *Gospel Doctrine,* 339.
9. *Gospel Doctrine,* 339.
10. In James R. Clark, comp., *Messages of the First Presidency of The Church of Jesus Christ of Latter-day Saints,* 6 vols. (1965–75), 5:97.
11. "Testimony," *Improvement Era,* Aug. 1906, 808–9.
12. *Gospel Doctrine,* 337.
13. *Gospel Doctrine,* 340.
14. *Gospel Doctrine,* 46.
15. *Gospel Doctrine,* 371.
16. *Gospel Doctrine,* 271.
17. *Gospel Doctrine,* 118–19.
18. *Gospel Doctrine,* 413–14.
19. *Gospel Doctrine,* 338.
20. *Gospel Doctrine,* 338–39.
21. *Gospel Doctrine,* 2.

# Yield to the Promptings of the Spirit

*Every person in the Church has the right to the inspiration of the Holy Ghost for personal guidance.*

## From the Life of Joseph F. Smith

President Joseph F. Smith, in company with Bishop Charles W. Nibley, was returning home by train from a trip to the east. Near Green River, Wyoming, he had just stepped out onto the platform at the end of the car when he heard a voice that said, "Go in and sit down." He went back into the train, hesitated a moment, and then said to himself, "Oh, pshaw, perhaps it is only my imagination." He then heard the voice say again, "Sit down." Responding immediately, President Smith took his seat. Just then the train lurched as a broken rail caused the engine and most of the cars to be thrown from the track. Bishop Nibley said that if President Smith had not acted as he did, he would have been seriously injured, for although his car remained on the track, all of the cars were "jammed up together pretty badly."

President Smith said of this experience, "I have heard that voice a good many times in my life, and I have always profited by obeying it."

"[President Smith] lived in close communion with the Spirit of the Lord," observed Bishop Nibley, "and his life was so exemplary and chaste that the Lord could easily manifest himself to his servant. Truly he could say, 'Speak, Lord, for thy servant heareth.' [1 Samuel 3:9.] . . . The heart of President Smith was attuned to the Celestial melodies—he could hear, and did hear."[1]

# Teachings of Joseph F. Smith

## All Church members have the right to receive personal guidance from the Holy Ghost.

The spirit of inspiration, the gift of revelation, does not belong to one man solely; it is not a gift that pertains to the Presidency of the Church and the Twelve apostles alone. It is not confined to the presiding authorities of the Church, it belongs to every individual member of the Church; and it is the right and privilege of every man, every woman, and every child who has reached the years of accountability, to enjoy the spirit of revelation, and to be possessed of the spirit of inspiration in the discharge of their duties as members of the Church.[2]

Every individual in the Church has just as much right to enjoy the spirit of revelation and the understanding from God which that spirit of revelation gives him, for his own good, as the bishop has to enable him to preside over his ward. Every man has the privilege to exercise these gifts and these privileges in the conduct of his own affairs, in bringing up his children in the way they should go, and in the management of his farm, his flocks, his herds, and in the management of his business . . . ; it is his right to enjoy the spirit of revelation and of inspiration to do the right thing, to be wise and prudent, just and good in everything that he does. I know that this is a true principle.[3]

It is the right of individuals to be inspired and to receive manifestations of the Holy Spirit for their personal guidance to strengthen their faith, and to encourage them in works of righteousness, in being faithful and observing and keeping the commandments which God has given unto them; it is the privilege of every man and woman to receive revelation to this end, but not further. The moment an individual rises up assuming the right to control and to dictate, or to sit in judgment on his brethren, especially upon those who preside, he should be promptly checked, or discord, division and confusion will be the result. Every man and woman in this Church should know better than to yield to such a spirit.[4]

President Joseph F. Smith, left, and Presiding Bishop Charles W. Nibley
at a railroad stop. On such a train trip with Bishop Nibley, President Smith was
spared injury because he listened to the whisperings of the Spirit.

We should live so near to the Lord, be so humble in our spirits, so tractable and pliable, under the influence of the Holy Spirit, that we will be able to know the mind and will of the Father concerning us as individuals and as officers in the Church of Christ under all circumstances.[5]

We should . . . ever live so that the Holy Ghost may be within us as a living spring, calculated to lead us to perfection in righteousness, virtue and integrity before God, until we accomplish our earthly mission, performing every duty that may be required at our hands.[6]

---

**Revelation comes to us most often through the still, small voice of the Spirit.**

It is not by marvelous manifestations unto us that we shall be established in the truth, but it is by humility and faithful obedience to the commandments and laws of God. When I as a boy first started out in the ministry, I would frequently go out and ask the Lord to show me some marvelous thing, in order that I might receive a testimony. But the Lord withheld marvels from me, and showed me the truth, line upon line, precept upon precept, here a little and there a little [see 2 Nephi 28:30], until he made me to know the truth from the crown of my head to the soles of my feet, and until doubt and fear had been absolutely purged from me. He did not have to send an angel from the heavens to do this, nor did he have to speak with the trump of an archangel. By the whisperings of the still small voice of the Spirit of the living God, he gave to me the testimony I possess. And by this principle and power he will give to all the children of men a knowledge of the truth that will stay with them, and it will make them to know the truth, as God knows it, and to do the will of the Father as Christ does it. And no amount of marvelous manifestations will ever accomplish this.[7]

You need never fear, my brethren and sisters, if you do not receive any very great or marvelous manifestation, or if you do not receive any very wonderful revelations from heaven, if you will only live so that God can reveal Himself to you if He will. You will be all right, you will have nothing to fear, you will have nothing lacking, so far as you are concerned, if you are in a position to receive the will of God whenever He is ready or desires to make it manifest to you. That is enough. And then God will only reveal to you that which is necessary for your development, for your growth and advancement in the knowledge of the truth.[8]

---

### Let us do what the Spirit directs.

I do not feel either physically or mentally able to perform the duties which are required of me without the assistance of the Spirit of the Lord. I do not know that any man is able to carry on the work of the Lord which may be required at his hand, independently of the Lord, or without the promptings and inspiration of the Spirit which comes from the Father of Light.[9]

When we live so that we can hear and understand the whisperings of the still, small voice of the Spirit of God, let us do whatsoever that Spirit directs without fear of the consequences. It does not make any difference whether it meet the minds of carpers or critics, or of the enemies of the kingdom of God, or not. Is it agreeable to the will of the Lord? Is it compatible with the spirit of the great latter-day work in which we are engaged? Is the end aimed at likely to advance the Church and to strengthen it in the earth? If its trend is in that direction, let us do it, no matter what men may say or think.[10]

It will not do for us to be content and satisfied with the mere knowledge of that which is right. Knowing that which is right, we must go to and do the right thing, whatever it might be, whatever [Jesus Christ] requires of us. If we know the right, if we know the truth, we must abide by the right and in the truth, and we must do the right thing, always, under all circumstances, and never yield to the tempter or deviate from the right way, the straight and narrow path that leads back into the presence of God.[11]

[Our] obedience must be voluntary; it must not be forced, there must be no coercion. Men must not be constrained against their will to obey the will of God; they must obey it because they know it to be right, because they desire to do it, and because it is their pleasure to do it. God delights in the willing heart.[12]

**By yielding obedience to the Spirit, we gain greater knowledge and grow in the power of discernment.**

Man is indebted to the Source of all intelligence and truth, for the knowledge that he possesses; and all who will yield obedience to the promptings of the Spirit, which lead to virtue, to honor, to the love of God and man, and to the love of truth and that which is ennobling and enlarging to the soul, will get a cleaner, a more expansive, and a more direct and conclusive knowledge of God's truths than anyone else can obtain.[13]

Men and women should become settled in the truth, and founded in the knowledge of the gospel, depending upon no person for borrowed or reflected light, but trusting only upon the Holy Spirit, who is ever the same, shining forever and testifying to the individual and the priesthood, who live in harmony with the laws of the gospel, of the glory and the will of the Father. They will then have light everlasting which cannot be obscured.[14]

The only safe way for us to do, as individuals, is to live so humbly, so righteously and so faithfully before God that we may possess his Spirit to that extent that we shall be able to judge righteously, and discern between truth and error, between right and wrong.[15]

How shall we know that [the counsel we receive from Church leaders] is right? By getting the Spirit of God in our hearts, by which our minds may be opened and enlightened, that we may know the doctrine for ourselves, and be able to divide truth from error, light from darkness and good from evil.[16]

To the faithful Latter-day Saint is given the right to know the truth, as God knows it; and no power beneath the celestial kingdom can lead him astray, darken his understanding, becloud his mind or dim his faith or his knowledge of the principles of the gospel of Jesus Christ. It can't be done, for the light of God shines brighter than the illumination of a falsehood and error; therefore, those who possess the light of Christ, the spirit of revelation and the knowledge of God, rise above all these vagaries in the world; they know of this doctrine, that it is of God and not of man.[17]

## When we live up to what has been revealed, the Lord will add to our light and intelligence.

There are many things yet to be revealed. There are things to be revealed which God will make known in his own due time which we do not now understand. For my own part, there is as much already revealed as it seems possible for me to understand. If I could only grasp all that God has revealed, and comprehend it as I should and apply it in righteousness in my life, I think I should then be prepared for something more, if I was still worthy of it. Why, bless your souls, there are people among us that are worrying and fretting over things that have never been revealed to the children of men. . . . If men would pay their tithing, if they would keep the word of wisdom, if they would say their prayers, if they would devote their lives to works of righteousness in the earth and study the gospel for themselves and obey it, they would have less necessity for asking questions, and don't forget the fact that they would know things better than they do.[18]

We know nothing, and we will preach nothing to the people except that which the Lord God has revealed, and we advise and counsel those who are in authority, and whose duty and business it is to teach and preach the principles of the gospel to the world and to the Latter-day Saints, to confine their teachings and their instructions to the word of God that has been revealed. There is a great deal that has been revealed that has not yet been lived up to, I assure you. There is a great deal yet remaining to be learned. There is a great deal that is yet to be taught in the spirit of instruction, and there is a great deal that has been revealed through the Prophet Joseph and his associates that the people have not yet received in their hearts, and have not yet become converted to as they should.

When we obey and are capable of observing the precepts of the gospel and the laws of God and the requirements of heaven, which have already been revealed, we will be far better off and nearer the goal of perfection in wisdom, knowledge and power than we are today. When that time comes, then there are other things still greater yet to be revealed to the people of God. Until we do our duty, however, in that which we have received, until we are faithful over the things that are now committed into our hands, until we live our religion as we have it now, as the Lord has given it to us, to add commandments, to add light and intelligence to us over that which we have already received, which we have not yet fully obeyed, would be to add condemnation upon our heads. It is enough for us to live in the light of present inspiration and present revelation and for each individual member of the Church to keep the commandments of the Lord and labor in the Church as the Spirit may give him and her guidance in the performance of duty. Every soul of us is entitled to inspiration from God to know what is our duty and how we are to do it.[19]

The thing for us to do is to live according to the light and intelligence that God has revealed to us in this dispensation, that we may be in harmony with the heavenly powers and with heavenly beings, and especially with our Lord Jesus Christ who stands at our head, who is our lawgiver, our exemplar, and the way of life and salvation to all the world; through whom we may enter into the celestial Kingdom of God, and without whom we can never enter that state of glory worlds without end. He is the way, the light and life of the world; and who soever will obey the commandments He has given, and do the works which He has done, and commanded us to do, shall not walk in the darkness, but shall have in them the light of life.[20]

## Suggestions for Study

- To whom is the "spirit of revelation" available?
- In what areas of our lives might we enjoy the personal guidance of the Spirit?
- Why do you think God guides us most often through the still, small voice of the Spirit rather than by "marvelous manifestations"? (See also 1 Kings 19:11–12.) In what ways does God guide us by the still, small voice?
- How can we know when we are being influenced by the Spirit of the Lord? (See also D&C 6:15, 22–23; 9:8–9; 11:12–14.)

272

- Why are we not coerced to follow the promptings of the Spirit? Why do you think that God "delights in the willing heart"?

- How must we live to be able to receive the guidance of the Spirit? What inhibits our ability to receive the promptings of the Spirit?

- When has the Spirit helped you expand your knowledge of God's truths?

- What blessings come to those who trust in the promptings of the Holy Spirit rather than depending on "borrowed or reflected light"?

- How can we prepare ourselves to receive more light and intelligence? (See also Alma 12:10.)

*Notes*

1. *Gospel Doctrine,* 5th ed. (1939), 523–24.
2. *Gospel Doctrine,* 34.
3. *Gospel Doctrine,* 34–35.
4. *Gospel Doctrine,* 41–42.
5. *Gospel Doctrine,* 58–59.
6. *Gospel Doctrine,* 60.
7. *Gospel Doctrine,* 7.
8. "President Joseph F. Smith on Revelation," *Millennial Star,* 6 Apr. 1905, 222.
9. In Conference Report, Oct. 1912, 2.
10. *Gospel Doctrine,* 59.
11. "Testimony," *Improvement Era,* Aug. 1906, 808.
12. *Gospel Doctrine,* 65.
13. *Gospel Doctrine,* 6.
14. *Gospel Doctrine,* 87.
15. *Gospel Doctrine,* 45.
16. *Deseret News: Semi-Weekly,* 3 Jan. 1893, 2.
17. *Gospel Doctrine,* 6.
18. In Conference Report, Oct. 1916, 6–7.
19. *Gospel Doctrine,* 35–36; paragraphing added.
20. *Deseret News: Semi-Weekly,* 31 Jan. 1882, 2.

*Prove Me Now Herewith,* by Glen S. Hopkinson, portrays faithful pioneer Saints bringing their tithes, which were often paid in commodities rather than money, to a tithing office near the Salt Lake Temple.

# Obedience to the Law of Tithing

*Those who obey the law of tithing help to accomplish the purposes of the Lord and are entitled to His blessings.*

## From the Life of Joseph F. Smith

At the end of the 1800s, the Church faced a staggering financial debt, exceeding one million dollars. This financial obligation weighed heavily on Joseph F. Smith's mind. At the October 1899 general conference he said: "We have had much valuable instruction in relation to our duties as Latter-day Saints, not only concerning the law of tithing, but also in reference to other things, which are as important in their place as the law of tithing. There is nothing, however, of greater importance to the welfare of the Church at present than the consideration of this law, by which means will be placed in the storehouse of the Lord, to meet the necessities of the people."[1]

One afternoon seven years later, President Smith came from his office and found his daughter Rachel in the front hall of the Beehive House.

" 'Where is your mother?' he inquired.

" 'I don't know.'

" 'Where could she be?'

" 'I don't know.'

" 'When will she be here?'

" 'I don't know, Papa. I don't know much. I just got home from school.'

" 'Well, baby,' he said, 'I wanted your mother to be the first to know, but since you don't know anything I will tell you.' In his hand he held a piece of paper.

" 'Do you see this paper?'

" 'Yes, sir.'

" 'It means the Church is at last out of debt.' He smiled. 'So now you really know something!' "2

# Teachings of Joseph F. Smith

### Obedience to the law of tithing affirms our loyalty to the kingdom of God.

God requires one-tenth of our increase to be put into His storehouse; and this is given as a standing law to all of the Stakes of Zion.3

By this principle (tithing) the loyalty of the people of this Church shall be put to the test. By this principle it shall be known who is for the kingdom of God and who is against it. By this principle it shall be seen whose hearts are set on doing the will of God and keeping his commandments, thereby sanctifying the land of Zion unto God, and who are opposed to this principle and have cut themselves off from the blessings of Zion. There is a great deal of importance connected with this principle, for by it it shall be known whether we are faithful or unfaithful. In this respect it is as essential as faith in God, as repentance of sin, as baptism for the remission of sin, or as the laying on of hands for the gift of the Holy Ghost.4

The law of tithing is a test by which the people as individuals shall be proved. Any man who fails to observe this principle shall be known as a man who is indifferent to the welfare of Zion, who neglects his duty as a member of the Church, and who does nothing toward the accomplishment of the temporal advancement of the kingdom of God. He contributes nothing, either, toward spreading the gospel to the nations of the earth, and he neglects to do that which would entitle him to receive the blessings and ordinances of the gospel.5

The observance of the law of tithing is voluntary. I can pay my tithing or not, as I choose. It is a matter of choice with me, whether I will do it or not do it; but, feeling as I do, loyal to the Church, loyal to its interests, believing that it is right and just to observe the law of tithing I do observe it—on the same principle that I think it is right for me to observe the law of repentance, and of baptism, for the remission of sins.[6]

We who have not paid our tithing in the past, and are therefore under obligations to the Lord, which we are not in position to discharge, the Lord requires that no longer at our hands, but will forgive us for the past if we will observe this law honestly in the future. That is generous and kind, and I feel grateful for it.[7]

I have said, and I will repeat it here, that a man or woman who will always pay his or her tithing will never apostatize. It does not make any difference how small or how large it may be; it is a law of the Lord; it is a source of revenue for the Church; it is God's requirement, and He has said that those who will not observe it are not worthy of an inheritance in Zion. No man will ever apostatize so long as he will pay his tithing. It is reasonable. Why? Because as long as he has faith to pay his tithing he has faith in the Church and in the principles of the Gospel, and there is some good in him, and there is some light in him. As long as he will do this the tempter will not overcome him and will not lead him astray.[8]

---

### Tithing is the Lord's law of revenue for His Church and for the blessing of the Saints.

The law of tithing is the law of revenue for the Church of Jesus Christ of Latter-day Saints. Without it, it would be impossible to carry on the purposes of the Lord.[9]

The Lord . . . gave the law of tithing, in order that there might be means in the storehouse of the Lord for the carrying out of the purposes he had in view; for the gathering of the poor, for the spreading of the gospel to the nations of the earth, for the maintenance of those who were required to give their constant attention, day in and day out, to the work of the Lord, and for whom it was necessary to make some provision. Without this law these things could not be done, neither could temples be built and maintained, nor the poor fed and clothed. Therefore the law of tithing is necessary for the Church, so much so that the Lord has laid great stress upon it.[10]

[Tithing] is being used to keep up the ordinances of the house of God in . . . temples. Thousands and thousands of dollars of it are being used in educating the youth of Zion and in maintaining the Church schools. Thousands of dollars are being expended to feed and clothe the poor, and to take care of those who are dependent upon the Church. They look to their "mother" for succor and support, and it is right and proper that the Church should provide for its own poor and indigent, feeble and helpless, so far as possible.[11]

The Lord has revealed how this means [tithing] shall be cared for, and managed; namely, by the Presidency of the Church and the High Council of the Church (that is, the Twelve Apostles), and the Presiding Bishopric of the Church. I think there is wisdom in this. It is not left for one man to dispose of it, or to handle it alone, not by any means. It devolves upon at least eighteen men, men of wisdom, of faith, of ability, as these eighteen men are. I say it devolves upon them to dispose of the tithes of the people and to use them for whatever purpose in their judgment and wisdom will accomplish the most good for the Church; . . . this fund of tithing is disposed of by these men whom the Lord has designated as having authority to do it, for the necessities and benefit of the Church.[12]

The Lord . . . especially demands of the men who stand at the head of this Church and who are responsible for the guidance and direction of the people of God that they shall see to it that the law of God [tithing] is kept. It is our duty to do this. . . . It becomes obligatory upon the leaders of the Church to say something upon this principle, that not only the people may do their duty in regard to this law, but that there may be something in the storehouse of the Lord with which to meet the necessities of the people; for the necessities of the Church are the necessities of the people. The members of the Church constitute the Church, and therefore whatever obligation the Church is under, it rests upon each individual member of the Church proportionate to his means. The Lord requires of us that we shall see that His law is kept among the people.[13]

*Captain Moroni Raises the Title of Liberty,* by Arnold Friberg.
Members of the Church in Book of Mormon times gathered to the title of liberty
to pledge that they would "maintain their rights, and their religion,
that the Lord God may bless them" (Alma 46:20).

## God does not interfere with our agency but permits us to experience the consequences of our choices.

The agency of man is not interfered with by Divine Providence. If men were not left free to choose the good and refuse the evil, or vice versa, there would be no righteousness or even reason in bringing them to judgment. In consequence of the power of volition they become responsible beings, and therefore will receive the results of their own doings. They will be rewarded or punished according to their works, when the books are opened and they are judged out of the things written therein.

God, doubtless, could avert war, prevent crime, destroy poverty, chase away darkness, overcome error, and make all things bright, beautiful and joyful. But this would involve the destruction of a vital and fundamental attribute in man—the right of agency. It is for the benefit of His sons and daughters that they become acquainted with evil as well as good, with darkness as well as light, with error as well as truth, and with the results of the infraction of eternal laws. Therefore he has permitted the evils which have been brought about by the acts of His creatures, but will control their ultimate results for His own glory and the progress and exaltation of His sons and daughters, when they have learned obedience by the things they suffer. The contrasts experienced in this world of mingled sorrow and joy are educational in their nature, and will be the means of raising humanity to a full appreciation of all that is right and true and good. The foreknowledge of God does not imply His action in bringing about that which He foresees, nor make Him responsible in any degree for that which man does or refuses to do.[6]

Many things occur in the world in which it seems very difficult for most of us to find a solid reason for the acknowledgment of the hand of the Lord. . . . The only reason I have been able to discover by which we should acknowledge the hand of God in some occurrences is the fact that the thing which has occurred has been permitted of the Lord. When two men give way to their passions, their selfishness and anger, to contend and quarrel with each other, and this quarrel and contention leads to physical strife and violence between them, it has been difficult for me to discover the hand of the Lord in that transaction; other than that the men who thus disagree, quarrel and contend with each other, have received from God the freedom of their own agency to exercise their own intelligence, to judge between the right and wrong for themselves, and to act according to their own desire. The Lord did not design or purpose that these two men should quarrel, or give way to their anger to such an extent that it would lead to violence between them, and, perhaps, to bloodshed. God has never designed such a thing as that, nor can we charge such things to the Almighty. . . .

The agency that [God] has given to us left us to act for ourselves—to do things if we will that are not right, that are contrary to the laws of life and health, that are not wise or prudent—and the results may be serious to us, because of our ignorance or of our determination to persist in that which we desire, rather than to yield to the requirements which God makes of us.[7]

You will suffer the consequences of your own mistakes, of your own errors, though they bring sorrow, or sickness, or death! So, I acknowledge the hand of the Lord in this free agency that he has given to the children of men; but I acknowledge the hand of man in the consequences of his own acts, following his disobedience to the law of God. I do not charge the weaknesses, the mistakes or errors, the crimes and wickedness of men, and the evils that exist in the world, to God the Father.[8]

It has been in [the] realm of freedom, and the exercise of human judgment that most of the evils that have occurred in the world have been done—the martyrdom of Saints, the crucifixion of the Son of God himself, and much of the apostasy and departure from the work of righteousness, and from the laws of God, have occurred in this realm of freedom and the exercise of human judgment. God in his boundless wisdom and gracious mercy has provided means, and has shown the way to the children of men whereby, even in the realms of freedom and the exercise of their own judgment, they may individually go unto God in faith and prayer, and find out what should guide and direct their human judgment and wisdom; and I do not want the Latter-day Saints to forget that this is their privilege.[9]

## The Church of Jesus Christ does not infringe upon individual liberty.

The Kingdom of God is a Kingdom of freedom; the gospel of the Son of God is the gospel of liberty.[10]

Can you find an organization, ecclesiastical or otherwise, that has the same perfection of government and organization in it as can be found in the church of Jesus Christ of Latter-day Saints, established by inspiration through the Prophet Joseph Smith? And what is the object of that organization? Is it to crush men? Is it to injure you? Is it to bow you down unto the earth? Is it to deprive you of your liberties, of your rights, of your privileges? Is it to make you slaves, menials, and degrade you unto the dust? Or is it to raise you up into the scale of intelligence and of manliness and increase your liberties, for there is no liberty like the liberty of the gospel of Jesus Christ? For I can tell you no man is free when he is under bondage of sin and of transgression, neither is any man free when he is under the bondage of ignorance in relation to the plan of life and salvation.[11]

I believe that there is not a freer, more independent nor a more intelligent people to be found anywhere in the world, who are more independent in choosing the course which they pursue, in the work that they perform and in everything that they have to do with, than the Latter-day Saints. There is not a member of the Church of Jesus Christ of Latter-day Saints, in good standing, anywhere in all the world today that is not such by reason of his independence of character, by reason of his intelligence, wisdom and ability to judge between right and wrong and between good and evil.[12]

The religion of the Latter-day Saints relates to present conduct as well as future happiness. It influences its votaries [believers] in everything that affects human character. It is for the body as well as for the spirit. It teaches people how to live and act in this world that they may be prepared for the realities of the world to come. The Church, therefore, instructs in things temporal as well as things spiritual, so far as they relate to the Church, its properties and institutions and the association of its adherents. But it does not infringe upon the liberty of the individual or encroach upon the domain of the state. The free agency of man is a fundamental principle which, according to the tenets of the Church, even God Himself does not suppress.[13]

---

### Obedience, the rightful exercise of agency, brings inestimable blessings.

There are . . . certain blessings which God bestows upon the children of men only upon the condition of the rightful exercise of this agency. For instance, no man can obtain a remission of his sins but by repentance, and baptism by one having authority. If we would be free from sin, from its effects, from its power, we must obey this law which God has revealed, or we never can obtain a remission of sins. Therefore, while God has bestowed upon all men, irrespective of condition, this agency to choose good or evil, he has not and will not bestow upon the children of men a remission of sins but by their obedience to law. . . .

All men are blessed with the strength of their bodies, with the use of their minds, and with the right to exercise the faculties with which they are endowed in a way that seemeth good to their sight, without regard to religion. But God has not and will not suffer the gift of the Holy Ghost to be bestowed upon any man or woman, except through compliance with the laws of God. Therefore, no man can obtain a remission of sins; no man can obtain the gift of the Holy Ghost; no man can obtain the revelations of God; no man can obtain the Priesthood, and the rights, powers and privileges thereof; no man can become an heir of God and a joint heir with Jesus Christ, except through compliance with the requirements of heaven. These are universal blessings, they are great and inestimable privileges which pertain to the gospel and to the plan of life and salvation, which are open and free to all on certain conditions, but which no persons beneath the heavens can enjoy, but through walking in the channel that God has marked out by which they can obtain them. And these privileges and blessings when obtained may be forfeited, and perhaps lost for all eternity, unless we continue steadfast in the course that is marked out for us to pursue. . . .

The sun shines upon the evil and the good; but the Holy Ghost descends only upon the righteous and upon those who are forgiven of their sins. The rain descends upon the evil and upon the good; but the rights of the Priesthood are conferred, and the doctrine of the Priesthood distils as the dews of heaven upon the souls of those only who receive it in God's own appointed way. The favor of heaven, the acknowledgment of the Almighty of his children upon the earth as his sons and his daughters, can only be secured through obedience to the laws which he has revealed.[14]

---

### The greatest measure of liberty comes through obedience to the gospel of Jesus Christ.

The gospel of Jesus Christ is the perfect law of liberty. It is calculated to lead man to the highest state of glory, and to exalt him in the presence of our Heavenly Father, "with whom is no variableness, neither shadow of turning." [James 1:17.][15]

We believe that God's will is to exalt men; that the liberty that comes through obedience to the gospel of Jesus Christ is the greatest measure of liberty that can come to man. There is no liberty that men enjoy or pretend to enjoy in the world that is not founded in the will and in the law of God, and that does not have truth for its underlying principle and foundation. It is error that makes bondsmen. It is untruth that degrades mankind. It is error and the lack of knowledge of God's laws and God's will that leaves men in the world on a par with the brute creation; for they have no higher instincts, no higher principle, no higher incentive, no higher aspiration, than the brute world, if they have not some inspiration that comes from a higher source than man himself.[16]

It is only by obedience to the laws of God, that men can rise above the petty weaknesses of mortality and exercise that breadth of affection, that charity and love, that should actuate the hearts and the motives of the children of men.[17]

Brethren and sisters, let us be free. I contend—and I think I have a right to do so—that I am a free man, in accordance with my observance of the commandments of God. If I do wrong, I am in bondage to that wrong. If I commit sin, I am in bondage to that sin. If I transgress the laws of God, I am responsible before the

Lord. But I contend that as to liberty, as to freedom of speech, freedom of will, freedom of action—as to everything that goes to make a free man in the midst of men, I do not believe there is another man on earth any freer than I am. Bless your soul, I can commit sin if I want to. I have as much liberty to commit sin as any man. No man has any right to commit sin; but all men have the liberty to do so if they will. God has given to them their agency. Is there any manhood displayed in my committing sin because I have liberty to do so? I have liberty to go to a saloon and drink liquor, if I choose, or go to a gambling [hall] and gamble. I possess just as much liberty in regard to these matters as any man living on earth. But the moment I should do such a thing as this I become a slave and a bondsman to iniquity. On the other hand, if I am not guilty of visiting saloons, or of playing cards, or of gambling, or of other crimes I am innocent of them and so far I am a free man. The truth has made me free in regard to this.[18]

We do not preach the gospel of fear. We do not seek to terrorize the souls of men. We do not ask a man to be righteous because of the terrors of the damned. We do not want you to be good because you fear the punishment of the wicked. We do not want you to do right because of the penalty that attaches to the doing of wrong. We want you to choose the right because it is right, and because your heart loves the right, and because it is choice above everything else. We want you to be honest, not merely because it is the best policy, but because in so doing you honor God and you carry out His purposes in your lives; for "an honest man," it is an old, and perhaps a hackneyed, saying—"is the noblest work of God." We want to be honest because we love God, and we cannot be the Saints of God [unless] we are. We should be good because we love to be good, and not because we fear the consequences of evil.[19]

The Lord does not accept obedience from men except that which they render cheerfully and gladly in their hearts, and that is all that is desired by his servants. That is the obedience we ought to render, and if we do not we are under condemnation.[20]

[Jesus Christ] not only had intelligence, but He applied that intelligence in the doing of good and in the making of men free from the errors of the world and the evil traditions of the fathers. He declared in words of truth and soberness, "If ye continue in my word, then are ye my disciples indeed; and ye shall know the truth, and the truth shall make you free." [John 8:31–32.] No man is like God unless he is free. God is free. Why? Because He possesses all righteousness, all power, and all wisdom. He also possesses His agency, and His agency is exercised in doing that which is good, and not that which is evil. So no man can be like unto Him until he can subject himself unto that which is righteous, pure, and good, and until he can forsake error and sin and overcome himself. . . .

He that is most pliant and submissive to the will of God shows the greatest wisdom among all men. He that sets up his opinion in opposition to the wishes and purposes of the Lord is of all men the farthest from God in that regard. Though he may be fashioned and formed in the image and likeness of the Father, yet he is most unlike the Son unless he can say in his heart, "Father, not my will, but thine, be done." [Luke 22:42.] It is the will of the Lord that we should possess this spirit, and understand this truth. It is true that there is to us but one God, the Father, and that all men will have to be subject unto Him and are required to obey His commandments, in order that they may be free and the disciples of Christ indeed.[21]

## Suggestions for Study

- What is agency? Who has agency? Why is agency a blessing?

- How does God expect us to use our agency? What does He promise us if we choose to obey Him? (See also D&C 58:28.)

- Why are we allowed to suffer the consequences of our actions? How would our mortal experience be diminished if God averted war, prevented crime, and destroyed poverty? How might you respond to someone who mistakenly attributes to God "the evils that exist in the world"?

- Although God "has permitted the evils which have been brought about by the acts of His creatures," what assurance do we have that He will "control their ultimate results"? (See also Romans 8:28; D&C 98:3.)

- What does it mean to "infringe upon the liberty of the individual"? How can parents and leaders in the Church help others to be obedient without infringing upon individual liberty? (See also D&C 121:34–46.)

- How does the Church help us to become truly free? How do sin and error restrict us?

- What "great and inestimable" blessings have you received when you have chosen to obey God's laws? (See also D&C 130:20–21.)

- How is it different to obey God's laws because of love rather than because of fear of punishment?

- How can we follow the example of the Savior in becoming more obedient to the will of the Father?

## Notes

1. *Deseret News: Semi-Weekly,* 11 Nov. 1873, 1.
2. In James R. Clark, comp., *Messages of the First Presidency of The Church of Jesus Christ of Latter-day Saints,* 6 vols. (1965–75), 4:144; the entire address is on pages 143–55.
3. *Gospel Doctrine,* 5th ed. (1939), 49.
4. *Deseret News: Semi-Weekly,* 3 Jan. 1871, 2.
5. In Brian H. Stuy, comp., *Collected Discourses Delivered by President Wilford Woodruff, His Two Counselors, the Twelve Apostles, and Others,* 5 vols. (1987–92), 2:297.
6. In *Messages of the First Presidency,* 4:325–26.
7. *Gospel Doctrine,* 56–57; paragraphing added.
8. In *Messages of the First Presidency,* 5:70–71.
9. *Gospel Doctrine,* 48.
10. *Deseret News: Semi-Weekly,* 2 Mar. 1867, 3.
11. In *Collected Discourses,* 5:143.
12. *Gospel Doctrine,* 492; paragraphing altered.
13. In *Messages of the First Presidency,* 4:79.
14. *Gospel Doctrine,* 49–50; paragraphing added.
15. *Gospel Doctrine,* 82.
16. *Gospel Doctrine,* 53–54.
17. In Conference Report, Oct. 1903, 2.
18. In *Collected Discourses,* 4:410–11.
19. In *Collected Discourses,* 3:217–18.
20. *Deseret News: Semi-Weekly,* 11 Nov. 1873, 1.
21. In *Collected Discourses,* 4:407.

In 1850, Mary Fielding Smith and her children lived in this
simple adobe home. In this home, Joseph F. Smith learned gospel truths
that blessed him throughout his life. The home now stands in the
Old Deseret Village at This Is the Place Heritage Park.

# Children: The Richest of All Earthly Joys

*We should cherish our children, bring them up
in the gospel of Jesus Christ, and teach them virtue,
love, and integrity.*

## From the Life of Joseph F. Smith

President Joseph F. Smith's love for the gospel was intertwined with his Christlike love for children—his own and all little ones. "The richest of all my earthly joys is in my precious children," he said. "Thank God!"[1]

Charles W. Nibley, Presiding Bishop of the Church, noted that President Smith's "love for little children was unbounded. During [a trip] through the southern settlements to St. George . . . , when the troops of little children were paraded before him, it was beautiful to see how he adored these little ones. It was my duty to try and get the company started, to make time to the next settlement where the crowds would be waiting for us, but it was a difficult task to pull him away from the little children. He wanted to shake hands with and talk to every one of them. . . .

"I have visited at his home when one of his children was down sick. I have seen him come home from his work at night tired, as he naturally would be, and yet he could walk the floor for hours with that little one in his arms, . . . loving it, encouraging it in every way with such tenderness and such a soul of pity and love."[2]

"He showed great tenderness and love for his large and honorable family. In his last address to his children, November 10, 1918, his heart's dearest sentiments were expressed to them in these words: 'When I look around me, and see my boys and my girls whom the Lord has given to me,—and I have succeeded, with His help, to make them tolerably comfortable, and at least respectable in the world—I have reached the treasure of my life, the whole substance that makes life worth living.' "³

# Teachings of Joseph F. Smith

## Teach children the gospel of Jesus Christ by precept and example.

A man and woman who have embraced the gospel of Jesus Christ and who have begun life together, should be able by their power, example and influence to cause their children to emulate them in lives of virtue, honor, and in integrity to the kingdom of God which will redound to their own interest and salvation. No one can advise my children with greater earnestness and solicitude for their happiness and salvation than I can myself. Nobody has more interest in the welfare of my own children than I have. I cannot be satisfied without them. They are part of me. They are mine; God has given them to me, and I want them to be humble and submissive to the requirements of the gospel. I want them to do right, and to be right in every particular, so that they will be worthy of the distinction that the Lord has given them in being numbered among his covenant people who are choice above all other people, because they have made sacrifice for their own salvation in the truth.⁴

"Children," we are told, "are a heritage of the Lord;" they are also, the Psalmist tells us, "his reward." [Psalm 127:3.] If children are cut off from their birthright, how shall the Lord be rewarded? They are not a source of weakness and poverty to family life, for they bring with them certain divine blessings that make for the prosperity of the home and the nation. "As arrows are in the hand of a mighty man; so are children of the youth. Happy is the man that hath his quiver full of them." [Psalm 127:4–5.]⁵

We are a Christian people, we believe in the Lord Jesus Christ, and we feel that it is our duty to acknowledge him as our Savior and Redeemer. Teach it to your children. Teach them that the Prophet Joseph Smith had restored to him the Priesthood that was held by Peter and James and John, who were ordained under the hands of the Savior himself. Teach them that Joseph Smith, the prophet, when only a boy, was chosen and called of God to lay the foundations of the Church of Christ in the world, to restore the holy Priesthood, and the ordinances of the gospel, which are necessary to qualify men to enter into the kingdom of heaven. Teach your children to respect their neighbors. Teach your children to respect their bishops and the teachers that come to their homes to teach them. Teach your children to respect old age, gray hairs, and feeble frames. Teach them to venerate and to hold in honorable remembrance their parents, and to help all those who are helpless and needy. Teach your children, as you have been taught yourselves, to honor the Priesthood which you hold, the Priesthood which we hold as elders in Israel.

Teach your children to honor themselves, teach your children to honor the principle of presidency by which organizations are held intact and by which strength and power for the well-being and happiness and upbuilding of the people are preserved. Teach your children that when they go to school they should honor their teachers in that which is true and honest, in that which is manly and womanly, and worth while. . . . Teach your children to honor the law of God and the law of the state and the law of our country.[6]

We read in the Book of Doctrine and Covenants that it is required of parents to teach their children "to understand the doctrine of repentance, faith in Christ the Son of the living God, and of baptism and the gift of the Holy Ghost by the laying on of the hands when eight years old." "And they shall also teach their children to pray and to walk uprightly before the Lord." And if the parents fail to do this, and the children go astray and turn from the truth, then the Lord has said that the sin shall be upon the heads of the parents [D&C 68:25, 28]. What a terrible thought it is that a father who loves his children with all his heart should be held responsible before God for having neglected those whom he has loved so dearly until they have turned away from the truth and have become outcasts. The loss of these children will be charged to the parents, and they will be held responsible for their apostasy and darkness. . . .

If I can prove myself worthy of an entrance into the kingdom of God, I want my children there; and I propose to enter into the kingdom of my God. I have set out for that, and I propose, with the help of the Lord and through humility and obedience, to complete my mission on this earth and to be true to God all my days. I have made up my mind to this, and am determined with the help of God that I will not fail. Therefore, I want my children with me. I want my family to accompany me, that where I go they may go also, and that they may share whatever exaltation I receive.[7]

Parents have an influence over their children; . . . and although we may not perceive that our example has any influence or weight, I assure you many times injury has been done by acts that we regarded as trifling through the influence they had upon our neighbors or children. . . . Yet we see fathers and mothers set an example before their children which they themselves condemn and warn their children against. The inconsistent conduct of parents has a tendency to blunt the sensibilities of children, and to lead them from the way of life and salvation, for if parents teach their children principles which they do not practice themselves, that teaching is not likely to have much weight or effect except for evil.

We do not look at and reflect upon these things as we should. What will a child, when he begins to reflect, think of a parent who, professing to believe that the Word of Wisdom is part of the gospel of Jesus Christ, and has been given by revelation, violates it every day of his life? He will grow up to believe that his parent is a hypocrite and without faith in the gospel. They who take such a course incur fearful responsibilities. We cannot be too consistent in our course, neither can we be too faithful in fulfilling promises.[8]

---

### We should bring up children in love and kindness.

Our children will be just about what we make them. They are born without knowledge or understanding—the most helpless creatures of the animal creation born into the world. The little one begins to learn after it is born, and all that it knows greatly depends upon its environment, the influences under which it is brought up, the kindness with which it is treated, the noble examples shown it, the hallowed influences of father and mother, or otherwise, over its infant mind. And it will be largely what its environment and its parents and teachers make it.

. . . A great deal depends upon the influence under which [a child] is brought up. You will observe that the most potent influence over the mind of a child to persuade it to learn, to progress, or to accomplish anything, is the influence of love. More can be accomplished for good by unfeigned love, in bringing up a child, than by any other influence that can be brought to bear upon it. A child that cannot be conquered by the lash, or subdued by violence, may be controlled in an instant by unfeigned affection and sympathy. I know that is true; and this principle obtains in every condition of life. . . . Govern the children, not by passion, by bitter words or scolding, but by affection and by winning their confidence.[9]

If you can only convince your children that you love them, that your soul goes out to them for their good, that you are their truest friend, they, in turn, will place confidence in you and will love you and seek to do your bidding and to carry out your wishes with your love. But if you are selfish, unkindly to them, and if they are not confident that they have your entire affection, they will be selfish, and will not care whether they please you or carry out your wishes or not, and the result will be that they will grow wayward, thoughtless and careless.[10]

Brethren and sisters . . . , I implore you to teach and control by the spirit of love and forbearance until you can conquer. If children are defiant and difficult to control, be patient with them until you can conquer by love, and you will have gained their souls, and you can then mould their characters as you please.[11]

---

### Guard children from growing wayward.

God forbid that there should be any of us so unwisely indulgent, so thoughtless and so shallow in our affection for our children that we dare not check them in a wayward course, in wrong-doing and in their foolish love for the things of the world more than for the things of righteousness, for fear of offending them. I want to say this: Some people have grown to possess such unlimited confidence in their children that they do not believe it possible for them to be led astray or do wrong. They do not believe they could do wrong, because they have such confidence in them. The result is, they turn them loose, morning, noon, and night, to attend all kinds of entertainments and amusements, often in company with those whom they know not and do not understand. Some of our children are so innocent that they do not suspect evil, and therefore, they are off their guard and trapped into evil.[12]

What are we doing in our homes to train our children; what to enlighten them? What to encourage them to make home their place of amusement, and a place where they may invite their friends for study or entertainment? . . . Do we take personal interest in them and in their affairs? Are we providing them with the physical knowledge, the mental food, the healthful exercise, and the spiritual purification, that will enable them to become pure and robust in body, intelligent and honorable citizens, faithful and loyal Latter-day Saints?

. . . We may well give our sons and daughters some time for recreation and diversion, and some provision in the home for satisfying their longing for legitimate physical and mental recreation, to which every child is entitled, and which he will seek in the street or in objectionable places, if it is not provided in the home.[13]

The character and variety of our amusements have so much to do with the welfare and character of our young people that they should be guarded with the utmost jealousy for the preservation of the morals and stamina of the youth of Zion.

In the first place they should not be excessive; and young people should be discouraged from giving themselves up to the spirit and frivolity of excessive mirth. . . . They should be trained to appreciate more and more amusements of a social and intellectual character. Home parties, concerts that develop the talents of youth, and public amusements that bring together both young and old, are preferable. . . .

In the second place, our amusements should be consistent with our religious spirit of fraternity and religious devotion. . . . The question of amusements is one of such far-reaching importance to the welfare of the Saints that the presiding authorities of every ward should give it their most careful attention and consideration.

In the third place, our amusements should interfere as little as possible with the work of the school-room. It is very desirable that the early education of our young people should be carried on with as little interruption as possible. . . .

Lastly, it is to be feared that in many homes, parents abandon all regulation respecting the amusement of their children, and set them adrift to find their fun wherever and whenever they can. Parents should never lose control of the amusements of their children during their tender years, and should be scrupulously careful about the companionship of their young people in places of amusements.[14]

---

### Teach children the value of patience and labor.

It is the duty of parents to teach their children the principles of the gospel and to be sober-minded and industrious in their youth. They should be impressed from the cradle to the time they leave the parental roof to make homes and assume the duties of life for themselves, that there is a seed time and harvest, and as man sows, so shall he reap. The sowing of bad habits in youth will bring forth nothing better than vice, and the sowing of the seeds of indolence will result invariably in poverty and lack of stability in old age. Evil begets evil, and good will bring forth good. . . .

Let the parents in Zion give their children something to do that they may be taught the arts of industry, and equipped to carry responsibility when it is thrust upon them. Train them in some useful vocation that their living may be assured when they commence in life for themselves. Remember, the Lord has said that "the idler shall not eat the bread of the laborer," but all in Zion should be industrious [see D&C 42:42]. Neither should they be given to loud laughter, light and foolish speeches, worldly pride and lustful desires, for these are not only unbecoming, but grievous sins in the sight of the Lord.[15]

Labor is the key to the true happiness of the physical and spiritual being. If a man possesses millions, his children should still be taught how to labor with their hands; boys and girls should receive a home training which will fit them to cope with the practical, daily affairs of family life.[16]

It is very gratifying to parents to be able to respond to the desires of their children, but it is undoubtedly a cruelty to a child to give it everything it asks for. Children may wisely be denied things which even in themselves are harmless. Our pleasures depend often more upon the qualities of our desires than upon the gratification. A child may be ladened with gifts which afford him little or no pleasure, simply because he has no desire for them. The education then of our desires is one of far-reaching importance to our happiness in life. . . .

God's ways of educating our desires are, of course, always the most perfect, and if those who have it in their power to educate and direct the desires of children would imitate his prudence, the children would be much more fortunate in combating the difficulties that beset men everywhere in the struggle for existence. And what is God's way? Everywhere in nature we are taught the lessons of patience and waiting. We want things a long time before we get them, and the fact that we wanted them a long time makes them all the more precious when they come. In nature we have our seedtime and harvest; and if children were taught that the desires that they sow may be reaped by and by through patience and labor, they will learn to appreciate whenever a long-looked-for goal has been reached.[17]

Above all else, let us train our children in the principles of the gospel of our Savior, that they may become familiar with the truth and walk in the light which it sheds forth to all those who will receive it. "He that seeketh me early," the Lord has said, "shall find me, and shall not be forsaken." [D&C 88:83.] It behooves us, therefore, to commence in early life to travel in the straight and narrow path which leads to eternal salvation.[18]

## Suggestions for Study

- How are the children who are entrusted to our care a "heritage of the Lord" and "his reward"? (Psalm 127:3). What divine blessings do children bring "that make for the prosperity of the home and the nation"?

- Why must parents teach their children to believe in the Lord Jesus Christ? What other significant doctrines and principles should children be taught? (See also Mosiah 4:14–15; D&C 68:25–28.) How might this teaching be done?

- What might be the results of failing to teach children the principles of the gospel?

- Why is it important that parents be unified and consistent in teaching their children? Why is it important that they set an example that is consistent with what they teach?

- Why is love the "most potent influence over the mind of a child"? How can parents win the confidence of their children? What might be the consequences of "selfish, unkindly" treatment of children?

- What does it mean to be "unwisely indulgent" in raising a child? What are the dangers of unwisely indulging children?

- What are "God's ways of educating" and directing His children? How can we follow His example in our own families?

- How can you follow President Smith's counsel in setting guidelines for family entertainment? How can children be taught to strive for worthwhile goals through "patience and labor"?

## Notes

1. *Life of Joseph F. Smith,* comp. Joseph Fielding Smith (1938), 449.

2. Charles W. Nibley, "Reminiscences," in *Gospel Doctrine,* 5th ed. (1939), 523.

3. Quoted in Edward H. Anderson, "Last of the Old School of Veteran Leaders," in *Gospel Doctrine,* 539–40.

4. *Gospel Doctrine,* 278.

5. *Gospel Doctrine,* 289.

6. *Gospel Doctrine,* 293; paragraphing added.

7. *Deseret News: Semi-Weekly,* 28 June 1898, 1; paragraphing added.

8. *Deseret News: Semi-Weekly,* 3 Jan. 1871, 2; paragraphing added.

9. *Gospel Doctrine,* 294–95; paragraphing altered.

10. *Gospel Doctrine,* 389.

11. *Gospel Doctrine,* 295.

12. *Gospel Doctrine,* 286.

13. *Gospel Doctrine,* 318–19.

14. *Gospel Doctrine,* 321.

15. *Gospel Doctrine,* 295–96.

16. *Gospel Doctrine,* 527.

17. *Gospel Doctrine,* 297–98.

18. *Gospel Doctrine,* 296.

The Vernal Utah Temple. In 1997, the Uintah Stake Tabernacle was
remodeled to become the Vernal Utah Temple.

# Sacred Temples of the Lord

*In holy temples we perform ordinances of salvation for the living and the dead and make covenants to which we should be true throughout our lives.*

## From the Life of Joseph F. Smith

At the August 1907 dedication service of the Uintah Stake Tabernacle in Vernal, Utah, President Joseph F. Smith told the assembled Saints that he would not be surprised if a temple were built in their midst someday.[1] In November 1997, the remodeled tabernacle was dedicated as the Vernal Utah Temple, the 51st temple of the Church.

Joseph F. Smith's life and ministry were closely tied to temple work. His personal experiences began in Nauvoo in the winter of 1845–46 when his mother and her sister, Mercy R. Thompson, "were much engaged in the work going on in the temple." President Smith said later, "It was there that my father's children were sealed to their parents."[2] He was present at the laying of the cornerstone of the Salt Lake Temple in 1853 and at the dedication of the temple in 1893.

In anticipation of the dedication, he said: "For forty years the hopes, desires, and anticipations of the entire Church have been centered upon the completion of this edifice. . . . Now that the great building is at last finished and ready to be used for divine purposes, need we say that we draw near an event whose consummation is to us as a people momentous in the highest degree?"[3] He served as president of the Salt Lake Temple from 1898 to 1911, nine of those years while he was President of the Church.

President Smith participated in the dedications of the St. George, Logan, and Manti Temples. In 1913 he dedicated the site for the sixth temple of the Church in Cardston, Alberta, Canada; and in 1915 he dedicated the land in his beloved adopted homeland, Hawaii, for the first temple outside North America. He recognized, however, that the Church was merely on the threshold of temple building: "I foresee the necessity arising for other temples . . . consecrated to the Lord for the performance of the ordinances of God's house, so that the people may have the benefits of the house of the Lord without having to travel hundreds of miles for that purpose."[4]

# Teachings of Joseph F. Smith

### Temples are for the performance of sacred, saving ordinances.

We are engaged in temple work. We have built four temples in this land, and we built two temples in the eastern country before we came here. During the lifetime of the Prophet Joseph Smith one of the two was built and dedicated, and the foundation of the other was laid and the walls had well progressed when he was martyred. It was finished by the efforts of the people under the most trying circumstances, and in poverty, and was dedicated unto the Lord. The ordinances of the house of God were administered therein as they had been taught to the leading authorities of the Church by the Prophet Joseph Smith himself. . . . The same gospel prevails today, and the same ordinances are administered today, both for the living and for the dead, that were administered by the Prophet himself, and delivered by him to the Church.[5]

We hope to see the day when we shall have temples built in the various parts of the land where they are needed for the convenience of the people; for we realize that one of the greatest responsibilities that rests upon the people of God today is that their hearts shall be turned unto their fathers, and that they shall do the work that is necessary to be done for them in order that they may be joined together fitly in the bond of the New and Everlasting Covenant from generation to generation.[6]

The temples are not open to the public. They are for the performance of sacred ordinances, having in view the salvation of the living and the dead. The principal ceremonies are baptisms, endowments, marriages, sealings. . . . Much of this work, that in behalf of the dead, is of a vicarious character. With the Latter-day Saints there is hope of salvation for those who have departed this life without obeying the gospel, if they will yield obedience to its requirements in the other world, the place of departed spirits. The gospel will be preached to them by servants of the Lord who have entered into paradise, and they who manifest faith and repent there can be baptized for here, receiving in like manner other ministrations, to the end that they may be exalted and glorified.[7]

No man can enter into the Kingdom of God but by the door and through the means that Jesus Christ has offered to the children of men. . . . Not a soul that has ever lived and died from off the face of this earth shall escape a chance to hear the gospel of Jesus Christ. If they receive it and obey it, the ordinances of the gospel will be performed for and in their behalf, by their kindred, or their posterity in some generation of time after them, so that every law and every requirement of the gospel of Jesus Christ shall be carried out, and the promises and requirements fulfilled for the salvation of the living and also for the salvation of the dead.[8]

The man or woman, therefore, among the Latter-day Saints, who does not see the necessity for the ordinances of the House of God, who does not respond to the requirements of the gospel in all its rites and ordinances, can have no proper conception of the great work which the Latter-day Saints have been called upon to perform in this age, nor can he or she enjoy the blessing that comes from the virtue of obedience to a law higher than that of man.[9]

Let no one treat lightly the ordinances of the house of God.[10]

We are not living only for the few miserable years that we spend on this earth, but for that life which is interminable; and we desire to enjoy every blessing throughout these countless ages of eternity, but unless they are secured to us by that sealing power which was given to the Apostle Peter by the Son of God, we cannot possess them. Unless we secure them on that principle, in the life to come we shall have neither father, mother, brother, sister, wife, children, nor friends, nor wealth nor honor, for all earthly "contracts, covenants, bonds, obligations, oaths, vows, connections, and associations," [see D&C 132:7] are dissolved in the grave, except those sealed and ratified by the power of God.[11]

---

**Let us enter the temple with faithful determination to carry out the will of God.**

A certain man . . . came with his recommendation from the Bishop . . . and desired the privilege of being baptized for a number of his dead, and as he came properly recommended, he received the privilege. He was baptized for his dead. Then he was permitted to go forward and perform other ordinances in their behalf. As soon as the work was done he announced his determination to withdraw from the Church. Now, I rather admired that poor fellow, because he was determined to do all he could for his dead friends before he deprived himself of the privilege of doing it. Some one may say, "Will that labor be accepted of the Lord?" Well, perhaps it will, so far as the dead are concerned, the record is kept and the ceremony was performed according to the law that God has instituted. Everything was done in the proper way, and under the direction of the proper authority, therefore why should it not be all right so far as the dead are concerned? But how much credit will that man obtain for what he did? Not much. "For what shall it profit a man, if he shall gain the whole world, and lose his own soul?" [Mark 8:36.]

The application of this to the man who is seeking to obtain privileges in the house of the Lord under false pretense, is this: Men who are trying to deceive God by pretending to be what they are not, in order that they may steal privileges and blessings from the house of God, will not be benefited in the long run. If we desire to receive the blessings and ordinances of the house of God, let us receive them in honest hearts, and let us enter into that house with a faithful and honest determination to carry out the will of God in all these things, not temporarily, but to do as He commands us all the days of our lives. So long as we continue in the enjoyment of the right spirit, these blessings will remain with us, and we shall be acknowledged of God as His children; and only when we depart from the right way and fail to do our duty, will God withdraw His spirit from us and leave us to ourselves. . . .

If I felt in my heart that I had wronged one of my brethren; or disobeyed any of the laws of God; or that I had dishonored any member of the Church, or any man that presides over me in the Church of God, I should feel that it was my duty to go and make it right before I go into that house. . . . If I have done you any wrong; if I have robbed you of any right; if I have not been true to my promise with you; or if I have done anything that has in any measure debased me in the sight of God or my brethren, I ought to go and try to make reparation before I attempt to go into the house of God. Yet I would not want to do this simply for the purpose of going into that house. I should want to do it because it is my duty to do it; and in order that I might be worthy to go there, and stand at any time after in sacred places before the Lord, I ought to make all things right with any brother that I may have wronged.

I ought to show honor to those unto whom honor is due. I ought to honor God my Heavenly Father, *now,* and from this time, henceforth, and forever. That is the principle upon which I should do right, make recompense and settle difficulties. I have heard of brethren associated together in family ties, as well as in the bonds of the new and everlasting covenant, who are at variance with each other, with bitter feelings existing in their hearts, one toward the other, and neither will humble himself to go to the other and acknowledge his faults, or to try to bring about a reconciliation, each one magnifying the weaknesses of his neighbor, and at the same time unmindful of his own faults and weakness. Yet . . . if they were denied the privilege of going into the house of God, they would feel that a great wrong had been done them.

But let me ask you, Are such men worthy to go there? Is a man that has bitterness in his heart towards his neighbor and will not forgive him nor seek reconciliation, worthy to go into the house of God? And yet you cannot deny him. There will be hundreds go there in this condition, in spite of all that we can do or say. Can they expect God will be present with them, and that His glory will shine upon them? Do not deceive yourselves. When we are worthy, God will manifest Himself unto us. When we are prepared, we shall see Him as He is, and we shall know Him. And we shall be known as we are, too. But this will be when we are worthy, and not until then.[12]

---

### Be true to the covenants you make in the house of the Lord.

In regard to our religion, or our eternal covenants, we have no compromise to make, nor principles to barter away; they emanate from God and are founded upon the rock of eternal ages; they will live and exist when empires, powers and nations shall crumble and decay; and with the help of the Almighty we will guard sacredly our covenants and maintain our interests and be true to our God, while time exists or eternity endures.[13]

Now, the Lord bless you, and in the name of the Lord I bless you—this congregation, the covenant people of the Lord, just as truly as ancient Israel were the covenant people of God, for you have entered into the solemn covenant of the Gospel of Jesus Christ, that you will keep the commandments of God, that you will eschew evil and wickedness. You know what you have done; you know the nature of the covenants you have entered into before God and witnesses and before the angels of heaven; and, therefore, you have entered into the bond of the new and everlasting covenant and are indeed the covenant people of God in the latter days.[14]

As the Lord has helped me in the past to be true to my covenants, that I have entered into with Him and with you, . . . so by His help and by His blessing I propose to be true throughout the future of my life, whether I am permitted to live long or short; it matters not to me. While I live, I hope to be a true man, an honest man, a man who can face all mankind and, at last, who can stand before God, the Judge of the quick and the dead, and not quail for what I have done in the world.

. . . I pray you to be true to your covenants; be true to those covenants that you made in the waters of baptism, to those covenants you made in the house of the Lord, and true to every righteous obligation that devolves upon you. To be Latter-day Saints, men or women must be thinkers, and workers; they must be men and women who weigh matters in their minds, men and women who consider carefully their course of life and the principles that they have espoused. Men cannot be faithful Latter-day Saints unless they study and understand, to some extent at least, the principles of the gospel that they have received. . . . When people understand the gospel of Jesus Christ, you will see them walking straightforward, according to the word of the Lord, and the law of God, strictly in accordance with that which is consistent, just, righteous, and in every sense acceptable to the Lord, who only accepts of that which is right and pleasing in His sight; for only that which is right is pleasing unto Him.[15]

## Suggestions for Study

- Why do we build temples? What blessings do we receive when we attend the temple and keep the covenants we make there? (See also D&C 109:10–23.) How do you feel when you attend the temple?

- In what ways do people sometimes "treat lightly the ordinances of the house of God"?

- What does it mean to you to "enjoy every blessing throughout these countless ages of eternity"? How do temple ordinances help us do this? How can temple attendance help us keep in our minds "the solemnities of eternity"? (D&C 43:34).

- What does it mean to be worthy to go to the house of God? What can we do to better prepare ourselves to attend the temple? Why can we not "steal privileges and blessings from the house of God"?

- What do you feel is required of you to be true to the covenants you have made in the temple?

- What can we do to meet President Smith's challenge to be "thinkers, and workers"?

- How can we show honor to the house of God? How can parents help their children learn to honor the temples?

311

## Notes

1. See Uintah Stake Historical Record: 1905–1909, Quarterly Conference, 25 Aug. 1907, Historical Department Archives, The Church of Jesus Christ of Latter-day Saints, 246.

2. *Gospel Doctrine,* 5th ed. (1939), 197.

3. In James R. Clark, comp., *Messages of the First Presidency of The Church of Jesus Christ of Latter-day Saints,* 6 vols. (1965–75), 3:241–42.

4. In Conference Report, Apr. 1901, 69.

5. *Gospel Doctrine,* 470.

6. *Gospel Doctrine,* 471.

7. In *Messages of the First Presidency,* 4:249–50.

8. "Latter-day Saints Follow Teachings of the Savior," *Scrap Book of Mormon Literature,* 2 vols. (n.d.), 2:561–62.

9. *Gospel Doctrine,* 213.

10. *Gospel Doctrine,* 5.

11. *Deseret News: Semi-Weekly,* 11 Nov. 1873, 1.

12. *Deseret News: Semi-Weekly,* 21 Mar. 1893, 2; paragraphing added.

13. In *Messages of the First Presidency,* 2:346–47.

14. In *Messages of the First Presidency,* 4:186.

15. In Conference Report, Oct. 1910, 3–4.

# Seek to Be Educated in the Truth

*We are to seek diligently for truth and strive to learn and improve each day.*

## From the Life of Joseph F. Smith

Although President Joseph F. Smith had few opportunities for formal education, he was greatly influenced by the doctrine that the "glory of God is intelligence" (D&C 93:36), and he encouraged the Saints to obtain as much education as possible in both spiritual and temporal truths. President Smith continued to support the Church academies program, which provided secondary school training and religious education for many Saints. He also laid the foundation for today's extensive Church Educational System by establishing the seminary program. The first seminary was opened in 1912, adjacent to Granite High School in Salt Lake City, Utah.

As President of the Church, he encouraged the Church auxiliaries—the Relief Society, the Sunday School, the Primary, and the Mutual Improvement Association (today the Young Men and Young Women programs)—in their mission of teaching the gospel. During his administration, uniform courses of study were established for children and adults in the Church auxiliaries, and the magazines published by the Church contained plans for weekly lessons. He served for many years as the editor of the *Improvement Era,* which preceded the *Ensign* magazine; and the *Juvenile Instructor,* which was published for the Sunday School organization, writing many articles and editorials that clarified Church doctrine. "He loved to write," remembered one of his friends, "and often expressed the wish that he could have more time to devote to the *Era.*"[1]

As President Smith expressed, "To the Latter-day Saints, salvation itself, under the atonement of Christ, is a process of education. . . . Knowledge is a means of eternal progress."[2]

# Teachings of Joseph F. Smith

### All truth is included in the gospel.

There is no truth in any other religious society or organization, which is not included in the gospel of Jesus Christ as taught by Joseph Smith, the Prophet, and after him by the leaders and elders of this Church; but it requires some effort on our part, some exertion, some devotion, to learn of and to enjoy these things. If we neglect them, we are, of course, not the recipients of the blessings that follow effort, and that come from a thorough understanding of these principles. Hence it is that others may come in among us and advocate their ideas which, though not comparing with ours in plainness, instruction, and truth, are yet listened to by people who are made to believe that all these things are new, and not contained in the gospel of Jesus Christ as taught by the Latter-day Saints. This is a fearful fallacy, and one that should be guarded against by everyone who loves the gospel.[3]

If you love the truth, if you have received the gospel in your hearts and love it, your intelligence will be added upon; your understanding of truth will be expanded, larger than in any other way. Truth is the thing, above all other things in the world, that makes men free—free from indolence and carelessness, free from the fearful consequences of neglect, for it will be a fearful consequence, if we neglect our duty before the living God. If you will learn the truth and walk in the light of truth you shall be made free from the errors of men . . . ; you will be above suspicion and above wrong-doing of every description. God will approve of you and bless you and your inheritances, and make you prosper and flourish like a green bay tree.[4]

He that hath the privilege of learning and embracing the knowledge of God, and the way of life . . . is more fortunate than the finder of wealth, or of the hidden treasures of the earth. . . . His mind is free to accept the plain and precious truths revealed for the redemption and the life of man from the fountain head,

This building housed the Church's first seminary, opened in 1912
adjacent to Granite High School in Salt Lake City, Utah.

and his heart is—or should be—wholly devoted to the great and glorious cause of human redemption.[5]

Where would you have people go who are unsettled in the truth? The answer is plain. They will not find satisfaction in the doctrines of Men. Let them seek for it in the written word of God; let them pray to him in their secret chambers, where no human ear can hear, and in their closets petition for light; let them obey the doctrines of Jesus, and they will immediately begin to grow in the knowledge of the truth. This course will bring peace to their souls, joy to their hearts, and a settled conviction which no change can disturb. They may be well assured that "he that heareth in secret will reward them openly." [See Matthew 6:6.][6]

---

**Unlike the theories of men, the word of God
is always true, always right.**

Our young people are diligent students. They reach out after truth and knowledge with commendable zeal, and in so doing

315

they must necessarily adopt for temporary use, many theories of men. As long, however, as they recognize them as scaffolding useful for research purposes, there can be no special harm in them. It is when these theories are settled upon as basic truth that trouble appears, and the searcher then stands in grave danger of being led hopelessly from the right way. . . .

The Church holds to the definite authority of divine revelation which must be the standard; and that, as so-called "Science" has changed from age to age in its deductions, and as divine revelation is truth, and must abide forever, views as to the lesser should conform to the positive statements of the greater, and, further, that in institutions founded by the Church for the teaching of theology, as well as other branches of education, its instructors must be in harmony in their teachings with its principles and doctrines. . . .

The religion of the Latter-day Saints is not hostile to any truth, nor to scientific search for truth. "That which is demonstrated, we accept with joy," said the First Presidency in their Christmas greeting to the Saints, "but vain philosophy, human theory and mere speculations of men we do not accept, nor do we adopt anything contrary to divine revelation or to good common sense, but everything that tends to right conduct, that harmonizes with sound morality and increases faith in Deity, finds favor with us, no matter where it may be found." ["Words in Season from the First Presidency," *Deseret Evening News,* 17 Dec. 1910, 3.]

A good motto for young people to adopt, who are determined to delve into philosophic theories, is to search all things, but be careful to hold on only to that which is true. The truth persists, but the theories of philosophers change and are overthrown. What men use today as a scaffolding for scientific purposes from which to reach out into the unknown for truth, may be torn down tomorrow, having served its purpose; but faith is an eternal principle through which the humble believer may secure everlasting solace. It is the only way to find God.[7]

Science and philosophy through all the ages have undergone change after change. Scarcely a century has passed but they have introduced new theories of science and philosophy, that supersede the old traditions and the old faith and the old doctrines entertained by philosophers and scientists. These things may undergo continuous changes, but the word of God is always true, is always right.[8]

Education that has for its highest ideals the pursuit of worldly ambitions is wanting in that free and unrestrained flow of the spirit which makes for higher freedom and a more wholesome life. As we ripen in years and in experience, our spiritual lives have more and more to do with our real happiness. Our thoughts are more frequently turned inward as we contemplate the approaching end of this life and the unfolding of the greater life to come.[9]

---

## We are to improve and advance in the scale of intelligence.

We are not "ever learning and never coming to a knowledge of the truth." [See 2 Timothy 3:7.] On the contrary, we are ever learning and are ever drawing nearer to a proper comprehension of the truth, the duty and the responsibility that devolve upon members of the Church who are called to responsible positions in it. Not only does this apply to those members who are called to act in responsible positions, but it applies to . . . [all] members of the Church of Jesus Christ of Latter-day Saints.

Who is there, under the circumstances that exist around us, that is not growing? Who is there of us that is not learning something day by day? Who is there of us that is not gaining experience as we pass along, and are attending to the duties of membership in the Church, and to the duties of citizens . . . ? It seems to me that it would be a very sad comment upon the Church of Jesus Christ of Latter-day Saints and her people to suppose for a moment that we are at a standstill, that we have ceased to grow, ceased to improve and to advance in the scale of intelligence, and in the faithful performance of duty in every condition in which we are placed as a people and as members of the Church of Christ.[10]

One of the greatest evils existing . . . is that of ignorance, coupled with indifference. I presume that if the ignorant were not so indifferent to these facts and to their condition they might be prompted to learn more than they do. The trouble with men and

Students at the Latter-day Saints' University in Salt Lake City, Utah, 1903.
President Joseph F. Smith exhorted the Saints to "enrich your minds with the
best of knowledge and facts. . . . No man can be saved in ignorance"
(*Gospel Doctrine,* 206).

women is that they too frequently close their eyes to the facts that
exist around them, and it seems to be very difficult for many of the
people to learn and adapt to their lives those simple truths that
should be in fact the household words and precepts of every
Latter-day Saint, and of every home of a Latter-day Saint. How shall
we stem the tide of this evil, this indifference, this consequent ignorance? It appears to me that the only way to do it is to wake up
and become interested, or to interest ourselves in those things
which are so important and necessary to the happiness and well-
being of the children of men, especially that which is so needful
for the happiness and well-being of ourselves individually.

It isn't all that is necessary, to learn the truth or to cease to be
ignorant. Following that comes the application of the understanding and knowledge that we gain, to those works and things
that are needful for our protection and for the protection of our
children, our neighbors, our homes, our happiness.[11]

Search out the truth of the written word; listen for and receive the truth declared by living prophets and teachers; enrich your minds with the best of knowledge and facts. Of those who speak in his name, the Lord requires humility, not ignorance. Intelligence is the glory of God; and no man can be saved in ignorance [see D&C 93:36; 131:6].[12]

Service in the Lord's cause is a means towards obtaining a true education, and an education that is worth the name widens the fields of its possessor's usefulness, and imparts zest and energy to all his undertakings.[13]

Fix in your minds noble thoughts, cultivate elevated themes, let your aims and aspirations be high. Be in a certain degree independent; to the degree of usefulness, helpfulness and self-reliance, though no human beings can be said truly to be independent of their fellow beings, and there is no one reckless enough to deny our utter dependence on our heavenly Father. Seek to be educated in the highest meaning of the term; get the most possible service out of your time, your body and brains, and let all your efforts be directed into honorable channels, that no effort shall be wasted, and no labor result in loss or evil.

Seek the very best society; be kind, polite, agreeable, seeking to learn whatever is good, and comprehend the duties of life that you may be a blessing to all those with whom you associate, making the very most and best of your lot in life.[14]

---

### In all our educational and worldly endeavors, we should hold to the iron rod.

It is very important that the Latter-day Saints should always keep before them that recognized standard of religious and moral life which modern revelation has set up for their guidance. They should, in other words, keep a firm hold upon what has been beautifully described as the "iron rod."

In these times when commercial, social and business organizations are taking strong hold upon the people, . . . the duties and obligations of the Latter-day Saints cannot safely be set aside for other standards of living.

It is to be feared that men accept for their guidance too frequently the general conduct of those by whom they are surrounded. If questionable practices are indulged in and the want of proper restraint is felt in any of these business, social and political organizations, it is no reason why those who profess to be Latter-day Saints should cut themselves loose from their moorings and drift with those who are indifferent, wayward, or immoral. . . .

We should never forget that we are, or should be, distinctly Latter-day Saints, wherever our lot in life might be cast, and we should never lose sight of that moral and spiritual guidance which the Gospel imposes upon us. Some of our young men who have made shipwreck of their lives may trace their misfortune and downfall to the first step they took in their willingness to be like those with whom they were associated in their temporal pursuits.

There are periods of excitement which rise often to such an extent that men and women apparently are completely carried away with it and forget everything but that which gives them temporary pleasure or worldly gain. Some, indeed, have no higher standard of morals than that which panders to worldly popularity. When these waves of excitement pass over they find themselves not only drifting aimlessly but sometimes hopelessly submerged among the debris or driftwood of wayward humanity. . . .

It is imperatively necessary, at all times, and especially so when our associations do not afford us the moral and spiritual support which we require for our advancement, that we go to the house of the Lord to worship and mingle with the Saints that their moral and spiritual influence may help to correct our false impressions and restore us to that life which the duties and obligations of our conscience and true religion imposes upon us.

. . . Let us, therefore, in the midst of our worldly callings and associations not forget that paramount duty which we owe to ourselves and to our God.[15]

## Suggestions for Study

- What experiences have taught you that all truth is "included in the gospel of Jesus Christ"?

- What must we do to learn the principles of truth? What are the dangers of neglecting this duty? What rewards are promised to those who learn the truth and walk in its light?

- What is the position of the Church regarding the scientific search for truth? How do the theories and philosophies of men contrast with the word of God?

- What are the dangers of pursuing an education only to satisfy "worldly ambitions"?

- In what ways do people cease "to improve and to advance in the scale of intelligence"? How can we ensure that we are continuing to learn something day by day? (See also D&C 130:18–19.)

- Why is ignorance of the truth "one of the greatest evils"? How can we "stem the tide of this evil"?

- How can you "get the most possible service out of your time, your body and brains"? What attitudes and habits can help us make "the very most and best of [our] lot in life"?

- What are the dangers of accepting for our guidance "the general conduct of those by whom [we] are surrounded" in our educational and temporal pursuits?

- In the "midst of our worldly callings and associations," what can we do to "not forget that paramount duty which we owe to ourselves and to our God"?

## Notes

1. "Editor's Table," *Improvement Era,* Dec. 1918, 174.
2. In James R. Clark, comp., *Messages of the First Presidency of The Church of Jesus Christ of Latter-day Saints,* 6 vols. (1965–75), 4:146–47.
3. *Gospel Doctrine,* 5th ed. (1939), 122–23.
4. "A Journey to the South," *Improvement Era,* Dec. 1917, 102.
5. "Foreign Correspondence," *Millennial Star,* 25 Mar. 1878, 187.
6. *Gospel Doctrine,* 126.
7. *Gospel Doctrine,* 38–39.
8. *Gospel Doctrine,* 39.
9. *Gospel Doctrine,* 353.
10. *Gospel Doctrine,* 342.
11. *Gospel Doctrine,* 342–43.
12. *Gospel Doctrine,* 206.
13. "Counsel to Returning Missionaries," *Millennial Star,* 2 Oct. 1913, 646.
14. *Gospel Doctrine,* 351–52.
15. "Editorial Thoughts: Our Religious Identity," *Juvenile Instructor,* Mar. 1912, 144–45.

*Daniel Refusing the King's Meat and Wine,* by Del Parson.
Daniel and his friends refused to eat the Babylonian king's food and drink his wine
because they knew it would not be good for them. They grew healthy and strong and
were blessed with wisdom because they chose to eat food that was better for them.

# The Word of Wisdom: A Law for the Physical and Spiritual Health of the Saints

*Observance of the Word of Wisdom will strengthen our bodies, ennoble our souls, and bring us nearer to God.*

## From the Life of Joseph F. Smith

President Joseph F. Smith taught that the Word of Wisdom was more than a prohibition against tea, coffee, tobacco, and alcohol; it contained practical counsel for good health and spiritual growth, and those Saints who obeyed it would draw nearer to the Lord and become more like Him. To remind the Saints of the importance of the Word of Wisdom, he sometimes read Doctrine and Covenants 89 in its entirety in a meeting. "Now, it may seem altogether unnecessary and out of place, perhaps, to many, for me to occupy the time of this vast congregation in reading this revelation," he once said, but read every word of it anyway to emphasize the great value of the message.[1]

He said: "I recollect a circumstance that occurred three years ago in a party that I was traveling with. There were one or two who persisted in having their tea and coffee at every place they stopped. I preached the Word of Wisdom right along; but they said, 'What does it matter? Here is So-and-so, who drinks tea and coffee.' . . . I said at one time, 'Oh, yes, you say it is a good thing to drink a little tea or coffee, but the Lord says it is not. What shall I follow?' The Lord says that if we will observe the Word of Wisdom we shall have access to great treasures of knowledge, and hidden treasures; we shall run and not be weary, we shall walk and not faint; and the destroying angel shall pass us by, as he did the children of Israel, and not slay us. . . . I will pray for you and earnestly beseech you, my brethren and sisters, . . . to cease practicing these forbidden things, and observe the laws of God."[2]

# Teachings of Joseph F. Smith

### We are to observe the Word of Wisdom for our benefit and prosperity.

We see great reasons for the principles contained in this chapter of the book of Doctrine and Covenants [section 89] being taught to the world, and especially to the Latter-day Saints. It is nothing more nor less than that simple Word of Wisdom that was given in 1833, for the benefit, the help, and the prosperity of the Latter-day Saints, that they might purify and prepare themselves to go nearer into the presence of the Lord, that by reason of keeping this law they might fit themselves to enjoy the blessings that He is more than willing to bestow upon them, if they are worthy. . . .

I simply want to say to you my brethren and sisters, that there is no other course that we can take in the world, in relation to our temporal welfare and health, better than that which the Lord God has pointed out to us. Why can we not realize this? Why will we not come to a perfect understanding of it? Why will we not deny ourselves that which our craven appetites desire? Why can we not observe more closely the will of the Lord as made known to us in this revelation? . . . If this commandment were observed by the whole people, the vast amount of money that now goes out to the world for strong drink and these other things forbidden in the word of wisdom, would be saved at home, and the health, prosperity and temporal salvation of the people would be correspondingly increased. No man can violate the laws of God with reference to health and temporal salvation, and enjoy those blessings in the same degree that he could do and would do if he would obey the commands of God. . . .

No member of the Church of Jesus Christ of Latter-day Saints can afford to do himself the dishonor or to bring upon himself the disgrace, of crossing the threshhold of a liquor saloon or a gambling hall. . . . No Latter-day Saint, no member of the Church can afford it, for it is humiliating to him, it is disgraceful in him to do it, and God will judge him according to his works. The man or woman who truly believes in the doctrines of the Church or professing to have membership in the Church, who believes and practices the principles contained in this "Word of Wisdom," will never be numbered among those who will bring this disgrace upon them, upon their neighbors or upon the Church to which they belong; they will never do it.

. . . The Lord does not delight in intemperance, in drunkenness, nor can He have pleasure in the poverty, in the degradation and ruin that such practices bring upon their votaries and upon those who are dependent upon them, the ruin of manhood, the ruin of family organizations and the degradation of those that are engaged in it and that bring poverty, destruction, and death upon themselves and upon their families. Every member of the Church, male and female, ought to set his or her face as flint against intemperance and against anything that is in violation of the laws of God, that they might never be overcome or yield to the temptation of evil. We ought to have purer communities, communities that are not ridden by vice, by pernicious habits and practices. . . .

Perhaps those who are accustomed to these habits think this is a very trivial or very unimportant thing to talk about to a vast congregation like this, but I never see a boy or a man, young or old, addicted to this habit and practicing it openly but I am forced to the conclusion to the conviction in my mind that he is either ignorant of God's will concerning man or he is defiant of God's will and does not care anything about the word of the Lord, and that alone is sufficient to bring sorrow to the heart of any man who has any regard or respect for the word or will of the Lord and would like to see it obeyed. . . .

. . . We pray God to heal us when we are sick, and then we turn round from our prayers and partake of the very things that He has told us are not good for us! How inconsistent it is for men to ask God to bless them, when they themselves are taking a course to injure and to bring evil upon themselves. No wonder we don't get our prayers answered more than we do, and no wonder our health is no better than it is, when we are addicted to practices that God has said are not good for us, and thereby entail evils upon our life and physical being; and then to turn to the Lord and ask Him to heal us from the consequence of our own folly, and pernicious practices; from the effects of the evil that we have brought upon ourselves and that we knew better than to do. How foolish it is![3]

When I see a man professing to be a Latter-day Saint, or even professing to be a member of the Church, . . . befouling his breath with intoxicating drink, with the fumes of tobacco, or unnecessarily indulging in stimulants, it grieves my spirit, my soul goes out for him in pity and in sorrowful regret, and I wonder why it is that we, individually, cannot realize our own folly, our own degradation in yielding to these pernicious habits that are neither useful or ornamental, nor in the least degree beneficial, but indeed are harmful. Why cannot we rise to that degree of intelligence that would enable us to say to the tempter, "Get behind me," and to turn our backs upon the practice of evil. How humiliating it must be to a thoughtful man to feel that he is a slave to his appetites, or to an over-weening and pernicious habit, desire, or passion.[4]

---

### By putting the Word of Wisdom into practice, we will be able to appreciate it.

We should observe the Word of Wisdom that has been given to us. . . . The drunkard becomes a slave to his drink; others become slaves to the use of tea, coffee and tobacco, and therefore they consider them necessary to their happiness; but they are not really necessary to their happiness nor to their health. Indeed, they are injurious to health. . . . It is by putting the word of the Lord into practice that we will be able to appreciate it, not by simply looking upon it without doing it. When we do the will of the Lord, then shall we know of the doctrine, that it is of God; then shall we build upon the rock; then when the floods descend and the storms beat upon the house, it will not fall.[5]

In the mad rush of life for worldly honors and for the possession of the perishable things of this earth men do not stop before they get weary, and they do not rest before they become faint.

They appear to think that what is necessary for them when they become weary and faint is to take stimulants to refresh themselves, that they may be able to run a little farther for a few moments. In this way the man of business braces himself up by taking strong drinks. The housewife and the mother who has the care of her family upon her hands, after she has toiled until she has become faint, feels that she must, in order to keep up her strength, take a cup of tea, and thus brace up her nerves and strengthen herself for a little while that she may be able to finish her day's work. Now, if the pure intelligence of the Spirit of God were substituted for the stimulating influence of the tea and the liquor; if we could by some means get a sufficient portion of the Spirit of the Lord within us that would cause us to know just what to do when we felt weariness and faintness coming upon us, without resorting to the aid of stimulants and drugs that go far to injure our systems and make us slaves, to an acquired appetite, it would be a great deal better for us. . . .

I would rather feel tired and exhausted by labor, and let nature have a chance to restore itself, than I would attempt to doctor myself by the use of narcotics and drugs that would sap the foundation of my physical and spiritual health. But inasmuch as we do not observe the Word of Wisdom, how shall we have wisdom, knowledge and understanding by which we may be governed in our own conduct? The promise is that if we will observe this we shall have knowledge, and the destroyer shall pass us by, and we shall escape those evils that are coming upon the wicked.[6]

### Abiding by the Word of Wisdom brings us nearer to becoming like the Lord.

I believe that we are coming nearer to the point where we shall be able to observe that great and glorious law of temperance which the Lord Almighty has given unto us, wherein He has said that strong drink is not good, that tobacco is not for the habitual use of man, not for the stomach. . . . We are coming to the conclusion that the Lord knew best, when He delivered to the Church, through the Prophet Joseph Smith, that "Word of Wisdom," contained in the book of revelations from the Lord. . . .

The great majority of the people of the Church of Jesus Christ of Latter-day Saints are coming nearer and nearer to a proper observance of the law which the Lord has given to us for our health, for the preservation of our lives; that we may be in harmony with His Spirit and His will, that we may be clean and undefiled, that we may be nearer like unto Him Who was without sin, Who was indeed pure and holy as God is pure and holy.[7]

The young man who would cope with the world, who would be full of vigor, and fresh for the battle of life, will find his strength in living according to the word of the Lord; for the promise is that all "who remember to keep and do these sayings, walking in obedience to the commandments, shall receive health in their navel, and marrow to their bones, and shall find wisdom and great treasures of knowledge, even hidden treasures; and shall run and not be weary, and shall walk and not faint; and I, the Lord, give unto them a promise, that the destroying angel shall pass by them, as the children of Israel, and not slay them." [See D&C 89:18–21.][8]

Are these glorious promises not sufficient to induce us to observe this Word of Wisdom? Is there not something here that is worthy our attention? Are not "great treasures" of knowledge, even "hidden treasures," something to be desired? But when I see men and women addicting themselves to the use of tea and coffee, or strong drinks, or tobacco in any form, I say to myself, here are men and women who do not appreciate the promise God has made unto them. They trample it under their feet, and treat it as a thing of naught. They despise the word of God, and go contrary to it in their actions. Then when affliction overtakes them, they are almost ready to curse God, because he will not hear their prayers, and they are left to endure sickness and pain.[9]

Now, I do wish with all my heart—not because I say it, but because it is written in the word of the Lord—that you would give heed to this Word of Wisdom. It was given unto us . . . for our guidance, for our happiness and advancement in every principle that pertains to the kingdom of God, in time and throughout eternity, and I pray you to observe it. It will do you good; it will ennoble your souls; it will free your thoughts and your hearts from the spirit of destruction; it will make you feel like God, who sustains even the sparrow, that it does not fall to the ground without his notice; it will bring you nearer to the similitude of the Son of God, the Savior of the world, who healed the sick, who made the lame to leap for joy, who restored hearing to the deaf and sight to the blind, who distributed peace, joy, and comfort to all with whom he came in contact.[10]

# Suggestions for Study

- For what purposes is the Word of Wisdom given to us? (See also D&C 89:1–4.)

- How do habit-forming substances or practices chain our bodies and dull our sensitivity to the Spirit's influence?

- What kinds of "degradation and ruin" often accompany disobedience to the Word of Wisdom? When people disregard the counsel in the Word of Wisdom, how do their loved ones often suffer?

- How does observing the Word of Wisdom help us have "purer communities, communities that are not ridden by vice, by pernicious habits and practices"?

- In what ways have you learned to appreciate the Word of Wisdom by "putting the word of the Lord into practice"? (See also John 7:17.)

- How have you seen the promises given in Doctrine and Covenants 89 fulfilled in your own life or the lives of others? (See also D&C 89:18–21.)

- How does observance of the Word of Wisdom help us have the "wisdom, knowledge and understanding" by which we can govern our conduct?

- How does observance of the Word of Wisdom ennoble our souls? How does it free our thoughts and hearts from the spirit of destruction? How does observance of this law bring us "nearer to the similitude of the Son of God"?

## Notes

1. In James R. Clark, comp., *Messages of the First Presidency of The Church of Jesus Christ of Latter-day Saints,* 6 vols. (1965–75), 4:180–81.

2. *Gospel Doctrine,* 5th ed. (1939), 366–67.

3. In *Messages of the First Presidency,* 4:179–80, 182–85; paragraphing added.

4. In Conference Report, Apr. 1908, 4.

5. *Deseret News: Semi-Weekly,* 20 Nov. 1894, 1.

6. *Deseret News: Semi-Weekly,* 7 Apr. 1895, 1; paragraphing altered.

7. In Conference Report, Apr. 1908, 4.

8. *Gospel Doctrine,* 241.

9. *Gospel Doctrine,* 366.

10. *Gospel Doctrine,* 365–66.

# Sons and Daughters of the Eternal Father

*We are the children of God, formed in His divine image and capable of becoming like Him.*

## From the Life of Joseph F. Smith

In November 1909, President Joseph F. Smith and his Counselors in the First Presidency, John R. Winder and Anthon H. Lund, issued a statement titled "The Origin of Man" to answer inquiries arising "from time to time respecting the attitude of the Church of Jesus Christ of Latter-day Saints . . . in relation to the origin of man. It is believed that a statement of the position held by the Church upon this important subject will be timely and productive of good." The statement includes these words:

" 'God created man in his own image, in the image of God created he him; male and female created he them.' [Genesis 1:27.] In these plain and pointed words the inspired author of the book of Genesis made known to the world the truth concerning the origin of the human family."[1] This chapter contains excerpts from "The Origin of Man."

President Smith frequently affirmed the literal reality of the fatherhood of God: "As I know, and as I have reason to know, that I am here and that I live, so I believe and I have reason to know that God, my Father, lives."[2]

## Teachings of Joseph F. Smith

### We are the spirit children of our Heavenly Father.

We want to know where we came from, and where we are going. Where did we come from? From God. Our spirits existed before they came to this world. They were in the councils of the heavens before the foundations of the earth were laid. We were there. We sang together with the heavenly hosts for joy when the foundations of the earth were laid, and when the plan of our existence upon this earth and redemption were mapped out. We were there; we were interested, and we took a part in this great preparation. We were unquestionably present in those councils . . . when Satan offered himself as a savior of the world if he could but receive the honor and glory of the Father for doing it. But Jesus said, "Father, thy will be done, and the glory be thine forever." Wherefore, because Satan rebelled against God, and sought to destroy the agency of man, the Father rejected him and he was cast out, but Jesus was accepted.

We were, no doubt, there, and took part in all those scenes, we were vitally concerned in the carrying out of these great plans and purposes, we understood them, and it was for our sakes they were decreed, and are to be consummated. These spirits have been coming to this earth to take upon them tabernacles, that they might become like unto Jesus Christ, being "formed in his likeness and image," from the morn of creation until now, and will continue until the winding up scene, until the spirits who were destined to come to this world shall have come and accomplished their mission in the flesh.[3]

We behold . . . man, the crowning work of God, on this earth, the masterpiece, if you please, whom inspiration teaches us, is the offspring of that eternal being who is the Creator of all things, he being the most perfect in his organization, possessing greater attributes, powers of reason, and intelligence than all other beings, constituting him the "lord of creation," and the nearest in resemblance to the Creator. We look at these things and we cannot but come to the conclusion that this is *not* the work of chance, but the result of matured omniscient designs and purposes, that man is the son of God, possessing the attributes and image of his Father, and in the beginning much of this intelligence, insomuch that he was the companion and associate of God and dwelt with him, and knew no sin. The Lord gave him the earth as a possession and an inheritance, and laws for his government, that he might fill the measure of his creation and have joy therein.[4]

*Adam and Eve in the Garden,* by Lowell Bruce Bennett. President Smith taught that Adam was "the first man of all men" (Moses 1:34).

The written standards of scripture show that all people who come to this earth and are born in mortality, had a pre-existent, spiritual personality, as the sons and daughters of the Eternal Father. . . . Jesus Christ was the first-born. A spirit born of God is an immortal being. When the body dies, the spirit does not die. In the resurrected state the body will be immortal as well as the spirit.[5]

---

## We are created in the image of God.

What was the form of man, in the spirit and in the body, as originally created? In a general way the answer is given in [these] words. . . . "God created man in his own image." It is more explicitly rendered in the Book of Mormon thus: "All men were created in the beginning after mine own image" (Ether 3:15). It is the Father who is speaking. If, therefore, we can ascertain the form of the "Father of spirits," "The God of the spirits of all flesh," we shall be able to discover the form of the original man.

Jesus Christ, the Son of God, is "the express image" of His Father's person (Hebrews 1:3). He walked the earth as a human being, as a perfect man, and said, in answer to a question put to Him: "He that hath seen me hath seen the Father" (John 14:9). This alone ought to solve the problem to the satisfaction of every thoughtful, reverent mind. The conclusion is irresistible, that if the Son of God be the express image (that is, likeness) of His Father's person, then His Father is in the form of man; for that was the form of the Son of God, not only during His mortal life, but before His mortal birth, and after His resurrection. It was in this form that the Father and the Son, as two personages, appeared to Joseph Smith, when, as a boy of fourteen years, he received his first vision.

Then if God made man—the first man—in His own image and likeness, he must have made him like unto Christ, and consequently like unto men of Christ's time and of the present day. That man was made in the image of Christ, is positively stated in the Book of Moses: "And I, God, said unto mine Only Begotten, which was with me from the beginning, Let us make man in our image, after our likeness; and it was so. . . . And I, God, created man in mine own image, in the image of mine Only Begotten created I him, male and female created I them" [Moses 2:26–27].

The Father of Jesus is our Father also. Jesus Himself taught this truth, when He instructed His disciples how to pray: "Our Father which art in heaven," etc. Jesus, however, is the firstborn among all the sons of God—the first begotten in the spirit, and the only begotten in the flesh. He is our elder brother, and we, like Him, are in the image of God. . . .

"God created man in His own image." This is just as true of the spirit as it is of the body, which is only the clothing of the spirit, its complement; the two together constituting the soul [see D&C 88:15]. The spirit of man is in the form of man, and the spirits of all creatures are in the likeness of their bodies. This was plainly taught by the Prophet Joseph Smith (Doctrine and Covenants, 77:2). . . .

When the divine Being whose spirit-body the brother of Jared beheld [see Ether 3:6–16], took upon Him flesh and blood, He appeared as a man, having "body, parts and passions," like other men, though vastly superior to all others, because He was God, even the Son of God, the Word made flesh: in Him "dwelt the fulness of the Godhead bodily." [Colossians 2:9.] And why should He not appear as a man? That was the form of His spirit, and it must needs have an appropriate covering, a suitable tabernacle. He came into the world as He had promised to come (III Nephi 1:13), taking an infant tabernacle, and developing it gradually to the fulness of His spirit stature. He came as man had been coming for ages, and as man has continued to come ever since. Jesus, however, as shown, was the only begotten of God in the flesh.

Adam, our great progenitor, "the first man," was, like Christ, a pre-existent spirit, and like Christ he took upon him an appropriate body, the body of a man, and so became a "living soul." The doctrine of the pre-existence,—revealed so plainly, particularly in latter days, pours a wonderful flood of light upon the otherwise mysterious problem of man's origin. It shows that man, as a spirit, was begotten and born of heavenly parents, and reared to maturity in the eternal mansions of the Father, prior to coming upon the earth in a temporal body to undergo an experience in mortality. It teaches that all men existed in the spirit before any man existed in the flesh, and that all who have inhabited the earth since Adam have taken bodies and become souls in like manner.

It is held by some that Adam was not the first man upon this earth, and that the original human being was a development from lower orders of the animal creation. These, however, are the theories of men. The word of the Lord declares that Adam was "the first man of all men" (Moses 1:34), and we are therefore in duty bound to regard him as the primal parent of our race. It was shown to the brother of Jared that all men were created in the *beginning* after the image of God; and whether we take this to mean the spirit or the body, or both, it commits us to the same conclusion: Man began life as a human being, in the likeness of our heavenly Father.

True it is that the body of man enters upon its career as a tiny germ or embryo, which becomes an infant, quickened at a certain stage by the spirit whose tabernacle it is, and the child, after being born, develops into a man. There is nothing in this, however, to indicate that the original man, the first of our race, began life as anything less than a man, or less than the human germ or embryo that becomes a man.[6]

---

### We become like God our Father through obedience to the principles of the gospel.

God originated and designed all things, and all are his children. We are born into the world as his offspring; endowed with the same attributes. The children of men have sprung from the Almighty, whether the world is willing to acknowledge it or not. He is the Father of our spirits. He is the originator of our earthly tabernacles. We live and move and have our being in God our heavenly Father. And having sprung from him with our talents, our ability, our wisdom, we should at least be willing to acknowledge his hand in all the prosperity that may attend us in life, and give to him the honor and glory of all we accomplish in the flesh. . . .

. . . [Man] is made in the image of God himself, so that he can reason, reflect, pray, exercise faith; he can use his energies for the accomplishment of the desires of his heart, and inasmuch as he puts forth his efforts in the proper direction, then he is entitled to an increased portion of the Spirit of the Almighty to inspire him to increased intelligence, to increased prosperity and happiness in the world; but in proportion as he prostitutes his energies for evil, the inspiration of the Almighty is withdrawn from him, until he becomes so dark and so benighted, that so far as his knowledge of God is concerned, he is quite as ignorant as a dumb brute.

. . . We must become like [God]; peradventure to sit upon thrones, to have dominion, power, and eternal increase. God designed this in the beginning. . . . This is the object of our existence in the world; and we can only attain to these things through obedience to certain principles, through walking in certain channels, through obtaining certain information, certain intelligence from God, without which no man can accomplish his work or fulfill the mission he has come upon the earth to fulfill. These principles are the principles of the gospel of eternal truth, the principles of faith, repentance, and baptism for the remission of sins, the principle of obedience to God the eternal Father; for obedience is one of the first principles or laws of heaven.[7]

Man is the child of God, formed in the divine image and endowed with divine attributes, and even as the infant son of an earthly father and mother is capable in due time of becoming a man, so the undeveloped offspring of celestial parentage is capable, by experience through ages and aeons, of evolving into a God.[8]

## Suggestions for Study

- How does it make you feel to know that you are literally the offspring of God? How does this understanding influence your everyday choices and actions?

- Where did we first hear the plan of our Heavenly Father for our eternal progression? For what purposes did we come to earth?

- What attributes do we possess as children of God? What are the consequences of misusing our God-given attributes and abilities?

- What scriptural testimonies do we have that God the Father and His Son, Jesus Christ, have bodies in the form of men? How are these testimonies of value to you?

- How does the doctrine of the premortal existence pour "a wonderful flood of light" on questions about our origin?

- How does revealed truth about the origin of mankind differ from the theories of men on this subject?

- Why is it important to give our Father in Heaven "the honor and glory of all we accomplish in the flesh"?

- What principles must we obey in order to become like our Heavenly Father?

## Notes

1. "The Origin of Man, by the First Presidency of the Church," *Improvement Era,* Nov. 1909, 75.

2. In Conference Report, Oct. 1909, 3.

3. *Gospel Doctrine,* 5th ed. (1939), 93–94; paragraphing added.

4. *Deseret News: Semi-Weekly,* 18 Feb. 1873, 2.

5. In James R. Clark, comp., *Messages of the First Presidency of The Church of Jesus Christ of Latter-day Saints,* 6 vols. (1965–75), 4:264.

6. "The Origin of Man, by the First Presidency of the Church," 77–80; paragraphing added.

7. *Gospel Doctrine,* 62–64.

8. "The Origin of Man, by the First Presidency of the Church," 81.

# Serving in the Church

*Let us serve faithfully in our callings under the direction of priesthood authority.*

## From the Life of Joseph F. Smith

When President Joseph F. Smith had served as an Apostle for 44 years and as President of the Church for 9 years, he stood in the October 1910 general conference and said, "I feel happy, this morning, in having the privilege to say to you that in the days of my childhood and early youth, I made a pledge with God and with his people that I would be true to them." He explained that since that time he had served faithfully in every calling given to him:

"In looking over the experiences of my life, I cannot now discern, and do not remember a circumstance, since the beginning of my experience in the world, where I have felt, for a moment, to slacken or relax in the pledge and promise that I made to God and to the Latter-day Saints, in my youth. . . . As an elder in Israel I tried to be true to that calling; I tried to my utmost to honor and magnify that calling. When I became a seventy, I felt in my heart to be true to that calling, and I strove, with all the intelligence and fervor of my soul, to be true to it. I have no knowledge nor recollection of any act of mine, or any circumstance in my life where I proved untrue or unfaithful to these callings in the Priesthood of the Son of God. Later in my life, when I was called to act as an apostle, and was ordained an apostle, and set apart to be one of the Twelve, I strove to honor that calling, to be true to it, and to my brethren, to the household of faith, and to the covenants and obligations involved in receiving this holy Priesthood which is after the order of the Son of God. I am not aware that I ever violated one of my obligations or pledges in these callings to which I have been called. I have sought to be true and faithful to all these things."[1]

President Smith admonished the Saints to commit themselves to the work of the Lord and to serve devotedly—in priesthood callings, in the auxiliaries of the Church, and in other kinds of unselfish service—always honoring the priesthood authority by which they were called and directed.

# Teachings of Joseph F. Smith

### The priesthood is given for the ministry of service.

Priesthood is not given for the honor or aggrandizement of man, but for the ministry of service among those for whom the bearers of that sacred commission are called to labor. Be it remembered that even our Lord and Master, after long fasting, when faint in body and physically weakened by exhausting vigils and continued abstinence, resisted the arch tempter's suggestion that he use the authority and power of his Messiahship to provide for his own immediate needs.

The God-given titles of honor and of more than human distinction, associated with the several offices in and orders of the Holy Priesthood, are not to be used nor considered as are the titles originated by man; they are not for adornment nor are they expressive of mastership, but rather of appointment to humble service in the work of the one Master whom we profess to serve.[2]

I have known Elders, who, all their lives, have been "minute men;" they have never stopped a moment to question the calls that have been made upon them, neither have they stopped to consider their own temporal interest, they have gone and come at the request of their brethren in the service of the people and the Lord. . . . They were on hand, like the ready watchman, scarcely stopping to think of themselves. . . . This they have done with all their hearts, and their labors have never been regarded as burdensome; but on the contrary, they afforded them joy, pleasure and constant satisfaction. . . . They are still ready and willing to go or come, or do whatever may be required of them, regarding, at all times, their duties in the priesthood of greater moment than any personal considerations.[3]

The weekly meetings of the priesthood quorums . . . will not only increase the proficiency of the priesthood by reason of its educative features, but by bringing all the brethren together once a week they will acquire the habit of regular activity as servants of the Lord.[4]

O God, bless the Holy Priesthood, the noble men, pure men, just men, men of honor, men of integrity, men who have gathered out, many of them, from the nations of the earth for the love of the gospel; and many of them have been born under the covenant of the Holy Priesthood, and I pray God to bless you, my brethren, with an abundance of His goodness, of His mercy and loving kindness, that you may prosper in the land, that you may be indeed truly His servants.[5]

---

### Auxiliary organizations allow all to serve under the presiding authority of the priesthood.

The Priesthood stand at the head. They preside over all things. It is the duty of those that bear the Priesthood to look after all the organizations of the Church; not only the organization of the Priesthood, but also all the organizations instituted for the benefit of the people at large—our Relief Societies, Mutual Improvement Associations [Young Men and Young Women], Primaries, . . . and all our organizations that have been devised for the building up of the people of God and the prosperity of truth and righteousness in the land. All of these should receive the supervisory and fatherly care and attention and the deep and abiding interest of the authorities of the Church, whether in the ward or in the general authorities of the Church, because the Priesthood are interested in the welfare of the people of God and the building up and establishment of Zion on the earth. And all these organizations that have been framed, established and ordained of God should look to these presiding authorities and operate in harmony with them; honoring them in their places.[6]

There is no government in the Church of Jesus Christ separate and apart, above, or outside of the holy Priesthood or its authority. We have our Relief Societies, Mutual Improvement Associations, Primary Associations and Sunday Schools, . . . but these organizations are not quorums or councils of the Priesthood, but are auxiliary to, and under it; organized by virtue of the holy Priest-

341

hood. They are not outside of, nor above it, nor beyond its reach. They acknowledge the principle of the Priesthood. Wherever they are they always exist with the view of accomplishing some good; some soul's salvation, temporal or spiritual.[7]

I would like to say that it is expected of the Relief Society, especially the general [officers] of that great organization, that they will have a watchcare over all its organizations among the women of Zion. They stand at the head of all such; they ought to stand at the head, and they should magnify their calling.[8]

Through [the] auxiliary organizations we have been able to reach out a guiding hand, and to exert an influence for good over many of our young men and women, whom it would have been difficult to reach by the organizations of the Priesthood. So far, these organizations have accomplished a most excellent primary work.[9]

I pray God to bless all our auxiliary organizations, from the first to the last, that they may do their duty, that they may not sit idly down and neglect to work. . . . We are only safe when we are doing, when we are at work, when we are in earnest, when we are engaged in the discharge of our duty, and when this condition exists with us we are safe, for then we are in the hands of God and not in the hand of the adversary.[10]

---

## We should all labor for the welfare and salvation of others.

If we are in the line of our duty, we are engaged in a great and glorious cause. It is very essential to our individual welfare that every man and every woman who has entered into the covenant of the gospel, through repentance and baptism, should feel that as individuals it is their bounden duty to use their intelligence, and the agency which the Lord has given them, for the promotion of the interests of Zion and the establishment of her cause, in the earth.[11]

We should all be willing to labor for the welfare and salvation of the people—to sacrifice our own desires and feelings for the good of the whole, being perfectly willing to do the bidding of the Almighty, with no will of our own but to serve the purposes of the Lord. . . . We are laboring for the salvation of souls, and we should feel that this is the greatest duty devolving upon us. Therefore, we should feel willing to sacrifice everything, if need be, for the love of God, the salvation of men, and the triumph of the kingdom of God upon the earth.[12]

We expect to see the day . . . when every council of the Priesthood in the Church of Jesus Christ of Latter-day Saints will understand its duty; will assume its own responsibility, will magnify its calling, and fill its place in the Church, to the uttermost, according to the intelligence and ability possessed by it. . . . The Lord designed and comprehended it from the beginning, and he has made provision in the Church whereby every need may be met and satisfied through the regular organizations of the Priesthood. It has truly been said that the Church is perfectly organized. The only trouble is that these organizations are not fully alive to the obligations that rest upon them. When they become thoroughly awakened to the requirements made of them, they will fulfil their duties more faithfully, and the work of the Lord will be all the stronger and more powerful and influential in the world.[13]

Every man should feel in his heart the necessity of doing his part in the great latter-day work. All should seek to be instrumental in rolling it forth. More especially is it the duty of every one who possesses any portion of the authority of the holy Priesthood to magnify and honor that calling, and nowhere can we begin to do so to better advantage than right here, within ourselves and when we have cleaned the inside of the platter, cleansed our own hearts, corrected our own lives, fixed our minds upon doing our whole duty toward God and man, we will be prepared to wield an influence for good in the family circle, in society, and in all the walks of life.[14]

The men and the women who are honest before God, who humbly plod along, doing their duty, paying their tithing, and exercising that pure religion and undefiled before God and the Father, which is to visit the fatherless and the widows in their afflictions and to keep oneself unspotted from the world [see James 1:27], and who help look after the poor; and who honor the holy Priesthood, who do not run into excesses, who are prayerful in their families, and who acknowledge the Lord in their hearts, they will build up a foundation that the gates of hell cannot prevail against; and if the floods come and the storms beat upon their house, it shall not fall, for it will be built upon the rock of eternal truth [see Matthew 7:24–27].[15]

## Suggestions for Study

- What does the example of Jesus Christ teach us about the use of priesthood authority?

- How is ordination to the priesthood an "appointment to humble service"?

- What are the purposes of the auxiliary organizations of the Church? How do they bless the members of the Church? Why is it important to know that the auxiliaries function under the direction of the priesthood?

- What are the benefits of sustaining and honoring one another in our responsibilities and callings in the Church?

- How should we feel about "laboring for the salvation of souls"? What are some sacrifices that others have made to labor for your salvation? What are you willing to sacrifice for the benefit of others?

- What does it mean to become "thoroughly awakened" to our obligations? What will be the results if this happens?

- What does it mean to "humbly plod along"? What blessings come to those who do so?

### Notes

1. *Gospel Doctrine,* 5th ed. (1939), 504.
2. Joseph F. Smith, Anthon H. Lund, Charles W. Penrose, "On Titles," *Improvement Era,* Mar. 1914, 479.
3. *Deseret News* (weekly), 10 Dec. 1879, 2.
4. In James R. Clark, comp., *Messages of the First Presidency of The Church of Jesus Christ of Latter-day Saints,* 6 vols. (1965–75), 4:195.
5. In Conference Report, Oct. 1911, 132.
6. *Deseret Weekly,* 9 Jan. 1892, 70.
7. *Gospel Doctrine,* 144.
8. *Gospel Doctrine,* 386.
9. *Gospel Doctrine,* 393.
10. In Conference Report, Oct. 1911, 131–32.
11. *Deseret News: Semi-Weekly,* 28 Nov. 1876, 1.
12. *Deseret News* (weekly), 10 Dec. 1879, 2.
13. *Gospel Doctrine,* 159–60.
14. *Gospel Doctrine,* 168.
15. *Gospel Doctrine,* 7–8.

———————— ⌘⌘⌘ ————————

# Strengthening Families in Family Home Evenings

*Family home evenings strengthen love within the family and faith in the heart of each family member.*

## From the Life of Joseph F. Smith

To President Joseph F. Smith, his family was precious, indeed priceless. He spoke often and eloquently of the "divinely ordained home" and said that "the very foundation of the kingdom of God, of righteousness, of progress, of development" is established in the home.[1]

In 1915 President Smith and his Counselors introduced a weekly home evening program to the Church, urging parents to use the time to instruct their children in the word of God. Later, when describing the home evening program, President Smith called for families to "spend an hour or more together in a devotional way—in the singing of hymns, songs, prayer, reading of the Scriptures and other good books, instrumental music, family topics, and specific instructions on the principles of the Gospel and on the ethical problems of life, as well as the duties and obligations of children to parents, the home, the Church, society and the nation."[2]

This home evening program represented President Smith's fervent belief that a "great and important duty devolving upon this people is to teach their children, from their cradle until they become men and women, every principle of the gospel, and endeavor, as far as it lies in the power of the parents, to instil into their hearts a love for God, the truth, virtue, honesty, honor and integrity to everything that is good."[3]

In 1917 President Smith reported to the Saints that home evenings were "being observed by many families, and very interesting and profitable evenings [were] being spent."[4] Today, the Church continues to emphasize many of the essential features of the original program instituted by President Smith.

# Teachings of Joseph F. Smith

### Teach your family to love God and the principles of the gospel.

The very foundation of the kingdom of God, of righteousness, of progress, of development, of eternal life and eternal increase in the kingdom of God, is laid in the divinely ordained home.[5]

The typical "Mormon" home is the temple of the family, in which the members of the household gather morning and evening, for prayer and praise to God, offered in the name of Jesus Christ. . . . Here are taught and gently enforced, the moral precepts and religious truths, which, taken together, make up that righteousness which exalteth a nation, and ward off that sin which is a reproach to any people.[6]

Teach your children the love of God. Teach them to love the principles of the Gospel of Jesus Christ. Teach them to love their fellowmen, and especially to love their fellow members in the Church, that they may be true to their fellowship with the people of God. Teach them to honor the priesthood, to honor the authority that God has bestowed upon His Church for the proper government of His Church. The house of God is a house of order, and not a house of confusion. . . . No house would be a house of order if it were not properly organized as the Church of Jesus Christ of Latter-day Saints is organized.[7]

There is too little religious devotion, love and fear of God, in the home; too much worldliness, selfishness, indifference and lack of reverence in the family, or these never would exist so abundantly on the outside. Then, the home is what needs reforming. . . . Let love, and peace, and the Spirit of the Lord, kindness, charity, sacrifice for others, abound in your families. Banish harsh words, envyings, hatreds, evil speaking, obscene language and innuendo, blasphemy, and let the Spirit of God take possession of your hearts. Teach to your children these things, in spirit and power, sustained and strengthened by personal practice. Let them see that you are earnest, and practice what you preach. Do not let your children out to specialists in these things, but teach them by your own precept and example, by your own fireside. Be a specialist yourself in the truth. Let our meetings, schools and organizations, instead of being our only or leading teachers, be supplements to our teachings and training in the home.[8]

---

### In home evenings, teach your family to walk uprightly before the Lord.

We counsel the Latter-day Saints to observe more closely the commandment of the Lord given in the 68th section of the Doctrine and Covenants (25–28):

"And again, inasmuch as parents have children in Zion, or in any of her stakes which are organized, that teach them not to understand the doctrine of repentance, faith in Christ the Son of the living God, and of Baptism and the gift of the Holy Ghost by the laying on of hands when eight years old, the sin be upon the heads of the parents;

"For this shall be a law unto the inhabitants of Zion, or in any of her stakes which are organized;

"And their children shall be baptized for the remission of their sins when eight years old, and receive the laying on of the hands.

"And they shall also teach their children to pray and walk uprightly before the Lord."

The children of Zion should also observe more fully the commandment of the Lord given to ancient Israel, and reiterated to the Latter-day Saints: "Honor thy father and mother: that thy days may be long upon the land which the Lord thy God giveth thee." [Exodus 20:12.]

These revelations apply with great force to the Latter-day Saints, and it is required of fathers and mothers in this Church that these commandments shall be taught and applied in their homes.

To this end we advise and urge the inauguration of a "Home Evening" throughout the Church, at which time fathers and mothers may gather their boys and girls about them in the home and teach them the word of the Lord. They may thus learn more fully the needs and requirements of their families; at the same time familiarizing themselves and their children more thoroughly with the principles of the Gospel of Jesus Christ. This "Home Evening" should be devoted to prayer, singing hymns, songs, instrumental music, scripture-reading, family topics and specific instruction on the principles of the gospel, and on the ethical problems of life, as well as the duties and obligations of children to parents, the home, the Church, society and the nation. For the smaller children appropriate recitations, songs, stories and games may be introduced. Light refreshments of such a nature as may be largely prepared in the home might be served.

Formality and stiffness should be studiously avoided, and all the family participate in the exercises.

These gatherings will furnish opportunities for mutual confidence between parents and children, between brothers and sisters, as well as give opportunity for words of warning, counsel and advice by parents to their boys and girls. They will provide opportunity for the boys and girls to honor father and mother, and to show their appreciation of the blessings of home so that the promise of the Lord to them may be literally fulfilled and their lives be prolonged and made happy. . . .

We . . . request that all the officers of the auxiliary organizations throughout the Church support this movement and encourage the young people to remain at home that evening, and devote their energies to make it instructive, profitable and interesting.

If the Saints obey this counsel, we promise that great blessings will result. Love at home and obedience to parents will increase. Faith will be developed in the hearts of the youth of Israel, and they will gain power to combat the evil influence and temptations which beset them.[9]

Throughout the Church a spirit of unity, devotion, and faith prevails. . . . The introduction of the home-meeting movement has been an aid in this direction. One evening a week . . . for home family recreation, improvement and enjoyment, conducted in order and under a religious spirit, proves successful in the desired direction, and is to be heartily recommended everywhere.[10]

Family members at the home of President Joseph F. Smith in Salt Lake City in 1891. He said, "I would like my children, and all the children in Zion, to know that there is nothing in this world that is of so much value to them as the knowledge of the Gospel" (*Deseret News: Semi-Weekly,* 28 June 1898, 1).

## We should discharge our duties faithfully as parents in Zion.

We read in the Book of Doctrine and Covenants that it is required of parents to teach their children "to understand the doctrine of repentance, faith in Christ the Son of the living God, and of baptism and the gift of the Holy Ghost by the laying on of the hands when eight years old." "And they shall also teach their children to pray and to walk uprightly before the Lord." And if the parents fail to do this, and the children go astray and turn from the truth, then the Lord has said that the sin shall be upon the heads of the parents [D&C 68:25, 28]. . . .

We should look well to our ways, and see to it that we discharge our duties faithfully as parents in Zion. The wives should be united with their husbands, and the husbands with their wives, in exerting their influence over their children in this direction. . . . My children must not and will not turn away with my consent. If they do turn away, it must be over my protest, and against my example. I will plead with my children; I will endeavor with all the power I possess to have them as true and faithful to this Gospel as it is possible for me to be; because without all of them in the kingdom of God I would feel that my household was not perfect. . . .

I would like my children, and all the children in Zion, to know that there is nothing in this world that is of so much value to them as the knowledge of the Gospel as it has been restored to the earth in these latter days through the Prophet Joseph Smith. There is nothing that can compensate for its loss. There is nothing on earth that can compare with the excellency of the knowledge of Jesus Christ. Let, therefore, all the parents in Zion look after their children, and teach them the principles of the Gospel, and strive as far as possible to get them to do their duty—not mechanically, because they are urged to do it, but try to instill into the hearts of the children the spirit of truth and an abiding love for the Gospel, that they may not only do their duty because it is pleasing to their parents, but because it is pleasing also to themselves.[11]

My dear brothers and sisters, take care of your children; teach them in their childhood the principles of truth; teach them to live pure lives, to have faith in God, and to call upon the Lord in faith that they may obtain full fellowship with the Lord and become heirs of salvation in His kingdom.[12]

## Suggestions for Study

- In what ways is the "very foundation of the kingdom of God" established in the home? What important principles should be taught in the home that can serve to strengthen our society?

- How can we teach our children to love God and to love other people? How can we teach them to honor the priesthood?

- What counsel did President Smith give for increasing the religious devotion and decreasing the worldliness in our homes? How have you tried to make worldly considerations secondary in your home?

- How can family home evenings help parents fulfill the commandments given by the Lord in Doctrine and Covenants 68:25–28? How can family home evenings help children fulfill the commandment given in Exodus 20:12?

- What practices have helped you to hold more effective family home evenings? What guidelines did President Smith give for family home evenings?

- What blessings come to those who hold family home evenings? What can be the consequences of not holding them?

- Why must we never give up in our responsibilities as parents to bring our families to the truth? (See also 3 John 1:4; Mosiah 27:14.)

- Why should husbands and wives be "united . . . in exerting their influence over their children"? How can husbands and wives cultivate this unity?

## Notes

1. "Editorial Thoughts," *Juvenile Instructor,* Nov. 1916, 739.
2. In James R. Clark, comp., *Messages of the First Presidency of The Church of Jesus Christ of Latter-day Saints,* 6 vols. (1965–75), 5:89.
3. *Gospel Doctrine,* 5th ed. (1939), 292.
4. In *Messages of the First Presidency,* 5:89.
5. *Gospel Doctrine,* 304.
6. "An Address: The Church of Jesus Christ of Latter-day Saints to the World," in Conference Report, Apr. 1907, 7.
7. In Conference Report, Apr. 1915, 5.
8. *Gospel Doctrine,* 301–2.
9. In *Messages of the First Presidency,* 4:337–39.
10. In *Messages of the First Presidency,* 4:347.
11. *Deseret News: Semi-Weekly,* 28 June 1898, 1; paragraphing added.
12. "Discourse by President Joseph F. Smith," *Millennial Star,* 30 Aug. 1906, 545–46.

This stained-glass window, created in 1913 for the Adams Ward meetinghouse in Los Angeles, California, depicts the appearance of God the Father and His Son, Jesus Christ, to Joseph Smith.

# The Father and the Son

*Modern revelation teaches us great, eternal truths about our Father in Heaven and His Son, Jesus Christ.*

## From the Life of Joseph F. Smith

President Joseph F. Smith often bore powerful testimony of Heavenly Father and His Son, Jesus Christ, the supreme objects of our faith. He said, "I believe with all my soul in God the Father and our Lord and Savior Jesus Christ."[1] While he was President of the Church, he sought to clarify the identity and roles of the Father and the Son, especially since some scripture passages designate Jesus Christ as Father. In an effort to help the Saints better understand certain scriptures concerning the Father and the Son, the First Presidency and the Quorum of the Twelve issued a doctrinal exposition on 30 June 1916 titled "The Father and the Son." This declaration affirmed the unity between God the Father and His Son, Jesus Christ, and clarified the distinct roles of each in the plan of salvation. It also explained the ways in which the term *Father* is applied in the scriptures to both our Father in Heaven and Jesus Christ.

Several excerpts from the exposition are cited in this chapter along with other teachings of President Smith, who affirmed that to gain "the knowledge of God, and of his Son Jesus Christ, . . . is the first and last lesson of life."[2]

## Teachings of Joseph F. Smith

### To know God and Jesus Christ is life eternal.

It is a scriptural truth, that this is life eternal to know the only true and living God and Jesus Christ whom thou hast sent [see John 17:3]. I believe that the Latter-day Saints, through the teachings of the scriptures and through the revelations that have come to them by the voice of the Prophet Joseph Smith, are able to learn the true and living God and know Him and also His Son whom He has sent into the world, whom to know is life eternal.[3]

Not only is it necessary to have faith in God, but also in Jesus Christ, his Son, the Savior of mankind and the Mediator of the New Covenant; and in the Holy Ghost, who bears record of the Father and the Son, "the same in all ages and forever."[4]

---

### The Father of our spirits is an eternal being with a body of flesh and bones.

God has a tabernacle of flesh and bone. He is an organized being just as we are, who are now in the flesh. . . . We are the children of God. He is an eternal being, without beginning of days or end of years. He always was, he is, he always will be.[5]

I do not believe in the doctrine held by some that God is only a Spirit and that he is of such a nature that he fills the immensity of space, and is everywhere present in person, or without person, for I can not conceive it possible that God could be a person, if he filled the immensity of space and was everywhere present at the same time. It is unreasonable, a physical, a theological inconsistency, to imagine that even God the eternal Father would be in two places, as an individual, at the same moment. It is impossible. But his power extends throughout the immensity of space. His power extends to all his creations, and his knowledge comprehends them all, and he governs them all and he knows all.[6]

God the Eternal Father, whom we designate by the exalted name-title "Elohim," is the literal Parent of our Lord and Savior Jesus Christ, and of the spirits of the human race. Elohim is the Father in every sense in which Jesus Christ is so designated, and distinctively He is the Father of spirits.[7]

[We] pray unto the Father of our Lord and Savior, Jesus Christ, in whose image and likeness we are made, or were born into the world, and in whose likeness and image we are, for we are God's children, and therefore must resemble his Son in person, and also spiritually, so far as we will obey the principles of the gospel of eternal truth. For, we were foreordained . . . to become conformed to his likeness through the wise and proper use of our free agency.[8]

God, the eternal Father, is constantly mindful of you. He is mindful of his people throughout all this land, and he will reward you according to your faithfulness in observing the laws of righteousness and of truth.[9]

---

### God our Heavenly Father is the Creator.

The Lord Almighty is the Creator of the earth, he is the Father of all our spirits. He has the right to dictate what we should do, and it is our duty to obey, and to walk according to his requirements. This is natural, and perfectly easy to be comprehended.[10]

The scriptures plainly and repeatedly affirm that God is the Creator of the earth and the heavens and all things that in them are. In the sense so expressed, the Creator is an Organizer. God created the earth as an organized sphere; but He certainly did not create, in the sense of bringing into primal existence, the ultimate elements of the materials of which the earth consists, for "the elements are eternal" (Doc. & Cov. 93:33).[11]

[Man] is indebted to the Lord Almighty for his intelligence, and for all that he has; for the earth is the Lord's and the fulness thereof [see Psalm 24:1]. God originated and designed all things.[12]

Beware of men who . . . would make you to think or feel that the Lord Almighty, who made heaven and earth and created all things, is limited in his dominion over earthly things to the capacities of mortal men.[13]

---

### Jesus Christ is the Firstborn in the spirit and the Only Begotten Son of God in the flesh.

Among the spirit children of Elohim, the first-born was and is Jehovah, or Jesus Christ, to whom all others are juniors.[14]

Jesus Christ is not the Father of the spirits who have taken or yet shall take bodies upon this earth, for he is one of them. He is the Son, as they are sons or daughters of Elohim.[15]

[Jesus Christ] is essentially greater than any and all others, by reason (1) of His seniority as the oldest or firstborn; (2) of His unique status in the flesh as the offspring of a mortal mother and of an immortal, or resurrected and glorified, Father; (3) of His selection and foreordination as the one and only Redeemer and Savior of the race; and (4) of His transcendent sinlessness.[16]

There is no doubt in the minds of Latter-day Saints in relation to the existence and personage of the Lord God Almighty, who is the Father of our Lord and Savior Jesus Christ. There is no doubt in the minds of Latter-day Saints that Jesus is the Son of God, being begotten of the Father in the flesh.[17]

Jesus Christ is the Son of Elohim both as spiritual and bodily offspring; that is to say, Elohim is literally the Father of the spirit of Jesus Christ and also of the body in which Jesus Christ performed His mission in the flesh, and which body died on the cross and was afterward taken up by the process of resurrection, and is now the immortalized tabernacle of the eternal spirit of our Lord and Savior.[18]

Jesus Christ was born of his mother, Mary. He had a fleshly tabernacle. He was crucified on the cross; and his body was raised from the dead. He burst the bonds of the grave, and came forth to newness of life, a living soul, a living being, a man with a body, with parts and with spirit—the spirit and the body becoming a living and immortal soul.[19]

God the Father . . . is the Father of our spirits, and . . . the Father in the flesh, of his Only Begotten Son, Jesus Christ, who joined divine immortality with the mortal, welded the link between God and man, made it possible for mortal souls, on whom the sentence of death had been placed, to acquire eternal life, through obedience to his laws. Let us, therefore, seek the truth and walk in the light as Christ is in the light, that we may have fellowship with him, and with each other, that his blood may cleanse us from all sin.[20]

---

### The Father and the Son are one.

" . . . I am in the Father, and the Father in me, and the Father and I are one." [3 Nephi 11:27.] I do not apprehend that any intelligent person will construe these words to mean that Jesus and his Father are one person, but merely that they are one in knowledge, in truth, in wisdom, in understanding, and in purpose; just as the Lord Jesus himself admonished his disciples to be one with him, and to be in him, that he might be in them. It is in this sense that I understand this language, and not as it is construed by some people, that Christ and his Father are one person. I declare to you that they are not one person, but that they are two persons, two bodies, separate and apart, and as distinct as are any father and son.[21]

[The Father and the Son] are one—in attributes. They are one in love, one in knowledge, one in mercy, one in power, one in all things that make them united and powerful, glorious and great, because in them is perfected all truth, all virtue and all righteousness.[22]

---

### Jesus Christ is called the Father.

The term "Father" as applied to Deity occurs in sacred writ with plainly different meanings.[23]

### *Jesus Christ is the Father of heaven and earth.*

Jehovah, who is Jesus Christ the Son of Elohim, is called "the Father," and even "the very eternal Father of heaven and of earth" [see Mosiah 15:4; 16:15; Alma 11:38–39; Ether 4:7]. With analogous meaning Jesus Christ is called "The Everlasting Father" (Isaiah 9:6; compare 2 Nephi 19:6). . . .

. . . Jesus Christ, whom we also know as Jehovah, was the executive of the Father, Elohim, in the work of creation. . . . Jesus Christ, being the Creator, is consistently called the Father of heaven and earth . . . ; and since His creations are of eternal quality He is very properly called the Eternal Father of heaven and earth.[24]

### *Jesus Christ is the Father of those who abide in His gospel.*

[Another] sense in which Jesus Christ is regarded as the "Father" has reference to the relationship between Him and those who accept His Gospel and thereby become heirs of eternal life. . . .

That by obedience to the Gospel men may become sons of God, both as sons of Jesus Christ, and, through Him, as sons of His Father, is set forth in many revelations given in the current dispensation [see D&C 11:28–30; 34:1–3; 35:1–2; 39:1–4; 45:7–8]. . . .

A forceful exposition of this relationship between Jesus Christ as the Father and those who comply with the requirements of the Gospel as His children was given by Abinadi, centuries before our Lord's birth in the flesh: ". . . And who shall be [Christ's] seed? Behold I say unto you, that whosoever has heard the words of the prophets, . . . and believed that the Lord would redeem his people, and have looked forward to that day for a remission of their sins; I say unto you, that these are his seed, or they are the heirs of the kingdom of God . . . " (Mosiah 15:10–13). . . .

Men may become children of Jesus Christ by being born anew—born of God, as the inspired word states [see 1 John 3:8–10].

Those who have been born unto God through obedience to the Gospel may by valiant devotion to righteousness obtain exaltation and even reach the status of Godhood [see D&C 76:58; 132:17, 20, 37]. . . .

By the new birth—that of water and the Spirit—mankind may become children of Jesus Christ, being through the means by Him provided "begotten sons and daughters unto God" [D&C 76:24; see also 1 Corinthians 4:15; D&C 84:33–34; 93:21–22]. . . .

If it be proper to speak of those who accept and abide in the Gospel as Christ's sons and daughters—and upon this matter the scriptures are explicit and cannot be gainsaid nor denied—it is consistently proper to speak of Jesus Christ as the Father of the righteous, they having become His children and He having been made their Father through the second birth—the baptismal regeneration.[25]

[Jesus Christ] is the foundation and chief cornerstone of our religion. We are his by adoption, by being buried with Christ in baptism, by being born of the water and of the spirit anew into the world, through the ordinances of the gospel of Christ, and we are thereby God's children, heirs of God and joint heirs with Jesus Christ through our adoption and faith.[26]

# Teachings of Joseph F. Smith

## We believe in direct revelation from God to man.

We believe . . . in the principle of direct revelation from God to man.

This is a part of the gospel, but it is not peculiar to this dispensation. It is common in all ages and dispensations of the gospel. The gospel cannot be administered, nor the Church of God continue to exist, without it. Christ is the head of his Church and not man, and the connection can only be maintained upon the principle of direct and continuous revelation. It is not a hereditary principle, it cannot be handed down from father to son, nor from generation to generation, but is a living, vital principle to be enjoyed on certain conditions only, namely—through absolute faith in God and obedience to his laws and commandments. The moment this principle is cut off, that moment the Church is adrift, being severed from its ever-living head. In this condition it cannot continue, but must cease to be the Church of God and, like the ship at sea without captain, compass or rudder, is afloat at the mercy of the storms and the waves of ever contending human passions, and worldly interests, pride and folly, finally to be wrecked upon the strand of priestcraft and superstition.[3]

It should be understood that the servants of God have the right in their administrations to obtain immediate divine guidance, and thus, in their faith, they couple divine wisdom as the directing force to their labors, and when that is done it must render a people invincible in enterprises they undertake in the service of God.[4]

I do know that every principle of the Gospel of Jesus Christ that has been revealed through Joseph Smith, the prophet, in these last days is of God and is true, and will stand for ever—that is, on its merit, as to its truth; it can never be overthrown. I know this with all my being. God has made me doubly assured by the presence and influence of His Spirit, and by the inspiration awakened in my soul to love that which is good, and to desire to forsake that which is evil.[5]

### God reveals His will to men as much in our day as at any time in history.

The Latter-day Saints . . . bear testimony to all the world that God lives and that he reveals his will to men who believe in him and who obey his commandments, as much in our day as at any time in the history of nations. The canon of scripture is not full. God has never revealed at any time that he would cease to speak forever to men. If we are permitted to believe that he has spoken, we must and do believe that he continues to speak, because he is unchangeable. . . .

What is revelation but the uncovering of new truths, by him who is the fountain of all truth? To say that there is no need of new revelation, is equivalent to saying that we have no need of new truths—a ridiculous assertion. As well, too, might we say that the revelations which Abraham received were sufficient for the prophets; that the revelations given to Enoch were sufficient for Noah, whose mission was to build the ark and preach repentance; or that the words spoken to Moses were sufficient for all time; or that what Abraham received would be ample for his children through all the ages. But not so. Notwithstanding Abraham was favored with great promises, the word of God was not denied to his son Isaac, nor to his grandson Jacob. Why? Because these could not have performed their missions on the word of the Lord alone to their father and to others. And how could the Father of the Faithful have accomplished his work on the instructions received by Noah? Of what personal use were the revelations of prior patriarchs and prophets to Balaam or to Paul? It is true, they were of use as historical truths or lessons, but not sufficient for them individually.

So we moderns stand in need, oh so greatly! of constant revelation, that we individually may fill our missions acceptably to our Father, and that we may the better work out our own salvation; and also that we may know the will of God concerning his Church, his people, and his purposes in regard to the nations. These are a few of the thousand needs that exist for revelation.[6]

### God reveals Himself to the world through the legally appointed channels of the priesthood.

Through Joseph [Smith], . . . the Lord revealed himself to the world, and through him he chose the first elders of the Church—men who were honest in their hearts; men who he knew would receive the word, and labor in connection with Joseph in this great, important undertaking; and all that have been ordained to the Priesthood, and all that have been appointed to any position whatever in this Church have received their authority and commission through this channel, appointed of God, with Joseph at the head. This is the order, and it could not be otherwise. God will not raise up another prophet and another people to do the work that we have been appointed to do. He will never ignore those who have stood firm and true from the commencement, as it were, of this work, and who are still firm and faithful, inasmuch as they continue faithful to their trust. There is no question in my mind of their ever proving themselves unfaithful, as a body, for if any of them were to become unworthy in his sight, he would remove them out of their place and call others from the ranks to fill their positions.[7]

The moment a man says he will not submit to the legally constituted authority of the Church, whether it be the teachers, the bishopric, the high council, his quorum, or the First Presidency, and in his heart confirms it and carries it out, that moment he cuts himself off from the privileges and blessings of the Priesthood and Church, and severs himself from the people of God, for he ignores the authority that the Lord has instituted in his Church. These are the men that generally get crotchets [eccentric opinions] in their heads, that get inspiration (from beneath), and that are often so desirous to guide the Church, and to sit in judgment upon the priesthood. The only safe way for us to do, as individuals, is to live so humbly, so righteously and so faithfully before God that we may possess his Spirit to that extent that we shall be able to judge righteously, and discern between truth and error, between right and wrong.[8]

It has sometimes been sorrowful to see respected members of the Church, men who should know better, allow themselves to become the tools of seductive spirits. . . . It seems difficult for men to comprehend the workings of the Priesthood, its legitimate authority, its scope and power; and yet by the light of the Spirit it is easily comprehended, but not understanding it, men are easily deceived by seductive spirits that are abroad in the world. They are led to believe that something is wrong, and the next thing that transpires, they find themselves believing that they are chosen specially to set things right. It is very unfortunate for a man to be taken in this snare; for be it understood by the Latter-day Saints that as long as the servants of God are living pure lives, are honoring the Priesthood conferred upon them, and endeavoring to the best of their knowledge to magnify their offices and callings, to which they have been duly chosen by the voice of the people and the priesthood, and sanctioned by the approval of God, so long as the Lord has any communication to make to the children of men, or any instructions to impart to his Church, he will make such communication through the legally appointed channel of the priesthood; he will never go outside of it, as long, at least, as the Church of Jesus Christ of Latter-day Saints exists in its present form on the earth.

It is not the business of any individual to rise up as a revelator, as a prophet, as a seer, as an inspired man, to give revelation for the guidance of the Church, or to assume to dictate to the presiding authorities of the Church in any part of the world, much less in the midst of Zion, where the organizations of the priesthood are about perfect, where everything is complete, even to the organization of a branch.[9]

In secular as well as spiritual affairs, Saints may receive Divine guidance and revelation affecting themselves, but this does not convey authority to direct others, and is not to be accepted when contrary to Church covenants, doctrine or discipline, or to known facts, demonstrated truths, or good common sense. No person has the right to induce his fellow members of the Church to engage in speculations or take stock in ventures of any kind on the specious [deceptive] claim of Divine revelation or vision or dream, especially when it is in opposition to the voice of recognized authority, local or general. The Lord's Church "is a house of order"

President Joseph F. Smith with missionaries and members of the
Swiss German Mission, August 1910. President Smith counseled the Saints to
unite and "hearken to the voices of the servants of God that are sounded
in their ears" (*Gospel Doctrine,* 261).

[D&C 132:8]. It is not governed by individual gifts or manifestations, but by the order and power of the Holy Priesthood as sustained by the voice and vote of the Church in its appointed conferences.[10]

### The spirit of revelation can unite the whole human family in the kingdom of God.

The Lord has told us in a revelation through the Prophet Joseph Smith, that except we are one we are not His [see D&C 38:27]. He has said that we must be united. We must be one.[11]

If we did act under [the Spirit's] influence and followed its dictation continually, we would be one, and bickering, strife and selfishness would be laid aside, and we would look after and be as zealous for our neighbor's as for our own good. But we still see in our midst controversies, differences of thought and opinion, one up and another down, and the same thing regarded in a different light by different persons, etc. Why is this? Because the gospel net has gathered in of every kind, and because we are only children in the school; because we have learned on the first letters, as it were, in the great Gospel plan, and that but imperfectly. And one cause of the diversity in our thoughts and reflections is that some have had greater experience and comprehend the truth more perfectly than others. But does this prove that the gospel we have embraced does not contain those principles necessary to unite all mankind in the truth? No, it does not. What are these great principles that are calculated to unite the whole human family, and to cause them to worship the same God, adhere to the same counsel and be governed by the same voice? They are the principle of revelation, the power of God revealed to His people, the belief in the hearts of the people that it is God's right to rule and dictate, and that it is not the right of any man to say it shall be thus and so; nor are the people required to obey these principles blindly—without knowledge.[12]

Let the Saints unite; let them hearken to the voices of the servants of God that are sounded in their ears; let them hearken to their counsels and give heed to the truth.[13]

Seek to have the fellowship and union of the Holy Ghost. Let this spirit be sought and cherished as diligently within the smallest and humblest family circle as within the membership of the highest organization and quorum. Let it permeate the hearts of the brothers and sisters, the parents and children of the household, as well as the hearts of the First Presidency and Twelve. Let it mellow and soften all differences between members of the Stake Presidencies and the High Councils, as well as between neighbors living in the same ward. Let it unite young and old, male and female, flock and shepherd, people and Priesthood in the bonds of gratitude and forgiveness and love, so that Israel may feel approved of the Lord, and that we may all come before Him with a conscience void of offense before all men. Then there will be no disappointment as to the blessings promised those who sincerely worship Him. The sweet whisperings of the Holy Spirit will be given to them and the treasures of Heaven, the communion of angels, will be added from time to time, for His promise has gone forth and it cannot fail![14]

# Suggestions for Study

- What is revelation? What does it mean to say that revelation is "a living, vital principle"?

- What would happen to the Church without direct and continuing revelation?

- What is the significance to us that the canon of scripture is not yet full? How can we prepare our hearts to accept further revelation through the appointed channels of the priesthood?

- Why was continuing revelation important in the days of such prophets as Noah and Moses? What are the blessings of having a living prophet today? How does the living prophet help us meet the challenges of our day?

- Why must revelation for the Church come only through appointed priesthood channels? Although individuals "may receive Divine guidance and revelation affecting themselves," why does this not convey authority to direct others? (See also D&C 42:11.)

- In what ways are Church members sometimes deceived in their understanding of priesthood authority? How can members avoid being deceived in this way?

- How can members of the Church throughout the world be united as one in purpose and truth? How does the influence of the Holy Ghost enable us to be more unified? Why is it so important that we be one? (See also D&C 38:27.)

## Notes

1. In Conference Report, Oct. 1918, 2.
2. "President Joseph F. Smith on Revelation," *Millennial Star*, 6 Apr. 1905, 222.
3. *Gospel Doctrine*, 5th ed. (1939), 104–5.
4. "President Joseph F. Smith on 'Mormonism,' " *Millennial Star*, 19 June 1902, 387–88.
5. In Conference Report, Apr. 1909, 6.
6. "Editor's Table: Modern Revelation," *Improvement Era*, Aug. 1902, 805–7; paragraphing added.
7. *Gospel Doctrine*, 42.
8. *Gospel Doctrine*, 45.
9. *Gospel Doctrine*, 40–41.
10. In James R. Clark, comp., *Messages of the First Presidency of The Church of Jesus Christ of Latter-day Saints*, 6 vols. (1965–75), 4:285–86.
11. *Deseret News* (weekly), 13 Aug. 1884, 466.
12. *Deseret News* (weekly), 6 Mar. 1867, 74.
13. *Gospel Doctrine*, 261.
14. In *Messages of the First Presidency*, 3:244.

*Ruth and Naomi,* by Judith Mehr.
Ruth found peace and happiness by living a life of purity and
obedience to God's laws.

# Let Us Conquer Ourselves

*Lasting happiness is derived not from gratification of our physical desires nor from worldly pleasures, but from virtue, purity of life, and obedience to God's laws.*

## From the Life of Joseph F. Smith

During his administration from 1901 to 1918, President Joseph F. Smith became increasingly concerned about the encroachment of worldly influences into the lives of the Latter-day Saints. He was not blind to the worldly ways around him. He observed the immodesty, he heard the profanity, and he sorrowed at many of the social practices that were prevalent. He urged the Saints to exercise self-mastery in facing these influences and to live lives of morality, virtue, and purity.

The importance of restraint in the Saints' amusements and social pastimes and the evils of profanity, gambling, backbiting, and immodesty were all subjects about which he spoke. In September 1916 the First Presidency sent a letter to the auxiliary organizations of the Church stating that "there exists a pressing need of improvement and reform among our young people, specifically in the matter of dress and in their social customs and practices" and charging these organizations to take action to create a reformation in these matters.[1]

While giving instructions to these organizations, he also recognized that "home influences . . . above all others, should direct in moral, social and dress reforms. The home should lead in the work being done by the organizations which are only auxiliary to the home."[2]

He cautioned: "Our first enemy we will find within ourselves. It is a good thing to overcome that enemy first and bring ourselves into subjection to the will of the Father, and into strict obedience to the principles of life and salvation which he has given to the world for the salvation of men."[3]

## Teachings of Joseph F. Smith

### Let us follow the Savior by mastering ourselves.

It seems to me that the example which was set to us by our Savior is the example we should seek to follow. Did He [misuse] His intelligence for the gratification of the lusts of the flesh? Or did He go about doing good—healing the sick, opening the eyes of the blind, giving speech to the dumb, hearing to the deaf, cleansing the lepers, forgiving sin, relieving the distressed? Was not that the example He set before the world? Was not that the course He commanded His disciples to pursue? I think it was. There is something in such a course that is praiseworthy and noble. It will bring true and lasting pleasure; while the pleasures of the world are only temporary and fleeting.[4]

No man is safe unless he is master of himself; and there is no tyrant more merciless or more to be dreaded than an uncontrollable appetite or passion. We will find that if we give way to the groveling appetites of the flesh and follow them up, that the end will be invariably bitter, injurious and sorrowful, both to the individual and society. It is hurtful in example as well as in its individual effects; dangerous and hurtful to the unwary; while the denial of these appetites . . . and an aspiration for something noble; whenever possible, doing good to our fellow creatures, hoping for the future, laying up treasures in heaven, where moth and rust cannot corrupt, and where thieves cannot break through and steal [see Matthew 6:19–20]—all these things will bring everlasting happiness; happiness for this world and the world to come.[5]

For my part I do not fear the influence of our enemies from without, as I fear that of those from within. An open and avowed enemy, whom we may see and meet in an open field, is far less to be feared than a lurking, deceitful, treacherous enemy hidden within us, such as are many of the weaknesses of our fallen human nature, which are too often allowed to go unchecked, beclouding our minds, leading away our affections from God and his truth, until they sap the very foundations of our faith and debase us beyond the possibility or hope of redemption, either in this world or that to come. These are the enemies that we all have to battle with, they are the greatest that we have to contend with in the world, and the most difficult to conquer. They are the fruits of ignorance, generally arising out of unrebuked sin and evil in our own hearts. The labor that is upon us is to subdue our passions, conquer our inward foes, and see that our hearts are right in the sight of the Lord, that there is nothing calculated to grieve his Spirit and lead us away from the path of duty.[6]

Many are lovers of pleasure and lust more than lovers of God. They delight in the lusts of the flesh, the gratification of their appetites, having virulent desires, living in corruption, debauchery, revelry and all manner of wickedness. Many people do not know how to be happy, not knowing how to use the blessings that God has given unto them. If they had all the world, they would use it for the gratification of their own base passions and desires, to their own destruction. But if they possessed the right spirit, they would seek to promote the peace and happiness of mankind and extend the influence of the Gospel of light and truth to all the world. They would love purity, virtue, honesty, sobriety and righteousness.[7]

---

### Amusement is not the purpose of life but only to give variety.

Tell me what amusements you like best and whether your amusements have become a ruling passion in your life, and I will tell you what you are.[8]

Our amusements should be characterized by their wholesome social environments. We should have proper regard to the character of those with whom we associate in places of amusement; and we should be governed by a high sense of responsibility to our parents, to our friends and to the Church. We should know that the pleasures which we enjoy are such as have upon them the stamp of divine approval. . . . Amusements which, in themselves, and in commendable social surroundings, may be proper and wholesome, should be avoided unless associates are unquestionable and the places are reputable and are conducted under proper restraints.

There are limits in our recreations beyond which we cannot safely go. They should be guarded in character and curtailed in frequency to avoid excess. They should not occupy all, nor even the greater part of our time; indeed, they should be made incidental to the duties and obligations of life, and never be made a controlling motive or factor in our hopes and ambitions.[9]

All excess is detrimental. Temperance should govern in everything. Amusement is not the purpose of life, it should be indulged in only by way of variety. When people accustom themselves to constant or oft-repeated rounds of pleasure, the true objects of human existence are forgotten and duty becomes irksome and detestable.[10]

---

### Let us lead pure lives, avoid excesses, and cease from sin.

*Profanity and vulgarity are gross sins in the sight of God.*

We should stamp out profanity, and vulgarity, and everything of that character that exists among us; for all such things are incompatible with the gospel and inconsistent with the people of God.[11]

Language, like thought, makes its impression and is recalled by the memory in a way that may be unpleasant if not harmful to those who have been compelled to listen to unseemly words. Thoughts that in themselves are not proper may be exalted or debased by the language used to express them. If inelegant expressions should be eschewed, what shall be said of profanity?[12]

The habit . . . which some young people fall into, of using vulgarity and profanity . . . is not only offensive to all well-bred persons, but it is a gross sin in the sight of God, and should not exist among the children of the Latter-day Saints.[13]

I say to the fathers and mothers of Israel, and to the boys who have been born in the Church of Jesus Christ of Latter-day Saints: I say it to men and boys throughout the world, as far as my words may go—I plead with you, I implore you not to offend the Lord, nor to offend honorable men and women, by the use of profanity.[14]

*The desire to get something for nothing is pernicious.*

Among the vices of the present age gambling is very generally condemned. . . . Nevertheless, in numerous guises the demon of chance is welcomed in the home, in fashionable clubs, and at entertainments for worthy charities, even within the precincts of sacred edifices. . . .

The desire to get something of value for little or nothing is pernicious; and any proceeding that strengthens that desire is an effective aid to the gambling spirit, which has proved a veritable demon of destruction to thousands. Risking a dime in the hope of winning a dollar in any game of chance is a species of gambling.[15]

*Backbiting is contrary to the spirit of the gospel.*

In a letter recently received by me, the following request and question were submitted for my opinion: "I would like you to define backbiting. There seems to be a difference of opinion respecting the meaning of the term. Some claim that so long as you speak the truth about a person, it is not backbiting, no matter what you say or how you say it. Would it not be better, if we knew a person had faults, to go to him privately and labor with him, than to go to others and speak of his faults?"

Nothing could be farther from the spirit and genius of the gospel than to suppose that we are always justified in speaking the truth about a person, however harmful the truth to him may be. The gospel teaches us the fundamental principles of repentance, and we have no right to discredit a man in the estimation of his fellowmen when he has truly repented and God has forgiven him. . . .

As a rule, it is not necessary to be constantly offering advice to those who in our judgment are possessed of some fault. In the first place, our judgments may be in error, and in the second place, we may be dealing with a man who is strongly imbued with the spirit of repentance, and who, conscious of his weakness, is constantly struggling to overcome it. The utmost care, therefore, should be observed in all our language that implies a reproach of others. As a general rule, backbiting is better determined by the spirit and purpose that actuate us in speaking of things we consider faults in others than in the words themselves.

A man or woman who possesses the Spirit of God will soon detect in his or her own feelings the spirit of backbiting, as that spirit is present in the remarks that are made concerning others. The question of backbiting, therefore, is probably best determined by the ancient rule that, "the letter killeth but the spirit giveth life." [2 Corinthians 3:6.][16]

### Immodesty should be frowned upon by all people.

Immodesty in dress should be frowned down by parents and all decent people. The shameless exhibitions of the human form purposely presented in modern styles of dress, or rather undress, are indications of that sensuous and debasing tendency toward moral laxity and social corruption which have hurried nations into irretrievable ruin. Let not the brilliant prospects of a glorious millennium be clouded with such shadows as are threatened by customs and costumes and diversions of these licentious days.[17]

In my sight the present-day fashions are abominable, suggestive of evil, calculated to arouse base passion and lust, and to engender lasciviousness, in the hearts of those who follow the fashions, and of those who tolerate them. . . . It is infamous, and I hope the daughters of Zion will not descend to these pernicious ways, customs and fashions, for they are demoralizing and damnable in their effect.[18]

We hear it reported, from time to time, that some . . . mutilate their garments, rather than to keep them holy and undefiled. . . . We see some of our good sisters coming here to the temple occasionally decorated in the latest and most ridiculous fashions that ever disgraced the human form divine. They do not seem to realize that they are coming to the house of God.[19]

### Wholesome dancing is permitted among the Saints.

We think it timely to draw attention to the subject of dancing parties, a diversion permitted to Latter-day Saints, but under certain rules that ought to be strictly observed. . . . Intoxicants should be barred entirely from dancing halls and their vicinity. Those dances that require or permit the close embrace and suggestive movements . . . ought to be utterly prohibited.[20]

*Books are companions for good or for bad.*

Books constitute a sort of companionship to everyone who reads, and they create within the heart feelings either for good or for bad. It sometimes happens that parents are very careful about the company which their children keep and are very indifferent about the books they read. In the end the reading of a bad book will bring about evil associates.

It is not only the boy who reads this strange, weird and unnatural exciting literature who is affected by its influence, but in time he influences others. This literature becomes the mother of all sorts of evil suggestions that ripen into evil practices and bring about an unnatural and debased feeling which is ever crowding out the good in the human heart and giving place to the bad. . . . When our children are reading books that are creating strange and unusual and undesirable thoughts in their minds we need not be surprised to learn that they have committed some unusual, some strange, or unnatural act. It is in the thoughts and feelings that we have to combat the evils and temptations of the world, and the purification of our thoughts and feelings should be made the special effort of every father and mother. . . .

A story is told of an English officer in India, who one day went to the book shelf to take down a book. As he reached his hand up over the volume his finger was bitten by an adder. After a few hours the finger began to swell. Later on the swelling went into his arm, and finally the whole body was affected, and in a few days the officer was dead. There are adders concealed in many a cheap and trashy book. . . . Their effects upon our souls are poisonous, and in time they are sure to produce a moral and spiritual death. . . . Let the Saints beware of the books that enter their homes, for their influences may be as poisonous and deadly as the adder which brought death to the English officer in India.[21]

### What manner of people ought we to be?

It is only by obedience to the laws of God that men can rise above the petty weaknesses of mortality and exercise that breadth of affection, that charity and love, that should actuate the hearts and the motives of the children of men. The gospel as it has been restored is intended to make [people] free indeed, free to choose the good and forsake the evil, free to exercise that boldness in their choice of that which is good, by which they are convinced of right, notwithstanding the great majority of the people of the world may point at them the finger of scorn and ridicule. It requires no especial bravery on the part of men to swim with the currents of the world.[22]

The Lord bless you my brethren and sisters. We endorse any movement looking to temperance, looking to virtue tending to purity of life and to faith in God and obedience to His laws. . . .

. . . What manner of people ought we to be; what manner of individuals should we be? Should we not set an example worthy of our profession? Should we not live pure lives? Should we not be upright, virtuous, honest, God-fearing and God-loving in our souls every day of our lives and in every position in which we may be called to act; ought we not to set an example for good? Ought we not to be Christ-like, manly, true to every principle of the Gospel, and honorable out in the world and at home . . . ? That is indeed the kind of people we ought to be. God help us to be such is my prayer.[23]

# Suggestions for Study

- In what ways did the Savior set an example of self-mastery? What is the "enemy we will find within ourselves"? (See also Mosiah 3:19.) How can we follow the Savior's example in conquering this enemy?

- When we are not masters of ourselves, how can we hurt ourselves and others? When we are masters of ourselves, how can we bless others?

- How might amusements become a "ruling passion" in our lives? How might they reveal what we are? What role should amusements play in our lives?

- Why is "using vulgarity and profanity . . . a gross sin in the sight of God"? If those around you are using profanity, how might you let them know that it is offensive to you?

- Why is backbiting contrary to the spirit of the gospel? What course of action should we take rather than speaking about the faults of others?

- How does dressing modestly encourage righteous living? How can some of today's fashions be "suggestive of evil" and "demoralizing" in their effect?

- How does President Smith's counsel about books apply to the entertainment of today, such as video presentations, music, television, movies, magazines, and the Internet? (See also D&C 88:118.) In what ways is bravery required if we are to swim against "the currents of the world"?

- How would you answer the question "What manner of people ought we to be"? (See also 3 Nephi 27:27.)

## Notes

1. In James R. Clark, comp., *Messages of the First Presidency of The Church of Jesus Christ of Latter-day Saints,* 6 vols. (1965–75), 5:37.

2. In *Messages of the First Presidency,* 5:40.

3. *Gospel Doctrine,* 5th ed. (1939), 253.

4. *Deseret Evening News,* 8 Mar. 1884, 1.

5. *Gospel Doctrine,* 247.

6. *Gospel Doctrine,* 341.

7. *Deseret News: Semi-Weekly,* 24 Apr. 1883, 1.

8. *Gospel Doctrine,* 330.

9. *Gospel Doctrine,* 320.

10. In *Messages of the First Presidency,* 3:123.

11. *Gospel Doctrine,* 241.

12. *Gospel Doctrine,* 265.

13. In *Messages of the First Presidency,* 3:112–13.

14. "A Sermon on Purity," *Improvement Era,* May 1903, 504.

15. *Gospel Doctrine,* 326–27.

16. *Gospel Doctrine,* 263–64; paragraphing added.

17. In *Messages of the First Presidency,* 4:281.

18. *Gospel Doctrine,* 332–33.

19. *Gospel Doctrine,* 333.

20. In *Messages of the First Presidency,* 4:280–81.

21. *Gospel Doctrine,* 324–25.

22. *Gospel Doctrine,* 211.

23. In *Messages of the First Presidency,* 4:185–86.

Hyrum Smith, father of President Joseph F. Smith,
left a lasting impression on his son, even though the boy was
just five years old when Hyrum was martyred.

# Fathers in the Home

*Every father should rise to the dignity of his holy office as head of his family.*

## From the Life of Joseph F. Smith

Throughout his life, Joseph F. Smith carried with him the memory of his martyred father, Hyrum Smith. On 27 June 1918, President Smith presided at the Salt Lake City Cemetery, where a monument had been erected in honor of his father. On that occasion, he said: "I am blessed today with thirty-five children living, all of whom, so far as I know, have a standing in the Church of Jesus Christ of Latter-day Saints, and I believe their hearts are in the work of the Lord. I am proud of my children. I have today over eighty-six grandchildren. . . . I am rich; the Lord has given me great riches in children and in children's children. . . . I want you to just take a look here at a little flock of my grandchildren—right here, every one of them. I love them. I know them all. I never meet them but what I kiss them, just as I do my own children."[1]

Later his son Joseph Fielding Smith, who would serve as President of the Church from 1970 to 1972, observed that his father's love for his family "was boundless in its magnitude and purity. The world did not know—could not possibly know—the depths of his love for them. The wicked and the depraved have ridiculed and maligned him; but the true condition of his family life and wonderful love for his family is beyond their comprehension. O how he prayed that his children would always be *true*—true to God, true to their fellow men; true to each other and true to him! . . . Let them, one and all, be true to him and true to the cause which he represented so faithfully for the period of his mortal life, and which was the dearest thing to him in all his life."[2]

# Teachings of Joseph F. Smith

## There is no substitute for the home.

There is no substitute for the home. Its foundation is as ancient as the world, and its mission has been ordained of God from the earliest times. . . . The home then is more than a habitation, it is an institution which stands for stability and love in individuals as well as in nations.

There can be no genuine happiness separate and apart from the home, and every effort made to sanctify and preserve its influence is uplifting to those who toil and sacrifice for its establishment. Men and women often seek to substitute some other life for that of the home; they would make themselves believe that the home means restraint; that the highest liberty is the fullest opportunity to move about at will. There is no happiness without service, and there is no service greater than that which converts the home into a divine institution, and which promotes and preserves family life.

Those who shirk home responsibilities are wanting in an important element of social well-being. They may indulge themselves in social pleasures, but their pleasures are superficial and result in disappointment later in life. The occupations of men sometimes call them from their homes; but the thought of homecoming is always an inspiration to well doing and devotion.[3]

In the ideal home the soul is not starved, neither are the growth and expansion of the finer sentiments paralyzed for the coarse and sensual pleasures. The main aim is not to heap up material wealth, which generally draws further and further from the true, the ideal, the spiritual life; but it is rather to create soul-wealth, consciousness of noble achievement, an outflow of love and helpfulness.

It is not costly paintings, tapestries, priceless bric-a-brac, various ornaments, costly furniture, fields, herds, houses and lands which constitute the ideal home, nor yet the social enjoyments and ease so tenaciously sought by many; but it is rather beauty of soul, cultivated, loving, faithful, true spirits; hands that help and hearts that sympathize; love that seeks not its own, thoughts and acts that touch our lives to finer issues—these lie at the foundation of the ideal home.[4]

---

### In the home the presiding authority is vested in the father.

There is no higher authority in matters relating to the family organization, and especially when that organization is presided over by one holding the higher Priesthood, than that of the father. The authority is time honored, and among the people of God in all dispensations it has been highly respected and often emphasized by the teachings of the prophets who were inspired of God. The patriarchal order is of divine origin and will continue throughout time and eternity. There is, then, a particular reason why men, women and children should understand this order and this authority in the households of the people of God, and seek to make it what God intended it to be, a qualification and preparation for the highest exaltation of his children. . . .

This authority carries with it a responsibility and a grave one, as well as its rights and privileges, and men can not be too exemplary in their lives, nor fit themselves too carefully to live in harmony with this important and God-ordained rule of conduct in the family organization. Upon this authority certain promises and blessings are predicated, and those who observe and respect this authority have certain claims on divine favor which they cannot have except they respect and observe the laws that God has established for the regulation and authority of the home.[5]

I desire . . . to impress upon the officers of the Church the necessity of consulting fathers in all things that pertain to the calling of their sons to the Priesthood, and to the labors of the Church, that the respect and veneration which children should show for parents may not be disturbed by the Church, nor overstepped by its officers. In this way harmony and good will are made to prevail; and the sanction of the families and the family life, on which the government of the Church is based and perpetuated, will thus be added to the calls of the holy Priesthood, insuring unity, strength and power in its every action.[6]

---

## **Fathers, do your full duty to your families.**

If [fathers] have the Spirit of the Lord with them in the performance of their temporal duties, they will never neglect the mothers of their children, nor their children. They will not fail to teach them the principles of life and set before them a proper example. Don't do anything yourselves that you would have to say to your boy, "Don't do it." Live so that you can say, "My son, do as I do, follow me, emulate my example." That is the way fathers should live, every one of us; and it is a shame, a weakening, shameful thing for any member of the Church to pursue a course that he knows is not right and that he would rather his children should not follow. What a shameful thing it is for a man to place upon himself an embargo, a handicap against doing his full duty to those that love him and whom he should love above his own life, by yielding to appetites that are wrong and to passions that are base, and doing things that he ought not to do, and that he would feign keep his children from doing. Do your duty, my brethren, and the Lord will do His for you.[7]

Brethren, there is too little religious devotion, love and fear of God, in the home; too much worldliness, selfishness, indifference and lack of reverence in the family, or these never would exist so abundantly on the outside. Then, the home is what needs reforming. Try today, and tomorrow, to make a change in your home by praying twice a day with your family; call on your children and your wife to pray with you. Ask a blessing upon every meal you eat. Spend ten minutes in reading a chapter from the words of the Lord in the Bible, the Book of Mormon, the Doctrine and Covenants, before you retire, or before you go to your daily toil. Feed your spiritual selves at home, as well as in public places. Let love, and peace, and the Spirit of the Lord, kindness, charity, sacrifice for others, abound in your families. Banish harsh words, envying, hatreds, evil speaking, obscene language and innuendo, blasphemy, and let the Spirit of God take possession of your hearts. Teach to your children these things, in spirit and power, sustained and strengthened by personal practice. Let them see that you are earnest, and practice what you preach.[8]

ble, and the day that cometh shall burn them up, saith the Lord of Hosts, that it shall leave them neither root nor branch." [Malachi 4:1.] Again, Moroni quoted the 11th chapter of Isaiah, in which are these words on this subject: "But with righteousness shall he judge the poor, and reprove with equity for the meek of the earth; and he shall smite the earth with the rod of his mouth, and with the breath of his lips shall he slay the wicked." [Isaiah 11:4.]

Again, Acts, 3d chapter, 22d and 23d verses—quoted by Moroni just as they read in the New Testament—"A prophet shall the Lord your God raise up unto you. . . . Him shall ye hear in all things whatsoever he shall say unto you, and it shall come to pass that every soul which will not hear that prophet shall be destroyed from among the people." Now this is strong language, and to the point. Moroni declared that this prophet was Christ at his second coming; that this scripture was not fulfilled, but was about to be fulfilled in the literal coming of the Son of Man to reign upon the earth and to execute judgment upon the world. Moroni also quoted Joel, 2d chapter, 28th to the 32d verses, declaring that this scripture was also shortly to be fulfilled: "And I will show wonders in the heavens and in the earth, blood, and fire, and pillars of smoke, &c. And it shall come to pass that whosoever shall call on the name of the Lord shall be delivered, for in Mount Zion and in Jerusalem shall be deliverance, as the Lord hath said, and in the remnant whom the Lord shall call." [See Joseph Smith— History 1:36–41.]

Now, it seems to me that none of the interest or importance of this vital subject are lost in the fact that we are not left to the traditions of the fathers nor to the written word solely, nor to any uncertain means for the verification of these predictions, but rather our interest should be awakened from the fact that an angel from heaven, an actual messenger from the presence of God, has reiterated these very predictions to man on the earth in this generation.

Some of these passages of scripture quoted by the angel were presumed to have been fulfilled in the days of the ancient apostles. Thus the world was in ignorance respecting them. All uncertainty upon this subject is now, however, dispelled, and the truth is made plain to all. For Moroni declared to Joseph Smith that these scriptures had not been fulfilled, but that the set time had come when they would be fulfilled, every whit, and the coming of Christ, the execution of the judgements, and the ushering in of the final reign of peace therein referred to, should be consummated in this dispensation. The power of the wicked nations of the earth will be broken. Thrones shall totter, and kingdoms fall, while Zion shall arise and shine, and put on her beautiful garments, and be clothed with power, wisdom, majesty and dominion upon the earth. Babylon must fall to rise no more.[4]

### The righteous will heed the signs and prepare themselves for the Savior's coming.

The many eruptions, earthquakes and tidal waves which have occurred . . . are signs which the Savior declared should foreshadow his second coming, although he said his advent should be as a thief in the night, still he gave certain signs which would indicate as surely his coming as the budding trees the coming of summer. The wise and prudent will heed the warning and prepare themselves that they be not taken unawares. Not the least of the signs of the times is this, that the gospel is being preached unto the poor, as a witness unto all nations.[5]

The Latter-day Saints . . . believe in the statements of the Holy Scriptures, that calamities will befall the nations as signs of the coming of Christ to judgment. They believe that God rules in the fire, the earthquake, the tidal wave, the volcanic eruption, and the storm. Him they recognize as the Master and Ruler of nature and her laws, and freely acknowledge his hand in all things. We believe that his judgments are poured out to bring mankind to a sense of his power and his purposes, that they may repent of their sins and prepare themselves for the second coming of Christ to reign in righteousness upon the earth.

We firmly believe that Zion—which is the pure in heart—shall escape, if she observes to do all things whatsoever God has commanded; but, in the opposite event, even Zion shall be visited "with sore affliction, with pestilence, with plague, with sword, with vengeance, and with devouring fire" (Doctrine and Covenants 97:26). All this that her people may be taught to walk in the light of truth and in the way of the God of their salvation.

We believe that these severe, natural calamities are visited upon men by the Lord for the good of his children, to quicken their devotion to others, and to bring out their better natures, that they may love and serve him. We believe, further, that they are the heralds and tokens of his final judgment, and the schoolmasters to teach the people to prepare themselves by righteous living for the coming of the Savior to reign upon the earth, when every knee shall bow and every tongue confess that Jesus is the Christ.

If these lessons are impressed upon us and upon the people of our country, the anguish, and the loss of life and toil, sad, great and horrifying as they were, will not have been endured in vain.[6]

I . . . testify, that unless the Latter-day Saints will live their religion, keep their covenants with God and their brethren, honor the priesthood which they bear, and try faithfully to bring themselves into subjection to the laws of God, they will be the first to fall beneath the judgments of the Almighty, for his judgments will begin at his own house.

Therefore, those who have made a covenant with the Lord by baptism, and have broken that covenant, who profess to be saints and are not, but are sinners, and covenant-breakers, and partakers of the sins of Babylon, most assuredly will "receive of her plagues," for it is written that the righteous will barely escape [see Revelation 18:4; D&C 63:34]. This is my testimony in relation to these matters. We rely upon the word of the Lord in these things, and not upon the word of man, for not only have angels, but God Almighty has spoken from the heavens in this our own age of the world, and we know his word is true.

That we as a people may be prepared not only for the judgments, but for the glory and coming of our Lord, that we may escape the calamities to be poured out upon the wicked, and receive the welcome plaudit of the faithful servant, and be counted worthy to stand in the presence of the Lord in his glorious kingdom, is my prayer.[7]

We hear about living in perilous times. We are in perilous times, but I do not feel the pangs of that terror. It is not upon me.

I propose to live so that it will not rest upon me. I propose to live so that I shall be immune from the perils of the world, if it be possible for me to so live, by obedience to the commandments of God and to his laws revealed for my guidance. No matter what may come to me, if I am only in the line of my duty, if I am in fellowship with God, if I am worthy of the fellowship of my brethren, if I can stand spotless before the world, without blemish, without transgression of the laws of God, what does it matter to me what may happen to me? I am always ready, if I am in this frame of understanding mind and conduct. It does not matter at all. Therefore I borrow no trouble nor feel the pangs of fear.

The Lord's hand is over all, and therein I acknowledge his hand. Not that men are at war, not that nations are trying to destroy nations, not that men are plotting against the liberties of their fellow creatures, not in those respects at all; but God's hand is not shortened. He will control the results that will follow. He will overrule them in a way that you and I, today, do not comprehend, or do not foresee, for ultimate good.[8]

---

### Obedience to the gospel will prepare the world for the coming of the Savior.

Obedience to the Gospel will save the world from sin, abolish war, strife and litigation, and usher in the millennial reign. It will restore the earth to its rightful owner, and prepare it for the inheritance of the just. These are all principles of [the] Gospel of Christ, and the effects which will flow from their acceptance and adoption by mankind.[9]

The gospel is salvation, and without it there is nothing worth having. We came naked into the world and shall go hence the same. If we were to accumulate half the world, it would avail us nothing so far as prolonging life here, or securing eternal life hereafter. But the gospel teaches men to be humble, faithful, honest and righteous before the Lord and with each other, and in proportion as its principles are carried out so will peace and righteousness extend and be established on the earth, and sin, contention, bloodshed and corruption of all kinds cease to exist, and the earth become purified and be made a fit abode for heavenly beings; and for the Lord our God to come and dwell upon, which he will do during the Millennium.[10]

The Church of Jesus Christ of Latter-day Saints . . . regards it as part of its mission to prepare the way for the literal and glorious coming of the Son of God to the earth, to reign over it and dwell with His people. As part of that work of preparation the Saints believe that Israel, so long scattered among the nations of the earth, will be gathered together and restored to the lands promised to their fathers as an everlasting inheritance. . . .

. . . Those who have received the Gospel in the world . . . will be factors in carrying out God's purposes. They will be conjoint laborers with Him in bringing to pass not only their own salvation in time and in eternity, but the salvation of all Israel and of the Gentiles who will receive the Gospel. They will be fulfillers of ancient prophecies. Isaiah, in the glow of the inspiration of God, saw them and their labors when he cried aloud: "It shall come to pass in the last days that the mountain of the Lord's house shall be established in the top of the mountains, and shall be exalted above the hills, and all nations shall flow unto it" (Isaiah ii:2–3). Of them Jeremiah was speaking when he repeated God's promise to Israel to be fulfilled in the last days: "I will take you, one of a city and two of a family, and I will bring you to Zion, and I will give you pastors according to mine heart, which shall feed you with knowledge and understanding" (Jeremiah iii:14–15).[11]

The Lord . . . decreed a decree which He said His people should realize: That they should begin from that very hour to prevail over all their enemies and, inasmuch as they continued to be faithful in keeping His laws He had given unto them, it was decreed that they should prevail until all enemies were subdued—not subdued by violence or the spirit of contention or of warfare but subdued by the power of eternal truth, by the majesty and power of Almighty God. . . . The increased power of the righteous and of the upright covenanted people of God should be magnified and increased, until the world shall bow and acknowledge that Jesus is the Christ, and that there is a people preparing for His coming in power and glory to the earth again [see D&C 103:5–8].[12]

The Church of Jesus Christ of Latter-day Saints is no partisan Church. It is not a sect. It is *The Church of Jesus Christ of Latter-day Saints.* It is the only one today existing in the world that can and does legitimately bear the name of Jesus Christ and his divine authority. I make this declaration in all simplicity and honesty before you and before all the world, bitter as the truth may seem to those who are opposed and who have no reason for that opposition. It is nevertheless true and will remain true until he who has a right to rule among the nations of the earth and among the individual children of God throughout the world shall come and take the reins of government and receive the bride that shall be prepared for the coming of the Bridegroom.[13]

# Suggestions for Study

- Why is it important to us that God's prophets "in modern as in ancient times" have foretold the Second Coming of the Savior?

- Why have we been given signs of the Second Coming? Who will recognize these as signs of the Savior's coming? How can we apply the information about these signs to our lives?

- In what ways might natural calamities be "for the good of [God's] children"? How should we respond when they fall upon us?

- What must we do to "escape the calamities to be poured out upon the wicked"?

- What blessings would come to the world if people would obey the principles of the gospel?

- In what ways does God "overrule" the results of evil "for ultimate good"?

- How will the Saints finally subdue all their enemies?

- Why is the Second Coming both a "great" and a "dreadful" day? (D&C 110:16).

- What can each of us do to help prepare the world for the Second Coming of the Savior?

## Notes

1. In James R. Clark, comp., *Messages of the First Presidency of The Church of Jesus Christ of Latter-day Saints,* 6 vols. (1965–75), 4:154.

2. In *Messages of the First Presidency,* 3:287.

3. In *Messages of the First Presidency,* 4:294.

4. In Conference Report, Apr. 1880, 95–96; paragraphing added.

5. In *Messages of the First Presidency,* 4:132.

6. *Gospel Doctrine,* 5th ed. (1939), 55.

7. In Conference Report, Apr. 1880, 96.

8. *Gospel Doctrine,* 89.

9. *Deseret News: Semi-Weekly,* 19 Feb. 1878, 1.

10. *Gospel Doctrine,* 84–85.

11. "President Joseph F. Smith on 'Mormonism,' " *Millennial Star,* 19 June 1902, 385–86.

12. In Conference Report, Apr. 1902, 2.

13. *Gospel Doctrine,* 137.

*Two Thousand Stripling Warriors,* by Arnold Friberg. Helaman wrote of the young men whom he led into battle: "They did think more upon the liberty of their fathers than they did upon their lives; yea, they had been taught by their mothers, that if they did not doubt, God would deliver them" (Alma 56:47).

# The Gospel Brings Peace to the World in Troubled Times

*The gospel of Jesus Christ brings peace to the world during troubled times.*

## From the Life of Joseph F. Smith

In the years just before his death, President Joseph F. Smith often lamented the sorrows associated with World War I. Many Church members were drawn into the war on opposite sides, and hundreds lost their lives. Several of President Smith's own sons served in the armed forces, and one was twice wounded in action.

In a Christmas message to the Saints during this time, the First Presidency said: "While rejoicing over the birth of the Incomparable One, the light of our gladness is overshadowed with the warclouds that have darkened the skies of Europe, and our songs and salutations of joy and good will are rendered sadly discordant by the thunders of artillery and the groans of the wounded and dying, echoing from afar, but harrowing to our souls as the awful tidings come sounding o'er the sea. Nations rising against nations, brothers against brothers, 'Christians' against 'Christians,' each invoking the aid of the God of love in their gory strife and claiming fellowship with the Prince of peace! What an awful spectacle is thus presented before the angelic host, a band of whom sang the immortal song of 'good will toward men' at the birth of the babe of Bethlehem!"[1]

President Smith lived to hear the news of the signing of the armistice that brought an end to hostilities and the destruction of life and property. The armistice was signed on 11 November 1918, just eight days before his death.

He taught the Saints during this period that true peace comes only through accepting and living the gospel of Jesus Christ.

Joseph Fielding Smith, who would later become President of the Church, said of his father: "His spirit was gentle and kind. A more sympathetic soul, one who suffered with the sufferer, who was more willing to help the helpless to carry his burden, and the downtrodden to regain his feet, could not be found in all the borders of Israel. He was a peace-maker, a lover of peace."[2]

# Teachings of Joseph F. Smith

## Only the gospel of Jesus Christ can bring peace to the world.

There is only one thing that can bring peace into the world. It is the adoption of the gospel of Jesus Christ, rightly understood, obeyed and practiced by rulers and people alike. It is being preached in power to all nations, kindreds, tongues and peoples of the world, by the Latter-day Saints, and the day is not far distant when its message of salvation shall sink deep into the hearts of the common people, who, in sincerity and earnestness, when the time comes, will not only surely register their judgment against a false Christianity, but against war and the makers of war as crimes against the human race. For years it has been held that peace comes only by preparation for war; the present conflict [World War I] should prove that peace comes only by preparing for peace, through training the people in righteousness and justice, and selecting rulers who respect the righteous will of the people.[3]

We want peace in the world. We want love and good will to exist throughout the earth, and among all the people of the world; but there never can come to the world that spirit of peace and love that should exist, until mankind will receive God's truth and God's message unto them, and acknowledge his power and authority which is divine, and never found in the wisdom only of men.[4]

The Lord loveth peace. The doctrine of the Savior of men was "Peace on earth, good will to men," love, love unfeigned. The greatest of all the commandments that was ever given to the children of men is: "Thou shalt love the Lord thy God with all thy heart, and with all thy soul, and with all thy mind. This is the first and great commandment. And the second is like unto it, Thou shalt love thy neighbor as thyself. On these two commandments hang all the law and the prophets." [Matthew 22:37–40.] If in the central nations of the earth this spirit of love had existed, this principle of the gospel of Jesus Christ; if this glorious admonition had been taken to heart by the rulers of those nations, there never would have been any war, there never would have been any bloodshed, there never would have been the devastation and ruin and evil conditions that exist today. It is because the people of the world have not the gospel. It is because they do not obey the truth. It is because they have not Christ, and therefore they are left to themselves, and the results that we see are the consequences of their own misbehavior and of their own wicked deeds.[5]

There is just one power, and one only, that can prevent war among the nations of the earth, and that is true religion and undefiled before God, the Father. Nothing else will accomplish it. . . . There is but one remedy that can prevent men from going to war, when they feel disposed to do it, and that is the Spirit of God, which inspires to love, and not to hatred, which leads unto all truth, and not unto error, which inclines the children of God to pay deference to him and to his laws and to esteem them as above all other things in the world.

The Lord has told us that . . . wars would come. We have not been ignorant that they were pending, and that they were likely to burst out upon the nations of the earth at any time. We have been looking for the fulfilment of the words of the Lord that they would come. Why? Because the Lord wanted it? No; not by any means. Was it because the Lord predestined it, or designed it, in any degree? No, not at all. Why? It was for the reason that men did not hearken unto the Lord God, and he foreknew the results that would follow, because of men, and because of the nations of the earth; and therefore he was able to predict what would befall them, and came upon them in consequence of their own acts, and not because he has willed it upon them, for they are but suffering and reaping the results of their own actions.

. . . "Peace on earth, and good will to men," is our slogan. That is our principle. That is the principle of the gospel of Jesus

Christ. And while I think it is wrong, wickedly wrong, to force war upon any nation, or upon any people, I believe it is righteous and just for every people to defend their own lives and their own liberties, and their own homes, with the last drop of their blood. I believe it is right, and I believe that the Lord will sustain any people in defending their own liberty to worship God according to the dictates of their conscience, any people trying to preserve their wives and their children from the ravages of the war. But we do not want to be brought into the necessity of having to defend ourselves.[6]

## When called to serve, keep yourself pure and unspotted from the world.

I exhort my friends . . . to maintain above all other things the spirit of humanity, of love, and of peace-making, that even though they may be called into action they will not demolish, override and destroy the principles which we believe in, which we have tried to inculcate, and which we are exhorted to maintain: peace and good will toward all mankind, though we may be brought into action with the enemy. I want to say to the Latter-day Saints who may enlist, and whose services the country may require, that when they become soldiers of the State and of the Nation that they will not forget that they are also soldiers of the Cross, that they are ministers of life and not of death; and when they go forth, they may go in the spirit of defending the liberties of mankind rather than for the purpose of destroying the enemy.[7]

When our boys . . . are called into the army . . . , I hope and pray that they will carry with them the Spirit of God, not the spirit of bloodshed, of adultery, of wickedness, but the spirit of righteousness, the spirit which leads to do good, to build up, to benefit the world, and not to destroy and shed blood.

Remember the passage of scripture . . . in the Book of Mormon, concerning the pure young men that abjured war and the shedding of blood, lived pure and innocent, free from contaminating thought of strife, of anger, or wickedness in their hearts; but when necessity required, and they were called to go out to defend their lives, and the lives of their fathers and mothers, and their homes, they went—not to destroy but to defend, not to shed blood but rather to save the blood of the innocent and of the unoffending, and the peace-lovers of mankind [see Alma 56:45–48].

Will those men who go out from . . . the Church of Jesus Christ of Latter-day Saints forget their prayers? Will they forget God? Will they forget the teachings that they have received from their parents at home? Will they forget the principles of the gospel of Jesus Christ and the covenants that they have made in the waters of baptism, and in sacred places? Or will they go out as men, in every sense—pure men, high-minded men, honest men, virtuous men, men of God? That is what I am anxious about.

I want to see the hand of God made manifest in the acts of the men that go out from the ranks of the Church of Jesus Christ . . . to help to defend the principles of liberty and sound government for the human family. I want to see them so live that they can be in communion with the Lord, in their camps, and in their secret places, and that in the midst of battle they can say: "Father, my life and my spirit are in thine hand!"

I want to see the boys that go away from here in this cause, go feeling just as our missionaries do when sent out into the world, carrying with them the spirit a good mother feels when she parts with her boy, on the morning of his departure for his mission. She embraces him with all the mother's love in her soul!

. . . If our boys will only go out into the world this way, carrying with them the spirit of the gospel and the behavior of true Latter-day Saints, no matter what may befall them in life, they will endure with the best. They will be able to endure as much as anybody else can possibly endure of fatigue or of suffering, if necessary, and when they are brought to the test they will stand it! Because they have no fear of death! They will be free from fear of the consequences of their own lives. They will have no need to dread death, for they have done their work; they have kept the faith, they are pure in heart, and they are worthy to see God![8]

There are many evils that usually follow in the wake of marshaled armies equipped for and engaged in war, far worse than honorable death which may come in the conflict of battle. It matters not so much when our young men are called, or where they may go, but it does matter much to their parents, friends and associates in the truth, and above all to themselves, how they go. They have been trained all their lives as members of the Church to keep themselves pure and unspotted from the sins of the world, to respect the rights of others, to be obedient to righteous principles, to remember that virtue is one of the greatest gifts from God. Moreover, that they should respect the virtue of others and rather die a thousand times than defile themselves by committing deadly sin. We want them to go forth clean, both in thought and action, with faith in the principles of the gospel and the redeeming grace of our Lord and Savior. We would have them remember that only by living clean and faithful lives can they hope to attain the salvation promised through the shedding of the blood of our Redeemer.[9]

---

### We strive to live at peace with all men.

We admonish the Latter-day Saints to live their religion; to remember their covenants made at the waters of baptism; to honor the Lord and keep His commandments; not to be overcome by the follies of the world, but to seek the guidance of the Holy Spirit, [and] live at peace with all men.[10]

The new year and future years invite the inhabitants of all lands to unite in the establishment of peace and the realization of universal brotherhood. Strife, enmity, selfishness, immorality are evils to be eradicated from the individual life. No one is too lowly or insignificant to help. Let each man love his neighbor as himself and the present tragedies will pass away, future terrors will be averted, and "every man in every place will meet a brother and a friend."

An illustrious model of right living and noble fellowship was given to the world twenty centuries ago in Jesus Christ. His message was peace and good will. His law was founded on justice wisely exercised and righteousness intelligently applied. Light was His standard and truth His creed.[11]

In spite of "man's inhumanity to man," so awfully manifested in the dreadful struggle between nations now impending, we rationally take cognizance of present causes for gladness and thanksgiving, and look through the clouds of direful war to the sure and certain fulfilment of the promises of permanent peace in the approaching advent of our Lord and King.[12]

I . . . stand upon this principle, that the truth is in the gospel of Jesus Christ, that the power of redemption, the power of peace, the power for good will, love, charity and forgiveness, and the power for fellowship with God, abides in the gospel of Jesus Christ and in obedience to it on the part of the people. I therefore admit, and not only admit but claim, that there is nothing greater on earth, nor in heaven, than the truth of God's gospel which he has devised and restored for the salvation and the redemption of the world. And it is through that that peace will come to the children of men, and it will not come to the world in any other way.[13]

## Suggestions for Study

- Why is the gospel of Jesus Christ the only thing that can bring peace to the world? What can we do to help bring about peace in the world?

- Where does peace begin? How does observing the two great commandments lead to peace at home and abroad?

- How can those who go into military service be "ministers of life and not of death"?

- How can members carry with them into military service "the spirit of the gospel and the behavior of true Latter-day Saints"?

- When members are called into military service, what beliefs and attitudes will help them not to fear death?

- What can we each do to more fully "live at peace with all men"?

- What does the example of the Savior teach us about living with peace and goodwill?

## Notes

1. In James R. Clark, *Messages of the First Presidency of The Church of Jesus Christ of Latter-day Saints*, 6 vols. (1965–75), 4:319.
2. *Life of Joseph F. Smith,* comp. Joseph Fielding Smith (1938), 440.
3. *Gospel Doctrine,* 5th ed. (1939), 421.
4. *Gospel Doctrine,* 417–18.
5. In Conference Report, Apr. 1918, 170.
6. *Gospel Doctrine,* 418–19; paragraphing altered.
7. In *Messages of the First Presidency,* 5:52.
8. *Gospel Doctrine,* 423–25.
9. *Gospel Doctrine,* 426.
10. In *Messages of the First Presidency,* 4:211.
11. In *Messages of the First Presidency,* 5:1–2.
12. In *Messages of the First Presidency,* 4:348.
13. *Gospel Doctrine,* 420.

# Redeeming Our Dead through Temple Service

*Through temple service, we become saviors on Mount Zion for those who have died.*

## From the Life of Joseph F. Smith

"My soul is rent asunder. My heart is broken, and flutters for life! O my sweet son, my joy, my hope! . . . O God, help me!"[1] lamented President Joseph F. Smith at the unexpected death of his oldest son, Hyrum M. Smith, a member of the Quorum of the Twelve Apostles. Hyrum was 45 years old. Six months later President Smith presided at the Salt Lake City Cemetery when a monument was erected in honor of his father, Hyrum. It was 27 June 1918, the anniversary of the martyrdom of his father and his uncle, the Prophet Joseph Smith.

The Spirit of the Lord must have stirred his soul as he contemplated the deaths of his loved ones. A few months later, only weeks before his own death, President Smith recorded: "I sat in my room pondering over the scriptures; And reflecting upon the great atoning sacrifice that was made by the Son of God, for the redemption of the world. . . . While I was thus engaged, my mind reverted to the writings of the apostle Peter [see 1 Peter 3:18–20; 4:6]. . . . As I pondered over these things which are written, the eyes of my understanding were opened, and the Spirit of the Lord rested upon me, and I saw the hosts of the dead, both small and great" (D&C 138:1–2, 5, 11).

He then received the vision of the redemption of the dead, recorded in Doctrine and Covenants 138, which taught him new truths and reaffirmed doctrines he had believed and taught for decades.

# Teachings of Joseph F. Smith

### Jesus Christ was foreordained and anointed to save the living and the dead.

[The Savior] was sent not only to preach the gospel to those dwelling in mortality, but he was foreordained and anointed of God to open the doors of the prison house to those in bondage and to proclaim his gospel to them.[2]

On the third of October, in the year nineteen hundred and eighteen, I sat in my room pondering over the scriptures;

And reflecting upon the great atoning sacrifice that was made by the Son of God, for the redemption of the world;

And the great and wonderful love made manifest by the Father and the Son in the coming of the Redeemer into the world;

That through his atonement, and by obedience to the principles of the gospel, mankind might be saved. . . .

As I pondered over these things which are written [see 1 Peter 3:18–20; 4:6], the eyes of my understanding were opened, and the Spirit of the Lord rested upon me, and I saw the hosts of the dead, both small and great.

And there were gathered together in one place an innumerable company of the spirits of the just, who had been faithful in the testimony of Jesus while they lived in mortality. . . .

While this vast multitude waited and conversed, rejoicing in the hour of their deliverance from the chains of death, the Son of God appeared, declaring liberty to the captives who had been faithful;

And there he preached to them the everlasting gospel, the doctrine of the resurrection and the redemption of mankind from the fall, and from individual sins on conditions of repentance. . . .

And as I wondered, my eyes were opened, and my understanding quickened, and I perceived that the Lord went not in person among the wicked and the disobedient who had rejected the truth, to teach them;

But behold, from among the righteous, he organized his forces and appointed messengers, clothed with power and authority,

President Joseph F. Smith's son, Elder Hyrum M. Smith of the Quorum
of the Twelve Apostles, died in 1918, shortly before President Smith received
the vision of the redemption of the dead that became section 138
of the Doctrine and Covenants.

and commissioned them to go forth and carry the light of the gospel to them that were in darkness, even to all the spirits of men; and thus was the gospel preached to the dead.

And the chosen messengers went forth to declare the acceptable day of the Lord and proclaim liberty to the captives who were bound, even unto all who would repent of their sins and receive the gospel.

Thus was the gospel preached to those who had died in their sins, without a knowledge of the truth, or in transgression, having rejected the prophets.[3]

Jesus had not finished his work when his body was slain, neither did he finish it after his resurrection from the dead; although he had accomplished the purpose for which he then came to the earth, he had not fulfilled all his work. And when will he? Not until he has redeemed and saved every son and daughter of our father Adam that have been or ever will be born upon this earth to the end of time, except the sons of perdition. That is his mission.[4]

---

### The living and the dead labor together to bring the gospel to all of God's children.

We will not finish our work until we have saved ourselves, and then not until we shall have saved all depending upon us; for we are to become saviors upon Mount Zion, as well as Christ. We are called to this mission. The dead are not perfect without us, neither are we without them [see D&C 128:18]. We have a mission to perform for and in their behalf; we have a certain work to do in order to liberate those who, because of their ignorance and the unfavorable circumstances in which they were placed while here, are unprepared for eternal life; we have to open the door for them, by performing ordinances which they cannot perform for themselves, and which are essential to their release from the "prison-house," to come forth and live according to God in the spirit, and be judged according to men in the flesh [see D&C 138:33–34].

The Prophet Joseph Smith has said that this is one of the most important duties that devolves upon the Latter-day Saints. And why? Because this is the dispensation of the fulness of times, which will usher in the millennial reign, and in which all things spoken by the mouths of holy prophets, since the world began, must be fulfilled, and all things united, both which are in heaven and in the earth. We have that work to do; or, at least all we can of it, leaving the balance to our children, in whose hearts we should instill the importance of this work, rearing them in the love of the truth and in the knowledge of these principles, so that when we pass away, having done all we can do, they will then take up the labor and continue it until it is consummated.[5]

The same principles that apply to the living apply also to the dead. . . . And so we are baptized for those that are dead. The living cannot be made perfect without the dead, nor the dead be made perfect without the living. There has got to be a welding together and a joining together of parents and children and children and parents until the whole chain of God's family shall be welded together into one chain, and they shall all become the family of God and His Christ.[6]

This gospel revealed to the Prophet Joseph is already being preached to the spirits in prison, to those who have passed away from this stage of action into the spirit world without the knowledge of the gospel. Joseph Smith is preaching that gospel to them. So is Hyrum Smith. So is Brigham Young, and so are all the faithful apostles that lived in this dispensation under the administration of the Prophet Joseph [see D&C 138:36–37, 51–54]. They are there, having carried with them from here the holy Priesthood that they received under authority, and which was conferred upon them in the flesh; they are preaching the gospel to the spirits in prison; for Christ, when his body lay in the tomb, went to proclaim liberty to the captives and opened the prison doors to them that were bound [see D&C 138:27–30]. Not only are these engaged in that work but hundreds and thousands of others; the elders that have died in the mission field have not finished their missions, but they are continuing them in the spirit world [see D&C 138:57]. Possibly the Lord saw it necessary or proper to call them hence as he did. I am not going to question that thought, in the least, nor dispute it. I leave it in the hand of God, for I believe that all these things will be overruled for good, for the Lord will

411

suffer nothing to come to his people in the world that he will not overrule eventually for their greater good.[7]

I have always believed, and still do believe with all my soul, that such men as Peter and James and the twelve disciples chosen by the Savior in his time, have been engaged all the centuries that have passed since their martyrdom for the testimony of Jesus Christ, in proclaiming liberty to the captives in the spirit world and in opening their prison doors [see D&C 138:38–50]. I do not believe that they could be employed in any greater work. Their special calling and anointing of the Lord himself was to save the world, to proclaim liberty to the captives, and the opening of the prison doors to those who were bound in chains of darkness, superstition, and ignorance. . . .

. . . The things we experience here are typical of the things of God and the life beyond us. There is a great similarity between God's purposes as manifested here and his purposes as carried out in his presence and kingdom. Those who are authorized to preach the gospel here and are appointed here to do that work will not be idle after they have passed away, but will continue to exercise the rights that they obtained here under the Priesthood of the Son of God to minister for the salvation of those who have died without a knowledge of the truth.[8]

## We can become saviors upon Mount Zion by performing saving ordinances for the dead in temples.

Teach your children and let yourselves be taught the fact that it is necessary for you to become saviors upon Mount Zion for those who have died without the knowledge of the gospel, and that the temples of God in these mountains, and that are being reared in other lands, have been built and are designed expressly for the performance of these sacred ordinances which are necessary for those who have passed away without them. Do not forget these things. Keep them in mind for they are necessary for us.[9]

This great work for the redemption of our dead, the uniting together of the living and the dead, the sealing power . . . and all the ordinances that have been revealed to be performed in the sacred edifices called temples, which we are under commandment

President Smith dedicated the site for the temple
at Cardston, Alberta, Canada, in 1913.

from God always to build unto His holy name, . . . these things have been revealed to us in this dispensation in greater fulness and in greater plainness than ever before in the history of the world so far as we know.[10]

We hope to see the day when we shall have temples built in the various parts of the land where they are needed for the convenience of the people; for we realize that one of the greatest responsibilities that rests upon the people of God today is that their hearts shall be turned unto their fathers [see Malachi 4:5–6; D&C 2], and that they shall do the work that is necessary to be done for them in order that they may be joined together fitly in the bond of the New and Everlasting Covenant from generation to generation. For the Lord has said, through the Prophet, that this is one of the greatest responsibilities devolving upon us in this latter day.[11]

In relation to the deliverance of spirits from their prison house, of course, we believe that can only be done after the gospel has been preached to them in the spirit, and they have accepted the same, and the work necessary to their redemption by the living be done for them. That this work may be hastened so that all who believe, in the spirit world, may receive the benefit of deliverance, it is revealed that the great work of the Millennium shall be the work in the temples for the redemption of the dead; and then we hope to enjoy the benefits of revelation . . . by such means as the Lord may reveal concerning those for whom the work shall be done. . . . It stands to reason that, while the gospel may be preached unto all, the good and the bad, or rather to those who would repent and to those who would not repent in the spirit world, the same as it is here, redemption will only come to those who repent and obey.[12]

Great activity has been manifest . . . on the part of the saints in their temple work. The spirit to work for the redemption of the dead is resting upon them, and an increased interest has been shown in this work of divine love. This work is, the Prophet Joseph tells us, "essential to our salvation, as Paul says concerning the fathers, 'that they without us cannot be made perfect, neither can we without our dead be made perfect.' " [D&C 128:15.] The command of God is for the saints to labor with their might for the redemption of their dead. . . .

. . . The Spirit which moves the saints to work for the redemption of the dead is the planting in the hearts of the children the promises made to the fathers. This same spirit seems to be moving upon the hearts of honorable men of the earth who are spending their time and means in collecting and compiling genealogical records. . . . The saints should take advantage of every opportunity to obtain the records as far as possible of their ancestors, that their redemption through the ordinances of the House of God might be obtained. We commend the saints for their diligence in this most important and essential work.[13]

We carry to the world the olive branch of peace. We present to the world the law of God, the word of the Lord, the truth, as it has been revealed in the latter day for the redemption of the dead and for the salvation of the living.[14]

# Suggestions for Study

- What is the "work" and the "mission" of the Savior? What did the Savior do in the spirit world to help fulfill this great work? (See D&C 138:11–12, 18–19, 29–30.)

- How is missionary work performed in the spirit world? Who are the missionaries? (See D&C 138:29–34, 57–59.)

- What can we do to open the "prison doors to those who [are] bound in chains of darkness, superstition, and ignorance"? What has helped you in your efforts to find information about your ancestors and have their temple ordinances completed?

- How can we "become saviors upon Mount Zion"? Why is this work "one of the greatest responsibilities that rests upon the people of God today"?

- What are some of the purposes of temples? What blessings have come to you because you have done work for others in the temple or submitted names so that work could be done?

- What will be "the great work of the Millennium"? How can we participate in this work now?

- How has the knowledge of God's plan for redeeming the dead blessed your life? What does this plan tell us about God's love for all of His children?

## Notes

1. *Life of Joseph F. Smith,* comp. Joseph Fielding Smith (1938), 474.
2. *Gospel Doctrine,* 5th ed. (1939), 460.
3. Doctrine and Covenants 138:1–4, 11–12, 18–19, 29–32.
4. *Gospel Doctrine,* 442.
5. *Gospel Doctrine,* 442.
6. "Discourse by President Joseph F. Smith," *Millennial Star,* 4 Oct. 1906, 628–29.
7. *Gospel Doctrine,* 471–72.
8. *Gospel Doctrine,* 460–61.
9. In Conference Report, Apr. 1917, 6.
10. In Conference Report, Oct. 1913, 9–10.
11. *Gospel Doctrine,* 471.
12. *Gospel Doctrine,* 438.
13. In James R. Clark, comp., *Messages of the First Presidency of The Church of Jesus Christ of Latter-day Saints,* 6 vols. [1965–75], 4:193–94.
14. *Gospel Doctrine,* 74.

# Integrity: Living Our Religion with All Our Hearts

*Those who maintain their integrity by daily putting the things of God first and enduring in trials will gain eternal life.*

## From the Life of Joseph F. Smith

On 10 November 1918, the 17th anniversary of the day he was sustained as President of the Church, Joseph F. Smith gathered his family together and spoke of his life and what he had learned. All came to the occasion fasting and in the spirit of prayer. President Smith said, "If there is anything on earth I have tried to do as much as anything else, it is to keep my word, my promises, my integrity, to do what it was my duty to do."[1]

This was his last formal counsel. Nine days later, on 19 November 1918, President Joseph F. Smith died. An influenza epidemic prohibited a formal public funeral service. In tribute to this great leader, all public assemblies, entertainments, and official meetings were suspended. Theaters and many local businesses were closed. Thousands of citizens of Salt Lake City, Church members and nonmembers, thronged the streets to honor Joseph F. Smith as the funeral cortege made its way up South Temple to the Salt Lake City Cemetery. As the procession passed the Catholic Cathedral of the Madeleine, the bells in the cathedral tower tolled in tribute to this venerable leader who had influenced so many.

President Joseph F. Smith loved the right; he championed the cause of truth; he lived fully the principles he preached; and he was respected and revered for such integrity.

# Teachings of Joseph F. Smith

## We manifest our integrity by daily putting the things of God first.

The religion which we have espoused is not a Sunday religion; it is not a mere profession. . . . It is the most important thing in the world to us, and the results to us in this world and in the world to come will depend upon our integrity to the truth and our consistency in observing its precepts, in abiding by its principles, and its requirements.[2]

It is a joy to me always to have the privilege of meeting with men and women who have embraced the truth and who are true to it in their daily life, for after all, we establish the standard of our integrity and our fidelity to the truth by our daily works. The tree is known by its fruits, and we do not gather grapes of thorns nor figs of thistles. When you see a number of individuals, a community, or an entire people, who have embraced the gospel of Jesus Christ, consistent with their professions, true to their covenants, true in every respect to their faith, you will see men and women who are bearing good fruit and worthy in all respects.[3]

It is for us to do our duty and live our religion on one day the same as any other. Let us serve the Lord in righteousness all the day long and He will be our Father and Friend, and our enemies shall have no power over us.[4]

We all need love in our souls, all the time: first, for God our heavenly Father, who is the giver of all good—love which encompasses our souls, our thoughts, our hearts, our minds, our strength, insomuch that we would willingly, if he required, give our lives as well as our time, talents, and substance in this world to the service of the living God who gives us all that we have. . . . We [should] have that love in our hearts, so much that we will love God more than business, more than money, more than earthly pleasures; that is, enjoy greater pleasure in the worship and love of God than we have in any other thing in the world.[5]

Everywhere men hear the word success dwelt upon as if success were defined in a word, and as if the highest ambition of men and women was the advancement of some worldly ambition. . . . After all, one's success must be determined more by the eternal (as well as the present) needs of man, than by temporary standards which men erect in pursuance of the spirit of the age in which they live. Certainly nothing is more fatal to our well being than the notion that our present and eternal welfare is founded upon the wealth and honors of this world.

The great truth enunciated by the Savior seems very generally to be lost sight of in this generation, that it will profit a man nothing though he should gain the whole world, if he lose his own soul [see Matthew 16:26]. The standard of success as declared by the word of God, is the salvation of the soul.[6]

The essence of true membership in the Church of Jesus Christ of Latter-day Saints is this—that you and I, independent of every other person in the world, will live our religion and do our duty, no matter what other people do. As Joshua expressed himself in olden times, "As for me and my house, we will serve the Lord." [Joshua 24:15.] . . . The true measure of our standing in this Church is that we will do right, no matter who else does right or does wrong. Therefore let us seek to get that spirit upon us and live by that rule.[7]

The first and highest standard of correct living is to be found in that individual responsibility which keeps men good for the truth's sake. It is not difficult for men who are true to themselves to be true to others. Men who honor God in their private lives do not need the restraint of public opinion which may not only be indifferent, but positively wrong. It is by the individual responsibilities which men feel that they are able to place themselves on the right side of all public questions. Those who neglect the inner life are dependent upon public guidance which leads them into all sorts of inconsistencies.[8]

The fruits of the Spirit of God—the fruits of the spirit of true religion—are peace and love, virtue and honesty, and integrity, and fidelity to every virtue known in the law of God.[9]

Our duty is to keep steadily on—on and upward in the direction that the Lord Almighty has marked out for us to pursue. Keep the faith; honor the name of God in your hearts; revere and love the name of Him whose blood was shed for the remission of sins for the world; honor and hold in the highest esteem him whom God raised up in his childhood to lay the foundations of this great latter-day work.[10]

---

### Our integrity will be tried and tested.

My childhood and youth were spent in wandering with the people of God, in suffering with them and in rejoicing with them. My whole life has been identified with this people, and in the name and by the help of God it will be to the end. I have no other associations or place of abode. I am in this respect like Peter when the Savior, on seeing the people turn away from Him, asked him, Will ye go also? Said Peter, Lord, if I leave Thee whither can I go, Thou hast the words of eternal life. [See John 6:67–68.] We have nothing else to do save to keep in the narrow path that leads back to God our Father. That is the channel He has marked out for us to pursue, and it is our duty to press on; we cannot turn aside, we cannot switch off; there is no side track, it is a "through train" and its destiny is already fixed and mapped out.

We have got to meet opposition as it presents itself, battling against it with the weapons of truth which God has placed in our hands. And we must make up our minds that this world with all its pleasures is as dross compared with the excellency of the knowledge of God. He intends to try us and prove us, and He has a right to do it, even to the death if need be, and only those who endure to the end, who will not flinch, but will maintain their integrity at the risk and sacrifice of their all, if need be, will gain eternal life, or be worthy of the reward of the faithful.[11]

My prayer has been constantly, not that I might be spared trials, but that I might have wisdom and judgment, patience and endurance given unto me, to bear the trials that I might be called to pass through. While I cannot say truthfully that I have been tried in my faith in the Gospel of Christ, yet I can say truthfully that I have been tried in many ways. My patience has been tried, my love has been tried, my integrity has been tried.[12]

I believe [our pioneer forefathers] built better than they knew. I believe they were led by the power of God, step by step, and were taught precept upon precept, line upon line. In this way He proved their integrity and their devotion. He proved them unto death; yes, and even beyond death; for death to many of them would have been sweet, it would have been peaceful, happy rest, compared with the toil and trouble they had to endure.[13]

Many a man has gone to the stake in obedience, as he believed, to the commandments of God. Not one of the ancient disciples who were chosen of Jesus Christ, escaped martyrdom, except Judas and John. Judas betrayed the Lord, and then sacrificed his own life; and John received the promise of the Lord that he should live until He came again to the earth. All the others were put to death, some crucified, some dragged in the streets of Rome, some thrown from pinnacles, and some stoned to death. What for? For obeying the law of God and bearing testimony to that which they knew to be true. So may it be today. But let the spirit of this gospel be so imbedded in my soul that though I go through poverty, through tribulation, through persecution, or to death, let me and my house serve God and keep his laws.[14]

---

**We show our integrity by serving the Lord,
no matter what may befall.**

The Lord told the young man who loved the world, that if he desired to be perfect, he should sell all that he had and give it to the poor, then said the Lord, "Come and follow me." [Matthew 19:21.] This may be a very simple manner of expression, but there is a great deal of truth in it, there is an essential principle involved in it. It is the putting of that which is sacred and divine, that which is of God, that which makes for the peace and happiness of the souls of men, before our riches, before all our earthly honors and possessions. The Lord Almighty requires this of the Latter-day Saints; and every man and woman who has embraced the Gospel ought to feel in his and in her heart today, and in their souls always, that "whatsoever the Lord requireth of me, that will I do," or that will I give, no matter what it is.[15]

If He should require me to give all I possess unto him, I wish to feel that it should be done cheerfully and willingly, as Job, and also Abraham, felt when the Lord called upon them for expres-

The Beehive House in Salt Lake City, where President Smith lived for many years. He died here on 19 November 1918.

sions of their faith. Abraham was called upon to offer up his son—a child of promise—did he stop to reason or argue with the Almighty? No, he went to, without complaint or murmuring, to do what he was commanded. He may have had peculiar feelings, and no doubt he was tried to the very core; his tenderest affections were tested, but for all that he proposed obeying the behest of the Almighty. Abraham did not, however, execute the command, for the Lord, seeing his integrity and willingness, prevented it. [See Genesis 22:1–18.] . . .

Now, how many of us have the confidence in the Lord that Abraham had? Supposing, He were to ask from you your first born, or any of your loved ones, or your wealth, could you endure it without murmuring? . . . Can we expect to attain a celestial exaltation if we have some corner—something put away—upon which our hearts or dearest affections are set? Ask yourselves, if you are worthy to receive exaltation in the celestial kingdom of God?[16]

Job was a righteous man, perfect in all his ways. There were none like him in all the earth. . . . He did not curse the Sabeans

421

for carrying off his cattle, nor the fires of heaven for consuming his flocks, nor the winds of heaven for destroying his habitation and children. He did not swear and blaspheme and deny the Lord because of this. But he said, "The Lord gave, and the Lord hath taken away; blessed be the name of the Lord." [Job 1:21.] . . .

. . . Here is exemplified the principle that should underlie all the faith, the hope, the charity, the love, the labor, the desire of all mankind—that they will serve God, no matter what may befall them. Though they suffer imprisonment, though they suffer persecution, though they suffer poverty, though God should try them to the very core, and put them to the utmost test to prove their integrity, they should say like Job, "Naked came I out of my mother's womb, and naked shall I return thither; the Lord gave, and the Lord hath taken away; blessed be the name of the Lord." [Job 1:21.] Thus magnify God, love Him with all thy heart, might, mind and strength; then love our neighbor as ourselves; that when trials come we may endure them and not complain, but wait until God shall develop His purposes. Then we will see that there is no love like that of God for His suffering children; there is no mercy so broad, no purpose so grand, and great and noble as the purpose of God concerning His children. If we will do this, we will learn this eventually and we will bless God with all our hearts.[17]

## Suggestions for Study

- What is integrity? How do we "establish the standard of our integrity . . . by our daily works"? What situations in your daily life cause you to choose whether to put the things of God first?

- How can we develop the ability to "enjoy greater pleasure in the worship and love of God" than in the love of business, money, or other earthly pleasures? When you have faced tests in putting "that which is sacred and divine" ahead of "earthly honors and possessions," how have you responded?

- What is the true standard of success in our lives? What other definitions of success sometimes keep us from pursuing this true standard? How does acting according to revealed truth contrast with acting according to "public guidance"?

- Why do trials and opposition often face us when we are striving to live the gospel? In what ways have you been tried and proven in your efforts to do the will of God? How have you responded?

- How do the examples of faithful disciples like Abraham and Job help us better understand how to "serve God, no matter what may befall"? How has your testimony been strengthened by their examples? What things can prepare us to serve God in this way during our times of trial?

- How can developing and maintaining personal integrity bless and strengthen our families? our communities?

## Notes

1. *Life of Joseph F. Smith,* comp. Joseph Fielding Smith (1938), 477.
2. *Gospel Doctrine,* 5th ed. (1939), 107.
3. In Conference Report, Oct. 1916, 2.
4. *Deseret News: Semi-Weekly,* 8 Aug. 1884, 1.
5. In James R. Clark, comp., *Messages of the First Presidency of The Church of Jesus Christ of Latter-day Saints,* 6 vols. (1965–75), 5:91.
6. *Gospel Doctrine,* 123–25; paragraphing altered.
7. *Deseret News: Semi-Weekly,* 21 Mar. 1893, 2.
8. *Gospel Doctrine,* 253.
9. *Gospel Doctrine,* 75.
10. In Conference Report, Apr. 1904, 3.
11. *Deseret News: Semi-Weekly,* 25 Apr. 1882, 1; paragraphing added.
12. *Deseret News: Semi-Weekly,* 27 Apr. 1897, 1.
13. *Deseret News: Semi-Weekly,* 9 Aug. 1898, 1.
14. *Gospel Doctrine,* 251.
15. In Conference Report, Apr. 1909, 4–5.
16. In Brian H. Stuy, comp., *Collected Discourses Delivered by Wilford Woodruff, His Two Counselors, the Twelve Apostles, and Others,* 5 vols. (1987–92), 2:279.
17. *Deseret News: Semi-Weekly,* 19 Dec. 1893, 1; paragraphing altered.

President Joseph F. Smith, 1838–1918. He taught, "In proportion to your fidelity, your faithfulness, your advancement in the knowledge of God, shall you be able to enjoy happiness, unalloyed and unsullied, for it is the Gospel that brings true joy" (*Millennial Star*, 30 May 1907, 349).

◦◦◦◦◦ ▲▲▲ ◦◦◦◦◦

# Finding Rest in Christ

*Those who receive the testimony of Jesus Christ
find rest and peace in their souls.*

## From the Life of Joseph F. Smith

President Joseph F. Smith died on 19 November 1918, having
served as President of the Church since 1901. Vigorous, steadfast,
and sincere in doing the work of the Lord, he had given his life to
teaching the truths of the gospel of Jesus Christ. He was a preacher
of righteousness, a prophet of God, who urged the Saints, "Follow
me as I follow our head, the Redeemer of the world."[1]

President Heber J. Grant, who succeeded Joseph F. Smith as
President of the Church, said at his graveside service: "For 36 years
I have been with him, first when he was a counselor, and later
when he was President of the Church. During all these years I have
never known of anything in his life, in either word or act, that was
not worthy of a real man. I could say in all sincerity, 'He was the
kind of man I'd like to be.' Standing here by his grave, I desire
more than language can tell, the power and ability to be as kind,
as considerate, as forgiving, as brave and noble, and true, and to
walk in very deed in his footsteps. I could ask nothing more.

" . . . For no man that ever lived had a more powerful testimony of the living God and of our Redeemer than Joseph F.
Smith. From my earliest childhood days he has thrilled my very
being with the testimony that he has borne to all those with
whom he has come in contact, bearing witness that he knew that
God lives and that Jesus is the Christ, the Son of the living God,
the Redeemer of the world. The very spirit of inspiration that
was with this man found lodgment in my heart and in the hearts
of many others. I loved Joseph F. Smith as I never loved any
other man that I have ever known. May God bless his memory."[2]

The following testimony is taken from an address that President Smith delivered in Provo, Utah, on 13 January 1907.[3]

# Teachings of Joseph F. Smith

### We enter into the rest of the Lord as we yield our souls to Him and His gospel.

I desire to read from the writings of Moroni, wherein he quotes the teachings of his father, Mormon.

"And now I, Moroni, write a few of the words of my father, Mormon, which he spake concerning Faith, Hope, and Charity. . . .

" . . . I would speak unto you that are of the Church, that are the peaceable followers of Christ, and that have obtained a sufficient hope, by which ye can enter into the rest of the Lord, from this time henceforth, until ye shall rest with him in heaven." [Moroni 7:1, 3.]

. . . What does it mean to enter into the rest of the Lord? Speaking for myself, it means that through the love of God I have been won over to Him, so that I can feel at rest in Christ, that I may no more be disturbed by every wind of doctrine, by the cunning and craftiness of men, whereby they lie in wait to deceive; and that I am established in the knowledge and testimony of Jesus Christ, so that no power can turn me aside from the straight and narrow path that leads back into the presence of God, to enjoy exaltation in His glorious kingdom; that from this time henceforth I shall enjoy that rest until I shall *rest* with Him in the heavens.

I desire to impress this thought upon your minds, for I want you to understand that this is the meaning intended to be conveyed by the words, "entering into the *rest* of God." Let me assure you that that man who is not thoroughly established in the doctrine of Christ, who has not yielded his whole soul unto the Lord, and to the Gospel He has taught to the world, has not yet entered into that rest. He is still at sea, so to speak, wandering, unstable, lacking firmness, lacking the faith that cannot be moved, ready to be overtaken by the cunning and craftiness of him who lies in wait to deceive and mislead into error and darkness. While he that has received the testimony of Jesus Christ in his heart, he that has yielded his all to the kingdom of God and to the will of the Father, is so established. His heart is fixed; his mind is made up; doubts have been dispelled; fears have all been removed; he knows in whom to trust; he is thoroughly established in his purposes and in his determination that, as for him and his house he will serve God, keep His commandments and walk, as far as it is possible for human creatures to walk, in purity of life, in honor, fidelity, and uprightness before the Lord.

I thank my God that this spirit and feeling of unrest has been removed from my thoughts and mind with reference to the work in which we are engaged; and that the Lord has given me assurance that is beyond all other things in relation to this matter. I rejoice in the Gospel; I rejoice in the testimony of the Spirit of God in my heart; I rejoice in the testimony of the Prophet Joseph Smith; I rejoice in every principle of the Gospel of Jesus Christ that we have become acquainted with, so far as my knowledge goes. I cannot ask for, I do not want anything better than the principles of life and salvation revealed in this great plan of redemption restored to the earth in the latter days. . . .

---

## We strive to follow the high moral standard established by our Savior.

. . . If our hearts are fixed with proper intent upon serving God and keeping His commandments, what will be the fruits of it? What will be the result? . . . Men will be full of the spirit of forgiveness, of charity, of mercy, of love unfeigned. They will not seek occasion against each other; nor will they take advantage of the weak, the unwary, or the ignorant; but they will regard the rights of the ignorant, of the weak, of those who are dependent and at their mercy, as they do their very own; they will hold the liberties of their fellow-men as sacred as their own liberties; they will prize the virtue, honor and integrity of their neighbors and brothers just as they would appreciate and prize and hold sacred their own.

We cannot reach at once that high moral standard of perfection that was promulgated by Him. And while we are conscious of the fact that we cannot at present attain to that perfection, and cannot grasp the whole as we should, yet the mark is there, the standard is before our eyes. We are looking forward to the time when we may reach that glorious and exalted standard set for us by the example, the life, and mission of the Lord Jesus Christ. Though we fail to come up to the perfect standard that God manifested through Jesus Christ, yet we will repent of our failure, and will renew our determination, and double our diligence tomorrow. Aye, this moment we will double our diligence, try to overcome our weaknesses, and come nearer to the example set us by the Son of God.

This is the Gospel of Jesus Christ, and it is true doctrine. The man who will obey it, who will enter into the spirit of it, and cherish the spirit of it in his heart; who has this desire in his soul and seeks for that desire to become paramount to all other desires, will go on from faith to faith, from hope to knowledge, from understanding to wisdom and power, and finally to exaltation and glory in the kingdom of our God; and there is no power beneath the celestial kingdom that can stay him in his progress, if he will but strive to keep the laws and commandments of God. . . .

. . . When we make up our minds, as did Joshua of old, that we will serve God this day, and from this day henceforth we will serve Him and keep His commandments, then we are beginning to be able to divide the darkness from the light, the good from the evil, the right from the wrong, that which is pure from that which is impure; and from that moment your desire for good will grow stronger and stronger, and you will become more proficient in doing good and in accomplishing the purposes of God, in overcoming your own weaknesses, in proportion as you are diligent in forsaking evil and choosing good, by desiring good and eschewing evil, and turning away from the world and from the appetites of fallen human nature, and assist in doing that which is calculated to exalt mankind, to exalt the aspirations of man, exalt his purposes and enlarge his charity, his love and his forgiveness. Then you are able to discern the light, as the prophet has said; you may do it just as clearly, as unmistakably as you can discern the light of day from the darkness of night. [See Moroni 7:14–15.] . . .

### We grow from grace to grace until we receive a fulness and become joint heirs with Jesus Christ.

Let me read you this:

"Verily, thus saith the Lord, it shall come to pass that every soul who forsaketh their sins and cometh unto me, and calleth on my name, and obeyeth my voice, and keepeth my commandments, shall see my face and know that I am." [D&C 93:1.]

This is the word of the Lord. It is not easy for a man to see God's face and know that He is, who forsaketh not sin, cometh not unto God, who calleth not on His name, who obeyeth not the voice of God, who keepeth not His commandments. Shall he see the face of God, and shall he know that He is? No, there is no such promise; but to the contrary. It is he that "cometh unto me;" he that "forsaketh his sins;" he that "calleth on my name;" he that "obeyeth my voice;" he that "keepeth my commandments." It is he that "shall see my face," says God, and it is he who shall "know that I am," and not only "know that I am," but he shall know that "I am the true light that lighteth every man that cometh into the world." [D&C 93:2.]

What a glorious promise is held out to the children of God. . . . If Jesus Christ, the only begotten of the Father in the flesh, received not a fulness at first, and thereby was called the Son, but continued to receive grace for grace, adding grace unto grace until He received a fulness, it is clear that he that will walk in His footsteps, who will obey His precepts, and will adopt His plan for life and salvation, may receive grace for grace, may continue from grace to grace; may grow out of imperfection into perfection, and may receive here a little and there a little until he shall receive the fulness as the Son of God received a fulness; and thus become like Christ the Son of God, an heir of God, and joint heir with Jesus Christ. [See D&C 93:11–14.] I feel incapable of giving utterance to the thought and feeling that is burning in my soul, awakened by this word of Christ, this glorious opportunity that is granted unto me through obedience to the commandments of God, through keeping the word of the Lord, that of becoming possessed, by and by, of the fulness of God's glory, a fulness of knowledge of the truth, a fulness of power, a fulness of wisdom, of possessing power and dominion and glory like unto the Father.

Does not this give you something to live for, something to hope for? Is there not here a prize that is priceless held out unto you; offered to you through your obedience, your faithfulness, your accepting the light, walking in the light as Christ is in the light; that you may have fellowship with Him, and that the blood of Jesus Christ may cleanse you from all sin? I thank my God for this holy Gospel; I thank Him for this aspiration, and this hope that is inspired in my soul to become worthy of my Father and my God; worthy to dwell with Him, worthy of exaltation in His kingdom, and of enjoying His presence and His favor throughout the countless ages of eternity.

I know that it is the Gospel of Jesus Christ that will enable me to attain to this exaltation, and there is no other way given by which man can be saved; no other plan revealed in the world by which man can be exalted and return again to the presence of God. There is no other way. . . .

Have all things been revealed? No. Has God yet other things to reveal to His children? Yes, many; but we are not yet prepared for any greater light than has come; for where much is given much is required; and much has already been given to us, and God requires more of us to-day than we give Him. We will not walk in the light as He is in it; we will not obey the truth as He requires us to obey it. We yield to our own weakness; we yield to the temptations that beset us, to our own appetites, to our own selfishness, and to our own human desires instead of rising above the weakness of mortality and saying in our souls, "As for me, I will serve my God, keep His commandments, and walk blameless before Him." We do not do it; yet the Latter-day Saints are the best people in the world. We are living nearer to this standard than any other people in the world to-day, with all our weaknesses and imperfections.

---

### All peace and happiness is possible through the gospel of Jesus Christ.

Now, the Lord bless you. May peace abide with you, my brethren and sisters. Get the faith of the Gospel in your hearts. Learn that this religion that is given to you through Joseph Smith the prophet is God's religion, is God's law and God's requirements of His children upon the earth, and that this is above everything else. It is above self; it is above the world; it is above gold and silver, houses, and lands; it is above mortal life itself, because in it we are not only secured in our person and in our rights and privileges, but we are secured in the gift of eternal life, which is the greatest gift of God.

There is nothing to compare with it. It is the biggest thing in the world—the greatest thing on earth—it is the most momentous thing for us in all this world—[it] is God's truth, the religion of Jesus Christ, the doctrine of redemption and of salvation from sin, from our own weaknesses, and of a thorough and perfect engrafting of the spirit, and of the work, and knowledge, and power, and wisdom of God, the giver of all good. Peace be unto you, and may the blessings of health and love abound with you, in every walk of life, in every capacity in which you act, that you may have the fear of God before your eyes all the time.

But I do not want you to think for a moment that the religion of Jesus Christ is burdensome or heavy upon you. Not so. God has said, "My yoke is easy and my burden is light." [Matthew 11:30.] It is redemption from sin. The slave is not he who has been redeemed and lifted out of the bondage of sin, but it is he who remains a debtor and a prisoner to sin. He is the slave; he is the bondman; such as he needs our pity, our sympathy, and our commiseration. It is he that we should try to raise above the bond of slavery and sin, to enjoy freedom from sin and transgression.

Jesus Christ, the Son of God, is capable, and was capable while He dwelt in the flesh, and is capable today, of enjoying everything that is possible for righteous persons to enjoy; and there is not one thing of which He was deprived that is worth while. The same is possible with the Latter-day Saints. "Oh," says one, "if I would live your religion as you point it out to me, I would have no more enjoyment, my pleasures would cease." O, thou fool. I can enjoy every legitimate, every righteous pleasure that any man on God's earth can enjoy; and if I am more faithful than my brother in keeping the commandments of God, I may enjoy more than it is possible for him to enjoy. In proportion to your fidelity, your faithfulness, your advancement in the knowledge of God, shall you be able to enjoy happiness, unalloyed and unsullied, for it is the Gospel that brings true joy, and true liberty and freedom from the bonds of iniquity, and the gall of bitterness.

God help us to see the truth, and the light as in the day time and to discern it as clearly as we can discern the light of day from the darkness of night, is my prayer, in the name of Jesus. Amen.

## Suggestions for Study

- What does it mean to "enter into the rest of the Lord"? How can we obtain this rest?

- How can we yield our whole souls to the Lord and His gospel?

- What can we do to better reach for the "exalted standard" set for us by the Savior?

- What does it mean to grow "from grace to grace"? What can we do to ensure that we continue to grow in this way until we receive a fulness?

- What glorious promises are made to those who strive to become like the Savior?

- As your faith in Jesus Christ has grown, how has He lightened your burdens and given you rest? (See also Matthew 11:28–30.)

- What experiences have helped you to understand that all peace and happiness can be found through the gospel of Jesus Christ?

- How has your study of the gospel of Jesus Christ, as taught by President Joseph F. Smith, helped you to learn more about God? feel true joy and peace? become more like the Savior?

### Notes

1. In Conference Report, Apr. 1915, 5.
2. Quoted in Preston Nibley, *The Presidents of the Church* (1947), 260–61.
3. "At Rest in Christ," *Millennial Star,* 30 May 1907, 337–49; paragraphing altered.

# Index

Doctrine, false. *See* False doctrine

Doctrine and Covenants
read often to find truth, 44–46
reveals glorious principles, 44
testifies of Christ, 42–44, 204–5
*See also* Scriptures

Dream about being clean, 95–96

Dress, immodesty in, 376

**E**

Economy. *See* Finances, wisdom in

Educated, education, 313–21
apply what we learn, 317–19
divine revelation is the standard, 315–17
hold to the iron rod in, 319–20
role of science and philosophy, 315–17
seek to be, in truth, 313–21
should be continually learning, 317–19

Elders. *See* Missionaries

Elohim. *See* God the Father

Enemies
of Church will not triumph, 261–62
Joseph F.'s forgiveness of, xvii–xviii
leave in God's hands, 262–63
mercy for, 259–61
not ours, but the Lord's, 262

Entertainment. *See* Recreation

Eternal life. *See* Exaltation

Evil, God permits, 286–87

Exaltation
through Atonement and faithfulness, 100–101
children of God can become like Him, 336–37
families part of, 385–86
growing from grace to grace, 429–30
marriage is for our, 174–77, 181
must know God and Jesus Christ, 353–54
necessary to become parents of spirit offspring, 92
plan of salvation leads to, 148–51
repentance and baptism necessary for, 64–65
sacrifice necessary for, 57

Example
fathers should set, 384
Jesus Christ our great, 151–52, 427–28
necessary in missionary work, 84
in teaching children, 296–98
valiant, of early Church leaders, 109–11

**F**

Faith, 49–57
Abraham's example of, 54–55
courage of, 56, 106–9
defined, 50–53
enter into God's rest through, 56–57
gift of God to man, 53–54
God teaches us, 52
in God the Father and Jesus Christ, 50–53
obtained by obedience, 53–54
sustains us in adversity, 54–56

Fall of Adam
brought spiritual death, 96
brought temporal death, 87–89
overcome by Atonement, 89–92

False doctrine, avoid, 115–19

be sociable, 80
have humility, 77–78
Joseph F.'s belongings burned
as, 76–77
Joseph F.'s prayer for, 27–28
must pray, 77–78
responsibilities of returned,
83–84
teach with simplicity, 80–83
teach with the Spirit, 77–78,
80–82

Missionary work, 76–84
how to teach gospel, 80–83
necessary at home, 83–84
qualifications of missionaries,
77–80
responsibilities of returned
missionaries, 83–84

Money. *See* Finances, wisdom in

Mortgages, cautions urged in,
164–68

Mothers, 31–37
help from the Holy Ghost, 34, 37
influence generations, 32–33
love of, is like love of God, 35–36
responsibility to teach children,
33–34
should not be abused, 252–53
truest greatness, 386
will raise little children who
die, 132
*See also* Children, teaching of

Mutual Improvement Associations, service of, 341–42

**N**

Needy. *See* Poor and needy

Neighbor, love as yourself,
194–96

Nibley, Charles W., 163, 192, 265

**O**

Obedience
brings inestimable blessings,
289–92
inspired by testimony of Jesus
Christ, 206–7
leads to greater knowledge,
270–72
necessary for exaltation, 64–65,
152–53
necessary for faith, 53–54
necessary to work out salvation,
243–44
prepares for Second Coming,
394–96
to voice of Spirit, 269

Opposition
standing courageously against,
106–9
*See also* Adversity

Ordinances, temple
necessary for salvation, 306–8
perform worthily, 308–10

"Origin of Man," First Presidency
statement, 331

Oxen, Mary Fielding Smith's
prayer for, xiv, 21–22

**P**

Parents. *See* Children, teaching
of; Fathers; Mothers

Patience, teaching children,
301–2

Patriarchal order, 139–40, 383

Patriotism, Latter-day Saints have,
123–25

Paul, had courage of faith, 107

Peace, 399–405
Jesus' example of, 404–5

**R**

Recreation
not on the Sabbath, 233–34
not purpose of life, 373–74
parents should regulate
children's, 299–301
should be wholesome, 373–74

Redeemer. *See* Jesus Christ

Redemption of the dead. *See*
Family history work; Vision of
redemption of the dead

Relief Society, 183–91
care for the needy, 185–87
directed by the priesthood, 190
example of early leaders,
188–89
instituted by God, 184
instruct and build faith in
sisters, 185–90
Joseph F.'s prayer at 50th
anniversary, 183
service of, 341–42

Religious hobbies, avoid, 118–19

Repentance, 59–65
definition of true, 61–62
necessary for salvation, 60–62,
64–65
of sexual sin, 160–61

Rest, 425–32
all happiness possible through
gospel, 430–32
in Christ, 425–32
enter into, through faith, 56–57
follow Savior's example, 427–28
grow from grace to grace,
429–30
on the Sabbath, 231–34
scriptures lead to, 40
yield souls to Jesus Christ,
426–27

Restoration of gospel, 12–14

Resurrection
Atonement makes possible,
89–92
form of body in, 91–92
of Jesus Christ, 4–6
of little children, 130–32

Revelation, 265–72, 362–69
to all Church members, 266–68
continuous, 363–64
direct from God to man, 363
gain testimony through, 202–3
need for modern, 364
obedience leads to greater,
270–72
personal, 366
President receives, for the
Church, 226–27
through priesthood channels,
116–17, 365–67
through small voice of Holy
Ghost, 268–69
unites all people, 367–68

**S**

Sabbath, 230–38
blessings of observing, 237–38
desecration leads to loss of the
Spirit, 235–36
God has hallowed, 231
Saturday evening is introduction to, 235
what to do on, 231–34

Sacrament, remember Atonement
during, 101–2

Sacrifice
all to maintain integrity, 419–22
necessary for eternal life, 57
of our desires for others,
198–99
for welfare of others, 342–44

# Notes